The Complete

DACHSHUND

▼

By

MILO G. DENLINGER

Dachshunds, from *La Venerie*, by Jacques du Fouilloux, 1561.

The Complete

DACHSHUND

By
MILO G. DENLINGER

Revised by
WILLIAM W. DENLINGER

Drawings by
EDWIN MEGARGEE

Fourth Edition

Published by
DENLINGER'S
Middleburg, Va.
1958

FOREWORD

First and Second Editions

In order to meet the demand of the fancy for a publication on the Dachshund which would be complete and afford information not only to the novice but also to the professional breeder, I have endeavored to include in the compilation of this book information not usually obtained, such as a list of champions and the translation of the German vocabulary pertaining to canine terms.

It is not generally known by even the most advanced fancier the method used to make a champion in Germany, and it was through Anne FitzGerald Paramoure and her collection of German studbooks that this information was correctly assembled.

I wish to express my sincere appreciation to Miss Gerda Umlauff of Germany for the chapters on the status of the Dachshund in the country of its origin since the cessation of hostilities in 1945; to Walter L. DeVolld for his translation in substance of the famous German book by Dr. Fritz Engelmann; to Mrs. Mildred L. Hill for her chapter on famous Dachshunds and kennels, large and small; and last but not least to the many fanciers who so kindly submitted photographs of their good Dachshunds for reproduction in this book.

1947-1949   Milo G. Denlinger.

FOREWORD

Third Edition

It is with the greatest pleasure that I present the third edition of *The Complete Dachshund*. The first and second editions were received with such overwhelming enthusiasm by the Dachshund fancy that I felt it well worth while to expand the contents of the book and include information on the breed's progress and development since the publication of the previous edition.

In this edition are enlarged and up-to-date lists of champions and winning dogs; entirely new chapters on the character and temperament of the Dachshund; the principles involved in breeding for coat colors as they apply specifically to the Dachshund breed; training, and preparing the Dachshund for shows; current information on the Dachshund in foreign countries; and a revised chapter on famous Dachshunds and kennels in America.

I wish to express my sincere appreciation to Mrs. Mildred L. Hill for her extensive research in revising the latter chapter. Her thoroughness and her attention to details are reflected in the completeness with which she has covered an involved and extremely note-worthy subject. I also wish to thank the many Dachshund owners who have permitted me to include pictures of their outstanding dogs.

I feel sure that Dachshund owners everywhere will appreciate and profit by the wealth of information which has been included here.

1954   WILLIAM W. DENLINGER.

TABLE OF CONTENTS

PART I

Dachshund History ----------------------------------- 9
Early German Dachshunds----------------------------- 19
Der Dachshund ------------------------------------- 25
Dachshunds In Germany Since 1945-------------------- 51
Early English Dachshunds---------------------------- 67
The Dachshund As A Sporting Dog-------------------- 85
Description and Standard of Points------------------- 95
The Dachshund In A Nutshell------------------------ 105
The Blueprint of the Dachshund--------------------- 109
Soundness and Unsoundness-------------------------- 139
Fundamental Breeding Principles-------------------- 147
The Character and Temperament of the Dachshund---- 159
Obedience Training, and Preparation For the
    Show Ring ------------------------------------- 163
How German Champions Are Made--------------------- 167
A Short Explanation of German Grammar------------- 171
German Vocabulary --------------------------------- 175
German Terms and Abbreviations-------------------- 185
Champion Dachshunds and Famous Kennels----------- 189
    Long-haired Dachshunds ----------------------- 261
    Dappled Dachshunds --------------------------- 281
    Miniature Dachshunds ------------------------- 285
    Wire-haired Dachshunds ----------------------- 297
List of Champions--------------------------------- 317

PART II

Preliminary Training, Care, Feeding, Breeding,
    Medical -- 353

Clark Gable and his Dachshund Techelheim Red Russ,
a son of Ch. Bavarian Russ

Dachshund History

HE Dachshund is the only dog classified as a sporting dog by the American Kennel Club which is neither a Hound nor a dog exclusively used with the gun. That it is used occasionally as a Hound in the sense that it follows rabbits and hares by scent as does a Beagle, does not alter the fact that it is essentially a dog that goes to earth and is therefore a Terrier. Its name of Badger Dog is all the evidence needed on that point. That it can be used as a Beagle does not alter the fact that it is properly an earth dog, any more than the occasional use of Fox Terriers for rabbit coursing makes them Whippets.

The Dachshund is now recognized as essentially a dog of Germany, although there can be no doubt that it was found throughout Western Europe at an early date. The description of the French dogs, given in the old French sporting books copied by early English writers as applying to English Terriers, leaves no doubt as to the Dachshund's being then a dog known and used in France. It is very true that they were called Bassets, but what we know as Bassets could not have gone to earth, and the name was at that time merely indicative of their being low dogs, though it must be admitted that the name was also applied to the taller, rough dog. Apparently the French gave up the small, smooth,

9

crooked-legged dog, and it remained for the Germans to continue his use and develop him into the Teckel, or Dachshund, whose peculiar formation has turned many a penny for the comic newspaper illustrator.

Notwithstanding the distinctly German origin of the modern Dachshund, it is due the English fanciers to state that they were the pioneers in giving the dog the distinction of a specialty club, for as early as 1881 there was a Dachshund Club in England, and that was not established until the breed had been recognized for eight years as entitled to individual classification. The Crystal Palace show of 1873, not Birmingham in 1872 as stated by Mr. Marples in "Show Dogs," was the first to give a class for the breed which, from 1866 up to that time, had been included in the class for foreign sporting dogs. Later, in 1873, Birmingham followed the Kennel Club lead and gave its first class for Dachshunds. The meaning of the German word "hund" not being so well known as it should have been in England, led to the breed's being given a class in the studbook of 1874 under the title of "Dachshunds (or German Badger Hounds)," in place of Badger Dogs, and this led to their being considered Hounds and bred for Hound heads in place of the correct Terrier type. Indeed, it was not until the winter of 1883-84 that Mr. George Krehl, returning from a visit to Germany, took up the question of type and led the change to that of the German dog.

Undoubtedly, the Dachshund had been brought to America in the early '70's, but we think the first systematic importation of the dog for use in the field was made by Dr. Twadell, of Philadelphia, who got them for rabbitting, and there was a good deal of discussion as to their merits as compared with the longer legged Beagles. Dr. Downey, of Newmarket, Maryland, and Mr. Seitner, of Dayton, Ohio, then became interested in them, and we have always been of the opinion that the "bench-legged Beagles" of Delaware and Maryland had their origin in crosses of these early importations with Beagles. The Dachshunds' use as field dogs soon died out in favor of Beagles, and since then they have been regarded primarily as show dogs, although it must be admitted that they are favorite dogs with many

10

Germans who go afield after rabbits with their Waldmans and Gretchens.

Whether Dr. Motschenbacker, of New York, had such a very strong kennel that he had but one opponent of any consequence, we cannot say, but on his shoulders and those of Mr. and Mrs. Kellar had fallen the duty of upholding the breed so far as the Eastern shows were concerned. It was seldom that any other exhibitor got in ahead of these exhibitors who had done wonders in breeding and showing winners from their own kennels.

The one exception in the East was Mr. R. Murray Bohlen, who had kept Dachshunds for a good many years, and the puppies he showed at the Atlantic City exhibition proved that he had some good breeding material.

The Dachshund is such an exaggeration that it is much easier to show by reproductions of old photographs what the best dogs looked like, than to convey a clear impression to any person who has never seen one. The one distinct peculiarity is also that of the Basset, the crooked forelegs, which is nothing but a deformity. That this deformed foreleg is of any practical use in digging underground, we cannot believe. Perhaps we should say that its being better than the short, straight leg of the Terriers which go to ground is not our opinion, and we put that idea away with the old-time belief that the loose dewclaw of the St. Bernard helped the dog to walk in, or on, the snow. It appears from some remarks of Mr. Marples that there was an attempt at doing away, in a great measure, with the Dachshund front by English breeders. He wrote as follows: "In these later days, there has been a tendency in England to moderate the crook of the Dachshund . . . I cannot, however, go so far in the craze for sound fronts as to accept a straight-legged Dachshund, as some judges do." In this, Mr. Marples was quite correct, for it is purely a fancy breed, and whether these fronts are deformities or not does not matter, usage and Standards have made them properties of the Dachshund, and it is just as easy to breed sound fronts as straight fronts; that is, legs that are properly crooked, so that the dog stands true on his feet and does not "run over," as a man does who fails to put his foot down squarely as he walks. We recognize it as a

11

part of the breed, while we dissent from the claim that it is essentially useful in digging underground.

The German Standard goes to great length in describing the Dachshund, indulging in technicalities and minuteness of detail. There seems also to be a great deal of difficulty in getting a good translation into language common to dog Standards. The combination of a dog man who thoroughly understands German and has an equally good English education does not seem to have been secured for the translation of this Standard. The English long have had a short, clearly written Standard, but it differs in several points from the German code, and, as the latter is the one in use here, that alone will be of service. We have seen three translations, and the one which seems clearest is the one we give. It is better in its division into paragraphs, and clearer in its phraseology. The best part of the German Standard is the illustrations, which show the ideal, also the faulty, conformation.

Of Historical Interest

Some of the old type of Dachshund were much more of Terrier type than those of today, and many resembled the Basset Hound.

General Appearance.—Dwarfed, short legged, elongated, but stiff figure, muscular. Notwithstanding the short limbs and long body, neither appearing stunted, awkward, incapable of movement, nor yet lean and weasel-like; with pert, saucy pose of the head and intelligent expression.

Head.—Elongated, and, as seen from above and from the side, tapering toward the point of the nose, sharply outlined and finely modelled, particularly in profile.

Skull.—Neither too wide nor too narrow, only slightly arched, and running gradually without break (stop) [the less the break (stop) the better the type], into a well-defined and slightly arched nasal bone.

Eyes.—Medium sized, oval, set obliquely, clear and energetic expression. Except the silver color of the gray and spotted dogs and the yellow eyes of the brown dogs, the color is a transparent brown.

Nose.—Point and root long and slender, very finely formed.

Lips.—Tightly stretched, well covering the lower jaw, neither deep nor snipey, with corner of mouth slightly marked.

Jaws.—Capable of opening wide, extending to behind the eyes.

Teeth.—Well developed, particularly the corner teeth; these latter fitting exactly. Incisors fitting each other, or the inner side of the upper incisors touching the outside of the lower.

Ears.—Relatively well back, high, and well set on, with forward edge lying close to the cheeks; very broad and long, beautifully rounded (not narrow, pointed, or folded), very mobile, as in all intelligent dogs; when at attention, the back of the ear directed forward and upward.

Neck.—Sufficiently long, muscular, lean, no dewlap, slightly arched in the nape, running in graceful lines between the shoulders, usually carried high and forward.

Shoulders.—Long, broad, and set sloping, lying firmly on fully developed thorax; muscles hard and plastic.

Chest.—Corresponding with his work underground,

muscular, compact; the region of chest and shoulders deep, long, and wide; breast bone, strong and so prominent as to show a hollow on each side.

Back.—In the case of sloping shoulders and hindquarters, short and firm; if steep (straight) shoulders and hindquarters, long and weak; line of back behind shoulders only slightly sunk and only slightly arched near the loins.

Trunk.—Ribs full, oval, with ample width for heart and lungs, deep and hanging low between forelegs, well sprung out toward loins, loins short and tight and broad, line of belly moderately drawn up, and joined to hindquarters with loosely stretched skin.

Hindquarters.—Rump round, full, broad, muscles hard and plastic; pelvic bone not too short, broad, and strongly developed, set moderately sloping.

Forelegs.—Upper arm of equal length with, and at right angles to, shoulders, strong boned and well muscled, lying close to ribs, but moving freely up to shoulder blade. Lower arm short, as compared with other animals, slightly inclined inward; strongly muscled and plastic toward front and outside, inside and back parts stretched by hard tendons.

Hind Legs.—Thigh bone strong, of good length, and joined to pelvis at right angles; thighs strong and with hard muscles; buttocks well rounded out; knee joint developed in length; lower leg short in comparison with other animals, at right angles to thigh bone, and firmly muscled; ankle bones well apart, with strong, well-sprung heel and broad Achilles tendons.

Feet.—Forefeet broad and sloping outward; hind feet smaller and narrower; toes always close together, with distinct bend in each toe; nails strong and regularly pointed outward; thick soles.

Tail.—Set on at medium height and firmly; not too long, tapering without too great curvature, not carried too high, well (but not too much) haired. (A brush tail is, however, better than one without, or with too little, hair; for to breed a weather-proof coat must always be the aim.)

Coat.—Short, thick as possible, glossy, greasy (not harsh and dry), equally covering entire body (never showing bare spots).

Color.—(a) Single-colored: Red, yellowish-red, yellow, or red or yellow with black points; but one color only is preferable, and red is better than yellowish-red, and yellow. White is also allowed. Nose and nails black, red also permitted, but not desirable.

(b) Two-colored: Deep black, or brown, or gray, each with yellow or reddish-brown spots over the eyes, on the sides of the jaws and lower lips, on the inner rim of ear, on the breast, on the inside and back of legs, under the tail, and from there down one-third to one-half of the underside of the tail. Nose and nails black in black dogs, brown in brown dogs, gray in gray dogs, and also flesh color.

In one- and two-colored dogs, white is permissible, but only to the smallest possible extent, such as spot or small streaks on breast.

(c) Spotted: Ground is a shining silver gray, or even white with dark, irregular spots (large spots are undesirable) of dark gray, brown, yellowish-red, or black.

Neither the light nor the dark colors should predominate. The main factor is such a general appearance that, at some distance, the dog shall show an indefinite and varied color which renders him particularly useful as a hunting dog. The russet-brown marks are darker in darker-spotted dogs, and yellower in the lighter ones, and there may be an indication of these in the case of a white ground color. Light eyes are permitted; when the ground color is white, a flesh-colored or spotted nose is not a fault. White marks are not desirable in dark dogs, but are not to be regarded as faults which disqualify.

Height at Shoulder.—7⅛ to 8⅝ inches.

Weight.—Divided into three classes: Light-weight: Dog under 16½ lbs.; bitches under 15½ lbs. Medium-weight: Dogs from 16½ to 22 lbs.; bitches, 15½ to 22 lbs. Heavy-weight: Dogs and bitches over 22 lbs.

Defects.—Too weak or crippled, too high or too low on legs; skull too wide, too narrow, or too much arched; ears set on too high, too heavy, or too short, also set on too low and narrow, or long or slack; stop too pronounced; goggle-eyes; nasal bone too short or pressed in; lips too pointed or too deep; overshot; short, developed neck; forelegs badly

16

developed, twisted, or poorly muscled; hare-footed or flat-spread toes; too deeply sunk behind shoulders, *i.e.*, hollow backed; loins too much arched and weak; ribs too flat or too short; rump higher than shoulders; chest too short or too flat; loins arched like a Greyhound; hindquarters too narrow and poor in muscle; cowhocked; tail set on high, and carried too high or too much curled, too thin, long, or hairless (rat-tailed); coat too thick, too coarse, too fine, or too thin; color dead, dull, or too much mixed. In black dogs with russet-brown marks (tan), these latter should not extend too far, particularly on the ears.

WALDEMAN II

A winner at the turn of the century

Early German Dachshunds

OME seventy years ago, Herr
Beckmann, one of the German authorities, dealing with the
different types of the breed, wrote as follows:

"Having concentrated all varieties of the Badger Dog
to one single class—the crook-legged, short-haired dog, with
head neither Hound- nor Terrier-like, weight from eighteen
to twenty pounds, color black-tan and its variations—we
shall still meet many varying forms. With some attention
we shall soon distinguish the *common* breed and *well-* or
high-bred Dachshund. The first is a stout, strong-boned,
muscularly built dog, with large head and strong teeth; the
back not much arched, sometimes even straight; tail long
and heavy; forelegs strong and regularly formed; the head
and tail often appear to be too large in the dog; the hair is
rather coarse, thick-set, short, and wiry, lengthened at the
underside of the tail, without forming a brush or feather,
and covering a good deal of the belly. These dogs are good
workmen, and are less affected by weather than high-bred
ones; but they are very apt to exceed eighteen pounds and
even twenty pounds weight, and soon get fat if not worked
frequently. From this common breed originates the well-
and high-bred dog, which may at any time be produced
again from it by careful selection and inbreeding without

19

any cross. The *well-* and *high-bred* dog is smaller in size, finer in bone, more elegantly built, and seldom exceeds sixteen to seventeen pounds weight; the thin, slightly tapering tail is only of medium length; the hair is very short, glossy like silk, but not soft; the under part of the body is very thin haired, rendering these nervous and high-spirited dogs rather sensitive to wet ground and rain. These two breeds are seldom met with in their purity, the vast majority of Dachshunds in Germany ranging between the two, and differing in shape very much, as they are more or less well-bred or neglected. In this third large group we still meet with many good and useful dogs, but also all those aberrant forms, with pig snouts and short under jaws, apple-headed skulls, deep-set or staring eyes, short necks, wheel backs, ring tails, forelegs joining at the knees, and long hind legs bent too much in the stifles and hocks."

We quote from an old book of about 1880 an abstract by John Fisher:

"This breed of dog has long been used by the noble owners of the immense forests of Germany for hunting the badger, and Colonel Thornton, in his Sporting Tour in France, in 1802, also mentions them as being used for other purposes; but it is only of late years that they have gained a footing in this country (England), where they have not been much used for hunting the badger, but have been mostly kept as pets in the families of royalty and nobility. They are very cheerful and agreeable companions, being watchful and devoted in their attentions, and of great courage where defense is necessary, amiable in temper but withal jealous of favors, and admit the presence of a rival with but ill-bred grace.

"There is on the top of the Grand Duke of Baden's Jagdhaus, or hunting-lodge, near Baden-Baden, an historical life-sized statue of a red deer couchant, with a Dachshund in the act of seizing him by the throat—showing that the Hound has tracked a stag to his lair, and there seized upon him; and the Germans have a proverb: 'Wo ein Dachshund fangt er halt,' *i.e.,* 'Where a Dachshund bites he holds.'

"The chief characteristics of the breed may be thus described: The head is long and somewhat narrow, and

20

the 'stop' slight; the muzzle long, and broad to the end of the
nose; the teeth strong—those in the lower jaw slightly reced-
ing, the fangs large and recurvent; flews of medium size;
the ears, which are set low and far back, are thin and soft,
and fall gracefully over the cheeks; the eyes, of medium
size, and of the same color as the coat, are very lustrous,
tender and intelligent in expression; the neck being thick
and muscular; the chest broad with the brisket point well up
to the throat; the ribs are very widely sprung or rounded
behind the shoulders; the loin is long, slightly arched and
lithesome—enabling the dog to turn round, or serpent-like
to wriggle himself out of the earth or burrow. The forelegs
possess great bone, and are very muscular; the elbows are
turned out and the knees turned in, so that the ankles touch
when standing at ease; the shoulders are very loose and the
legs so supple that he can go to ground without going down
on his knees; the forefeet, which are very large and armed
with strong claws, are splayed outwards and are admirably
adapted for working in the earth; the thighs are short and
remarkably muscular, and the hocks straight, giving a great
power of leverage for drawing the quarry to daylight when
it is reached. The skin is remarkable for its thickness as
well as for its elasticity, which is so great that on whatever
part an adversary may seize, he can give skin enough to
enable him to return the compliment on the throat or foreleg, for the Dachshund always fights low and near the
ground, and will 'stand in' as long as any sportsman would
desire; indeed he never seems to realize the idea of leaving
off second best. The stern is of good length, strong at the
base, is carried Hound-like, and should not show any decided curl. The coat is short and moderately hard, the prevalent colors being black with tan markings, brown with
tawny markings, fallow red, and gray with blue or brown
flecks—and they mostly have a little white on the breast,
and sometimes on the toes, but the latter is not desirable.
The black-and-tans are the most plentiful and the fallow
reds the most fashionable colors. The late King of Hanover
had a fine pack of these dogs, from which we have drawn
supplies on several occasions; and having possessed dogs of
each of the above-mentioned colors, we give to the fallow-

reds a decided preference, as they possess more substance, are more hardy, and have, we think, more courage, and certainly show more nobleness of character and quality in the head than we have ever met in dogs of the other colors. The weight of dogs of this breed should be about twenty pounds, and of bitches, eighteen or nineteen pounds, and ought not to be less for drawing the badger from his stronghold, or for successfully competing with him in the open.

"Feldmann (see portrait), a fallow-red dog, was bred by H. S. H. the Prince Edward of Saxe-Weimar, from whom he was a gift to his present owner; weighs twenty-one pounds, and measures 38½ inches in length over all, of which the stern measures 9 inches. Height at shoulder, 10 inches. Height of chest from ground, 3½ inches. Width of chest, 6½ inches. Length from eye to nose, 3½ inches. Length of ear, 4¾ inches. From point to point of ears over cranium, 13¼ inches. Muzzle girth behind fangs, 8¾ inches. Girth of head in front of ears, 12½ inches. Girth immediately behind shoulders, 19 inches.

"Feldmann is acknowledged by many of the best judges of dogs, as well as by gentlemen acquainted with the best packs on the Continent, to be a very perfect specimen of the breed. He has gained thirty-two prizes, including Birmingham three years in succession, and has been exhibited at most of the principal dog shows in the kingdom (the Crystal Palace excepted).

"During the early part of his show career, his travelling box was kept at the railway station, which is three miles distant, and whenever he had to go to a show, he was taken down and put into his box and sent away without either keeper or guardian, instructions being given to the porters to let him out whenever he was returned from any show, and it was not long before he announced his arrival at home by sundry impatient barkings at the front door. But this state of things did not continue very long, for having to pass through two populous villages en route home, the boys took advantage of his loneliness, and pelted him with stones, which annoyed Master Feldmann so much that now he will not budge from the station without having a porter to escort him through the enemy's territory.

"Not very long ago, and early on a summer morning, we were walking through a village in Lancashire with Feldmann as a companion, when a working man, as we passed, threw open his bedroom window, thrust out his head, and gave such a stentorian Tally Ho! as not only awakened the early echo, but also his slumbering neighbors, who rushed to their windows *en deshabille* to ascertain what had happened, when the resident No. 1 responded, 'Eh! lads, it's many a yer sin' I seed a dog o' that breed, e Garmany; by the' mon! they can foight like bull-dogs—an' better'!! and the old cotton weaver yoicks'd and cheered so long as we continued in sight.

"As an instance of the pluck and tenacity of this breed, we may mention, that being out rabbitting last winter, an earth on a steep bank was challenged, but which was too small for any of the dogs except a red bitch puppy, which managed to enter with considerable difficulty, when the hubbub inside told that the hole was occupied by something more formidable than rabbits; presently she was seen backing out—the other dogs anxiously waiting on the bank for a grab at whatever might be brought to daylight, and in the melee which followed, they all—dogs and prey—rolled down the bank into a pool of water below. The puppy held her grip, and brought to land what turned out to be a full-grown hedgehog, which was soon despatched, when she returned and ultimately produced four other young hedgehogs from the same burrow, with two of which she got cold baths as with the first. With the exception of having been in at the breaking up of a rabbit or two, this puppy had not been previously entered to any kind of vermin."

Mr. Fisher's concept of the ideal Dachshund is long outdated. In a modern dog show either in Germany or America, a dog fitting this description, particularly with regard to the crooked front, would meet with small favor. Feldmann, however excellent he may have been considered in his own day, would today be considered but a poor specimen of the breed.

FELDMANN

THREE NOTED DOGS

Festus, Waldeman, and Schlupferle were three important dogs
at the end of the nineteenth century.

Der Dachshund

By Dr. Fritz Engelmann
as translated by
Walter L. DeVolld

HE material in this chapter and
Chapter II is based upon a translation of *Der Dachshund* by
Dr. Fritz Engelmann, who represents the German breeder
interested in the Dachshund primarily as a hunting dog.
His discussion of the history of the Dachshund is based
largely upon an earlier work by Maj. Emil Ilgner, who was
an early breeder and the first president of the Teckel Klub.
Thus, Dr. Engelmann's book represents one of our most
authoritative sources of historical information. One of the
chief values to be obtained from a close consideration of Dr.
Engelmann's discussion is an understanding of the development of the different types of Dachshund which the American breeder is likely to encounter in his work with the breed.
Many a person who is working to develop a dog that can win
in the present-day show ring is amazed to find in a litter one
or more dogs which seem completely different in type from
the sire and the dam of the litter. One pup may be high on
its legs and shallow chested, while another may have a
roached back and a gay tail. A study of Dr. Engelmann's
comments may help the breeder to understand the reasons
for such outcroppings.

It must be emphasized quite strongly that Dr. Engelmann wanted to produce hunting dogs in his own kennels,

that he was hardly interested in the show ring, or in prizes for beauty, as he put it. His Dachshund, or any that he admired, had to be a good burrower, trailer, and fighter, and had to be built for speed. Aggressive temperament is a quality that Dr. Engelmann desired almost more than any other.

In America today the average breeder wants a dog that is built along very different lines, and what the Germans call the beauty prizes are most avidly sought after. It is a matter of common knowledge here that the Dachshund, as a breed, has hunting abilities, but more Dachshunds will be found in steam-heated city apartments than in the field.

It is not our task or interest to promote Dr. Engelmann's ideas or those of the average American owner. The material is presented here as something of historical interest and significance.

Dr. Engelmann stated early in his discussion of the history of the Dachshund that it took many thousands of years to develop from the earliest wolf-like domestic dogs the wide variety of types of dogs which we now term breeds. And further, it has been within recent years that those dogs appeared which are thought of as Hounds, having typically pendant ears.

The Brache, which may be compared to some extent with the Limehound, is often taken as the German example of an early hunting dog whose chief function was to flush game, to penetrate dense undergrowth, and to guide the prey toward the hunter or the trap. Dr. Engelmann suggested that the name of this dog may be related to the German verb *brechen,* meaning to break, and he also commented that the past participle of the verb, *gebrochen,* is sometimes used to describe the crooked front legs with which some Dachshunds have been and are afflicted. However, we should hesitate to substantiate the etymological accuracy of his explanation. It might be possible to make a case for a word, *brake,* which came to us through the Anglo-Saxon, an early Germanic dialect, and which according to Webster's Collegiate Dictionary means a thicket, or underbrush. In German, *das Brack* means refuse or trash. It is known that words which came into English via Anglo-Saxon often retain a form similar to the original but alter the meaning slightly. An example of this is the German *Knabe,* a boy, and the English derivative, *knave,* a rascal or scoundrel. Thus it might be that the Brache was a dog that hunted in underbrush and derived his name from that fact. Following this development, a process of generalization took place and hunting dogs in general were termed Brache, and from there one proceeds again to the specialization encountered in Dachsbrache. Dr. Engelmann stated that in certain areas of Germany the Dachshund is still known as the Brache. He believed that the Brache is the forerunner of all Hound-eared dogs to be found in western Europe.

There have been a number of somewhat dubious explanations of the origin of the Dachshund. One, proposed by a Dr. Schame, was based upon some skull studies that he made. He attempted to establish a connection between the Pinscher (or Terrier) group and the Dachshund group. Had Dr. Schame taken into account the introduction of Pinscher blood to create the wire-haired Dachshund, he would have avoided the error of concluding that *all* Dachshunds are related to the Pinschers.

Another theory attempted to prove that the Dachshund is of ancient Egyptian origin, due to the coincidence that a representation of a short-legged dog found in an Egyptian tomb was accompanied by an inscription including the work *tekal* or *teckar.* It is true that the Dachshund is often given the name *Teckel* in Germany, but this word can be proved to have resulted from variation of the consonants *d* and *t* and of the vowels *a* and *e.* In south German dialects, a word like *Deutsch,* meaning German, will be spelled with a *t,* resulting in *Teutsch;* while in north Germany the *d* is retained. The difference between *a* and *e* may also often be nothing but a matter of dialect, or geographic variation. Other writers have pointed to the fact that it is doubtful whether any breed has been bred true from the time of the early Egyptians to the nineteenth century.

Dr. Engelmann also failed to find any connection between the "beaver dog" mentioned in the *lex bajuvarum,* a law of the fifth century protecting beaver dogs from human molestation, and the Dachshund. He also saw no resem-

27

blance between the Dachshund and the dogs portrayed in *La Venerie du Jacques du Fouilloux,* 1561. A woodcut, executed by Jost Ammon and dating from 1582, portrays a badger and rabbit hunt. Dr. Engelmann believed that the dogs portrayed in it suggest the *Kaninchenteckel,* Miniature Dachshund of today. Other early references to dogs that hunt rabbits, badger, and fox are cited, and one from Tantzer's *Hunting Secrets,* published toward the end of the seventeenth century, mentions a dog that is a "particularly bad-legged sort." However, Dr. Engelmann came to the conclusion that the dogs described have more in them of the idea of the work of the modern Dachshund than of its form.

In his work, *Georgica Curiosa,* about 1700, Holberg described a dog in such a way that for the first time one feels that here is a true ancestor of the Dachshund. He referred to badger dogs which the French called Bassets because of their low stature (*bas* meaning "low") and which had a long slender body, and stated that these dogs may occur in all sorts of colors.

Flemming's book *The Complete German Hunter,* 1719, has two illustrations which appear without doubt to represent a breed very like the modern Dachshund. And in 1734 a "small short-legged sharp dog that likes to trail" was mentioned by Parson. Dobel, in 1793, demanded sharp Dachshunds for work in the burrows of badger and fox.

In 1793 the celebrated French authority on natural history, Buffon, mentioned that there were straight- and crooked-legged Dachshunds and that they occurred in a variety of colors including white and dapple. Dr. Engelmann commented that, although Buffon's illustrations revealed over-developed Dachshunds in length of back and size, the chest was not exaggerated.

Dr. Walther said of Dachshunds in 1812 that they are snappish, often cunning, brave but pugnacious animals which are tenacious of life, and that they engage with any dog, be he ever so big.

About this time Dachshunds were mentioned which were wiry-coated, not so crooked- or short-legged as the smooth-hairs, while in 1820 Dietrich aus dem Winckell mentioned long-haired Dachshunds.

Dr. Reichenbach's mention (1836) of all varieties and many colors of Dachshunds is of more than usual interest in view of the fact that some varieties did not become popular until after 1900. Illustrations accompanying his discussion portray smooth-haired, wire-haired, long-haired, yellow, brown, black, dappled, brindle, crooked- and straight-legged dogs.

In Germany, the revolution of 1848 resulted in a period that was exceedingly unfavorable to the breeding of dogs or to any activities that were not of national political significance. To be sure, breeding continued, but not according to any unified plan, and it was the work of people often isolated by occupation and distance from other breeders, namely, the national foresters. Enough dogs had been bred, however, that when the national equilibrium had recovered somewhat, it was possible to carry on with the interrupted work.

A year that is of real importance in the history of the Dachshund is 1879, for it was then that a listing of desirable characteristics was made, and it became the basis of the present-day Standard. Fifty-four entries were included in the first German Studbook, which also included the names of famous breeders. Some of these are: G. Barnewitz, L. Beckmann, Prince Solms-Braunfels (who previously had organized and sponsored several groups of immigrants to this country and whose name is commemorated in the town of New Braunfels, Texas), v. Podewils, Fink, Meyer, Wilhelm v. Daacke, v. Nathusius, Count v. Waldersee, and Baron v. Knigge.

In 1883, v. Knigge's dogs received the highest award of the Berlin show, Kaiser Wilhelm I's golden medal.

For those who are more interested in red Dachshunds, Wilhelm v. Daacke, of Osterode, was a person of prime importance, for most of the good red dogs of today have in their ancestry dogs bred by von Daacke. Von Daacke, who began his work in 1868, had as his principal aim the breeding of good hunting dogs which could work both on and below ground. The weights which he felt to be most practical were seventeen to eighteen pounds for a male dog, and fourteen to fifteen pounds for a bitch.

29

Monsieur Schneidig, a von Daacke product, became famous and was much used for breeding. He competed with another famous dog at Berlin, Flott-Sonnenberg, and Dr. Engelmann expressed the opinion that Monsieur Schneidig was superior in shape of head to Flott. It is believed that von Daacke's dogs carried some blood of the best Harz mountain Bloodhounds, introduced to improve the Dachshund's trailing abilities.

The black-and-tan variety owes as much to Hundesports Waldmann and Schlupfer-Euskirchen as the reds owe to Monsieur Schneidig and Flott-Sonnenberg. These two black-and-tans can trace their lineage back to Dachs 16 whose ancestry has never been proved.

The Cologne show in 1889 was the starting point of many arguments over the superiority of Hundesports Waldmann, owned by E. von Otto and bred by Stech, of Schorndorf, and Schlupfer-Euskirchen, owned by Albert Latz, of Euskirchen. The argument, which was carried on in journals devoted to the fancy, if not conclusive, at least demonstrated that both dogs were good. Dr. Engelmann saw Hundesports Waldmann at Munich, and in a discussion of the dog he found much to praise, but he revealed his constant interest in light, quick-moving dogs when he said that he would have liked him more had he been a bit lighter and had he been built for easier movement.

It may be of interest to note briefly the names of some of the early breeders of the three main varieties of Dachshunds so that those who desire background material on one or the other variety may glean some additional information.

The smooth-haired Dachshunds were bred in a variety of colors, as will be indicated by the following:

Barnewitz, of Berlin—outstanding black-and-tan dogs: Berolina Frigga, Berolina-Waldmann-Mako, Berolina Waldhexe, and Berolina Waldteufel.

Benda bred these black-and-tans: Schlaula-Reinecke, Altremplin Reinecke.

Isermann, of Sonderhausen, bred Junker Racker vom Jagerhaus and Junker Schlupfer vom Jagerhaus.

Chocolates were usually bred by chance, but Bockelmann's Erda and Pucher's Traudel deserve mention.

The tiger dogs, known in America as dapples, were bred by von Daacke, whose Holle was worthy of note; and by Ilgner who produced good dogs, among them Hexe Erdmannsheim, Janke Erdmannsheim, and Hannemann Erdmannsheim.

Captain v. Brunau, of Bernberg, was an active breeder of long-haired Dachshunds. It was upon Brunau's Schnipp that the Standard for the variety was set. The principal points of the Standard are that the longhairs should have the colors allowable in smoothhairs but that the coat should be like that of the Spaniel.

Baron v. Cramm was a breeder of longhairs that won prizes in the shows from 1883 until 1890. Other longhair breeders and their hometowns were:

Wilhelmi, of Strehlen; E. Schaper, of Rohrsheim; Escherhaus, of Wesel; Franke, of Wanne; Reinhold, of Besigheim; Fischer, of Zwieselmuhle; Denner, of Erfurt; Herding, of Gelsenkirchen; Kramer, of Hochst; Schmitt, of Jena; and Engelmann, of Gera.

One of the first breeders of wirehairs was Captain v. Wardenburg, of Hamburg. His Mordax was one of the first to gain public interest. The name of this dog is interesting because of its meaning. *Mord* means "murder," and *ax* may be a shortened form of *Axt* meaning "axe." It is thus possible to pun upon the similar sound of Mord-Ax and Mord-Dachs. This is all the more interesting in view of the German custom of prefixing *Mord* to the word for "fellow" or "guy"; thus, *Mordskerl,* which means "he's a devil of a fellow" or "some guy" or "quite the boy." So a *Mord-Dachs* would be a "real Dachshund" or a Dachshund that kills badger, since *Dachs* means "badger." Mordax was exhibited at the Berlin show in 1883 and received a "prize of encouragement."

Wirehairs were produced by two main methods: 1. A smooth-haired Dachshund was crossed with a wire-haired Pinscher. 2. A smooth-haired Dachshund was crossed with one of the English Terriers, particularly the Dandie Dinmont. The first method resulted for some time in dogs with short heads, and coats that were a mixture of salt and

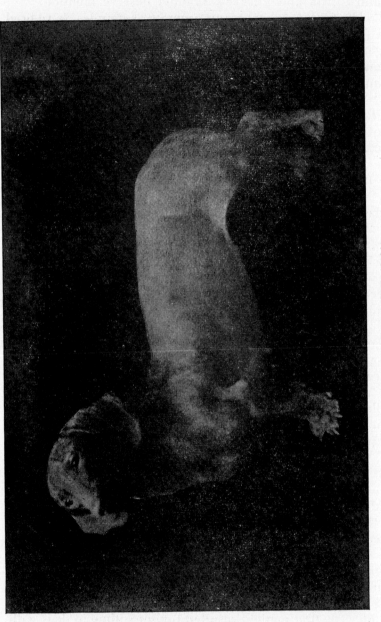

CHAMPION JANET (1890)

pepper, or similar to that of a wildcat. Dandie Dinmont crosses were responsible for soft, silky coats. In order to preserve the Dachshund conformation, smooth-haired blood was occasionally introduced.

Count Claus Hahn had bred a number of good wire-hairs. One of his products, Nesiehda, whose name incidentally means "Well, look there!" was sired by a Dandie Dinmont and was out of a smooth-haired Dachshund. His strain of dogs passed into the hands of R. Benda, of Wurttemberg, where the best wirehairs have been produced.

It is interesting to note that often the older breeders not only bred just one variety of Dachshund but also tended to favor a particular color. To my knowledge, this is not as often the case in America or elsewhere today.

Dr. Engelmann mentioned Franz Hof, of Stuttgart, as a breeder of red wirehairs, and Meinhold, of Dornap, as a breeder of black-and-tan wirehairs.

Wittmaack, of Hamburg, gained fame through his understanding of inbreeding which he carried out quite successfully with wirehairs. Some of his products were Mentor Ditmarsia (8060), Quickborn Ditmarsia (13631), and Kleines Dirndl Ditmarsia (11839).

To return to the general history of the breed, let us begin with a review of some of the developments from the 1880's on. One of the first important happenings was the founding of the Teckel Klub (Dachshund Club) in 1888. At the first general meeting on June 10, statutes were set up and a directorate was chosen. The chairman was First Lieutenant Ilgner; vice-president, Count Hahn; second vice-president, Lord Willmann. Negotiations were begun for some sort of cooperation with the Delegate Commission (comparable to our American Kennel Club), but these efforts finally had to be abandoned because of the Commission's lack of interest.

The Teckel Klub then set up its own studbook, thus precipitating the beginning of a split in the Dachshund fancy, since some dogs were listed in the Teckel Klub Studbook and some in that of the Delegate Commission. A number of local Dachshund Clubs were organized, among them the Munich Dachshund Club, the Frankfurt Dachs-

33

hund Club, the Dusseldorf Burrowing Club, the Lower Rhine Club of Dachshund Breeders, the Dachshund and Burrowing Club of Saxony, the Dachshund Burrowing Club of Munster. From the number of clubs that had arisen it is obvious that the Dachshund had grown in popularity.

Dr. Engelmann chose three years for discussion, since he felt it would be impossible to discuss fully all that occurred from 1895 to 1922. He expressed disappointment that in 1895 many breeders were more interested in what he termed "cynology" than in hunting dogs. By cynology he seemed to mean the breeding of dogs for standards of beauty alone and without consideration of the original purpose for which the Dachshund was developed. He regretted the increased size of the Dachshunds, increased depth of chest, and lessened agility. He spoke of a swing of the pendulum back toward the Dachshund as a hunter which began in 1905 with the "hunting Dachshund movement."

It will be of interest to some Dachshund breeders to note the name of an outstanding dog mentioned by Dr. Engelmann as being well received in the shows of 1895 and the names of some of his get which followed. Isolani Frankonia, who was later renamed Isolani Forst, was among the best at the Munich Show of 1895. Isolani was mated with a daughter of Schlupfer, Mauschen v. Wittringen, and the get was four pups, all of which became prize winners. They were: Wicht von der Bult, Gisela Erdmannsheim, Loni von der Bult, and Mauschen von der Bult.

The Dachshund Studbook of 1895 lists 489 dogs of both sexes which can be classified as follows:

Dogs	Bitches
56 red	85 red
90 black-and-tan	174 black-and-tan
12 brown	12 brown
1 silver gray	1 silver gray
8 dapples	14 dapples
9 wirehairs	14 wirehairs
8 longhairs	5 longhairs (among them the first brown long-haired bitch)

34

Dr. Engelmann commented that no brindle or white Dachshunds were listed in 1895. However, he gave ample evidence that a fairly large number of whites existed then and later. He mentioned specifically Berolina Wanda, Sylva Brunonia, Waldemar Brunonia, and the following persons as breeders of white Dachshunds: W. Muller, of Stendal; Hampe, of Braunschweig; and Seifert, of Plauen. They all seemingly encountered breeding difficulties and eventually gave up the effort of establishing a strain of white Dachshunds that would breed true. The problem of breeding a

TIGER-REINECKE—Dapple Dachshund
(Extract from the Journal Der Hunde-Sport)

white Dachshund today seems almost impossible of solution, but the breeder who could solve it would certainly make a name for himself and would, no doubt, find the type popular with hunters because of the color.

The registration of dogs in the Dachshund Studbook was made in a manner quite different from that followed in America today. Any member of the Dachshund Club could pass upon the suitability of a dog for registration and the dog was entered unless he was discovered to possess faults detrimental to his being used for breeding. However, a change was made later to the effect that a dog with rather serious faults could be entered provided he was the offspring of registered parents. The change resulted in a lessening of the value of registration as a factor in determining the quality of a dog.

From 1895 on, Dachshunds came to be the most numerous breed at the shows and an unfortunate trend began to make itself apparent. Some breeders began to seize upon characteristics of the breed and over-emphasize them. Length began to be sought after as a special virtue in itself and exaggeration was obtained. The same was true of depth of chest.

Earlier it was indicated that a counter-reformation began about 1905 in the form of a "hunting Dachshund movement." The breeders took sides and the directors of the Dachshund Club tried to satisfy both groups, thus losing for the Club its leadership in Dachshund affairs. The end result was that in 1910 the German Hunting Dachshund Club was formed and soon had a membership of over one hundred persons interested only in hunting. This group unselfishly dissolved itself in order to create a larger federation of local clubs interested in the Dachshund as a hunter, called the Federation of German Working Dachshund Clubs. The Federation wrote a Standard for the working Dachshund and established various tests in the different types of work such as burrowing, trailing, and bush-beating.

In 1905 the Club for the Breeding of the Miniature Dachshund was formed by Jager, Lutz, and Schultz. They believed they could attain their goal of developing a dog small enough to go underground after wild rabbits by disregarding purity of race in breeding. After ten years of trial, the Club disbanded, having failed to develop a true Dachshund type that would consistently produce the small dog they desired.

But the idea was not lost. Forester Kroepelin had a kennel of small Dachshunds and as a result of his energy and persuasiveness, another club was formed in 1905, the same year in which the previously mentioned club was founded. The new club was called the Miniature Dachshund Club (Kaninchenteckelklub). Co-founders were Senff, Nausester, and Dr. Engelmann. The latter referred those who wished to learn more about the Miniature Dachshund to a book by Forester Kroepelin, *Der Kaninchenteckel;* publisher, J. Neumann, of Neudamm, Germany.

In 1922 the Dachshund had survived another setback which came with World War I. The breeding of all three coat varieties was in full swing, and the demand was greater than the supply. There were four studbooks in which Dachshunds were registered, since each nationally organized club published its own studbook. These were the Delegate Commission (which registered all breeds), the Dachshund Club, the Working Dachshund Club, and the Miniature Dachshund Club. The chief value of the studbooks is in recording complete pedigrees, but they do not establish the quality of the dogs listed, with the exception of the Working Dachshund Club Studbook which lists only those dogs that passed certain tests set up by the Federation.

THE DEVELOPMENT OF SOME EARLY STRAINS

Anyone who is seriously interested in the background of the dogs he owns or raises will have encountered again and again the names of certain strains. Dr. Engelmann presented in some detail an account of the way in which some of these strains were developed. Of the smooth-haired strains, he discussed the Lichtenstein, Asbeck, and Gib Hals dogs. In long-haired, he described his own work with the Sonnenstein strain, and in wire-haired, he presented a thorough history of the Klausner products.

Dr. Engelmann commented early in his discussion that those breeders who sought only dogs that met their ideals in conformation had a much easier task than those who sought good hunting temperament combined with the physical structure that is the most practical for a hunting dog.

Widmann developed the Lichtenstein strain of smoothhaired Dachshunds, and he openly admitted that some of his dogs were not and could not be hunters, but he could stand for minutes at a time watching with admiration Hans v. Lichtenstein, because he was sure that it was impossible for Hans to knuckle over. When one sees pictures of some of the prize winners of that time, Widmann's pride is understandable. Dr. Engelmann stated that Widmann offered him his best dogs for stud service and that he was not offended when his offer was refused. He realized that Dr. Engelmann's chief interest was in hunting dogs and only commented, "Religion is a private matter."

The foundation bitch of the Lichtenstein dogs was Flora Gostenhof (11633), who was whelped in 1898. The descent of Flora is interesting since she is just four generations removed from the famous Hundesports Waldmann (37). Here is a partial pedigree:

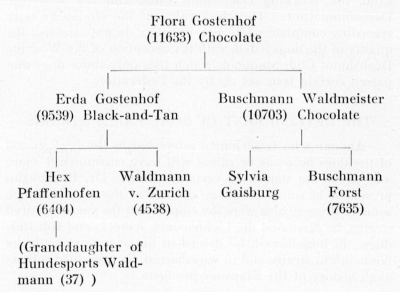

Flora Gostenhof
(11633) Chocolate

Erda Gostenhof
(9539) Black-and-Tan

Buschmann Waldmeister
(10703) Chocolate

Hex
Pfaffenhofen
(6404)

Waldmann
v. Zurich
(4538)

Sylvia
Gaisburg

Buschmann
Forst
(7635)

(Granddaughter of
Hundesports Wald-
mann (37))

38

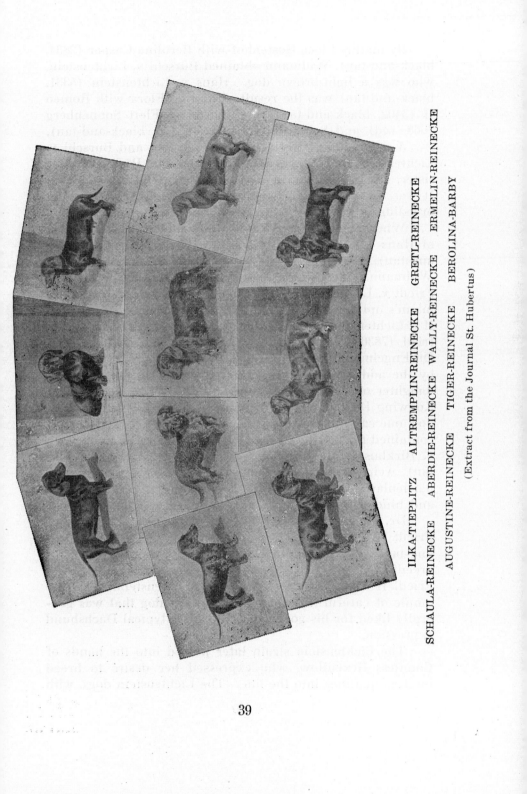

ILKA-TIEPLITZ ALTREMPLIN-REINECKE GRETL-REINECKE ERMELIN-REINECKE

SCHAULA-REINECKE ABERDIE-REINECKE WALLY-REINECKE BEROLINA-BARBY

AUGUSTINE-REINECKE TIGER-REINECKE

(Extract from the Journal St. Hubertus)

39

By mating Flora Gostenhof with Berolina Casper (2834, black-and-tan), Widmann obtained Burschl v. Lichtenstein, who was a light-brown dog. Hans v. Lichtenstein (5331, black-and-tan) was the result of mating Flora with Romeo II (3402, black-and-tan), a grandson of Flott Sonnenberg (668, red) and Schlupfer Euskirchen (76, black-and-tan).

A combination of Hans v. Lichtenstein and Burschl v. Lichtenstein blood was effected by breeding Burschl's litter sister, Erda v. Lichtenstein (5424, black-and-tan), to Hans. It was this union which became the basis of Lichtenstein breeding down through the years.

When Erda v. Lichtenstein was mated with a grandson of Hans v. Lichtenstein, Ramsch v. Seelberg (6545, black-and-tan), two pups resulted that were much admired by Widmann. They were Walter v. Lichtenstein (8429) and Friedl v. Lichtenstein (8364), both black-and-tan. In Widmann's opinion, Friedl could not be surpassed. But Friedl II v. Lichtenstein (122770, black-and-tan), a son of Ila Waldfried (7836, black-and-tan), was most admired by others. Dr. Engelmann felt that Friedl II would have been improved by the addition of more Birkbusch blood (his dam was a daughter of Mein Stern v. Birkbusch, 5950, black-and-tan). Knowing Dr. Engelmann's admiration for the light-weight dog, one can understand this feeling, for the Birkbusch line contained many Miniatures. In fact, the sire of Mein Stern v. Birkbusch, Mein Punkt v. Birkbusch (6276, black-and-tan), weighed only nine pounds. However, Friedl II was particularly admired for the good angulation of his forelegs and hind legs.

Dr. Engelmann found that one of the most attractive of Friedl II's offspring was Asbeck's Fernand (13669, black-and-tan), a dog bred by Asbeck, which was the result of breeding Friedl II to Schratel (10602), a granddaughter of Friedl II's litter brother, Walter v. Lichtenstein. This example of careful inbreeding produced a dog that was generally liked for his good angulation and typical Dachshund expression.

The Lichtenstein strain later passed into the hands of Countess Reventlow, who expressed her desire to breed hunting qualities into the line. The Lichtenstein dogs, with the exception of the red Kadarra v. Lichtenstein, were black-and-tans.

Carl Asbeck developed a strain of Dachshunds that was very similar to the Lichtenstein dogs, and he often used blood relatives of Widmann's dogs. Widmann had as his ideal a dog that weighed between twelve and fourteen pounds, but Asbeck wrote to Dr. Engelmann that he personally was not concerned with size. He also described a low Dachshund as one that did not have an excessively deep chest, but rather it was a dog with short legs which should be as straight as possible. He also sought a tight, well-arched foot. He wanted the shoulder to be as long and sloped as possible, so that it lay as far forward as possible on the rib cage; the upper arm as long as possible so that the whole front structure of the dog was pressed forward. Then this entire burden rested upon the foot and the ankle. Thus the weight of the body was distributed and the pressure relieved. These breed characteristics, he wrote, were something he had always striven for, and he never bred with faddish dogs that often had no Dachshund type. Square, short dogs were also avoided by Asbeck. In Hannover he was asked for his opinion of a dog of Saxon breeding. His reply was short and certainly to the point: "What the dog has too much of in width it lacks in length."

Asbeck felt that the chest of a Dachshund should not be deep like a keel, but drawn out and beautifully curved. His hind legs should be powerfully muscled and not cow-hocked.

Asbeck's last product, Asbeck's Rex (402/33K), was red. In his blood are many ancestors common to numerous present-day dogs. Among them are Zimmt, Monsieur Schneidig, Hundesports Waldmann, Schlupfer Euskirchen, and Flott Sonnenberg. He used the material that many others had employed, but he formed it differently according to his own ideas.

At this point Dr. Engelmann pointed out that, while inbreeding makes easier the task of developing uniformity in the physical structure of a breed, extreme caution must be exercised in order, by careful selection, to breed out typical family faults. To illustrate his point, he mentioned the

41

tendency in some Asbeck dogs toward high rear quarters, which, he explained, are the result of unnecessarily low shoulders.

Then Dr. Engelmann entered into a discussion of that thorny problem, the level top-line versus the slightly arched back. To support his own belief that some arch just over the kidney section is necessary for the greatest strength, Dr. Engelmann referred to statements made by Muller. The latter said that if the back of a Dachshund is intended to transmit smooth continuous motion, it cannot be flat or "negative" (apparently he meant sway-backed). Dr. Engelmann also noted that a correctly arched back appears to be shorter than a level one. One function of the back is to transmit the work of the powerful hindquarters to the fore-part of the body, and Dr. Engelmann believed that the arch contributes strength to the spine.

Quoting from someone who was acquainted with Wid-mann's dogs, Dr. Engelmann wrote: "These dogs could hardly jump up onto a chair, many couldn't; in a rocky terrain they would have been impossible." He admitted that there may well be some exaggeration in the statement, but it does give a good idea of the reasoning followed by those opposed to the level top-line. The lightly curved, powerfully arched backline in the kidney section was also supported by von Daackc, one of the master breeders.

Dr. Engelmann also told of some dogs that he owned when he was breeding for show competition. They would chase a cat into the haymow and then bark until someone came to carry them down the steps. Their chests were so deep that they struck the lower step before their short legs could reach it.

The opposite type from the Lichtenstein and Asbeck strains wcre the products of Selchow's Gib Hals kennels. From the pictures of Selchow's dogs one sees immediately that they all show strong family resemblances. Some of their characteristics are a shorter backline, a shallower chest, and an overall lighter structure. Modern breeders in America would think they were underfed, scrawny, and even Terrier-like, although they do seem to retain a rather typical Dachshund facial expression. As Dr. Englemann

42

stated it: "Where something could be saved and chiseled away of hindering substance, unnecessary chest volume, too heavy bone, too large, dangling ears, in fat, skin, and feet, that was done." Dr. Engelmann admired the agility and fleet movement of the Gib Hals dogs and their "strong spirit," by which he meant their aggressiveness. He commented that, on the reverse side of a photograph of Gib Hals Olaf, Selchow had written laconically, "Torn to bits alive by Gib Hals Excellenz."

The Gib Hals dogs were bred for work and not for beauty. Selchow used a very sharp stud as the basis of his program. He was Schlupfer v. Fehmarn (5774, red) and of his get the smallest and sharpest offspring were selected for breeding purposes. Dr. Engelmann thought his best product was Gib Hals Schrimm (8196, red), a son of Schlupfer v. Fehmarn. Some of the well-known dogs to be found in the Gib Hals background were Knopf, Coeur Konig v. Waldmannsruh, Flott Sonnenberg, Monsieur Schneidig, and repeatedly, Zimmt.

After considering these strains, which differ so much in type, Dr. Engelmann discussed his own work in establishing the Sonnenstein line. He believed that he followed a middle-of-the-road policy, and yet the outsider notes how strongly he leaned towards small, lightly built, sharp hunters.

He began with a smooth-haired bitch, Dinchen, and bred her to a long-haired stud. From this mating he obtained the long-haired bitch, Braune Hexe v. Sonnenstein (2163). She weighed just over twelve pounds and was a good hunter. Dr. Engelmann used her as the foundation bitch for his strain. To the other attributes which he sought in his Dachshunds, Dr. Engelmann added that of resistance to distemper. As far as possible, he bred only dogs that had never suffered the disease, although many of them had definitely been exposed along with others that succumbed to it. Braune Hexe liked water work, she was a trailer and, in a sense, a retriever, for she dragged to her master that which was too large for her to carry

Braune Hexe was mated with a sharp, long-haired stud, Etzel (2691), who was the son of a trailing Sieger named

43

Stromer. From their progeny, Dr. Engelmann chose without regard for beauty the sharpest pup, Erda v. Sonnenstein. He said that before long he made the error of selecting for beauty and discovered that the hunting ardor of his Dachshunds diminished and the size increased accordingly. He admitted that this may have been coincidence.

He looked around among long-haired studs for one that could restore hunting fire and small size to his strain but found none, and finally he resorted to a breeding with a smoothhair. Selchen v. Sonnenstein was the result of this breeding, and in her he found the type he wanted. However, since the smooth coat is dominant over the long coat, Dr. Engelmann lost the source of the longhairs that he admired.

Selchen was bred to Schwefelgezwerg v. Niflheim and the very small Herkules v. Sonnenstein resulted. When bred to Gib Hals Schrimm, Selchen produced the thirteen-pound Teckele v. Sonnenstein. A breeding with Raudl v. Seelberg brought Raudel v. Sonnenstein, whom Dr. Engelmann regarded as his best and most versatile worker.

In variance with the practice of most modern breeders, Dr. Engelmann cared little whether he bred with smoothhaired or wire-haired dogs. The sole test that he applied was performance in the field and burrow. He stressed soundness of structure and character, and, as previously mentioned, freedom from distemper. He did some inbreeding, but he selected carefully the dogs to be bred. He also followed a practice which he termed "transplanting." At times he bred to dogs which he had bred and sold to other kennels, or to the offspring of such dogs. He seemed to feel that his own strain which had been raised in a different geographic environment could contribute a refreshening influence to his own dogs. The dam was selected for soundness and character and not for beauty. Dr. Engelmann said that one admires the belle of the ball, but one doesn't marry her.

The qualities he sought are stated as follows: "The goal of my breeding remains an eleven- to thirteen-pound Dachshund, sound in body and character, with harsh smooth coat or the hardest wirehair, with elongated head and powerful teeth. Not high, not low, not short, not long. Ears only medium long, well set back; no heavy bones, and certainly no rickety ones; straight, Pointer-like, short tail. Sloping shoulder set, better straight than too crooked legs, closed feet. Briefly, intelligent, practical, and useful in every respect. Above all, I emphasize it again and again, hard, dry, hard as steel, carved from working Dachshund wood, in form and character. None at all of the soft-as-butter sort! Certainly not in personality nor in his back; the latter should be sturdy, never swayed or cut off in the rump."

Leaving his own work, Dr. Engelmann proceeded to consider the work that was done in breeding wirehairs unmixed with other coats. For a number of years it was thought that in order to keep Dachshund conformation, it was necessary occasionally to introduce smoothhair blood into the strain. However, the President of the Club for Wire-haired Dachshunds, Captain Zuckschwerdt, believed that it was possible to breed wire-haired dogs without resorting to smoothhair blood. Zuckschwerdt began his work with a black-and-tan smooth-haired bitch of Austrian breeding, but he felt that she was too heavy and too deep in the chest. He sought a stud that could counterbalance her faults, and in Mentor Ditmarsia, a wirehair, he felt he had found that stud. He was so pleased with the offspring of this mating that he decided to breed only wirehairs. Therefore he began to eliminate the smoothhairs from his strain.

By inbreeding with Mentor and his son, Klausner's Pan, Zuckschwerdt contrived to produce a strain characterized by excellent stance, hard coat, and good head. But fate worked against Zuckschwerdt. Just as he began to see the results he desired, the supreme naval command called him into active service in 1912. He spent seven years away from home, mostly in the South Seas and finally as an American prisoner. His dogs passed out of his hands and upon his return he had to start from the beginning again.

The Ditmarsia strain, by 1919, had moved to Sweden and the only person who had maintained some of its blood was Pabst, who was lighthouse keeper on the lonely island of Fehmarn. He used the kennel name of v. Alsen. Fiffi v. Alsen became the foundation dam of the Klausner wirehairs, but she had smoothhair blood on her sire's side, and that blood went back to the Lichtenstein strain. Helios v. Teck-eltreu, the only stud that had preserved the Ditmarsia blood over the war, was chosen to be bred to her. He carried wirehair blood from the Otting dogs and v. Annenhof smoothhair blood. But his sire, Quickborn Ditmarsia, was strong in Ditmarsia blood. The get from the breeding of Helios and Fiffi was three wirehairs and three smoothhairs. A salt-and-pepper wire-haired male died of distemper, but the two remaining reds, Klausner's Bautz and Klausner's Blida, became outstanding dogs. Bautz was bred back to his dam and he became the foundation sire of many wire-hairs to whom he usually gave a firm body, good muzzle, excellent coat, and outstanding hunting qualities. Bautz's ancestry can be traced through his dam to the wire-haired bitch, Cartouche v. d. Klause (3186), in whose blood he was inbred nine times. His great-grandsire on his sire's side, Mentor Ditmarsia (131), came from Murx (4597) out of Dirndl v. Klause (Wire-haired Dachshund Studbook, 20), who was also in the dam's line of Cartouche, while his great-granddam on his sire's side, Kleines Dirndl (542), was also derived from Mentor but out of his dam, Dirndl (20), and so he went back doubly to Cartouche. Heidelerche v. d. Olenberg (12836), the dam of Helios, came from the same dam's line, and that is also true of the granddam on the dam's side, Nelly v. Alsen (745R), who came from two litter mates which go back doubly to Cartouche. Bautz was the product of conscious family breeding and his chief value to wirehairs lay in his concentrated hunting blood and in the emphasis upon his ancestors' qualities that made them de-sirable for breeding. Bautz's best descendant is probably Klausner's Mentor (515Y), who was the result of breeding Bautz to his dam, Fiffi v. Alsen. Other outstanding Klausner dogs were Bautz's litter mate, Klausner's Blida, and the litter sisters of Mentor, Klausner's Maja, Mirza, Mona, and Mira, and a lightweight, dark salt-and-pepper, Klausner's Ayesha.

SHOWS

Dr. Engelmann included in his book a short chapter on shows and their purpose in which he granted that some breeders oppose exhibitions while others regard them as necessary evils. He listed a number of purposes that are served by planned and supervised exhibitions of dogs, as well as some disadvantages. These observations are as pertinent today as they were when they were written.

1. They provide the breeder the opportunity to compare his dogs with those of others, and he then has a basis for deciding whether or not he is proceeding correctly.

2. At a show it is possible to discover outside breeding material which may help to improve one's own dogs in their weak points.

3. The showing of one's stock is one of the best ways of advertising it.

4. There is no better place for the purchase and sale of dogs since many dogs are brought from distant parts of the country. The purchaser can see what he is buying, and the seller has his merchandise at hand to back up his sales talk. And, of course, any wins accrued at the show act as a further drawing card.

5. At shows breeders can compare notes and make new friendships, all of which encourages cooperation which in its turn will improve the breed.

6. The show gives the breeder a chance to win recognition for his work and places a stamp of impartial approval (with some few exceptions) upon the winning dogs. Dr. Engelmann called attention to a harmful effect upon the welfare of the breed if prizes are awarded to poor dogs because of lack of competition and the subsequent deception of the unknowing beginner.

7. Shows sometimes work to the disadvantage of a breed when too much emphasis is placed upon conformation to the detriment of temperament.

8. Unfortunately, some people regard success or failure at a show as a compliment or insult to their persons or social position and lose sight of the fact that it is the dogs that are being judged.

9. One great service of the dog show is that it helps to gain the interest of the public in the purebred dog and it makes known the advances that have taken place.

Dr. Engelmann concluded his discussion of shows with some observations that every present-day exhibitor can profit by. He urged the breeder to go to the show himself, to handle his own dog, to look at his dogs' competitors and to form his own opinions about them. However, he should accept the decision of the judge calmly. *After* the judging, he should discuss with the judge anything he does not understand. The dog owner should remember that, although the breed Standards are prescribed, the interpretation of them varies with the judge, which is only natural and must be expected.

ALL WHITE DACHSHUND
(From German book by Emil Ilgner, 1902)

The daughter of Kaiser Wilhelm and her Dachshund

Dachshunds In Germany Since 1945

By Gerda M. Umlauff, Germany

WAR and postwar chaos bring a crucial test to any breed and its fanciers. Hence it is interesting to observe what effects the recent conflict has produced on the Dachshund in Germany.

Chairman H. Grote of the old "Teckel-Verband" spoke on this theme at the March 1949 meeting of the "Verein der Hunderfreunde." Mr. Grote is manager of the Hamburg group of the "Deutscher Teckelklub e. v. gegr. 1888," which, since the end of the war, is again the official name of the German Dachshund Club. There are eighty-five groups in the "Deutscher Teckelklub," and of these the Hamburg group is one of the largest. Following are some of Mr. Grote's observations about the effect of the war on the Dachshund:

"Years of hunger naturally do not produce such catastrophic effects on small breeds as on large ones which require more food. While the breeding and raising of large dogs often became problems because of inadequate nutrition, for the most part the Dachshunds were sufficiently well-fed. This was true primarily because most Dachshund kennels were in small towns or in the country, and the owners of the Dachshunds were hunters who very likely had better access to food than dog owners in cities.

"The German Dachshund would have survived World War II without serious losses, except of course those occasioned by bombings and being deprived of essential medicines such as worm capsules, had it not been for the events of 1945. The flight of East German breeders and owners, and the erection of boundaries between the different zones caused pitiable losses among the little four-footed hunters. The East of Germany has long been famous for its hunting grounds, and therefore, there was considerable loss among the smooth-haired Dachshunds, much more among the wirehaired, and less among the long-haired variety."

The work of the Teckelklub was hindered in many ways because during the first postwar days the mail service could not be used by Germans. Permission was not granted for meetings of the members of the Club, and resignations followed together with the foundation of several new Clubs, most of which were smaller. In spite of these handicaps, fancy breeding and regular work were going on in German dogdom. The Teckelklub was anxious to arrange regular shows and trials, so several sporting events took place. The following facts give ample proof of activities:

The first postwar show took place on September 9, 1945, at Hamburg, with forty-five Dachshund entries among seven hundred dogs of all breeds. The Dachshund entries were all living in Hamburg or its environs. Thirty thousand visitors were reported to have attended this particular show. In November of the same year, the first field trial was held, and in May 1946 there was another show at Hamburg. On this occasion there were eighty-six Dachshunds in the catalogue. On August 9, 1946, at the same place, there was a championship show with ninety-nine Dachshund entries. On June 15, 1947, twenty field trials and fourteen forthcoming shows were announced, and since that time much progress has been made in the training of Dachshunds for hunting. From 1945 to 1948 nearly two hundred shows were held, and on these occasions from one hundred to two hundred fifty Dachshunds were on exhibition; in 1949 there were twenty-nine shows with 2,037 Dachshunds exhibited, 1,719 of which were awarded prizes; in 1951 there were only twenty shows with 1,043 Dachshunds exhibited, of which 872 were awarded prizes; in 1952 there were seventeen shows with 1,290 Dachshunds exhibited, of which 1,127 were awarded prizes.

The following list presents the German champions of recent years:

Champion Show, Hamburg, 1946:
  smooth-haired, black-and-tan, dog: Itzenplitz v. d. Trapp 390945 k
  wire-haired, pepper and salt, dog: Zaunkonig v. Konigshufen, 414894 r
  wire-haired, pepper and salt, bitch: Marotte v. Konigshufen, 425309 r
  long-haired, red, dog: Butz v. d. Goldenen Perle, 398346 l

Champion Show, Hamburg, 1947:
  smooth-haired, black-and-tan, dog: Magnat v. d. Sauhatz, 450563 k
  smooth-haired, red, dog: Billi v. Kyffhauserwald, 431322 k
  wire-haired, pepper and salt, dog: Zaunkonig v. Konigshufen, 414894 r
  wire-haired pepper and salt, bitch: Marotte v. Konigshufen, 425309 r
  long-haired, black-and-tan, dog: Stropp v. d. Eifelkraft, 457356 l
  long-haired, red, Miniature, dog: Bodo v. Kuxhof, 457126 l
  wire-haired, red, Miniature, bitch: Madi v. Bohlenbach, 2181/45 r

Champion Show, Munich, 1948:
  smooth-haired, red, bitch: Elli v. Rottal, 460131 k
  wire-haired, pepper and salt, dog: Zaunkonig v. Konigshufen, 414894 r
  wire-haired, pepper and salt, bitch: Modell v. Konigshufen, 443330 r
  long-haired, red, dog: Nicky v. Ainhofen, 439406 l
  long-haired, red, bitch: Halma v. Habichtshof, 457912 l

Champion Show, Dortmund, 1948:
  wire-haired, dead leaf brown, bitch: Anka v. d. Geest, 453153 r

53

long-haired, red, bitch: Olly v. Eichbruch, 427978 l

long-haired, red, Miniature, bitch: Linde aus Koln, 477230 l

Champion Show, Dortmund, 1949:

smooth-haired, black-and-tan, dog: Magnat von der Sauhatz, 450563 k

smooth-haired, black-and-tan, bitch: Edda von der Sauhatz, 480021 k

wire-haired, dead leaf brown, bitch: Nette von Heidefeld, 453119 r

wire-haired, black-and-tan, dog: Bob von Eschbachtal, 426513 r

long-haired, red, dog: Adi von Rothaargebirge, 477922 l

long-haired, red, bitch: Loni von Oldenburg, 467266 l

Champion Show, Frankfurt, 1950:

smooth-haired, red, bitch: Amsel (Centner), 480861 k

wire-haired, dead leaf brown, dog: Blitz von Weidehorst, 474521 r

wire-haired, black-and-tan, bitch: Minka von Eschbachtal, 474739 r

long-haired, red, dog: Gertrud's Axel, 447232 l

Champion Show, Aachen, 1951:

smooth-haired, red, dog: Juwel von Haus Hagen, 481622 k

smooth-haired, black-and-tan, bitch: Nora von der Sauhatz, 500421 k

long-haired, red, Miniature, dog: Arras von der Ulrichsburg, 488497 l

long-haired, red, dog: Clown von Brauck, 498544 l

wire-haired, dead leaf brown, dog: Horrido von der Fichtenhöhe, 474002 r

wire-haired, dead leaf brown, bitch: Sieggold's Susi, 502945 r

Champion Show, Dortmund, 1952:

smooth-haired, black-and-tan, dog: Fra Diavolo von der Sauhatz, 510879 k

smooth-haired, black-and-tan, bitch: Nora von der Sauhatz, 500421 k

wire-haired, dead leaf brown, dog: Ast von der Herzogsstadt, 503660 r

long-haired, black-and-tan, dog: Heiko von der Geier-
sheck, 490526 l

long-haired, red, Miniature, dog: Arras von der Ulrichsburg, 488497 l

wire-haired, red, Miniature, dog: Viktor von der Hermannsklause, 512201 r

Champion Show, Mannheim, 1953:

smooth-haired, black-and-tan, dog: Maxim von Schwarenberg, 510553 k

smooth-haired, black-and-tan, bitch: Maritza von
Schwarenberg, 510555 k

smooth-haired, black-and-tan, Miniature, bitch: Ariane
von der Hermannsklause, 501378

wire-haired, red, Miniature, dog: Viktor von der Hermannsklause, 512201 r

wire-haired, red, Miniature, bitch: Odette von der
Hermannsklause, 522826 r

long-haired, red, Miniature, dog: Ned. Ch. Arco von
der Gartenstadt Haan Winner, 509677 l

long-haired, red, Miniature, bitch: Varni von Drach-
enstein, 48764 l

smooth-haired, black-and-tan, Rabbit Dachshund, bitch:
Anke von der Holzheide, 511074 k

wire-haired, dead leaf brown, dog: Arko von Ueber-
feld, 513624 r

wire-haired, dead leaf brown, bitch: Xandra von Heidefeld, 485076 r

long-haired, black-and-tan, dog: Youp du Grand-Croe,
LOF 11 Tpl 500

long-haired, red, bitch: Ulla von Bockholzberg, 507768 l

The Teckelklub has increased the number of its groups
tremendously. In 1933 there were thirty-four groups; in
1947, thirty-nine groups; in 1948, sixty-three groups; and in
1954, eighty-five groups. Including members living in the
Russian zone of Germany and in foreign countries, the Club
had a total of 4,080 members at the end of 1952, and a total
of 4,382 members at the end of 1953.

From 1890 to 1953, membership in the German Teckelklub increased as follows:

KATHRIN v. KONIGSHUFEN
376363 R   VPI-Spl.-
Two times International Champion

SIEGER ZAUNKONIG v. KONIGSHUFEN
414394 R   G. T. 16/47
Three times Zone-Sieger
Austellungs-Sieger 1947, u. 1948   Gebraych-Sieger 1947
· Vp p Spl. BgDN

Year	No. of Members
1890	192
1933	1,149
1938	2,030
1947	1,643
1949	4,292
1951	3,933
1952	4,080
1953	4,382

Four officials work regularly in the Teckelklub office, and since January 12, 1946, the Club has published a monthly magazine, *The Dachshund,* which is distributed in twenty-one countries. To help promote the use of the Dachshund for hunting purposes, the Teckelklub published a book in 1953 which contains instructions for conducting trials. Subjects included are: work under ground; rousing game; developing ability to scent; following and barking on trail; following on leash; and making the dog shot proof (preventing the dog from becoming gun-shy).

All varieties of Dachshunds are permitted to participate in trials regardless of size, or type of coat, provided they have been registered in the studbook. Their ability in trials is rated as follows:

0—not sufficient
1—sufficient
2—good
3—very good
4—excellent

The Allied soldiers were much interested in German Dachshunds and bought some good dogs. Because of ignorance, however, they more often purchased dogs of inferior quality. Field Marshall Montgomery was one of the first Dachshund buyers. He bought a black-and-tan smooth-haired dog from the famous Asbeck kennel, and showed him at a later date at an exhibition in Great Britain.

The progress of different varieties of a breed can be observed through a study of the registrations in the studbook. The information given in the following table indicates how the popularity of the different varieties of Dachshunds has varied since 1890:

Year	Smooth-haired	Wire-haired	Long-haired	Total
1890	386	3	5	394
1933	1,577	780	1,105	3,462
1938	2,140	2,514	1,977	6,631
1947	1,475	3,009	4,433	8,917
1949	1,722	3,053	5,334	10,109
1951	1,275	2,151	4,628	8,054

The extraordinary popularity of the long-haired Dachshund is obvious. As the above figures indicate, there are more registrations for the long-haired variety than for the wire-haired and the smooth-haired together. The wire-haired Dachshund, although taking second place in the studbook, is considered by many to excel in qualifications as a hunter.

Red is the Dachshund color given preference in Germany today, for black-and-tan Dachshunds are not so numerous. The breeders are working, however, to produce more of the black-and-tan dogs, and some are trying to reproduce the almost forgotten chocolate brown Dachshund. Most of the Rabbit Dachshunds in Germany are red in color; very few black-and-tan dogs of this variety are to be found, although many hunters would prefer the black-and-tan Rabbit Dachshund, since by his color the dog could then be more easily distinguished from the red of the fox.

In the studbook of the German Teckelklub only those dogs are registered whose parents are already in it. The total loss of Dachshunds during the war was not so great as to make necessary any exceptions to this rule. Only one case is known where there has been any departure from this principle. It was discovered at the end of the war that one dog in Wurttemberg without a pedigree had been registered in the studbook. It is conceivable that other cases may appear in Berlin, but this will have no influence on the breed in the Western zones.

The high dog taxes imposed in many places have militated more against the Dachshund and the prosperity of the

Teckelklub than the new currency of June 1948. Nevertheless, the quality of the German Dachshund is now first-class
as has been attested by several foreign specialists who have
had the opportunity to make first-hand observations. Further proof is the fact that the Dachshund is again being
exported to Sweden and Switzerland, and fanciers in other
foreign countries are also anxious to buy Dachshunds in
Germany. Buyers from Austria, Sweden, and Norway ask
for wire-haired Dachshunds, while the English demand the
smooth- and long-haired. The buyers want Dachshunds
which not only manifest beautiful physical conformation
but also are useful as hunters. They must be keen and must
follow the trail of the hare with appropriate barking. As
often as it is possible, examinations must be given to prove
the dogs' abilities as hunters.

The motto of the German Teckelklub is: "Our dogs
must be both keen and handsome." The chief aim of breeders is to produce a dog whose beauty is commensurate with
his intelligence, who is alert, and whose endurance makes
him fit for hunting. In order to realize this ideal, the German
breeder gets much excellent advice from the Teckelklub,
which takes every precaution to bar from membership
breeders who are interested only in money. Breeders who
are vitally concerned with the welfare of the Dachshund
and in the prevention of the recurrence of his common faults,
are further assisted by rules which were announced in 1948.

These rules state that every kennel must be inspected
by a Teckelklub member who has practical knowledge of,
and experience with, breeding. Through visiting the different
kennels, he must be able to recognize possibilities of raising
properly bred dogs in his group. The inspector must decide
if the puppies are of sufficiently good quality to be registered,
and if they are not, they must be destroyed immediately.
Breeders may not keep unregistered Dachshunds, and dogs
may not be bred to bitches without pedigrees.

In order to produce better hunting Dachshunds, a special
studbook has been established. In it are registered all
Dachshunds which have been examined at fox-holes, either
natural or artificial, and which have passed other tests of
their hunting ability. Each qualified Dachshund is given a

MILO v. KONIGSHUFEN 395303 R
BhFN I   (German)

Zuchtgruppe v. Konigshufen
Marquis   Sieger Marotte   Five times Sieger Zaunkonig von Konigshufen

60

special number in this studbook, and this number together with his number in the other studbook appears with his pedigree. All Dachshunds which receive prizes in hunting tests also get the so-called *"Leistungszeichen"* which become parts of their names, and will be found with the pedigrees of all their descendants. If the Leistungszeichen is awarded when the Dachshund is under twelve months of age, "J" (abbreviation for the German word *Jugend,* meaning youth) becomes a part of the dog's name. The Leistungszeichen are:

BhF K—means dog has been examined at fox-hole (artificial)

BhD K—means dog has been examined at badger kennel (artificial)

BhF N—means dog has been examined at fox-hole (natural)

BhD N—means dog has been examined at badger kennel (natural)

W—means strangler (*Wurger*)

Sp—means dog has been examined: he barks on trail (*spurlaut*)

Schwh. K—means dog has been examined: he follows blood on artificial trail

Schwh. N—means dog has been examined: he follows blood on natural trail

Tv—means dog barks at the dead game (*Totverbeller*)

Tw—means dog leads to the dead game

Vp—means dog has had many-sided examination

KSchlH—means dog (Rabbit Dachshund) has shown ability to bring rabbit, either dead or injured, from burrow

KSprN—means dog (Rabbit Dachshund) has shown hunting ability comparable to that of larger variety of Dachshund, barks on trail, and is keen.

In order to achieve truly beautiful dogs, the German Teckelklub does not permit registration in the studbook of any dogs with the following faults: undershot, overshot, very loose shoulders, stump tail, one or both testicles undescended, or a bad chest. German show points are listed as

61

excellent, very good, good, sufficient, and deficient. The rating of excellent or very good is never given to a Dachshund manifesting the following faults: too weak, too tall, lacking compactness in the shoulders, having a too slender body, a too heavy or clumsy body which causes the dog to exhibit waddling movements, the position of the toes too much on the outside or the inside, spread toes, a carp-back, a hollow back, or overbuilt—that is if the croup is higher than the withers. The chest must not be too weak, and the hindquarters must be well muscled. Cowhocks, and light eyes in dogs other than gray or spotted dogs, and poor condition of the hair are also rated as serious faults.

Little faults which prevent a rating of excellent are: badly placed, folded ears; a forehead too heavy or too pointed; weak jaws; distemper teeth; a too broad, short head; goggle eyes; too light eyes in gray and spotted dogs; not sufficiently dark eyes in all other colored dogs; loose folds of skin at the neck; a short neck; and too thin hair. Being overweight is also a fault, for a dog should not weigh more than nine kg. (eighteen pounds).

The classification of the weight for shows is:

> heavy dogs—more than 7 kg.
> heavy bitches—more than 6½ kg.
> average dogs—under 7 kg.
> average bitches—under 6½ kg.
> Miniature dogs—under 4 kg.
> Miniature bitches—under 3½ kg.

These weights are for Dachshunds at least twelve months old. Miniature Dachshunds should have a chest measurement of 35 cm. (14 inches), and Rabbit Dachshunds should have a chest measurement of 30 cm. (12 inches). The chest is measured when the dog is at least twelve months old and is recorded on the dog's pedigree.

In recent years in Germany a number of faults in Dachshunds have been observable. In the smooth-haired we have seen long feet and folded parts quite as often as cowhocks, and in the wire-haired, very frequently the upper arm has been too short. For the most part, fortunately, the condition of the coat of the wire-haired has been very good—

that is at a distance it looks like the smooth-haired, showing short hair and as little beard as possible. The principal faults of the long-haired have been cowhocks, and, even in dogs from well-known kennels, overshot jaws. We can truthfully say, however, that seventy out of one hundred smooth-haired and wire-haired males would be rated excellent.

The smooth-haired Dachshund is no longer as popular as it was in the past. The long-haired variety is preferred despite the difficulties encountered in breeding to produce a satisfactory coat in this variety. The average and Miniature dogs are preferred to the heavy Dachshunds, and in South Germany, especially in the mountains, the Brachen, a breed related to the Dachshund, is used for hunting.

It is said that seventy-five percent of all dogs are of no value to their breed, because they either die when they are young or live in private homes where they are lost to the breed. The remaining twenty-five percent are used for the propagation of the species, and among them we find different bloodlines which guarantees that there shall not be too much inbreeding. Careful investigation reveals the following:

Formerly, regardless of the kind of hair, all Dachshund bloodlines led to a red, long-haired bitch, Braune Hexe v. Sonnenstein, who lived about 1889. The modern smooth-haired Dachshunds come from the bloodlines of the following kennels: von Erbenstein (breeds red color), von Hasselkopf, von der Geest, which all lead back to the famous male Burschel von Alderschroffen. The kennels Luitpoldsheim, Schwarenberg, and Schneid lead back to the kennel von der Sauhatz, and its best male, Magnat von der Sauhatz. In his bloodlines we find dogs who carry the names of Asbeck's and Lichtenstein. Today we find very good dogs among animals from the kennel von Wickrathsberg, von Stromberg, Flottenberg, and Behn von der Trapp.

Among the wire-haired Dachshunds there are four kennels which produce animals equally endowed with beauty and excellent qualifications for hunting. These are von Konigshufen, von Grobenhagen, von Moorberg, and St. Georg. In these kennels there are dogs whose pedigrees indicate two hundred and fifty times that they carry the

SIEGER MAROTTE v. KONIGSHUFEN, 425309 **R**
Many sided examined, also as strangler.
After Veronika Sandstrom of Sweden,
the best European Dachshund of today.
Sire: Five times Champion Zaunkonig v. Konigshufen
Dam: Milo v. Konigshufen

blood of the famous wire-haired male Raudel von Sonnenstein, who was the best wire-haired male at the time of the first world war. A notable exception among the wire-haired kennels is the well-known Ditmarsia kennel, whose dogs, without "Raudel" blood, lead back directly through Mentor Ditmarsia to Krott v. d. Klause and Kartusch v. d. Klause, and thence to the famous Munich kennel. One other kennel which should be mentioned is von Allertal, which was established with dogs from the Konigshufen, Klausner's, and von Hohentwiel bloodlines.

Among the best-known long-haired kennels are: von Eichbruch, von der Goldenen Perle, von Ainhofen, von Zinnowitz, von Fels, and Gertrud's.

Since 1950 the Miniature and Rabbit Dachshunds have improved tremendously, and the ideal Rabbit Dachshund of today not only should be a beautiful specimen of the breed, but also should be a good hunting dog. In 1951 the long-haired Miniatures were awarded the championship titles, whereas today, the smooth-haired and wire-haired Miniatures equal the long-haired in quality. German breeders have become more and more interested in the Miniature variety, and among the best of dogs of this variety produced in Germany today are the wire-haired black-and-tan dogs from the vom Hasegau kennel; the wire-haired dogs from the aus der Hermannsklause kennel; the long-haired red dogs from vom Teufelsstern kennel; and the long-haired red dogs from the vom Höhenberg and von der Haidloh kennels. Other Miniature and Rabbit Dachshund kennels of merit are: von Bohlenbach, von Kuxhof, vom Wedeberg, and von Waldhotel. The breeding place for the tiger Dachshund is the prominent von Tigerpark kennel.

Dachshunds, from *La Venerie*, by Jacques du Fouilloux, 1561.

Early English Dachshunds

HE following contribution, a complete history of the Dachshund and the leading kennels in England from 1870 to 1891, was written by Mr. Harry Jones (a noted English breeder) about 1895:

"The first Dachshunds that are recorded as winning prizes in England were Mr. H. Corbet's Carl and Grete; when at Birmingham in 1866, they were each awarded a prize in the 'Extra class for any known breed of sporting dogs.' And in these 'extra' classes, all Dachshunds had to compete until the show held at the Crystal Palace in June 1873, when, for the first time, a class was given for the breed, and the winners on this occasion were Mr. Hodge's Erdmann, first; Rev. G. F. Lovell's Satan, second; and Hon. Gerald Lescelles' Schnaps, third; but from 1866 to 1873, Dachshunds, whenever exhibited, were invariably winners in these 'extra' classes, the chief winners being Mr. Fisher's Feldmann, Mr. Seton's Dachs, Rev. G. F. Lovell's Satan and Mouse, and the Earl of Onslow's Waldmann. Birmingham gave a separate class in 1873, the winners being Mr. Fisher's Feldmann, first, and the Hon. Gerald Lescelles' Schnaps, second; this was a good class of fifteen entries, and they were judged by the late Mr. Lort.

"At the Kennel Club Show, held at the Crystal Palace in June 1874, two classes were given: 'Red' and 'Other than

Red,' and separate divisions were given during the year at Pomona Gardens, Manchester, at Nottingham, and at Belle Vue Gardens, Manchester; while at Birmingham two classes were given: 'Red' and 'Other than Red,' when Mr. Bass's Slap was first, and Rev. G. F. Lovell's Mouse second in reds, and Mr. Hodge's Erdmann first, and Hon. Miss E. Strutt's Thekla second in the other than red class.

"At the Kennel Club Show at the Crystal Palace in June 1875, Prince Albert Solms judged the Dachshunds and the classes were divided into 'Black-and-tan' and 'Other than Black-and-tan,' and there were thirty entries in the two. In the first-named class, H.R.H. the Prince of Wales won first with Deurstich, a dog five years old, bred at Sandringham, and the dam of Marguerite, the second prize winner, was bred by Her Majesty the Queen. In the second class, the Duke of Hamilton won with Badger, a nice red puppy eleven months old, bred by himself, and the Rev. G. F. Lovell was second with Pixie, a red bitch imported from Hanover. Pixie was very Houndy in head, compared with the Dachshunds then being shown, was smaller in size, with a beautiful arched loin. At Nottingham Mr. Hutton's Festus won first and also first at Birmingham, when he beat Slap, the 1874 winner. Festus won a large number of prizes; he was a very good-bodied dog, but was short in ear.

"In 1876, more Dachshunds were exhibited with the decidedly pronounced Hound type of head than had been previously shown; these included Xaverl, a most beautiful stamp of Dachshund, full of quality, particularly good in loin, imported from the Royal Kennels, near Stuttgart. Most of our best Dachshunds go back to Xaverl, and many of them are inbred to him. Xaverl first appeared at the Kennel Club Show at the Crystal Palace in June, when he was placed second, Pixie being first. But this decision was reversed at Brighton. Zeiten came out with Xaveral, and was awarded an extra prize. He was said to be the sire of Xaverl, though they were quite different in type. Most of Zieten's stock born in England had his square, lippy type of head, short cloddy body, with immense bone; whereas Xaverl was a most graceful dog, with beautiful neck and shoulders, magnificent loin, but light in bone.

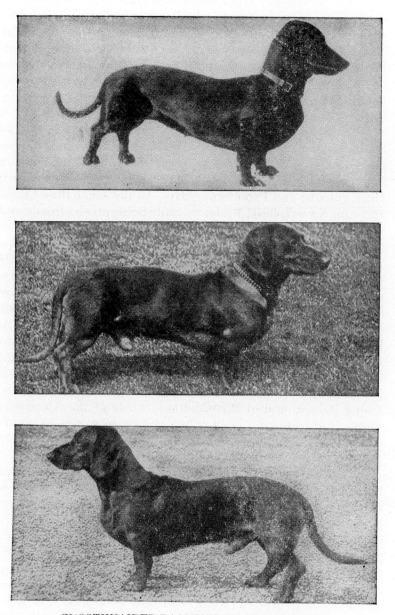

SMOOTHHAIRED DACHSHUNDS OF ABOUT 1910
Note improvement in type in recent years

"At Maidstone, Dina came out and was awarded an extra first. She had a lovely head, narrow and straight, with a beautiful skull, good skin and bone, but moved badly behind. Fritz also came out at Maidstone. He had particularly long ears, was rather large, but plain in head. He was not so low, nor with so much bone as Dina. At Darlington, Festus beat Xaverl, and again at Birmingham, but the judging of Dachshunds at this time was very inconsistent.

"At Brighton, in October, Dessauer, Chenda, Linda, and Schlupferle were new faces. Dessauer won first in black-and-tan dogs, and five prizes were awarded in black-and-tan bitches, *viz.*, Marguerite, first; Chenda, second; Linda, third; Dina, fourth; and Frou Frou, fifth. In the other than black-and-tan, Xaverl, first; Pixie, second; Schlupferle, third; and Gisella, fourth; the latter was a very small bitch, light in bone and toyish in head. Dessauer had a long punishing Terrier-like head, was too large, but very sound; Chenda was Houndy, but, like her dam, Waldine, lacking in quality; Linda was still larger, with a particularly long head, but flat in skull. Schlupferle was a large red bitch, with a good head, but wanting in length of ear, and short of quality. At Birmingham, 1876, Major Cooper's Waldmann, bred by Count Munster, came out, and only obtained h. c., but in the following year, 1877, he won first each time shown, *viz.*, at the Kennel Club Shows at the Agricultural Hall and Alexandra Palace, and at Birmingham; while at the Alexandra Palace the following year, when shown in excellent condition, he did not obtain even a card, such was the in-and-out judging of Dachshunds about this time.

"In 1877, the Dachshund classes at the Kennel Club Shows were divided by weight as well as by color, and few fresh faces appeared in the prize lists. In the class for 'over twenty pounds,' Olga, a nice red bitch, was first at the Agricultural Hall, with Dina second. Olga had won first at Bath the month previous; she was a Houndy bitch, too large, and not sound in front. Her blood is to be found in a very large number of our best Dachshunds, chiefly through Wag, her son by Bodo; bred to Fritz, she also produced that good bitch Flink. In 1878 another change was made in the division of the classes at the Kennel Club Shows, this time by color

70

and height. A large number of Dachshunds came out in 1878 that are to be found in the pedigrees of most of the Dachshunds of the present day, and others only distinguished themselves on the show bench. These include Mrs. Hoare's Faust; Mr. Arkwright's Hans, Otto, and Senta; Mr. Hutton's Haufmann; Mr. C. Goas's Teck; Captain Shaw's Von; Mr. Wootten's Zigzag and Zanah; and Mr. Byron's Beckah — these were all bred in England, except Haufmann and Teck. Faust came out, a seven-months-old puppy, at the Kennel Club winter show, when he was second to his sire Dessauer. Faust won a large number of prizes, and his stock, more especially from Zulette, were very successful on the show bench. Hans became famous chiefly through his daughter Hagar from Linda, although he sired several nice Dachshunds from other bitches. Mr. E. Hutton's Haufmann was a good-colored black-and-tan, another son of Dessauer, but better in head; though too large, he was a celebrated prize winner. He came out in a Dachshund class at Blaydon-on-Tyne, when he was placed equal with Xaverl, and at Birmingham he commenced the somewhat extraordinary performance of winning first for six consecutive years, *viz.*, 1878 to 1883; still, very few of the present prize winners go back to him in their pedigree. Otto came out as a ten-months-old puppy, and won at the Kennel Club Show at the Crystal Palace, beating his sire, Xaverl; he was a nice red puppy, but he lacked the quality of Xaverl, who turning the tables, beat him the same year at Bristol, at the Kennel Club Show, and at the Alexandra Palace. At this show Zigzag and Senta made their first appearance, the former only getting third, but as he was but eight months old, he had not let down and furnished, so appeared high on the leg; still, the awards were very inconsistent as regards any type: Xaverl, first; Von, second; Zigzag, third; Otto, v.h.c.; Von Jostik (Zieten), v.h.c.; and Teck, h.c.; the latter had won first the previous week at Birmingham. Von was much of the same type as his sire, Zieten, cloddy in body, and lacking the beautiful outline of Xaverl.

"Then Senta caused a flutter among Dachshund breeders; she had no difficulty in winning first in her class; her skull and ears were wonderful, and her skin and bone extraordinary, but she lacked the grand outline of body of her sire, Xaverl; it was a great loss to the breed that she was never bred from; Zanah, her litter sister, not at all good in head, became famous as the dam of a large number of winners. In 1879, champion classes were established, and Xaverl was the first winner at the Kennel Club Show at the Alexandra Palace in July 1879, beating Dessauer, old Erdmann arriving too late to compete; but his presence would have made no difference in the awards. At this show Otto was exhibited by Mr. Mudie, when he only obtained v.h.c.; he should have made a valuable stud dog; his sister Erdine bred a good dog in Mr. Parrot's Zanker, and also Mr. Southwell's Hannah.

"Olympia, a puppy by Otto, came out in the puppy class in this year; she was scarcely six months old, and won first, the writer's Blitz being second; Olympia was simply immense, much too large, coarse in head, but with wonderful ears, skin, and bone; whereas Blitz was very small, with a lot of quality, and excellent loin. The awards at the Kennel Club Show held in Brighton in November, upset all previous opinions of Dachshund type, when Olympia was placed over Xaverl and Zigzag, the latter being again beaten by Zanker at Birmingham. The new faces in 1880 included Rev. G. F. Lovell's El Zingaro and Segesta; Mr. Byron's Jonah, Alma, and Hilda; Mr. Arkwright's Ozone and Octavia; Mr. Mudie's Flink; the writer's Jager and Jezebel; and last, but by no means least in importance, Mr. Mudie's Thusnelda. Mr. Lovell's puppies were not sent to the Kennel Club Show at the Crystal Palace, but came out at Stratford-on-Avon in October, where El Zingaro was second to the writer's Jager. In the bitch class Segesta was second to Octavia—a nice red bitch with capital loin, but not quite sound; she was first exhibited by her breeder, Mr. Byron, at Chesterfield, when she obtained only v.h.c., but she followed up her Stratford victory by winning for Mr. Arkwright first Bristol and first Alexandra Palace. Jonah and Alma came out at Chesterfield; the latter, a litter sister to Olympia, was spoiled by her bad carriage of ears.

"Hilda, Flink, and Thusnelda all made first appearance at the Kennel Club Show at the Crystal Palace in June; the

THREE GOOD TYPES

Such fine specimens of the wire-haired variety as those shown above are 1 .
often seen. The wire-haired Dachshund is often quite different from the
smooth-haired Dachshund, sometimes giving the impression of being a
distinct variety.

former, a sister to Jonah and Octavia, won in the puppy class. She had a beautiful type of head and ears, good loin, but had four white feet and a good-sized patch of white on her throat and chest. Flink won first in red bitches, a good bitch with a coarse stern, like her sire, Fritz. The black-and-tan bitch class at this show was described by Mr. Arkwright, who judged them, as "a magnificent class"; and it is a question whether five black-and-tan bitches so good as Chenda, Beckah, Alma, Dina, and Thusnelda have ever competed together. Beckah came out at Oxford in June 1878, when she was equal second with Zillah to Major Cooper's Waldmann. She had the much coveted arched loin. Thusnelda was considered by some breeders as being small and light in bone, but she was credited with having won first Hanover, first Munich, first Elms, and first Ulm. She was small by comparison with the others in the class, but Dachshunds were undoubtedly being bred too large at this time, and an outcross of a small size of the Hound type was very much required, and Thusnelda proved to be the very thing. By the end of the year she had gone from Mr. Mudie's kennel to Mr. Arkwright's, and the following spring she was put to Ozone, and bred the famous litter consisting of Maximus, Superbus, and Mignonne, from which so many of our very best Dachshunds are descended.

"Jezebel, a small Zigzag-Zanah bitch, with an excellent loin, capital body, but failing in head, came out and won first at Manchester when seven months old. She bred to Maximus, Joan of Arc, Joubert, Jocelyn, Brownie, and others, all of which have bred winners. At Birmingham, Mr. Wootten brought out Zadkiel, litter brother to Jezebel, but neither Zadkiel nor his sire, Zigzag, obtained even a card.

"This inconsistent judging helped in some manner to bring about the formation of the Dachshund Club. On the day previous to the Kennel Club Show at the Alexandra Palace in January 1881, a meeting was held and the Club formed, those present at the meeting being Mr. Arkwright, Rev. G. F. Lovell, Mr. Wootten, and the writer.

"At the Kennel Club Show, Mr. Arkwright brought out Ozone, then seven months old, by Zigzag out of Zaidee (litter sister to Senta and Zanoh). Ozone was not entered in the open class, in which Mr. Wootten's Zadkiel won, but in a good puppy class of fifteen entries. Ozone was first and Zadkiel second; Zulette was h.c., and Jezebel c. In the competition for the cup for the best Dachshund in the show, in which the following competed—Zigzag, Mr. Baker's Handsel, Alma, Octavia, and Ozone, the latter won.

"During the various shows of 1881, a number of good Dachshunds came out. At the Kennel Club Show at the Crystal Palace, Jude (litter brother to the famous Hagar) won first in the open class and second in puppies (a large class of twenty-five) to Hannah, a puppy of Mr. Southwell's by Hans—Erdine (sister to Otto). Hannah had a good loin and nice type of head, but was deficient in bone. Jude, although possessing excellent type of head, with capital skin and bone, was too large and deficient in quality. At this show Ozone beat Senta for the cup for the best Dachshund in the show.

"Hagar came out at Chesterfield, bred by Mr. Byron and exhibited by Mr. Wootten. She won first in the bitch class, and afterwards beat the writer's Jude for the special. Hagar was certainly a very beautiful Dachshund, excellent in type of head, with capital skin and bone. She was on the big side, and not quite perfection in loin and stern. She has become celebrated in pedigree chiefly through her son Charkow and her daughter Rachel, that was bred to Graf III. Hagar carried all before her. At the Kennel Club show at the Alexandra Palace she beat Zigzag and Ozone for the best Dachshund in the show. Mr. Benson's Rosa (litter sister to Hagar) first appeared at this show, when she was placed second to Olympia. Rosa had a nice clean, long head, with a capital jaw, good body, but carried her stern badly. The writer's Julian and Juliet, by Hans ex Dina, were prize winners here. In fact, no less than three first prizes, four second prizes, the medal, and the cup were won at this show by Dachshunds that had Hans for their sire. And Hans was also exhibited, but he only obtained v.h.c. He was not exactly a show dog, but he proved himself a valuable stud dog. Juliet was nearly black with white forefeet, but she was Houndy in type, had an excellent skull, with nicely set ears and low carriage of ears. At Birmingham, Mrs. Price's Neva (a sister to Wag) won in the class for red bitches. She was long, with strong loin, and a very good type of head.

"In 1882 the division of the classes by color was abolished at Kennel Club Shows. At the Alexandra Palace in June, Mr. Arkwright brought out the famous litter—Maximus, Superbus, and Mignonne. Ozone, now shown by Mr. Walker, won in the champion class, beating Zanker and Faust. Maximus and Superbus were first and second in the dog class, and Mignonne first, and Zulette (now shown by Mrs. Hoare) second in the bitch class.

"The cup for the best Dachshund in the show was awarded to Mignonne. Of the brothers Maximus and Superbus, the former had more quality, was better in skull and loin, while Superbus had the better ears and more bone, and these qualities each dog seemed to transmit to his stock. Soon after this show, Superbus went to Mr. Hoare's kennel, and, after the Kennel Club Show in January 1883, Maximus went to Mr. Walker's kennel.

Grafin II came out at Sheffield, and won in the puppy class, and afterwards many other prizes. She had a nice type of head, her ears were set on well, but were short; she was remarkably low, but her feet were long. The writer's Juventa, a long red bitch of the right type and one of unusual breeding by Zigzag ex Rubina, was second in the bitch puppy class. Mr. Southwell's Seidel, a puppy by Malt ex Erdine, was first; this was a nice quality bitch, but her ears were set on rather high and she was light in bone. Mr. Litt brought out Olympian in the puppy class at Cirencester, when he won first. He afterwards went to Birmingham, where he was only commended; but at the Kennel Club, the following month, he won first, Superbus only getting third, being beaten by Faust III, a capital son of Faust and Zulette— capital body, legs, and feet, but short in ears. Mr. Wootten brought out a puppy in Zeyn, by Zigzag ex Hagar—very good type with powerful loin, but not nice in color. He won first in the puppy class and in the produce stakes. At the Kennel Club Show in July 1883, Mr. Arkwright's Lady made her debut, and won first in the puppy class, the Club sweepstakes, and the silver medal. She had a grand head, ears well carried, and long, good body, excellent bone; her elbows

76

developed; no stop; eyes intelligent, and somewhat small; follow body in color.

"*Ears*—Long, broad, and soft; set on low and well back; carried close to the head.

"*Jaw*—Strong, level, and square to the muzzle; canines recurvent.

"*Chest*—Deep and narrow; breast bone prominent.

"*Legs and Feet*—Forelegs very short and strong in bone, well crooked, not standing over; elbows well clothed with muscle, neither in nor out; feet large, round, and strong, with thick pads and strong nails. Hind legs smaller in bone and higher, hind feet smaller. The dog must stand true, *i.e.*, equally on all parts of the foot.

"*Skin and Coat*—Skin thick, loose, supple, and in great quantity; coat dense, short and strong.

"*Loin*—Well arched, long and muscular.

"*Stern*—Long and strong, flat at root, tapering to the tip; hair on underside coarse; carried low except when excited. Quarters very muscular.

"*Body*—Length from the back of head to root of stern, two and a half times the height at shoulder. Fore-ribs well sprung, back ribs very short.

"*Color*—Any color, nose to follow body color; much white objectionable.

"*Symmetry and Quality*—The Dachshund should be long, low and graceful, not cloddy.

Head and skull	12	Ears	6½
Jaw	5	Chest	7
Legs and feet	20	Skin and coat	13
Loin	8	Stern	5
Body	8½	Color	4
Symmetry and Quality	11		
	64½		35½

Grand Total_____100

"The weight: Dogs about 21 pounds, bitches about 18 pounds.

"The Dachshund Club does not advocate point judging, the figures are only used to show the comparative value of the features.

"It will be noticed in the above Club description that 'any color' is allowed, with only the proviso that 'much white is objectionable.' The accepted colors with us are red, black-and-tan, chocolate (or brown), and chocolate and tan. There is some variation in the shades of hue, especially among the reds, some of which are so pale as to be almost yellow. The black-and-tans and the deeper reds are the handsomest, and a white foot or feet and a little white on the breast are no detriment. Mouse-colored specimens are occasionally met, sometimes with tan shadings, sometimes without. This is not a desirable color, and 'wall-' or 'china-eyes' often accompany it. The Dachshund is what may be termed a whole-colored dog, at least, this is what we have made him here since his adoption.

"White as the ground color is as objectionable in Germany as with us, but on the Continent a greater variety of color is allowed, Herr Beckemann giving the legitimate colors, dividing them into four groups as follows:

"First, black, chocolate, light brown (red), hare pied, all with tan shadings. Secondly, the same color without the tan markings. Thirdly, slate, mouse, silver gray, either whole colored or with tan marks; eyes, bluish or colorless (wall-eyed); and fourthly, variegated, slate, mouse, silver gray with irregular black, chocolate or tan marks and blotches, with or without tan, and with one or two 'wall-eyes.' Any one of these colors is as good as another in the Fatherland, but in case two dogs are of equal merit in other respects, the black-and-tan is to be preferred, or the dog most richly colored and free from white.

"As to the voice or cry of the Dachshund, he is not, as a rule, so free with his tongue as either the Basset Hound or Beagle; but, of course, there are exceptions to this. One old hound, Mr. Harry Jones's Dina, was particularly musical in this respect, and her voice in addition to being loud, was beautifully deep and mellow. Her daughter, Juliet, though equally free, had a much less pleasing note.

"There is no doubt that where Dachshunds have been entered to work with Terriers and used for the duties usually ascribed to a Terrier, they are inclined to hunt with less music than if used as a pack or worked in connection with

Basset Hounds. Indeed, this is pretty much the case with all Hounds, and I have known a Foxhound to hunt pretty nearly mute when alone, but in company with his pack to be as free with his tongue as any other Hound.

"An instance occurs to me, that of Rally, a favorite Otter Hound bitch with the late Kendal pack. Bred by Mr. Coulter, one of the good old school of sportsmen, she had been entered almost single-handed, and for a time, even on the strongest line, ran quite mute. After a season or two with the pack, she came to throw her tongue with the best of its members, and proved a most reliable and careful Hound."

BEROLINA EDDA II AND HER PUPPIES
M. G. Barnewitz, Berlin
(Extract from Journal Der Hunde-Sport)

93

OLD TYPE DACHSHUNDS
(Note currently objectionable front)

94

Description and Standard of Points

RANSLATED from the Dachshund Standard of the *Fachschaft Dachshunde im Reichsverband fur das Deutsche Hundewesen*—a consolidation of all the Dachshund Clubs in Germany.

(Adopted by The Dachshund Club of America, Inc., and approved by the Board of Directors of the American Kennel Club, July 9, 1935.)

GENERAL FEATURES

General Appearance — Low to ground, short - legged, long-bodied, but with compact figure and robust muscular development; with bold and confident carriage of the head and intelligent facial expression. In spite of his shortness of leg, in comparison with his length of trunk, he should appear neither crippled, awkward, cramped in his capacity for movement, nor slim and weasel-like.

Qualities—He should be clever, lively, and courageous to the point of rashness, persevering in his work both above and below ground; with all the senses well developed. His build and disposition qualify him especially for hunting game below ground. Added to this, his hunting spirit, good nose, loud tongue, and small size, render him especially

95

suited for beating the bush. His figure and his fine nose give him an especial advantage over most other breeds of sporting dogs for trailing.

Conformation of Body—Head: Viewed from above or from the side, it should taper uniformly to the tip of the nose, and should be clean cut. The skull is only slightly arched, and should slope gradually without stop (the less stop the more typical) into the finely formed slightly arched muzzle (ram's nose). The bridge bones over the eyes should be strongly prominent. The nasal cartilage and tip of the nose are long and narrow; lips tightly stretched, well covering the lower jaw, but neither deep nor pointed; corner of the mouth not very marked. Nostrils well open. Jaws opening wide and hinged well back of the eyes, with strongly developed bones and teeth.

Teeth: Powerful canine teeth should fit closely together, and the outer side of the lower incisors should tightly touch the inner side of upper. (Scissors bite.)

Eyes: Medium size, oval, situated at the sides, with a clear, energetic, though pleasant expression; not piercing. Color, lustrous dark reddish-brown to brownish-black for all coats and colors. Wall- (fish or pearl) eyes in the case of gray or dapple-colored dogs are not a very bad fault, but are also not desirable.

Ears: Should be set near the top of the head, and not too far forward, long but not too long, beautifully rounded, not narrow, pointed, or folded. Their carriage should be animated, and the forward edge should just touch the cheek.

Neck: Fairly long, muscular, clean-cut, not showing any dewlap on the throat, slightly arched in the nape, extending in a graceful line into the shoulders, carried proudly but not stiffly.

Front—To endure the arduous exertion underground, the front must be correspondingly muscular, compact, deep, long, and broad. Forequarters in detail:

(a) Shoulder Blade: Long, broad, obliquely and firmly placed upon the fully developed thorax, furnished with hard and plastic muscles.

(b) Upper Arm: Of the same length as the shoulder

blade, and at right angles to the latter, strong of bone and hard of muscle, lying close to the ribs, capable of free movement.

(c) Forearm: This is short in comparison to other breeds, slightly turned inwards; supplied with hard but plastic muscles on the front and outside, with tightly stretched tendons on the inside and at the back.

(d) Joint Between Forearm and Foot (Wrists): These are closer together than the shoulder joints, so that the front does not appear absolutely straight.

(e) Paws: Full, broad in front, and a trifle inclined outwards; compact, with well-arched toes and tough pads.

(f) Toes: There are five of these, though only four are in use. They should be close together, with a pronounced arch; provided on top with strong nails, and underneath with tough toe-pads.

Trunk—The whole trunk should in general be long and fully muscled. The back, with sloping shoulders, and short rigid pelvis, should lie in the straightest possible line between the withers and the very slightly arched loins, these latter being short, rigid, and broad.

(a) Chest: The breastbone should be strong, and so prominent in front that on either side a depression (dimple) appears. When viewed from the front, the thorax should appear oval, and should extend downward to the mid-point of the forearm. The enclosing structure of ribs should appear full and oval, and when viewed from above or from the side, full-volumed, so as to allow by its ample capacity, complete development of heart and lungs. Well ribbed up, and gradually merging into the line of the abdomen. If the length is correct, and also the anatomy of the shoulder and upper arm, the front leg when viewed in profile should cover the lowest point of the breast line.

(b) Abdomen: Slightly drawn up.

Hindquarters—The hindquarters viewed from behind should be of completely equal width.

(a) Croup: Long, round, full, robustly muscled, but plastic, only slightly sinking toward the tail.

(b) Pelvic Bones: Not too short, rather strongly developed, and moderately sloping.

(c) Thigh Bone: Robust and of good length, set at right angles to the pelvic bones.

(d) Hind Legs: Robust and well muscled, with well-rounded buttocks.

(e) Knee Joint: Broad and strong.

(f) Calf Bone: In comparison with other breeds, short; it should be perpendicular to the thigh bone, and firmly muscled.

(g) The bones at the base of the foot (*tarsus*) should present a flat appearance, with a strongly prominent hock and a broad tendon of Achilles.

(h) The central foot bones (*Metatarsus*) should be long, movable towards the calf bone, slightly bent toward the front, but perpendicular (as viewed from behind).

(i) Hind Paws: Four compactly closed and beautifully arched toes, as in the case of the front paws. The whole foot should be posed equally on the ball and not merely on the toes; nails short.

Tail—Set in continuation of the spine, extending without very pronounced curvature, and should not be carried too gaily.

Note: Inasmuch as the Dachshund is a hunting dog, scars from honorable wounds shall not be considered a fault.

SPECIAL CHARACTERISTICS OF THE THREE COAT-VARIETIES OF DACHSHUNDS

The Dachshund is bred with three varieties of coat: (A) Short-haired (*or Smooth*); (B) Wire-haired; (C) Long-haired. All three varieties should conform to the characteristics already specified. The long-haired and short-haired are old, well-fixed varieties, but into the wire-haired Dachshund, the blood of other breeds has been purposely introduced; nevertheless, in breeding him, the greatest stress must be placed upon conformity to the general Dachshund type.

The following specifications are applicable separately to the three coat-varieties, respectively:

(A) *Short - haired* (*or Smooth*) *Dachshund* — Hair: Short, thick, smooth and shining; no bald patches. Special faults are: Too fine or thin hair, leathery ears, bald patches, too coarse or too thick hair in general.

Tail: Gradually tapered to a point, well but not too richly haired; long, sleek bristles on the underside are considered a patch of strong-growing hair, not a fault. A brush tail is a fault, as is also a partly or wholly hairless tail.

Color of Hair, Nose, and Nails: (a) One-Colored Dachshund: This group includes red (often called tan), red-yellow, and yellow, with or without a shading of interspersed black hairs. Nevertheless a clean color is preferable, and red is to be considered more desirable than red-yellow or yellow. Dogs strongly shaded with interspersed black hairs belong to this class, and not to the other color groups. No white is desirable, but a solitary small spot is not exactly disqualifying.

Nose and Nails: Black; red is admissible, but not desirable.

(b) Two-Colored Dachshund: These comprise deep black, chocolate, gray, and white; each with rust-brown or yellow marks over the eyes, on the sides of the jaw and underlip, on the inner edge of the ear, front, breast, inside and behind the front leg, on the paws and around the anus, and from there to about one-third to one-half of the length of the tail on the under side. (The most common two-col-

ored Dachshund is usually called black-and-tan.) Except
on white dogs, no white is desirable, but a solitary small spot
is not exactly disqualifying. Absence, or undue prominence
of tan markings is undesirable.

Nose and Nails: In the case of black dogs, black; for
chocolate, brown or black; for gray, gray or even flesh color,
but the last-named color is not desirable; in the case of
white dogs, black nose and nails are to be preferred.

(c) Dappled and Striped Dachshund: The color of
the dappled (or tiger) Dachshund is a clear brownish or
grayish color, or even a white ground, with dark irregular
patches of dark-gray, brown, red-yellow or black (large
areas of one color not desirable). It is desirable that neither
the light nor the dark color should predominate. The color
of the striped (brindle) Dachshund is red or yellow with a
darker streaking.

Nose and Nails: As for One- and Two-Colored Dachshunds.

(B) *Wire-haired Dachshund*—The general appearance is the same as that of the short-haired, but without
being long in the legs, it is permissible for the body to be
somewhat higher off the ground.

Hair: With the exception of jaw, eyebrows, and ears,
the whole body is covered with a perfectly uniform tight,
short, thick, rough, hard coat, but with finer, shorter hairs
(undercoat) everywhere distributed between the coarser
hairs, resembling the coat of the German Spiky-Haired
Pointer. There should be a beard on the chin. The eyebrows are bushy. On the ears the hair is shorter than on
the body; almost smooth, but in any case conforming to the
rest of the coat. The general arrangement of the hair should
be such that the wire-haired Dachshund, when seen from a
distance should resemble the smooth-haired. Any sort of
soft hair in the coat is faulty, whether short or long, or
wherever found on the body; the same is true of long, curly,
or wavy hair, or hair that sticks out irregularly in all directions; a flag tail is also objectionable.

Tail: Robust, as thickly haired as possible, gradually
coming to a point, and without a tuft.

Color of Hair, Nose, and Nails: All colors are admis-

100

sible. White patches on the chest, though allowable, are not desirable.

(C) *Long-haired Dachshund*—The distinctive characteristic differentiating this coat from the short- or smooth-haired Dachshund is alone the rather long silky hair.

Hair: The soft, sleek, glistening, often slightly wavy hair should be longer under the neck, on the underside of the body, and especially on the ears and behind the legs, becoming there a pronounced feather; the hair should attain its greatest length on the underside of the tail. The hair should fall beyond the lower edge of the ear. Short hair on the ear, so-called "leather" ears, is not desirable. Too luxurious a coat causes the long-haired Dachshund to seem coarse, and masks the type. The coat should remind one of the Irish Setter, and should give the dog an elegant appearance. Too thick hair on the paws, so-called "mops," is inelegant, and renders the animal unfit for use. It is faulty for the dog to have equally long hair over all the body, if the coat is too curly, or too scrubby, or if a flag tail; or overhanging hair on the ears is lacking; or if there is a very pronounced parting on the back, or a vigorous growth between the toes.

Tail: Carried gracefully in prolongation of the spine; the hair attains here its greatest length and forms a veritable flag.

Color of Hair, Nose, and Nails: Exactly as for the smooth-haired Dachshund.

Miniature Dachshund—Note: Miniature Dachshunds are bred in all three coats. They are not undersized or underdeveloped specimens of full-sized Dachshunds, but have been purposely produced to work in burrows smaller than light- and heavy-weight Dachshunds can enter. The limits set upon their weight and chest circumference have inevitably resulted in a more slender body structure. Depth of chest and shortness of leg proportionate to the regular conformation, would in these diminutive animals, prove impractical for their active hunting purposes.

The German specifications limit Zwergteckel (dwarf Dachshunds) to a chest circumference of 13.8 inches (35 centimeters) and to weights for males of 8.8 pounds advoir-

dupois (4 kilograms, 8 pfunde) and for females of 7.7 pounds (3.5 kg., 7 pfd.), and limit Kaninchenteckel (rabbit Dachshunds) to a chest circumference of 11.8 inches (30 cm.) and to weights for both sexes of 7.7 pounds, certified at a minimum age of twelve months. Rather than the ideal, these sizes represent instead the upper limit for Miniature registration; and thus in pedigrees provide an index to purity of Miniature breeding. For hunting, where Kaninchenteckel originated, in order to move freely through rabbit holes, weights from 6 to below 5 pounds are preferred. In the show ring, weights well below the above maxima, far from being penalized, represent the desired type.

Miniature Dachshunds have not been given separate classification in the United States. A class for "under nine pounds" at American shows permits Zwerg- and Kaninchenteckel to compete as Miniatures according to the German specifications. Within the limits imposed, symmetrical adherence to the general Dachshund conformation, combined with smallness, and mental and physical vitality should be the outstanding characteristics of the Miniature Dachshund.

A CHAMPION AND HIS FRIEND

A charming study of a dog and bitch belonging to Miss D. Spurrier, England. They are Saucy Sue and Ch. Dicker von Kornerpark, an attractive pair and representative of the breed.

Serious Faults (which may prevent a dog from receiving any show rating) : Overshot or undershot jaws, knuckling over, very loose shoulders.

SUMMARY OF DACHSHUND STANDARD

General Appearance—Short legged, long bodied, low-to-ground; sturdy, well muscled, neither clumsy nor slim, with audacious carriage and intelligent expression; conformation pre-eminently fitted for following game into burrows.

Head—Long, uniformly tapered, clean-cut; teeth well fitted, with scissors bite; eyes medium oval; ears broad, long, rounded, set on high and well back; neck long, muscular.

Forequarters—Muscular, compact. Chest deep, long, full and oval; breastbone prominent. Broad, long shoulder, and oblique humerus forming right angle; heavy, set close; forearm short, inclined slightly in. Foreleg straight and vertical in profile, covering deepest point of chest. Feet broad, firm, compact, turned slightly out.

Hindquarters—Well muscled and rounded. Pelvis, femur, and tibia oblique, forming right angles; tarsus inclined forward. Hip should be level with shoulder, back strong, neither sagged nor more than very slightly arched. Tail strong, tapered, well covered with hair, not carried gaily.

Varieties—Three coat types: *Smooth* or Short-haired, short and dense, shining, glossy. *Wire-haired,* like German Spiky-Haired Pointer, hard, with good undercoat. *Long-haired,* like Irish Setter. *Miniature,* symmetrical rather slender body conformation below maximum limits of 11.8 and 13.8 inches chest girth, 7.7 and 8.8 pounds weight at minimum age of 12 months.

Color—Solid red (tan) of various shades, and black with tan points, should have black noses and nails, and narrow black line edging lips and eyelids; chocolate with tan points permits brown nose. Eyes of all, lustrous, the darker the better.

Faults—Overshot or undershot, knuckling over, loose shoulders; high on legs; clumsy gait; long, splayed, or twisted feet; sagged or roached back; high croup; small, narrow, or short chest; faulty angulation of forequarters or hindquarters; weak loins; narrow hindquarters; bowed legs, cowhocks; weak or dish-faced muzzle; dewlaps; uneven or scanty coat.

Secondary Faults (which may prevent a dog from receiving a high show rating): A weak, long-legged, or dragging figure; body hanging between the shoulders; sluggish, clumsy, or waddling gait; toes turned inwards or too obliquely outwards; splayed paws, sunken back, roach-back (or carp-back); croup higher than withers; short-ribbed or too-weak chest; excessively drawn up flanks like those of a Greyhound; narrow, poorly muscled hindquarters; weak loins; bad angulation in front quarters or hindquarters; cowhocks; bowed legs; "glass" eyes, except for gray or dappled dogs; a bad coat.

Minor Faults (which may prevent a dog from receiving the highest rating in championship competition): Ears wrongly set, sticking out, narrow or folded; too marked a stop; too pointed or weak a jaw; pincer teeth, distemper teeth; too wide or too short a head; goggle eyes, "glass" eyes in the case of gray and dappled dogs, insufficiently dark eyes in the case of all other coat-colors; dewlaps; short neck; swan neck; too fine or too thin hair.

WHAT CAN IT BE?
Two youthful Smooth Dachshunds, the property of Mrs. Huggins, England, are here seen displaying an alert interest in something "off-stage." The keen expression is very typical.

The Dachshund in a Nutshell

Look For:	Avoid:
Low station, without dragging. (Too low is possible.)	Long legs, stiltiness; and legs so short that chest barely clears ground.
Head moderately long and lean. Wedge shaped.	Short head, thick skull.
Skull nearly flat, rounding to cheeks.	Skull dome-like, round, lumpy.
Mouth even, with scissors bite. Teeth large, strong, ivory.	Overshot or undershot bite. Teeth delicate, pearly, or small; brown or eroded.
Eyes moderate in size, set wide apart but within cheeks. Dark as possible. (Walleyes permissible in dapples.) Allowance made for slightly lighter eyes in reds and buffs.	Full or pop eyes; stingy, weasel-like eyes. Narrow eyes. Light or yellow eyes.
Ears pendant, set well up on head; active and attentive. Moderate size.	Dead ears, set low on skull, too large or too skimpy.
Stop absent or small.	Pronounced stop.
Top of muzzle in same plane as top of skull.	Dish face, or down face.
Lips dry and tight.	Pendant flews. Lippiness.
Cheeks flat.	Muscular bumpiness on cheeks.
Nostrils large, open.	Nostrils small or pinched.
Neck long, arched, muscular.	Short, weak neck; ewe-neck.
Muzzle filled under eyes.	Muzzle much chiseled. Snipiness.

LOOK FOR:	AVOID:
Throat free from surplus skin.	Dewlap or throatiness.
Shoulders sharply angulated and laid well back. Blades close together at withers.	Upright shoulder blades. Excess of width between withers.
Prominent forechest as seen from side. Generous width of chest.	Absence of forechest. Pinched or narrow chest.
Straight front legs, with only minute bend at pastern.	Crooked front legs with prominent pastern joints. Feet turning outward.
Big thorax, wide, deep and long. Ribs springing widely from spine and descending in shape of a very blunt heart.	Thorax deficient in any dimension. Barrel ribs.
Loin moderately short and very muscular. Little tuck-up.	Long, slack, weak loin, or one considerably tucked.
Back line level from withers to pelvis, short rather than long. Rise over loin tolerable if only minute.	Roach-back or sway-back, standing or moving. Cobbiness or elongation.
Hams big and muscular, wide and thick.	Skimpy or weak hams.
Stifle joints well bent.	Straight stifles.
Hocks upright with strong Achilles tendon.	Hocks angled under body. Long hocks. Straight hocks.
Feet small, deep, short, compact. Nails short.	Large, thin, or splayed feet.
Croup with only slight downward slope.	Croup either continuation of straight back line or sloping abruptly.

Look For:	Avoid:
Tail strong at insertion, tapering, neither excessively long nor short. Carried in slight curve, out from body.	Pipe-stopper tail; long, blunt, or carried over back.
Action, rather wide and straight forward with long steps, feet turned neither in nor out.	Narrow, cramped action. Choppy steps. Pigeon-toed or slew-footed, front or rear.
Coat (smooth variety) short, fine, thick, glossy, covering animal thoroughly.	Coat (smooth variety) shaggy, coarse, scant or dead.
Coat (long-haired variety) densely feathered, fine, straight, or wavy.	Coat (long-haired variety) scant or short, curly or woolly.
Coat (wire-haired variety) dense, stiff wiry, with piley undercoat. Bearded. (This variety requires trimming.)	Coat (wire-haired variety) soft, oily, or scanty.
Colors, various. Usual colors, clear red or rufous; or black with brilliant tan markings; also, dapple and chocolate.	White on feet, large spot on chest. Clear red preferred over muddy red. Straw-colored tan on black-and-tan. Insufficient tan.

LITTER OF EIGHT MINIATURE DACHSHUND PUPPIES

Born to Primrosepatch Zinia by Ch. Primrosepatch Diamond
four days after arriving in California from England

Owner: Miss Avis Mary Earle, Tinyteckel Kennel, North Hollywood, Calif.

LAURELEI, SUSIE AND FERDINAND v. MAGDEBURG
AT SIX MONTHS
WITH MOTHER, DIRNEL v. KONKAPOT

Owned and Bred by Katrina Walter

The Blueprint of the Dachshund

DO you wonder just how good a specimen of his breed your Dachshund may be? It may make no difference in your affection for him, in your loyalty to him and his to you, but wouldn't you like to know?

If you exhibit the dog for the purpose of finding out how good a Dachshund he is, his place in the prize list will show you only his excellence or inferiority as he may be compared to the small number of dogs in the class or classes in which he competes. The judge has not the time at his disposal to analyze your dog's faults and virtues for you. And, in any event, he wishes not to offend you and seeks to gloss over the exhibit's shortcomings as best he may. Prizes are often awarded on the basis of minor qualities of the dogs under comparison, and a dog that wins in one show may be defeated in a subsequent show by the one he has previously beaten.

The novice and amateur is baffled. He knows no more about his dog than he knew before. He appeals to the official Standard of the breed. It may or may not be lucid enough for judges and experienced fanciers, who are used to dealing with Standards and applying their specifications to living dogs. To the novice dog owner the Standard may seem like some kind of double talk. What does it mean, and why?

109

This chapter is designed to enable the amateur to interpret the Standard for himself, to make it possible for him to analyze and evaluate his own dog. It cannot and is not intended to make him a judge of dogs overnight. Neither is it intended to establish a new Standard to take the place of the official Standard, but rather to elucidate and explain the terms of the official standard in such a way that the amateur can understand its terms and at least some of the reasons for them.

The official Standard is included here, and what it may say must take precedence over anything that we may say about it that may appear to be in conflict with its terms. It is, as we say, official.

The translation of the German Standard of the Dachshund, included here along with the American Standard, is minute in its details. The German Standards of all the breeds of German origin or sponsorship are so specific in their descriptions of the various parts of the dog that in the analysis of the parts the manner in which the parts fit together to make the whole dog is lost sight of. After all, it is the complete, functioning whole that makes a dog a good one or a bad one, not the mere parts taken separately. The parts, however good they may be as parts, must fit together to make an efficient and beautiful animal.

Before we begin with an examination of the dog and the application of the terms of the Standard to the individual dog, we have to know a little about the theory of judging dogs, have to know why one dog of a breed is deemed to be a better dog than another of the same breed, why a Dachshund must not look like a Greyhound or like a Bulldog. Too often it is believed that a dog is a good or a bad specimen of its breed just because somebody in an assumed position of authority said so. The fact is that the Standards were long unwritten and that the ideals upon which they were formed grew along with the breed's development.

The breed was long a-forming. Long before kennel clubs and dog shows, men utilized dogs for various purposes—the hunting of this or that kind of game, a particular sport, the herding of sheep, the driving of cattle, the guarding of property. It became apparent that a dog of a certain size, type, and structure served for some particular purpose better than some other kind of dog. Simply for their usefulness, the various types were conventionalized and grouped together, assumed the stature of a specific breed and, as a breed, were given a name. That name was a loose term and applied to any dog used for the specific purpose. Later, when the fanciers of a breed were organized and dog shows began to be held, the terms were tightened, Standards were adopted officially to describe the breed, the best bitches were bred to the best dogs, pedigrees were recorded, greater and greater uniformity was achieved within the breed, and it became possible to examine a dog and declare with some assurance that it was a good or a fair or a bad specimen of its breed, accordingly as it conformed or failed to conform to the ideals that attached to the breed and were described, or presumed to be described, in its official Standard.

A breed of dogs is something more than a convention. It is the embodiment of an ideal; that ideal being the animal structurally best fitted to perform the work or purpose for which the breed is destined to be used. Except for the merely ornamental breeds, such as many of the toys, the ideal is not merely arbitrary or "fancy," not somebody's idea of what is "cute" or pretty.

We need a machine to perform a given function, and the mechanical engineer designs it, using cogs and pulleys, pinions and belts, and pieces of such dimensions and materials most suitable for the purpose and so assembled together as to produce the utmost of efficiency in the machine's performance of the purpose for which it is to be used. The pursuit plane is built for speed and maneuverability; the bomber for cargo capacity and distance. So with breeds of dogs. When a breed of dogs is demanded for a specific purpose, the breeders set about producing one with the greatest efficiency for the particular end. The Standard for the breed is written to describe such a dog, and when the efficiency of the breed for its function is evident enough, and when enough fanciers and breeders demonstrate an intense interest in it, the breed is officially recognized by the governing body (in America, The American Kennel Club) as a distinct and separate breed of dogs.

111

And breeds change. Just as there are advances and improvements in machines, so too are there improvements in the respective breeds of dogs. If experience or logic convinces the fanciers of a breed that the alteration of some detail of its structure increases its efficiency, that alteration will be gradually adopted as an attribute of the breed and will subsequently be included in the revision of the official Standard. Such changes, when they occur at all, are slow, and many times the fanciers are themselves unaware that they are making such a change, altering their ideal. The alteration in the official Standard occurs, if at all, only after it has been firmly established in the breed itself. This development trend is always slow and conservative.

The best dogs of the respective breeds of twenty-five years ago would receive short shrift in one of our mid-century dog shows. Cocker Spaniels have grown taller; the muzzles of many of the Terriers have grown longer; the fronts of the Dachshunds have straightened. It is not always that the changes made are for the better, but it is intended that they shall be and most are so in fact.

We have said that a breed is more than a convention, but it is also conventional. When the efficiency of a given structure for a given purpose is established, the breed jells into such form and thenceforth is judged by its conformation to that ideal. As the poet has so well expressed the idea: "Beauty is use; use, beauty. That's all we need to know." The mechanic finds beauty in the efficient engine; the horologist derives an esthetic lift from the works of an accurate chronometer; to the judge of dogs, the best dog is the one structurally fittest to serve the function for which its breed is intended.

About a dog there are details that may have nothing at all to do with the animal's efficiency. A dog may see as well with a light eye as with a dark one, but to most persons the darker eye color is more pleasant. A Dachshund may have as keen a sense of smell with a flesh-colored nose as with a black one, although the black nose is preferred. The dark eye and black nose are imperative in the show ring. The acceptable coat colors in that breed are many and varied. There is perhaps no difference in the usefulness of a black-

112

and-tan dog and a red one; these become matters of personal preference. In judging the breed, one is as good as the other.

That one dog is structurally fitter than another to perform a given kind of work does not always imply that it actually does that work better. A cowhocked dog, or one actually crippled, may prove more enduring in the field than a completely sound one. Theoretically the unsound dog tires more quickly than the sound one, and we therefore demand that our dogs must be sound. While some quality of heart or mind or temperament may enable an unsound individual dog to do the breed's work with greater efficiency and stamina than a sound one, it is in spite of the unsoundness and not because of it that he works so well. The occasional exceptions in practice do not invalidate the theory that, as a lot, sound animals are more serviceable than unsound ones; dogs that conform to their breed Standard are better able to do the work for which the breed was made than other dogs that fail so to conform.

The primary purpose of the Dachshund, as its name implies, is the finding and drawing of badgers. It is very unlikely that the owner of a Dachshund in America ever expects to hunt badgers or would know a badger if he should meet one on Fifth Avenue. The Dachshund in America is a pet and companion. His primary purpose is quite lost sight of, but he is judged upon his structural fitness to serve that purpose.

The owner of a Dachshund, without any intention to become a hunter of badgers, wants his dog to conform to the ideals and conventions of the breed; he wants to know that he is a good Dachshund. Along with the dog at the time of his purchase came a pedigree which its breeder assured him was a good one. Without familiarity with the dogs named in that pedigree, it is impossible for the amateur to know how good it is or is not. He has to take the breeder's word.

Moreover, the pedigree may appear excellent, even to the expert, but no pedigree is better than the dog to which it is attached. It is possible for two litter brothers with identical pedigrees to differ so greatly that one may become a great champion and the other be a veritable mutt. Most good dogs have first-rate pedigrees, but the possession of a first-

113

rate pedigree does not necessarily mean that the dog it represents is one of great excellence.

It may be logical to question why, if a presumed Dachshund is a good pet and companion and if its appearance is not offensive to its owner, it should make any difference whether or not it conforms to its breed Standard, why it should have to have a structure designed for a purpose for which it will never be used. The answer is that, with men's minds functioning as they do, we derive pride from the knowledge that our dog conforms to the conventions of the breed, just as we take pride in the correctness of our attire or the design of our automobile. A mutt dog might give the companionship that we demand from a dog, just as a pair of jeans might cover our nakedness and keep us warm, or a Model T might provide us with the transportation we require. However, if we are to have a Dachshund, we are concerned to know that it is a good specimen of its breed. This does not mean to imply that we should shoot a faithful dog just because he does not measure up to the ideals of the breed he is presumed to represent. It does mean that we may assume an added pride in the dog if he is a noteworthy specimen of his breed. This pride is so general and so widespread among persons who own dogs that we can well say that it is human nature.

We rather certainly do not intend to use our dog for the hunting of badgers, but we like to know, if he is presumed to be a badger dog, he is structurally suited for that sport. We may not intend to exhibit the dog in the dog shows, but we like to know that if he were exhibited he would not be scorned by the judge; and, above all, we wish to refrain from exhibiting him if he is not of exhibition merit.

Let us trot out the Dachshund and go over him, examine him in the light of what the Dachshund fancy demands in an accepted member of his breed. How good is he?

First, what about his condition? Is he clean and well brushed? Has he been soundly fed with the right kind of food to bring him into the hard, sound, muscular state that is demanded of a show dog, amply filled out but without any superfluous soft fat? Has he had the moderate, frequent, and regular exercise to harden him up and make him fit?

114

Are his teeth clean, his nails short, his skin free from eczema or infection, his eyes bright, his nose moist, his breath sweet? Is he free from intestinal worms? Is he happy and full of enthusiasm when on the lead?

This scrutiny the dog is about to undergo at your hands is not a dog show. You may wonder why his condition should be considered at this time. The answer is that no dog looks his best unless he can be made to feel his best. The soft, shy, wormy, dull-eyed dog must always give way to a somewhat poorer specimen in better physical tone.

If this examination should serve no other purpose it will at least impel the owner to consider the condition of his dog and to resolve to take the necessary measures to bring the animal to the optimum state of well-being. Whether in our examination the dog measures up to the highest ideals of the Dachshund breed or whether we are forced to conclude that his shortcomings are such that his classification as a Dachshund is only nominal, he should be, for the owner's sake and for his own, fed, exercised, treated, and cared for in such manner as to make him look and feel his very best. This is our duty to our good friend, whether he be fundamentally handsome and representative of his breed or not.

However, unless the dog is in good condition, let us not seek to reach a final conclusion about his merits until we have done all possible to make him fit and put him in fine fettle. Let us not condemn him for an attribute that can be altered. Let us judge him only at his best; and, moreover, let us bring him to his best that he may be judged.

Assuming that the dog is in good enough condition to be fairly judged, let us put him on the lead and take him into a smooth space large enough to permit of his activity and large enough that we can stand away from him and see him whole—an ample room, a lawn, a driveway, or sidewalk. It is better to have another person "handle" the dog, manipulate the lead, take the dog away and bring him back as may be required to examine his gait as well as his structure. Otherwise, we are likely to see our dog merely in pieces and not evaluate him as a whole.

The whole is greater, as we learned in elementary geometry, than any of its parts. Let us stand away from the dog, have him trotted past us, consider him as a complete organism. It is a fair question—what shall we look for? Symmetry, style, compactness, soundness, the fitting of the parts together. Judging dogs is essentially common sense. Employing our layman's knowledge of the fitness of things, is there anything about the animal that offends the eye? Is the head too big or too small for the body? Is the expression toyish? Does the muzzle appear weak? Does he so throw his legs in action as to appear loose, or overly constricted, or crippled? Is he too long, too short, too high, too low? Is he bench legged? That is, do his front feet turn outward from the pastern joints?

Especially about the Dachshund are there general misapprehensions about the correct type of the breed. Persons uninformed about the particular subject are prone to assume that because a Dachshund is considerably longer than he is high, he should be as long as it is possible for a dog to be; the longer the better, they believe. Such is not the case. Because a Dachshund is short of leg, it is frequently assumed that he should be as low as possible to the ground. This is another fallacy. As for bench legs, they were formerly encouraged and up to about twenty years ago were at least tolerated, and prizes used to be awarded to cripples that literally walked on their wrists. Their front legs were more like seal's flappers than like dog's legs. It has been impossible for breeders entirely to eliminate these crooked ankles from the Dachshund breed, but the ideal has so changed as to demand normal, straight fronts on Dachshunds, and few bench-legged ones find their way into modern dog shows. When they are shown at all, it is by uninformed novices who are unaware of the ideals of the breed.

The Dachshund has suffered at the hands of the cartoonists, who have drawn humor out of the length and lowness and the old crippled fronts which were formerly approved and even sought in the breed. The popular concept was reinforced by these draftsmen who confirmed the misapprehension.

The Dachshund is designed to fight and kill in the badger earth one of the most wily, tough, best-protected, and gamest animals that is found anywhere. The dog must be

116

long enough to be lithesome and flexible of body as he manipulates himself under the earth in the badger's hole, and at the same time he must be short enough and compact enough not to dissipate the propulsive power developed in the hind legs and transmitted through the spine to the forehand. There is that compromise in his structure. We want the maximum of sinuosity without loss of propulsion. Especially must a Dachshund not have a long, weak or slack loin. The further back the ribs extend, the better.

Few Dachshunds (this plural form is preferred in America over the German "Dachshunde") are too short of leg, but it is possible to be. Many more fail on the side of being too tall than too short. The dog must be low enough to slide with agility into the badger earth, but with enough leg to support himself to prevent his chest and brisket scraping on the floor of the earth to injure and impede him.

The bench-legged ideal had its origin in the belief that a dog could dig more efficiently with a crooked foreleg which enabled him to throw the soil rearward on either side. It is now known that the dog with the straight foreleg is a more powerful and lasting digger than the one with a crooked front and that the only purpose served by the crook of the leg is to slow down, by crippling, such breeds as are used by huntsmen on foot and might, if completely sound, so outstrip the hunters as to fail of their purpose. Despite the rapidity with which the Dachshund covers the ground, there is no need to limit his action by crippling his front, and the demand for bench legs has ceased to exist within the Dachshund fancy.

This is at variance with the Standard which, it will be noted, reads: "Forearm: This is short in comparison to other breeds, slightly turned inward . . ."; and in the next paragraph: "Joint between forearm and foot (wrists): These are closer together than the shoulder joints, so that the front does not appear absolutely straight." Despite this statement that remains as a part of the Standard, it may be said that the best judges of the breed prefer legs, looked at from the front, to be as straight as possible. Some of them, out of deference to the terms of the Standard, will tolerate a slight turn outward of the pastern, but it must be slight indeed, and the animal with no such deviation at all is to be preferred. Any front that approaches in shape to an inverted lyre is no longer acceptable and incurs a heavy penalty from judges that know the modern version of the Dachshund breed. Much worse even than such a lyre front is the dog that literally walks on his pastern joints with pasterns and feet like seal's flippers.

Novices in the breed are prone to fail to consider their dogs in their fitness for the breed's primary purpose, for which they have no more intention to employ their pet than the owner of the show Fox Terrier intends to enter him to use with a pack of Fox Hounds or the owner of a Bulldog intends to use him for the long outlawed sport of baiting bulls. The Dachshund must be judged upon his fitness for the drawing of badgers, however, and in any event must be a powerful, strong, vigorous, compact, and sound animal.

Above all, the Dachshund is not a freak. One that in his excessive length, lowness, or crook of front appears freakish, abnormal, clumsy, or slim may as well be dismissed as unrepresentative of his breed.

So far, in fact, from being freakish, a good Dachshund is about as symmetrical and logical in his construction as it is possible for a dog to be. Any attribute that detracts from his symmetry, anything that lessens his power and efficiency and soundness, may be charged against his merits as a specimen of his breed. It is not to be denied that the appearance of a good Dachshund is amusing, quite aside from the sense of humor he may manifest in his temperament; but our amusement at his looks is in its essence an amazement that the squat, doughty, honest little structure can be so sinuous and agile and powerful.

When a large class of Dachshunds enters the show ring to be judged, it requires hardly more than a glance at the lot for the expert to note certain entries and tab them for subsequent discard. These will include the leggy, the excessively long and slim, the crooked fronted, and the unsound movers. The examination the judge may later give them is, for the purpose of making his awards, unnecessary. It is a mere courtesy to the owner, who expects to have his entry carefully looked at and feels that it has been slighted if it is dismissed without ceremony. The dog, as a whole entity, fails to conform to the demands of the breed, and to analyze the various parts is a waste of time. No matter how good the body if the head is toyish or coarse. No matter how excellent the head if it is followed by a body, legs, and feet that fall far short of the breed's ideal, a lyre front, an upright shoulder blade, a long, weak, slack loin, cowhocked or bandy-legged quarters.

It is not to be anticipated that the novice Dachshund owner will recognize these deviations from the symmetrical as quickly as the expert with an eye trained by experience; but by standing away from his dog, having it led past him, away from him, and back toward him, concentrating upon its ensemble and action, he will sense quite as much as he will see wherein the dog may be a failure as an efficient machine, constructed of bony levers covered with muscles which serve to move them with the greatest economy of energy.

If the Dachshund passes this test examination of the whole dog, we may proceed to the examination of the respective parts, observe where and how they fit together and function. Later, if our admiration for the dog survives this analytic survey, we shall return to the whole dog, test again his manner of going away from us and coming back, in the light of what we have learned from the examination of the parts.

Now we shall want to handle the animal, to explore his structure with the hand as well as with the eye. There is a growing custom of judging Dachshunds on a table, which has some advantages. It saves squatting and stooping over a dog so low to the ground as the Dachshund, for one thing. Further, it enables the examiner to look more squarely at the dog's profile. A standing man looking at a Dachshund standing on the ground can see it only obliquely.

If the dog is to be placed on a table, let it be a solid one that does not shake or wobble and one large enough to permit the dog to stand without cramping his legs under him and not to arouse his anxiety of falling off. No dog looks his best if the table upon which he stands is unsteady or too small; the poor little fellow, in his effort to keep his balance

119

and not fall, fails to stand with that firm fore-squareness which is essential to a good Dachs.

In our examination of the individual parts of the dog, let us begin with the head, not because it is the most important, but a good head is essential. The excellence of any animal must be determined by all the parts taken together. While a bad head may spoil an otherwise good dog, we must not depend upon the head to put across a dog that fails badly elsewhere. The failure of some judges to consider the animal behind the head has been much censured, and rightly. It is in the head that the breeds of dogs differ most from one another, and the head is considered to be the index of the breed.

The ideal head of the Dachshund is long, but not so long as to appear weak. Length and leanness of head can be overdone, although the judges who fail to look behind the head are prone to look for as long and lean a head as they can find. It must balance the body and neck, and the dog as a whole must appear as a unit.

The top-skull should be moderately flat, just rounding to the cheeks, which should be flat, free from bunches of muscles, which spoil the contour. The head is essentially a cone, with the nose as its apex. The less stop the better. The mouth is well covered by the lips, but that is all. There should be no flews or drooping of the lip to cause the dog to slobber.

As seen in profile, a just perceptible rise and fall on the top of the muzzle is desirable. The term "ram's nose," as used in the Standard for this bump, is a misnomer, since it does not involve the whole length of the muzzle and is not ram-like. It is the mark of a highly sensitive olfactory equipment and is slightly motile, especially when the dog sniffs. The muzzle is filled up under the eye, and free from surplus skin.

The scissors mouth is preferred to the overshot or pincer mouth. By scissors mouth is meant one in which the lower incisors are just covered by the upper incisors, the inner surface of the upper playing on the outer surface of the lower. The pincer mouth, in which the cutting edges of the two jaws impinge upon one another, soon wears down the teeth. In a young dog that has just grown its second set of teeth, a slightly overshot mouth is admissible, since the lower jaw grows a trifle more rapidly than the upper jaw and such a mouth will probably be even at the dog's maturity.

The overshot jaw in the mature dog, if very pronounced, will be visible from the outside with the dog's mouth closed. It is a deformity only less to be condemned than the undershot jaw, which produces a petulant expression. These malformations may harm the individual dog not at all for a pet, but either is considered to be a bad fault in a show dog. The Dachshund with either an undershot or an overshot jaw should not be used for breeding because these faults are hereditary and are likely to reproduce themselves in the offspring.

The teeth must be clean, large, strong, and white, with great width between the canine teeth or tusks. The correct mouth is a formidable instrument and must look so.

The Standard says: "Jaws opening wide and hinged well back of eyes, with strongly developed bones and teeth." While this may be true, we may well inquire whether all canine jaws are not so hinged. It is something that need not arrest us in our evaluation of the dog.

The nose, also, unless the nostrils are markedly small or closed, need not bother us. The nose in the black-and-tan must be black, and in the red dog a black nose is preferred, but the preference is not so great as to prevent a good dog with a self-colored nose from winning even over a black nose. In the other colors, less frequently seen than the black-and-tans and reds, black noses are also preferred, although brown or black is acceptable in the chocolate, gray in the blue or gray dog, and flesh-colored noses do not disqualify in the dapples.

With the head structure as it is, the eyes should be rather wide apart, but inside the cheeks. If they are placed too close together, the dog will have a "varminty" expression, too intent upon the business in hand. The Dachshund is an extrovert and sees everything that goes on around him.

The eyes are neither large nor small, but normal. They must not appear prominent or about to pop out of the head, which makes a dog appear toyish. Such eyes are seldom found in a dog with a correct muzzle formation. And when the eyes are too big and round, another look should be taken at the muzzle. It will probably be found that it is weak and cut out under the eyes.

The darker the eyes, the better they are considered to be, no matter what the color of coat may be. A red or tawny dog can get by with a lighter eye than a black-and-tan, but even here the dark eye is preferred. They must in no case be yellow or light. In the gray dog, light eyes can hardly be avoided, but few gray dogs are seen and the alternative is a walleye, which is also acceptable in the dapple dog. Such eyes are freaks and are not desirable, but they are in such coat colors to be preferred to yellow.

The correct ear fits the dog. It is not conspicuous, but appears to belong. It is wide and long (but not too long), reaching somewhat beyond the corner of the mouth in length. It falls against the cheek lightly, but is motile and never dead or flabby. In texture the ear is light and silky. A coarse, common ear denotes a coarse, common dog.

The ear is placed moderately high on the head. Set on low, like a Spaniel, we may look for a rounded skull. We may expect the whole dog to be a unit, and one part of the structure (especially the skeleton) wrong may throw out of kilter the remainder of the parts of the animal.

The ear is placed well back on the head, rounded at the base, without folds, and does not obscure the eye by its hanging forward.

The neck depends much upon the shoulders and how they are laid. It is correctly long and muscular, somewhat arched, especially in the male, and without surplus skin or dewlap to break the lines of the junction of head and neck. It can hardly be too long, if it is powerful enough to carry the head up without tiring, and a long head on a graceful neck will carry a dog a long ways, sometimes beyond one with fundamentally better structure.

The length of the Dachshund is more apparent than real. The lowness of his station and shortness of his legs causes him to appear longer of back than he really is. The really good Dachshund is not long of back; on the contrary, the length from the tops of the shoulder blades to the pelvic bones is short, although the length of the dog over all, from the point of the shoulder to the rear of the buttocks, may be considerably more. The top-line of the dog that is too long is sure to fail.

That top-line is one of the most important attributes of the breed to be considered. Except for a just perceptible rise over the loin, it is horizontal from the shoulder blades to the droop of the tail. The dog must maintain such a top-line in action as well as standing still. Dogs that are too high at the rear have faulty hindquarters, and a sag in the top-line indicates a weak loin.

The dog's power is developed in his hindquarters and transmitted to his forequarters through the spine, and with a weakness of spine some of the power is dissipated.

The upper arm and shoulder blade on the Dachshund are long, of about equal length, and placed at right angles to each other. The forearm is comparatively short. It is this arrangement of the upper arm and shoulder blade that provides for the forechest, which causes the dog to appear long. By the forechest is meant that part of the body forward from the extension of a vertical line running through the front part of the leg. Without a good forechest, it may be assumed that the assemblage of the skeleton of the forehand is inadequate.

Many otherwise good Dachshunds fail because of the shortness of the upper arm, which is the bone that extends forward from the elbow to form the chest, and some of them win high prizes in spite of that fault.

Looked at from the front, the body should be both wide and deep. The forechest should protrude from the body, with a dimple on either side of the breastbone. The legs should drop straight down from the elbow, without knuckling over at the pastern. Neither should the pastern give in the other direction and show signs of weakness. Knuckling over is more than a merely local manifestation; its origin is to be found in a faulty upper arm and shoulder blade.

It is also essential that the shoulder be firmly affixed to the body and that it shall not be loose to wobble about. Any looseness of shoulders will betray itself in the dog's action.

123

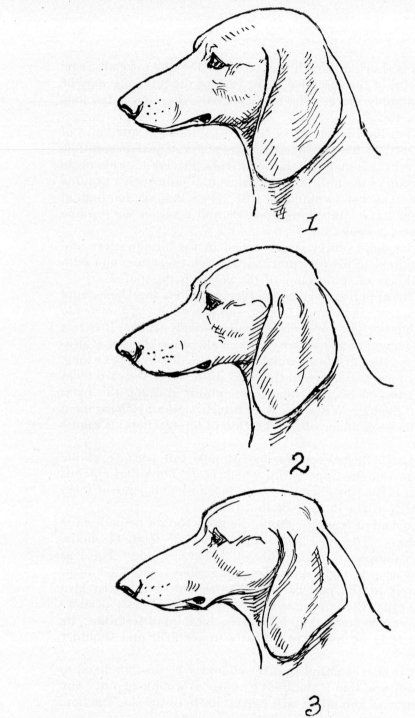

1. Correct head   2. Dish face—too much dome to skull
3. Down face, and very throaty; bad ear

124

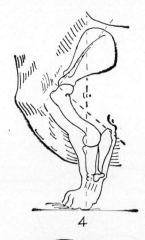

6

7

4 and 5. Correct Bone Structure
6. Correct outline, proper back   7. Sway back

8

9

8. Hindquarters higher than withers   9. Roach-back

126

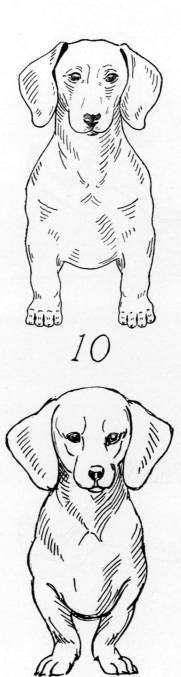

10

11

10. Correct front   11. Bad front and feet—wrinkled skin

13. Weak hindquarters

12. Correct hindquarters

128

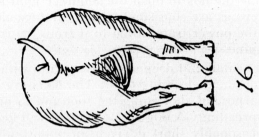

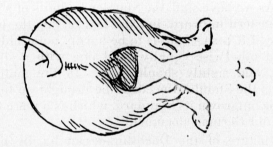

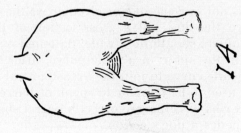

14. Correct rear view   15. Cowhocks   16. Bandy legs—toe in

Neither should the shoulder be tied so tightly to the body as to constrict the movement. The whole purpose of this fore-hand is to enable the dog to open the shoulder joint and to take as long steps as are consistent with its stature and not to lose any of the power transmitted to it from the rear by means of the spine.

The feet are small, but deep and closely knit, with thick pads and the toes held close together. The nails are short-en d for the purpose of shortening the foot and to prevent the toes from spreading. A dog with good feet will keep his own toenails reasonably short if given an opportunity for exercise out-of-doors, but even the best of natural feet may be artificially bettered for exhibition by reducing the nails as much as is possible without cutting into the quick.

The battle still rages about the straightness of the pas-tern joint, but for the advocates of the crooked front it is a losing one. As we have said, the Standard admits of a slight turn of the pastern outward, but the less of this the better. It may get by, if it is so slight as to be hardly noticeable, but even then an otherwise equally good dog with a straight pastern will, and rightly should, win. In the matter of straight fronts the Standard needs to be brought up to date. The breed has outgrown its Standard, which is a mere trans-lation of an old German document.

Bone structure of the Dachshund can hardly be too heavy. The correct Dachshund is heavier than it looks, and the body is wide as well as deep. Such a dog waddling about on legs too small to carry it appears top heavy and insecure. While a bitch can do with a trace less of bone than a dog, yet we may say the more the better.

The body is not sausage-like or circular, as the cartoon-ists have drawn the dog, but a cross-section of the body behind the shoulders should be a wide, flattened oval. The rib springs from the spine in a wide curve, after which it descends in a gentle curve to join the breastbone at the base of the oval. It used to be popular to speak of barrel ribs of a good dog, but ribs were never correctly barrel shaped. A bulging rib impedes a dog's action.

The cross-section of the chest should be as great as possible. There must be room for a big heart and capacious lungs, but not through roundness of rib.

The body should extend downward to midway of the forearm or even a little lower, although the lowness to the ground should not be overdone. When the dog extends itself in running, the body must not threaten to drag upon the ground.

If ribs are wide and heavy and the dog is "well ribbed back," the body may well be longer than that of a dog with a short rib and a long loin. The loin must not appear to be constricted, but neither should it appear long, in which case it is sure to be slack. It must be just long enough to permit of sinuosity without the sacrifice of the power transmission from the hindquarters that is lost with a long loin. If the dog is muscular and full through the loin this compromise between lithesomeness and power is easy without the failing of either factor.

The tuck-up of the loin is very little, just enough to guarantee that the belly doesn't sag. There is nothing Greyhound-like about it. In fact, it is just enough to relieve the body of a sausage aspect, and to accommodate the hardly perceptible rise over the loin, as seen in the back line. This slight drawing up of the belly is at least partly a matter of condition. Let a dog get fat and flabby and his belly will sag, although soft muscles to cover up a wasp-like waist will deceive nobody. It looks like exactly what it is—doubly wrong.

The sag in the waistline of an old bitch that has had several litters of puppies (or even in a young bitch that has just left puppies) is not to be penalized, so long as the muscles are hard and firm. Sometimes a litter of puppies will improve a bitch with tendency to too much tuck-up of loin.

The croup, extending from the top of the pelvic bones to the set on of tail, should slope downward ever so slightly. It is equally harmful that the croup shall be absolutely horizontal, with the tail set on vertically, as that it should slope too abruptly downward, with a slice off the corner of the dog. The sloping croup throws the hindquarters under the dog and destroys the power that could be developed there.

The tail is a mere continuation of the backbone, but is

not merely ornamental; it serves the dog as a rudder and balance staff. Without being coarse, the tail should be stout at the set on and taper gradually toward its end. In length, which to a fraction of an inch is unimportant, it should stop short of touching the ground when the dog stands upright and the tail is manipulated with the hand. It is better that it shall be a trifle too short than that it shall be too long.

In the smooth-haired Dachshund (the question is not likely to arise in dogs of the other kinds of coats), the complete coverage of the tail with hair is needful. Sparse hair on the tail is often found with thin or patched hair on other parts of the body and with hair too fine to serve as any protection for the dog. Coarse or common hair on the tail, with a long fringe, only serves to accentuate too heavy or coarse a tail itself and is frequently to be found on dogs that are coarse or common in their general type.

Not the least part of the Dachshund is its hindquarters, which are seldom found in perfection. Let us emphasize that the power of the dog is developed in the quarters and transmitted through the spine. The skeleton of the quarters is a series of right angles. The long thigh bone drops from its insertion into the pelvic bone, forms a right angle at the knee with the equally long second thigh, which in turn forms a right angle with the hock at the hock joint. This series of angles with their muscular covering constitute levers which drive the animal forward. The musculature is large and bulky, hardly possible that it shall be too large. The hock is vertical as the dog stands, never bent under the dog to form sickle hocks nor turned backward in a double-jointed manner. A vertical line from the rear of the buttock should fall through the front part of the hock joint, which should be short but strong and vigorous, with a powerful Achilles tendon.

The whole hindquarters formation should be massive in proportion to the size of the dog, the hams both broad and thick, the bones strong and well tied together. Loss of angulation is a loss of propulsion, and is apparent in a hindquarter that is a mere prop to the dog. On the other hand, saber hocks betray themselves in a tendency of the dog to go down at the heel and to walk like a rabbit. Opposite faults, they are equally to be avoided.

In this survey of the dog, it is well to have a dog of known excellence with which to compare the animal, but it must not be assumed that the sections wherein there are differences to be found are all to the discredit of the dog under survey. It is entirely possible that the dog being examined is on the whole better than the dog of known excellence or at least better in some parts or particulars. No specimen of any breed is perfect in all parts.

Failing the availability of a good dog with which to make the comparison, the pictures of good dogs set forth in this book may serve as well, or even better, for purposes of comparison. While the dogs pictured are all good ones, none must be accepted as perfect. Pictures have the advantage, however, inasmuch as the dogs are photographed in the best positions to hide whatever faults they may have and to accentuate their good points.

But pictures cannot move. Our survey of the individual parts of the dog has progressed far enough that we must now undertake to look at the animal in action, see how it goes away from us and how it returns toward us and look at it in profile to observe the top-line of the dog in action.

Squatting or kneeling to bring yourself down to the approximate level of the dog under examination, have your assistant lead the dog away from you for thirty or forty feet and return the dog directly toward you, first at a walk, afterward at a slow trot. Later, have it taken across your line of vision in profile, either directly back and forth or moved in a large circle around the examiner.

As the dog moves away from you, note the hindquarters. They should be wide apart without spraddling, hocks turned neither in nor out, the feet moving directly forward. Cow-hocks or bandy legs are equally objectionable. The hocks should move exactly parallel to each other. The step should be long and agile and well carried through.

The struggle of the dog on the lead may throw him off his stride; his pulling on his collar may cause him to appear cowhocked or bandy legged, may cause him to take short, mincing steps or throw him off his stride in some other way.

133

There is nothing to do in such a case but to wait until he can be moved freely on the lead and with alacrity. It may be necessary to adjourn the session altogether until he has learned the discipline of being led.

As the dog comes toward one, it should be observed whether his front legs are parallel with each other, whether the feet track immediately forward. The slight turn at the pastern joint (for which the Standard makes provision, but which is not desirable in the modern Dachshund) will cause the dog to turn out both front feet slightly. This must be tolerated, although it is by no means desirable. With shoulders too loose, the front legs will move in a paddle-like manner, with a movement outward on either side of the dog. When the shoulders are tied too tightly, the dog will weave, tending to cross the legs with every step. The latter fault is found less frequently than the former one.

In profile, the back should remain staunch and straight, with no undulation. Allowance may be made for a just perceptible rise over the loin, but no more than may serve as a "margin of safety" against a weak or flabby back. The absolutely horizontal back line is acceptable, if we can be sure that it is absolutely horizontal, but what seems like a horizontal back may be in fact a slight dip. The transmission of power from the quarters through the spine must be apparent and must not be wasted through any undulation of the back line. The forehand is but points of suspension that prevent the animal from falling on his face as he is propelled by the quarters. The forehand is none the less important in our consideration of the dog. The right angle of the shoulder blade and the humerus opens to admit of the maximum length of stride, but the power comes from the rear.

The matter of size in the Dachshund is presumed to be unimportant. The theory is that a good one cannot be of a bad size. However, observations of winning dogs show that Dachshunds of a medium size, from about fifteen to about twenty pounds, account for most of the show entries and most of the prizes. Dogs under those weights tend to lack type, to be pinched or snipey in muzzle, weak in bone structure, and generally weedy. This is not of necessity true, but the tendency is very definite. If the dog under examination

134

is a small one, it may be wise to give especial attention to his muzzle, evidences of stop, and prominence of eye, and to consider whether his lack of weight may not be due to a lack of bone and substance, rather than to smallness of stature.

On the other hand, extra large Dachshunds, as a lot, tend to coarseness of proportions and are likely to be too high on the leg. This is not intended to imply that the large Hound is not correct just because of its size, but merely to warn the amateur that excessive size is dangerous. Large dogs usually compensate for their coarseness by soundness fore and aft, but they are not likely to be found high in the prize lists at most shows.

The Germans have a race of Hounds much like the Dachshund, except for their greater size, longer legs, and slightly different head structure. They are used for trailing and hunting of game above ground. When we see an over-sized Dachshund in America, we may well suspect the admixture of some of this foreign blood in the extreme back reaches of the pedigree.

Miniature Dachshunds, classified as under nine pounds in American shows, are so much like the true Dachshunds that they can hardly be separated from the remainder of the breed, and so subtly different that they cannot be expected to win in the breed in competition with good specimens of the more normal size. In fact, few of them are ever exhibited, and few shows at this time open classes for them at all. Allowance must be made for their more fragile body structure, for their height on the leg, and for their toyish expressions.

While the Miniatures are presumed to be used for the hunting of rabbits, they are in fact little more than toys and might well be (although they are not) included in the toy group. The discussion of them in the official Standard needs no elaboration.

There are three varieties of Dachshund—the smooth or short-haired, the wire-haired, and the long-haired. The smooths are in great preponderance. All are alike in their fundamental type, the differences between them being entirely a matter of coat.

135

When we think of the Dachshund, we ordinarily think of the smooth variety, which was the first and primary variety. The long-haired and wire-haired varieties were later made by crossing the smooth with other breeds of dogs. It is presumed that the Cocker Spaniel was utilized in the manufacture of the long-haired variety, and that some Wire-haired Terrier variety was used in the wire-haired. It has been alleged that the Dandie Dinmont was the outcross that produced the wire-haired, but the nature of the coat of the Dandie makes it improbable that it was the sole outcross. In any event, except in unusual specimens of those varieties, the intensity of type found in the smooth Dachshund cannot be expected in either of the other varieties of the breed. In later years, due to persistent efforts, a few really notable dogs have appeared both in the wire-haired and the long-haired varieties, dogs fit to compete for top honors with the best of the smooth-haired dogs.

The wire-haired Dachshund may permissibly be actually a trifle longer of leg than the smooth dog, although it is not necessarily or markedly taller. The added coat on the chest, however, causes a dog to appear lower on the leg than it actually is.

Like any other wire-haired dog, the wire-haired Dachshund needs to be trimmed to pattern to present the best appearance.

The coat of the long-haired variety must be soft, straight or slightly wavy, never curly. It is the feather of the sporting Spaniel, not an excess of long hair all over the dog that is desired.

The specifications as laid down in the Standard to differentiate the varieties are entirely lucid and require no amplification.

Various colors are permissible and acceptable in Dachshunds, although the reds and rufous shades and the black-and-tans are by far the most numerous. Other colors are so infrequently found and are usually of so inferior type when they are found as hardly to merit discussion.

Rich, sound reds are most highly valued, although some of the greatest Dachshunds that have ever lived have been reds with a mixture of black in the coat that has been harmful to their beauty. Type must not be sacrificed to color but a "clear" red most takes the eye.

The darker and richer the red the better, although an inferior dog of that color must never be permitted to defeat a better-made one of some lighter rufous shade, even down to a light buff. All the reddish shades are classified as reds.

Black-and-tan dogs must be of sound black and rich rust tan. A light or faded tan is a frequently found fault, although faults of color are never to be considered as bad as faults of structure. The distribution of the tan is described in the Standard. An excess of tan markings is not considered as desirable, and it appears that such an excess of tan is accompanied with a comparative coarseness of type and a tendency to too much length of leg.

So few chocolate, gray, dappled, striped, and white dogs are ever seen that it is a waste of space to describe them more fully than they are described in the Standard itself. Gray and chocolate dogs are universally cursed with light yellow eyes, which are universally unpleasant and which have foredoomed the popularity those colors of the breed might have had.

Not the least of the virtues of a good Dachshund is its style, dash, carriage, alacrity, and readiness for whatever may occur. A dog that has such qualities, one that pulls itself together and exhibits itself with high-headed, clear-eyed confidence may and often does defeat another with better structure but lacking the verve and assurance that makes for greatness.

An animal in less than the optimum of condition cannot display such euphoria, but the quality is more fundamental than mere condition. It is a part of the dog's temper and temperament and is as much his own as is the color of his eyes. While it may be lessened or destroyed by bad food or neglect, good nurture cannot add it to a dog not fundamentally endowed with it.

A dog may be excellent without this "will to power," but he cannot be great. It appears to be an awareness of his own supremacy, a confidence that all is right with the world, an assurance that he can best all comers, that makes him valiant.

CH. KARL v. TENROC II
Owner: Dr. Louis A. Cornet

CH. HANS VON ARDOLIN
Owner: Dr. Louis A. Cornet

138

Soundness and Unsoundness

OUNDNESS in a dog is a somewhat tricky subject to discuss. This is true because there exists some differences in concept and opinion about what the word implies, and because the allegation of unsoundness as applied to a man's dog is the most heinous indictment it is possible to bring against the animal or its owner. Men resent with an absurd virulence the statement that their dogs are unsound. However, an absolutely sound dog is seldom to be seen.

Soundness, when it occurs, is a part of the correct structure, and is somewhat related to the correct type. Any part or feature of a dog's structure that restricts or constricts his action, or that in any way interferes with his performance of the function for which he is designed or intended, may be deemed, in any strict concept of the term, to be a degree of unsoundness. Utter, complete, and categorical soundness, the first quest in the show ring of any judge of dogs worthy of his license, is seldom found.

There are, of course, degrees of unsoundness; a dog with a mere symptom of being unsound is to be placed in the award list over another with a definite and patent kind or degree of unsoundness. Total blindness or total deafness of a dog, when detected, constitutes a cause for the disquali-

139

fication of the exhibit in the show ring, for either condition hampers efficiency in any activity in which the dog is employed. Classed, of course, as major unsoundness, total blindness and total deafness are, nevertheless, sometimes difficult for a judge to detect. A totally deaf dog, called in kennel parlance a "listener," is likely to be unusually alert, high headed, and showy in his effort and anxiety to know all that goes on around him. The word "listener" is applied to the deaf dog because he seems always to be on the *qui vive* to know what transpires. A totally deaf dog can detect minor vibrations, such as footfalls, seemingly with greater acuteness than a dog with all his faculties and certainly reacts with greater interest. Total blindness is sometimes equally difficult, even for an expert veterinarian, to be certain about. There have been many cases in which it has been impossible to ascertain whether a dog could discriminate between light and darkness.

Partial blindness and partial deafness are not causes for disqualification, although they are reasons to charge penalties, more or less severe according to their degree, to an exhibit in which they can be definitely detected. Blindness and deafness, either partial or total, are less frequently to be encountered in Dachshunds than in some other breeds. For instance, deafness is more frequently inherent in some strains of White Bull Terriers than in Dachshunds, and may be acquired in some breeds as a result of surgically cropping the ears. Pugs, English Toy Spaniels, Pekingese, Boston Terriers, and other breeds with large, prominent, or protruding eyes are more prone to ulcers and scars from ulcers on the eyeball than are Dachshunds. However they have been come by, whether inherited or acquired, whether partial or total, blindness and deafness may be definitely accepted as marks of unsoundness.

A lameness declared by a competent veterinarian to be only temporary may be passed over as not permanently hampering to a dog's activities and function. Any permanent lameness, however acquired, is an unsoundness; it may be congenital and inherited, or it may be acquired. If it is inherited, it may be transmissible to the dog's progeny, so to employ the animal for breeding purposes is inadvisable.

Permanent lameness acquired as the result of an accident or injury after the animal has been born may be depended upon as not transmissible to the immediate progeny or to any descendants. In the show ring, however, lameness must be deemed an unsoundness and penalized according to the degree of its severity. A broken bone in a leg, if improperly set and inadequately knit, may result in a lameness which may impair the dog's chances in the show ring, but in no manner affect his ability to breed and to produce sound progeny.

In breeds such as the Dachshund that are presumed to have an even mouth (that is, a scissors bite), an undershot or an overshot jaw is not merely a fault according to the breed Standard but is a kind of unsoundness. In breeds such as the Bulldog, Boston Terrier, or Pekingese, undershot jaws are accepted as correct and are not to be deemed unsoundnesses. Even in such breeds, the undershot jaw may interfere with the efficient tearing and mastication of food, but the ability to eat to the best advantage is, by common consent, sacrificed to the tenacity and strength of grip obtained by this kind of maloccludent teeth. In no breed is an overshot jaw admissible. Many puppies and very young dogs are very slightly overshot, but this is not to be charged against them as an unsoundness, since with maturity such dogs may usually be depended upon to develop a regulation scissors bite.

This failure of the incisors to meet and mesh correctly is inherited from one or more ancestors and is prone to transmission to the progeny in the first or second generation. It is, therefore, inadvisable to breed from an undershot or an overshot dog, if another with the desirable attributes plus an even mouth is available. Deliberately to breed uneven mouths into one's strain of Dachshunds must be patently undesirable for any serious breeder.

Cowhocks or bandy legs may be the results of rickets and, indeed, frequently are; on the other hand, they are even more frequently genetic in their source, in which latter case they are prone to be transmissible to progeny for several generations. It is impossible to overlook the fact that both cowhocks and bandy legs, the one the reverse forma-

141

ENGLISH DACHSHUNDS
Bred and owned by Mrs. Grosvenor Workman
Stoulton, Worcester, England

SILVAE BANJO
By Ch. Silvae Zebo ex Linda of Oldwill.

ENGLISH CHAMPION SILVAE ZEBO
By Ch. Zeusuom Schwarenberg ex Damascene of Dachswald.

tion to the other, are unsoundness. It is an amazing circumstance that, hard as serious dog breeders have striven to obtain good rear action in their dogs, some ninety percent or more of the dogs one sees on the streets, be they purebreds or mongrels, are either cowhocked or bandy legged. Even a large number of the dogs exhibited in the dog shows are more or less so afflicted. While cowhocks and bandy legs are somewhat less prevalent among Dachshunds than in some other breeds, there are still enough — and too many—of them. A few breeds, which it would be invidious to mention by name, have become so tainted with cowhocks or bandy legs that it is rare, even in the dog shows, to see a specimen of these breeds that can move away from one soundly.

A soft or swayed back may be in fact a kind of unsoundness, although it is rarely referred to as such unless it is glaring and patent. It is, of course, a fault and is universally recognized as a fault, but only the sticklers for soundness would try to justify calling an otherwise good dog with a slightly soft back unsound.

The most prevalent unsoundness in the case of the Dachshund is the turning out below the pastern joint of the front legs and feet in the manner of the Basset Hound. Indeed, the Basset is presumed to have been one of the progenitors of the Dachshund breed, and the crooked front legs of the latter, when they occur, may have been derived from the former. Time was when this kind of deformity was looked for and encouraged in the Dachshund, and the Standard still makes an allowance for a small degree of it. It was formerly believed, when the breed was included in the Terrier group and before it was transferred to the Hound group, that such a formation was of aid to the animal in his activity in digging his quarry from the ground. It has since that time been well proved that it was rather a hindrance to digging than a help, and that straight front legs are more serviceable in digging into the ground, just as they have long been recognized to be more serviceable in locomotion on top of it.

The American and German breeders were first to recognize the crooked pastern as a deformity, as it is now

143

accepted to be. The conservative English breeders still interpret the Standard literally and tolerate a slight turning out of the front feet. Even the English breeders and judges in recent years have been trying to eliminate from the breed this condition which still persists. It has been so long desired and bred for, that it is difficult to eradicate entirely when the fancy has made up its collective mind that crooked pasterns are no longer wanted. A liability to the dog in his activities both above ground and below, crooked pasterns may, therefore, be characterized as unsoundness.

There are two other conditions that are definitely unsoundness. These are cryptorchidism and monorchidism. They, of course, occur only in males. Cryptorchidism is the retention in the abdominal cavity of both testicles; monorchidism is the failure of only one testicle to descend into the scrotum. The cryptorchid dog is sterile. Despite the fact that he may be able to serve a bitch, he is unable to beget progeny. It is believed that the temperature inside the body cavity is so high as to impair the viability of the sperm cells.

Monorchid dogs may be fertile and beget live progeny, but their male progeny are subject to the probability of being monorchid or cryptorchid in the first filial or some subsequent generation. In any event, the monorchid is not to be considered a "whole" and normal dog and is therefore unsound.

It should be mentioned, however, that the buried testicles of young cryptorchids and monorchids sometimes descend into the scrotum at or before the animal's full maturity. When this occurs, the unsoundness, as such, no longer exists. There are hormone treatments for cryptorchidism and monorchidism that are sometimes successful in rectifying the conditions if administered while the dog is young. Such medication is wasted on a fully mature animal, so the earlier the treatment is begun, the greater the likelihood of its success. Any adequately trained veterinarian can offer a prognosis of the course of such treatment and, if favorable, administer it. It is worth-while only if the cryptorchid or monorchid dog is otherwise valuable.

One may detect in one's own dog an evidence of unsoundness and frankly call it that—unsoundness. There

144

will be no contradiction. In discussing the faults and virtues of the dog of some other person, it is wise to guard one's speech. If it becomes necessary to find fault at all with another's dog, it is much safer to say specifically that it is cowhocked, or has a crooked front, or is undershot, or whatever may be its failing, than to say that it is unsound. To say that another's dog is unsound is too often considered an insult to both the dog and the owner.

CH. GUNTHER v. MARIENLUST
Owner: Mrs. John W. Cross, Jr., New York, N. Y.

ENGLISH DACHSHUNDS
Bred and owned by Mrs. Grosvenor Workman
Stoulton, Worcester, England

SILVAE POST HORN (11 months)
By Ch. Silvae Zebo ex Silvae Error, winner of Res. Ch. Cert. to Lustre.

SILVAE SAILOR'S QUEST (10 months)
By Silvae Banjo ex Ch. Silvae Polish.
Winner of Challenge Cert. at 11 months.

Fundamental Breeding Principles

HEN the amateur owner or fancier decides to enlarge his canine interests and enter into the field of breeding, he is faced with two major problems: housing his breeding stock, and selecting the stock itself. Resolving these two problems depends in part upon the extensiveness of the projected breeding program—whether the potential breeder has unlimited financial means with which to purchase kennels and stock, or whether he must begin on a small scale with only the simplest housing facilities and but one or two dogs. In either case, there are certain fundamental principles which must be considered.

As a breed, Dachshunds are hardy, capable of withstanding extremes of temperature (both intense heat and severe cold), and capable of resisting many of the diseases which beset more delicate breeds that must be kenneled outside. In breeding Dachshunds, elaborate heated kennels and extremely specialized care are not necessary. The breeder must, of course, provide for his dogs' comfort, making sure that breeding stock is provided daily with sufficient nourishing food and a plentiful supply of fresh water; that the kennel is clean and snug; and that the dogs have sufficient daily exercise to maintain good physical condition. More explicit instructions on each of these points will be found in Part II of this book.

147

While the actual housing requirements of Dachshunds differ little from the housing requirements of other breeds of dogs, Dachshunds require more ample runs and greater opportunity for exercise than do some other breeds. Therefore, sufficient space must be provided so that the breeding stock may exercise enough to maintain good physical condition. It is unwise to permit breeding stock to wander unrestrained; stout pens designed to prevent contact with other dogs which might be disease-carriers are a necessity. Heavy steel fencing is the most desirable material for enclosing the runs, for neither adult dogs nor puppies will be able to break through it to wander away and become lost. The runs should provide sufficient space for the Dachshund to indulge his desire to burrow. Dachshunds confined to pens sometimes burrow under the fence and thus escape. To avoid this, or at least hinder the dog's escape, it is well to sink the fencing several inches below the surface of the ground. A narrow footing of concrete below the fencing is sometimes necessary to prevent the Dachshund's burrowing his way to freedom.

In selecting stock for a serious breeding program, the first point to consider is the form and type of the dog you wish to produce. You must formulate in your own mind a mental picture of your conception of the ideal Dachshund. This must not be a dog which you yourself have arbitrarily decided to term "ideal" but must be a composite picture of the various features which are generally conceded to represent the breed. It must be remembered that no perfect specimen of any breed has ever been produced, and it is extremely unlikely that a truly perfect dog ever will be produced. Nevertheless, nothing less than perfection should be your ultimate goal.

Since the Standard of any breed is presumed to describe the ideal specimen of that particular breed, it is wise to make a thorough study of the Dachshund Standard. The Standard does not describe each minute detail of every aspect of the dog, so to have a definite idea as to what constitutes a good Dachshund, you should also study the various dogs that have been declared to excel. The mere fact that a dog has been judged to be the best in a show does

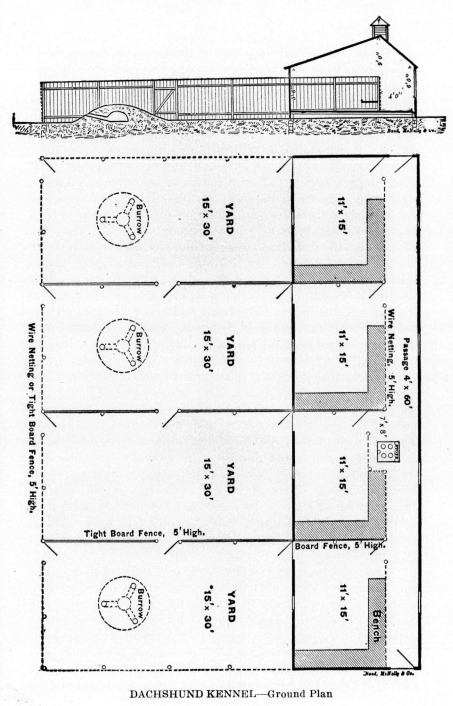

DACHSHUND KENNEL—Ground Plan

149

LIGUSTER von KONIGSHUFEN (d) Champion of Work
Breeder and Owner: Mr. Kurt Ruhnau, Stade, Germany

Litter of Puppies sired by Ch. Calidox Luigi ex Breezy Lane Pepper Pott
Breeder: Raymond S. Hill, Phoenix, Arizona

not mean that he excels in every respect. In addition to learning to discriminate between good and poor specimens of a breed, you must learn to discriminate between good and poor conformation of each distinct part of the dog.

After you have determined in your mind the size, type, variety, and general conformation of your "ideal," you must consider the problem of producing this dog. This dog will not be produced by a single mating, but will be the end product of successive matings which produce progeny that are a continuing improvement over their parents, each succeeding generation more nearly approximating the ideal. In order to realize your goal, you should begin your breeding program with the best dogs you can afford. By *best* is meant the dogs which most closely resemble your ideal, and which are most likely to produce desirable offspring.

In order to have some idea as to the progeny that may be expected from mating two dogs, you must have some knowledge of genetics, the science which deals with inheritance factors. An excellent reference book which explains this subject is *The Art of Breeding Better Dogs,* by Kyle Onstott, published by Denlinger's, the publisher of this book. A hit-or-miss program of carelessly mating any two dogs may occasionally produce some good offspring. It is, however, only through a working knowledge of the principles which govern the inheritance of the various features of the dog that truly satisfying progeny may be most consistently produced. Even when based on sound scientific principles, any breeding program will occasionally produce some progeny with features that are not desirable.

In the past there has been a good deal of controversy on the subject of inheritance. Some believed that the sire was completely responsible for how the progeny looked and developed. Others believed that the dam was responsible for these same things. Today we know that sire and dam are equally responsible, and that every aspect of type, form, coat, and color is determined by the combining of genes (the basic inheritance factors). The sire and the dam each contribute on a fifty-fifty basis, the genes which determine each individual feature of the dog. If one of the parents contributes a gene that is recessive while the other

151

contributes one that is dominant, the particular feature controlled by those genes will more nearly resemble the parent who contributed the dominant gene. If the parents differ widely in a particular feature controlled by a number of genes, each parent will contribute half the controlling genes, but in the particular feature, the offspring may resemble neither parent closely. Instead, the particular feature may represent a moderation or combination of two extremes.

It must be remembered that a desirable characteristic in one parent is not necessarily dominant over an undesirable characteristic in the other parent. In selecting the dogs to be used in any breeding program, it is not enough to select a dog that has the particular features that you want. To be more certain that these features will be dominant in the progeny to be produced, you should make a study of the ancestors of the dog. If, for several generations, the ancestors of the dogs you are considering have conformed fairly well to the ideal you have established in your mind, you may be fairly certain that the features you seek will be dominant in succeeding generations. Judicious inbreeding will further ensure the dominance of desirable qualities.

Inbreeding is a term commonly used to describe the mating together of dogs which have a close family relationship. For example, the mating of mother and son, father and daughter, brother and sister, etc. Theoretically, dogs so related are presumed to resemble each other and to have in common certain characteristics which would then be more likely to occur in the offspring. Since all dogs of a particular breed are related to some extent, mating of any two dogs of a breed might, in a broad sense, be termed inbreeding. Regardless of the family relationship shown on the pedigree, a brother and sister may be so different in their genetic potential that mating the two could not in any way be termed inbreeding. In the strictest sense, the word inbreeding should be used only to describe the mating of two dogs which are alike in many inheritable characteristics. Thus, two dogs whose pedigrees show no close family relationship may resemble each other so closely in genetic potential that the mating of these two dogs should actually be described as inbreeding.

152

The purpose of inbreeding is to intensify or fix the dominant inheritance factors controlling the characteristics which the breeder considers desirable and thus to produce more often progeny having such features or qualities. Studies of successive generations of inbred dogs have proved that inbreeding is the most potent force a breeder can use in producing a dog that approximates his preconceived ideal.

Through involved studies of innumerable matings, the dominance or recessiveness of genes controlling certain features or qualities has been determined. It is possible to theorize on paper what qualities a sire or dam will pass on to its progeny. The ability of any dog to reproduce in its offspring the characteristics considered desirable is termed "prepotency." Unfortunately, the actual prepotency, which is proved by the offspring produced, never coincides exactly with the theoretical prepotency of a dog. In order to be classified as "judicious," inbreeding must be based not on family relationship itself, but rather on the similarity of the prepotency of the dogs to be mated.

The many aspects of the subject of breeding are far too involved to be discussed in detail in a single chapter. The information given here, however, is sufficient to provide a basis for a sound program of breeding to produce a specific color strain in the Dachshund.

While there may be other features of a dog that are of more importance than color of coat, this characteristic is, without question, the one which forms the basis for the first impression, and perhaps the lasting impression, any Dachshund makes. A Dachshund with faulty color is immediately branded as less attractive than one of correct color and marking.

In the United States today, the red and the black-and-tan Dachshunds are more popular than the chocolate and the dapple. While white Dachshunds have been mentioned in the writings of various foreign authorities, apparently none are in existence today, and gray Dachshunds are seen only rarely. Although all these colors are, according to the Standard, correct, only the red, black-and-tan, chocolate, and dappled Dachshunds will be discussed here.

Although there are many variations in shade, correctly

colored Dachshunds are preferably a deep clear red; deep black with bright tan markings; deep chocolate and tan; or dappled. Dappled Dachshunds may have a ground color of any one of the other three color varieties. With the ground color should be intermingled small patches of white. The more evenly spaced these patches are, the more desirable the coat is. In poorly colored dapples the patches of white are fewer in number, more widely spaced, larger in size, and less distinct. Both the red and the black-and-tan Dachshunds should have dark points (eyes, noses, and nails) and narrow black lines edging the lips and eyelids. Chocolate Dachshunds almost always have light points. Those with dark points occur only rarely. Dappled Dachshunds may have light points, although dark points are preferable except in chocolate dapples. While walleyes are permissible in chocolate dapples, they are not considered desirable. Considered undesirable, though not disqualifying, in Dachshunds of any color are white toes or a single patch of white anywhere (other than a small patch on the chest which is permissible but not desirable). Such patches are conceded to be the result of dapple blood in previous generations. Very often the white spots on the chests of reds or black-and-tans disappear as the puppies mature. Prior to complete maturity Dachshunds of good conformation but bearing such spots should not be permanently discarded as potential breeding stock.

Many theories have been propounded as to the best method of producing offspring that are consistently of a clear deep red color. The method usually used by German breeders is to select dogs that have been bred pure red for generations and to continue to breed pure red to pure red. Many breeders believe that this will result in a gradual degeneration of the color of the points as well as of the color of the coat, resulting eventually in sandy-colored Dachshunds with eyes, nose, and nails of the same sandy hue. For this reason they cross red with black-and-tan once in every three generations, making sure that both sire and dam have really good black points. Recent studies have shown conclusively, however, that if the sire and dam are both from good red strains with the red color factor (gene)

CH. PETERMAN'S HUGH III
Sire: Message v. Marienlust   Dam: Peterman's Juliana
Breeder: Mrs. Sara E. Peterman, Montgomeryville, Penna.
Owner: Raymond S. Hill, Phoenix, Arizona

CH. VALENCIA OF HEYING-TECKEL
Sire: Int. Ch. Favorite v. Marienlust   Dam: White Gables Brenda
Owner: Raymond S. Hill, Phoenix, Arizona

155

dominant in both, succeeding generations may be bred red to red with no fading or degeneration of the color.

To correct faulty conformation, breeders of red Dachshunds occasionally resort to the use of a black-and-tan dog. Where sire and dam of good conformation and a good red strain are available, nothing will be gained through the introduction of a black-and-tan strain. Furthermore, the introduction of black-and-tan has been shown to produce, eventually, dogs with coats of a red color through which black is intermingled to an undesirable degree.

In the Dachshund, black-and-tan is recessive to red. When a dog of a pure red strain (pure dominant in the factor controlling color) is mated to a bitch that is either from a pure red or a pure black-and-tan strain, the offspring (first generation) will invariably be red, since a factor for red will be included in every sperm. On the other hand, if a red dog is only a hybrid dominant (that is, with black-and-tan in a previous generation), there will be black-and-tan genes in the color factor of some of the sperm. In a long-range breeding program where such a dog is bred to a black-and-tan bitch, approximately half the progeny will be black-and-tan and half will be red. These red dogs will then carry one gene for black-and-tan and over a period of years will produce black-and-tan as well as red offspring.

The offspring will always be black-and-tan when a dog of a pure black-and-tan strain is mated to a bitch of a pure black-and-tan strain. Many of the German breeders believe that the repeated breeding of black-and-tan to black-and-tan will tend to intensify the black coloring and that over a period of time the tan will become indistinct, eventually resulting in offspring that are entirely black. For this reason they occasionally introduce red into their black-and-tan breeding programs.

If both parents are black-and-tan but red has been introduced in a previous generation, one mating may produce only black-and-tan offspring while another mating of the same dogs may produce both black-and-tan and chocolate offspring.

Since few chocolate Dachshunds are bred in the United States, a discussion of the complexities of a long-range

156

breeding program to produce only chocolates will not be included here. It is a matter of conjecture whether a chocolate strain consistently breeding true could be produced by continuously breeding chocolate to chocolate. It is generally conceded that over a period of time such breeding would result in some offspring, both black-and-tan and red, which would have undesirable light points.

Careful planning is required in order to produce really good dappled Dachshunds. Only dapples, or dogs with dapples among their ancestors, produce dappled offspring. Dappled puppies will not occur in litters from red, black-and-tan, or chocolate Dachshunds with no dapples in their ancestry. A breeding program intended to produce only dogs with true dappled coats, evenly patterned with white, is certain of success only when both parents are dappled.

Considering the many difficulties involved in establishing a color strain, the amateur breeder would be wise to found his strain by using dogs whose pedigrees show only either black-and-tan or red dominant color factors. To attempt to breed-out an unwanted color factor is an extremely difficult task better left for the more experienced breeder, although the accomplishment of such an objective would, without a doubt, constitute a soul-satisfying victory.

Three Champions at Rock Manor Kennels, Walnut Creek, Calif.
AMER. & CAN. CH. SHIP'S MASCOT MISS PEACHES,
AMER. & CAN. CH. WHITE GABLES GADABOUT,
CH. WHITE GABLES PRUNES AND PRISMS

GUSTAV ALISCH

International Judge with his roughhaired Dachshund

"On Dec. 28, 1948 this well-known man died in Born/Darss. He was a master of his trade in every respect, one of Germany's leading dog breeders. All-round, special judge of numerous clubs, he was one of the few international judges whose expert advice was valued in every country. Shortly before the war, he trained dogs in Sweden and America. His international repute was not upset by the war because of his high esteem by other countries, who saw in the name of *Alisch*, the German guarantee. Through mediation of Col. F. D. Rossborough from American Kennel Club and American Dachshund Club, the Examining Organization for Export was built up in the spring of 1948. The aim was, even in the time of inflation, to give to other countries Germany's best purebred dogs."

158

The Character and Temperament
of the Dachshund

CHARACTER and temperament vary to some extent among individual dogs within any given breed, and environment and training have an undisputed effect upon the individual dog's inherited qualities. In many breeds, each dog differs so much in character and temperament that it is difficult to describe in general terminology the breed's instincts, habits, impulses, or emotions. A description of the various characteristics apparent in one dog might not be applicable as a description of any other member of the breed. In the Dachshund breed, however, the character and temperament of individual dogs vary but little. This is not meant to imply that the *behavior pattern* of individual Dachshunds fits exactly into a generalized pattern for the breed, for, on the contrary, each member of the breed has a distinct personality of his own. Rather, it implies that the average Dachshund usually conforms in character and temperament to the ideal established for the breed.

The primary purpose for which the Dachshund has been developed requires specific traits of character. Good Dachshunds, bred for generations for hunting purposes, must have courage, stamina, and perseverance beyond what is usually to be found in any other breed of hunting dog.

159

Although most breeds of dogs are developed with a view to conforming to a Standard which specifically prescribes only certain physical characteristics, the official Standard for the Dachshund outlines, in addition to physical qualities, the outstanding traits of character which one should expect to find in all good specimens of the breed. Generations of selective breeding combined with a ruthless weeding out of undesirable offspring have made the Dachshund a dog that, while friendly, affectionate, and loyal to those he knows, is always ready to attack with vigor those he considers his natural enemies.

With a confidence and courage bordering on rashness, the hunting Dachshund assumes a fight-to-the-finish attitude which usually brings him out on top, even though the larger size and the primitive instinct for self-preservation make his natural enemies, the badger and the fox, formidable adversaries indeed. Completely deserving his reputation as a savage fighter, the hunting Dachshund will pursue his prey underground, attack impetuously, and then fight to the limit of his physical capabilities.

In the United States today, the Dachshund more often serves as a house pet than as a burrowing hunting companion. Although he is not in the usual sense destructive of property, he has an unquenchable desire to dig that has dismayed many an amateur gardener who failed to provide his pet Dachshund with a suitable outlet for this overwhelming need to burrow underground—a need so strong that it may well be classed as an instinct. Indoors, the pet Dachshund may satisfy this need by burrowing under pillows, cushions, or rugs, particularly before a daytime nap and before retiring for the night.

Readily responding to discipline, the Dachshund may, in general, be considered extremely adaptable to the wishes of those he loves and wants to please. On the other hand, he will not adapt himself readily to a change of owners or surroundings. Once he has given his affection wholeheartedly to one master, he loyally refuses to transfer his affection to another. For this reason it is usually recommended that a pet Dachshund be acquired before he has become attached to any one person. Even though there is no change of ownership, a change of living quarters will sometimes make a pet Dachshund extremely unhappy. This is particularly true if he first becomes accustomed to living where he is permitted to roam freely and then later is forced to live where his natural inclination to wander must be curbed and his exercise is restricted to short walks on the leash.

Comparatively small in build, the Dachshund fits well into our modern efficiency apartments and compact homes. The Dachshund is a fastidious household companion whose desire to please, coupled with a lively intelligence and retentive memory, make him readily adaptable to training in habits of cleanliness. Gentle with those he loves, he is indisputably ideal as a companion for children. Certainly there is no breed with more endearing charm than this nimble little dog, quick and vivacious, whose every act and movement exude a spirit of mental alertness as well as an overwhelming joy of living.

CHAMPION "FIR TINKERGIRL,"
Owned by Mrs. Huggins of England

161

Milano 1939

(Foto Stucchi)

SOME ITALIAN DACHSHUNDS

RAZA: "DACHSHUND" (pelo corto)

"Jsar von Grünwald", 2o. premio. Sra. Srta.
Elisa J. Wharton

A CHAMPION OF ARGENTINA

162

Obedience Training, and Preparation
For the Show Ring

WHILE the intelligence of dogs in general is of a high caliber, no dog is born with an understanding of the language of humans, nor does any dog have the ability to read his owner's mind. Whether a dog is to serve only as a companion to his owner, is to be entered in bench competition, or is to be kenneled for breeding purposes, he can serve his particular purpose best only if he is given sufficient obedience training to understand what his owner expects of him.

The pet dog trained to understand his owner's wishes and to adapt himself to his owner's way of life is certainly a far greater pleasure to his owner than the puppy that has been allowed to develop undisciplined and with no regard for his owner's commands. Such a puppy proves in adulthood to be a nuisance and a disappointment rather than the faithful, devoted companion his owner seeks.

While the show dog is judged primarily on his physical conformation, even the best specimen of the breed will not show his physical attributes to the best possible advantage unless he has been taught how to act in the show ring.

The most desirable breeding stock is that which has not only been declared to excel in physical conformation but also has proved its adaptability by willingness to submit to the owner's commands.

163

In training a dog, the owner must be patient and persevering, if necessary, repeating the same lesson over and over. On the other hand, the daily training period must not be so lengthy that the dog becomes tired and confused. The owner must not become so anxious to accomplish all the various steps involved in fundamental obedience training that he moves too rapidly from one step to the next.

The value of systematic instruction and of appropriate and properly administered discipline must not be underestimated. By following implicitly the instructions in Part II of this book, even the owner inexperienced in fundamental training methods will be able to teach his dog the meaning of basic commands, developing a playful, clumsy, and uninhibited puppy into a well-behaved, obedient, and poised mature dog.

Many an owner has decided to enter a promising puppy in a show merely because the dog has reached show age (six months), without first considering whether the puppy is ready or mature enough for show competition. Age in itself is no criterion in determining whether the dog is mature, for mental and physical maturity in different dogs may vary a great deal. While one dog may be ready at six months to be entered in shows, another may not be.

A dog that is obedient at home often fails to show himself to the best advantage when he becomes distracted by the noise, commotion, and general air of excitement that are a part of any show. Before entering the dog in his first show, the wise owner will take the dog to a public place, such as a park, where the dog can become accustomed to crowds of people and learn to follow his owner's commands without being disturbed by the people and the noises about him. Only after the dog has thus proved himself, should the owner consider entering him in a show.

While there may not be as much prestige attached to wins in small shows, it is well to make the dog's first show a small one. Since the small shows are usually of shorter duration, the dog is less likely to become tired, nervous, or generally confused before taking his turn in the show ring. Once the dog has proved his ability to ignore the spectators and the other dogs at the small show, the owner may enter him in larger shows, confident that the dog will perform to the best of his ability.

The owner showing his dog for the first time should not become thoroughly disappointed and disgusted if his dog fails to win. Until the dog has been declared a poor specimen by a number of recognized authorities on the breed, the owner should continue to enter the dog in successive shows. By observing the winners and discussing his own dog with judges of the breed, the owner will be able to determine to his own satisfaction whether his dog is a good or a poor specimen.

While the breed Standard is, in a broad sense, a description of the breed and the basis for the comparison of the dogs that are entered, in the Dachshund breed individual dogs may vary widely in type and style, yet they will conform to the Standard in so far as their physical points are concerned. Before entering his own dog in any show, the wise owner visits shows and determines for himself which of the various types are currently popular and become the winning show dogs. The Standard permits a wide variation as far as size and weight are concerned. Thus a dog of good conformation but of a size that is not currently popular may lose to a dog that is no better in conformation but is considered to be a more desirable size. It must be remembered, too, that different judges may have different concepts as to what constitutes the most desirable size and that their opinions may change from year to year according to the general trend within the breed.

In addition, different judges may interpret the Standard in different ways. One judge may place more stress on some specific point of physical conformation than will another judge. While impartiality is very necessary in judging any breed of dogs, no judge is so machine-like in making his decisions that he can select what he considers the best dog entered in the show with a complete lack of personal feeling. A good judge is only human, and while he is unbiased as far as the owner of the dog is concerned, his personal preference for a particular size or type of dog may enter to some extent into his choice. It must also be remembered that the way the dog shows himself may vary from day to day, and that the quality of the dogs with which he competes will not always be the same. For these reasons, a dog declared a winner in one show may appear the poorest in the lot at a later show.

The show dog must be kept in the optimum of condition at all times. Regular exercise is an excellent means by which to increase the dog's stamina and prevent his tiring easily in the show ring. Conditioning, however, should be a gradual process. If he is permitted to exercise too much, the puppy may develop into a large, rangy adult dog, so until he is at least ten months of age, the Dachshund's exercise should be limited to running and burrowing in the kennel enclosure, or to short walks on the leash. Walking on pavements hardens the pads, makes the feet more compact, and strengthens the pasterns. Once he is ten months of age, the Dachshund may gradually be conditioned to more intensive exercise. In adulthood he may be allowed to run and burrow in the open fields for hours at a time. As a rule, the more exercise permitted but not forced upon a healthy mature Dachshund, the better.

Before the owner enters his dog in any show, he should make sure that the dog conforms generally to the Standard for the breed; that the dog is in top physical condition; that the dog is well-groomed; and that the dog knows how to act in the show ring. Only then is any owner justified in placing his dog in competition with others.

MINIATURE DACHSHUND AND PUPS
Mrs. M. Howard, England

How German Champions Are Made

HAMPIONSHIP titles in Germany have varied somewhat at different periods. Judging by the early stud books, around the year 1900, the term "champion" was used for a time, but was apparently superseded by the more native term "Sieger," which means literally a conqueror or victor. The Pinscher-Klub, founded in 1895, at Cologne, published the first volume of its studbook at the end of 1902. This contains minutes of its earliest meetings. At Erfurt on September 15, 1900, a decision was made regarding the awarding of Sieger titles. They were to be conferred on dogs winning three first prizes in the Open class, under three different approved judges at recognized shows and two first prizes in the Sieger class, and nonmembers of the Klub were eligible. This is the same requirement as in Volume I of the studbook of the Bayerischer Schnauzer-Klub, founded in 1907, which appeared in 1910. The Cologne and Munich clubs amalgamated in 1922 as the Pinscher-Schnauzer-Klub and their first studbook, published in 1923, states that the title of Sieger (or its feminine equivalent, Siegerin) shall be awarded to dogs winning three first prizes with the rating "excellent" under three different approved judges at recognized shows. The title of "Jahressieger" or Year Champion was to be awarded at the annual specialty show by an approved Klub judge to the best dog in all classes, with a rating of excellent." The same requirements applied to the "Jahressiegerin" title for bitches. By 1925 the term "Klubsieger" was applied to dogs receiving the first type award. There could be as many of these in a given year as fulfilled the requirements, and the Jahressieger was usually, though not always, a Klubsieger also. By 1925, likewise, Miniature Schnauzers were divided by color, so that a double set of Jahressieger titles was awarded, one for blacks and one for pepper and salts.

In 1902 Oberleutnant Emil Ilgner (retired) published "Gebrauchs-und Luxushunde." In this he lists 17 breed specialty clubs which published their own studbooks, in addition to the D.H.St.B., the all-breed stud book, comparable to the AKC studbook in this country, and the D.G.St.B., the all-breed studbook for working dogs. He does not state when the specialty clubs were founded but the Dachshund Club had already (in 1902) published ten volumes of its studbook, the German Wirehaired Pointers five, the Foxterriers nine, the St. Bernards and Collies three each, while the German Shepherd Dog Club was founded in 1899 and the Pinscher-Klub, as above stated, in 1895. The Deutschen Kartell für Hundewesen was founded by a group of clubs, among which the S.V. was a charter member. It corresponded to the AKC and even though the specialty clubs kept their own studbooks the AKC required the Kartell stamp on all German registrations before German dogs were accepted for registration over here. Probably the various clubs made their own rules for sieger titles, at least in the early days, but Ilgner makes no mention of what they were. The first volume of the Pinscher-Klub records the award of the title of "Champion" in 1899 at Cologne and also at Amsterdam in Holland in 1901. The S.V. for many years awarded only two titles annually, "Sieger" for dogs and "Siegerin" for bitches.

In 1933 the Nazi government muscled in on the dog fancy, as on so many other things. The Kartell became the Reichsverband für das Deutsche Hundewesen, in the Reichsfachgruppe Deutsches Hundewesen (RDH), and the specialty clubs belonging to it each became a Fachschaft or "Section." The Jahressieger title or its equivalent became Reichssieger, and was awarded at the annual Reichssieger show. The Klubsieger title became Fachschaftsieger. In 1937 the RDH became a member of the Reichsverband Deutscher Kleintierzüchter (German Reich Organization of Small Animal Breeders). Orders were given that in breeding both parents should have received the rating of "very good" or "excellent" from a judge approved by the Section. In the case of working breeds at least one parent must also have an "Ausbildungskennzeichen" or training certificate. This rule went into effect July 1, 1937, according to Felix Ebner in his "Schnauzer und Pinscher," published in that year. He also stated beginning January 1, 1938, a working certificate would be required for both parents.

The terms Siegeranwärter and Siegeranwärterin are used for a dog or bitch which has wins toward a title. Such a dog would correspond to a championship certificate winner in England. The title of Weltsieger (world champion) appears to be awarded at one important European show annually, with competition open to qualified dogs from various countries. The August, 1937, issue of the Mitteilungen of the Fachschaft für Schnauzer und Pinscher gives a report of the World Congress of the Fédération Cynologique Internationale (FCI) at Paris in July and in another item lists German Schnauzer winners at Paris, which included five Weltsieger and Weltsiegerin titles. In July, 1938, it was announced that the Antwartschaft for the Internationale Schönheits-Championat (International Bench Championship) as well as the Reichssieger titles would be competed for at Cologne in October. The report of the Paris show in 1937 mentions an Internationale Championats-Anwärterin. This would seem to indicate that these International Championships were awarded on a basis similar to the Fachschaft or Klubsieger titles and were not the same as the Weltsieger titles.

AM. AND CAN. CH. BRENTWALD JOSHUA W.
Sire: Ch. Lumpacius Hubertus   Dam: Ch. Jerry Hubertus
Owner: Mrs. Neville R. Stephens, Tubac, Arizona

CH. HAINHEIM'S NANCY
Wire-haired Dachshund
Sire: Ch. Brentwald Destiny   Dam: Ch. Starkrest's Nanette
Owner: Mrs. Neville R. Stephens, Tubac, Arizona

170

A Short Explanation of German Grammar

By Anne FitzGerald Paramoure

THE translation of foreign pedigrees and show reports is not easy, even for one who is well acquainted with the language in its everyday form. Just as the novice finds many English words used in an unfamiliar sense, so there is a special vocabulary employed by German-speaking breeders and exhibitors. To translate them it may be necessary to plow through ten or twenty variations of meaning in the unabridged dictionary, with no certainty that one will select the correct equivalent, even if it is included, while the ordinary abridged dictionary is likely to be no help whatever. Abbreviations are very frequently used, and may be fully as puzzling as an unfamiliar use of a familiar word.

All German nouns are capitalized, not merely proper names. Adjectives are not capitalized, even though they may form part of a kennel name, unless actually used in place of a noun. The formal second person "Sie" (meaning YOU) is also regularly capitalized. When an adjective is attached to the front of a noun so as to make a single word, however, it is capitalized instead of the noun to which it is attached, as in *Kleintierzuchter,* meaning small animal breeder.

171

German plurals are not formed by adding *S*, but in most cases by adding *er, e* or *en* to the root of the noun. Sometimes the root vowel is changed by the addition of an umlaut (··) over a, o or u, making it ä, ö, or ü. This may be the only change or it may be in addition to the plural endings already mentioned. The umlaut stands for an *e* which is not written. In proper names or in a word beginning with a capital the *e* is often written in place of the umlaut, and where printing is done with type which does not include the umlauts the *e* itself may likewise be used. The umlaut can be important for three reasons: it changes the pronunciation, it may be the only sign that a word is plural and not singular; in a German dictionary or index all names or words which contain an umlaut will be alphabetized as though the letter *e* were printed after the vowel over which it is used. This may mean that a name or word will be found several lines or even pages away from the same name or word without the umlaut. Moreover, the presence or absence of the umlaut may completely change the meaning of a word. For instance, *Mucke* means a whim, while *Mücke* is a gnat. Finally, the feminine of many nouns is formed by adding an umlaut to the vowel and the suffix *in* to the end of the word, so Hund, dog (general or masculine) becomes Hündin, bitch.

Other peculiarities which may confuse those not familiar with the language are: nouns have four cases, nominative, genitive (usually ending in *s* or *es* but sometimes in *e, en* or *ens*), dative and accusative. There are three genders, masculine, femine and neuter. Adjectives and pronouns also change their endings.

Another peculiarity is that the perfect participle of verbs is formed by adding *ge* to the *front* of the verb in most cases. Thus the participle of *decken* (meaning to breed) is *gedeckt* (bred) and the word will be found in a dictionary under *d* and not *g*. Compound verbs with *inseparable* prefixes do not add the augment *ge* for the participle, however. On the other hand, compound verbs with *separable* prefixes insert the *ge* between the prefix and the verb root, the participle of *anfangen* (to begin) being *angefangen*. In certain other

172

tenses the separable prefix of the verb in the main clause comes at the end of the phrase or sentence, as for instance, *ich fang an* (I begin) is a form of *anfangen*. As a compound verb may have quite a different meaning from the simple one from which it is formed, non-Germans unaccustomed to this usage find it extremely confusing to discover at the end of a sentence a prefix which may unexpectedly change the whole meaning. The Teutonic word order which frequently puts the verb at the end of the sentence instead of where other people would expect it is also confusing.

The names of German dogs, which are likely to appear dauntingly long and formidable to those who do not understand the language are much easier to remember if they are broken down into their separate parts. Most of them consist of an individual name, a preposition with or without an article, and a kennel name. Most if not all German breeds require litter registration, all puppies carrying the breeder's registered kennel name, while it is usual for all of a single litter to have individual names beginning with the same letter. Kennels' names often refer to the town, village or local area in which the breeder lives. Sometimes they are related to the name of the breed or the breeder, and puns are not uncommon. Thus Herr Berger, breeder of German Shepherds, used the kennel name *Bergerslust*, meaning "Shepherd's Delight" or "Berger's Delight" as one prefers. The impressive-sounding "Fiffi v. Rhein-Herne-Kanal" is only Fiffi of the Rhine Canal at Herne, where her breeder lived. Wilhelm Schwaneberg took the kennel name "v.d. Schwanburg," meaning "of or from the Swan Castle." The owners of "Neckar-lust," "Neckarstadt" and "Neckartal" all live along the Neckar River. "Zwergschnauzerheim" is nothing but "Home of Miniature Schnauzers."

Up to 1934 many of the larger German specialty clubs published their own studbooks. Included among these were the Verein für Deutsche Schaferhunde, devoted to German Shepherd Dogs, and the Pinscher-Schnauzer-Klub, which registered six breeds: Giant, Standard and Miniature Schnauzers, Smooth-haired Pinschers (not Dobermans), Miniature Pinschers, and Affenpinschers. The Deutsches

Kartell für Hundewesen (DKH) was the all breed club recognized by the AKC, and the papers of imported dogs had to be endorsed by them before they were accepted for AKC registration. In 1934 the Nazi government reorganized the dog fancy, like so many other things. The national organization became the Reichsverband für das Deutsche Hundewesen (RDH) and the specialty clubs were absorbed as Fachschafte or sections of the RDH, though they continued to publish their stud books and breed papers as before, at least up to 1938. What has happened during the war remains to be seen. On July 1, 1937, the RDH was reorganized as the Reichsverband Deutscher Kleintierzüchter (RDK). The old styles of *Sieger,* or *Jahressieger* were changed to Reichssieger, while the Klubsieger title became Fachschaftsieger. Bitch titles were similarly changed to Reichsiegerin and Fachschaftsiegerin.

CH. CID, JR., OF LAKELANDS

Sire: Ch. Cid v. Werderhavelstrand   Dam: Ch. Harriet v. Stahlhaus

White Gables Kennels, Mariam Van Court, Los Angeles, California

German Vocabulary

"Ablegen" ----------------------Lie down and lie still!

Abstammung ----------------Origin, descent, ancestry

Abzeichen ------------------Markings

Abzugeben ------------------Available, offered (e.g. for sale or at **stud)**

"Achtung" -------------------Look out! Watch! On guard!

Ahn, Ahnen ----------------Ancestors, ancestors

Ahnentafel ------------------Pedigree

Allgemeiner Deutscher
  Rottweilerklub e.V. --------German Rottweiler Club

Allgemeiner Eindruck -------General impression

Alter ----------------------Age

Altersklasse ----------------Open class

Amme ---------------------Foster mother

Angekört --------------------Inspected and certified suitable for breeding

Ankörung ------------------Official inspection for breeding suitability

Anwartschaft --------------Prospective championship; accumulated wins
                           toward a championship

"Apport" --------------------Fetch!

Apportierbock --------------Dumbbell (for training to carry and retrieve)

"Auf" ----------------------Up! (when the dog has been sitting or lying)

Aufbeisser ------------------Dog with undershot mouth

Augen ---------------------Eyes

"Aus" ----------------------Out! Let go!

Ausbildung ----------------Improvement or advancement of a breed

Ausbildungskennzeichen -----Standard

Ausstellung, Austellungen ---Show, shows

Band, Bände ----------------Volume, volumes (of stud book or magazine)

Befehl ----------------------Command, order (in training)

Befriedigend ----------------Satisfactory (used in rating on show points)

Begleithunde --------------Companion or house dogs

Begrenzte Klasse -----------Limit class

Behaarung ------------------Coat, hair

Beiesskorb ------------------Muzzle (worn by dogs)

Belassen --------------------Left (with dam after birth); kept

Belegt ----------------------Bred (of bitches)

Besitzer, Besitzerin --------Owner

Besitzwechsel --------------Change of ownership

Bewertung ------------------Qualification; value; rating (e.g.

Bild, Bilder ---------------- "excellent," "very good," "poor")
                           Picture, pictures

Blau ----------------------Blue; slate-grey

"Bleibsitzen" ----------------Stay! Keep sitting!

Blindenführer Hund --------Guide dog (for the blind)

Blindenführerhundprüfung --Guide dog trial or examination

Boxer-Klub e. V. -----------Boxer Club (incorporated)

175

Braun _____Brown
Braungestichelt (Elchfarbig) _Elk colored; mixed brown not solid color
"Bring" _____Fetch!
Bringbock _____Dumbbell (for carrying)
Bringen _____To fetch
Bruder, Brüder _____Brother, brothers
Brustfleck _____Spot on chest
Brustgeschirr _____Dog harness
"Daun" _____Down! Drop! (when dog off leash is to be
                    halted at a distance from trainer)
Decken _____To breed, to cover by a stud
Decken frei, zum _____At public stud (for the usual fee)
Decktag _____Breeding date
Der, dem, den _____The (declined like an adjective or pronoun
                    and agreeing in gender with its noun)
Deutsche Dogge _____Great Dane
Deutsche Pointer u. Setter-
  Verein _____German Setter and Pointer Association
Deutsche Schäferhund _____German Shepherd Dog
Deutsche Teckelklub e.V. ____German Dachshund Club (inc.)
Deutsche Vorstehende,
  Kurzhaarig _____Shorthaired German Pointers
Deutsche Vorstehende,
  Langhaarig _____Longhaired German Pointers
Deutscher Doggenclub e. V. i.
  Kartell _____Great Dane Club (inc.)
Deutscher Reichsverband für
  Polizei und Schutzhunde
  e. V. _____German Reich Association for police and
                    guard dogs (inc.)
Deutscher Schaeferhund
  Verband _____German Shepherd Dog Association (compara-
                    tively little known compared to the S.V.)
Deutsches Hundestammbuch _The official all-breed German stud book
Deutsches Kartells für
  Hundewesen _____Pre-Hitler all-breed German club correspond-
                    ing to the AKC.
Diensthund _____Service dog; trained dog in actual service
Dientsuchhund _____A tracker on active police duty
Dienstsuchhundprüfung _____A trial or contest for trained trackers
Dobermannpinscherverein ___Dobermann Pinscher Association
                    (commonly called D.V.)
Dogge _____Bulldog (see also *Deutsche Dogge*)
Drahthaarigen _____Wire-haired
Dressierung, Dressur _____Training
Dressurprüfung _____Training test, now colled Zuchtprüfung
Dritter _____Third
Dunkel _____Dark
Dunkelrot _____Dark red
Ehrenpreis _____Trophy

Eigentümer _____Owner
Eingetragener Verein _____Registered association (i.e. incorporated)
Eintragung _____Entry (at a show or in a stud book)
Eintragungsbestätigung _____Certificate of entry; registration
Elchfarbig _____Elk colored; a brownish mixture, not solid
     tan or chocolate
Ellenbogen _____Elbows
Eltern _____Parents
Enkel, Enkelin _____Grandson, granddaughter
Entwartung _____Cancellation
Ersatzpreis _____A prize given in special recognition of the
     runner-up to the prizewinners at a show
Erster _____First

Fachschaftssieger _____Formerly Klubsieger
Fachschaft _____Department; division; branch
Fachschaft für Schweizer
  Sennenhunde im R.D.H.____Swiss Sennenhund Division of the R.D.H.
Farbe, farbig _____Color, colored
"Fass" _____Take it!
Fédération Cynologique
  Internationale _____International Dog Federation which awards
     World championship titles
Fehler _____Faults
Fehlerhaft _____Faulty
Führer _____Handler
"Fuss" _____Heel!

Gau _____District
Gebrauchshund _____Working dog
Gedeckt _____Bred, covered
Gefleckt _____Spotted
Gelb _____Yellow
Genannt _____Called, alias, known as
Gesclecht _____Sex (also species, family, kind)'
Geschutzter _____Protected
Geschutzter Zuchtname _____Registered kennel name
Gesellschaft für
  Hundeforschung _____Association for dog research
Gestreift _____Brindled, striped
Gestrommt _____Brindle
Getötet _____Killed, destroyed (when a litter is too large
     to raise advantageously)
Gewinkelt _____Angulated
Gewolkt _____Clouded
Geworfen _____Whelped
"Gib laut" _____Speak!
Glanz _____Lustrous
Glattaarig _____Smooth coated

177

"Gradaus" _____Straight ahead! Forward! (for *gerade aus*)
Grau _____Grey
Gross _____Big, large
Grösse _____Size
Grosseltern _____Grandparents
Grossmutter _____Granddaf
Grossvater _____Grandshire
Gut _____Good

Haar _____Coat, hair
Hals _____Neck, throat
Halsband _____Collar
Hasenfarbig _____Hare colored, mixed brownish grey
Hauptgeschäftestelle _____Main office, headquarters
Hauptprüfung _____Championship contest or trial
Hauptpreishüten _____Herding championship trial
Heisst _____Called, known as
Hell _____Bright, light colored
Herdengebrauchshund
    (HGH) _____Trained herding dog
"Hier" _____Here! Come here!
Hinterhand _____Hindquarters
Hinterläufe _____Hind legs
Hirschrot _____Reddish fawn
Hitze _____Heat, season (in bitches)
"Hoch" _____Up! Over! (command for jumping)
"Hopp" _____Away! Over! (command for jumping)
Höchstlobende Erwähnung ___Very highly commended
Höhe _____Height
Holländische _____Dutch
Hund, Hunde _____Dog, dogs (male or in general)
Hundefreunde _____Dog lovers, fanciers
Hündin, Hündinnen _____Bitch, bitches

Inzucht _____Inbreeding

Jahressieger, Jahressiegerin _Dog and bitch winner of the annual specialty
                            championship show, thereby becoming
                            champions of the year. After Hitler called
                            Reichssieger and Reichssiegerin
Jahrgang _____Annual volumes, year's issue of stud book or
                            magazine
Jugendklasse _____Youth class (12-18 months for German Shep-
                            herds)
Jung _____Young
Junger, Junge _____Puppy, puppies, youngsters
Junghundklasse _____Junior class (18-24 months for German Shep-
                            herds)
Jungtier _____Young animal, youngster, puppy

Kampioen ------------------Champion (Dutch)

Katalog --------------------Catalog

Kind, Kinder ---------------Get (of a sire or dam)

Klein ----------------------Small

Kleintierzüchter -----------Small animal breeder

Klubsieger, Klubsiegerin -----Club champion dog or bitch. (Winner of First Open with rating of Excellent under three different judges.)

Knochen -------------------Bone

"Komm" -------------------Come!

Komondor-Klub im Kartell ---Komondor Club, affiliated with the D.K.H.

Konkurrenz ----------------Competition

Kopf ----------------------Head

Koppel-Klasse -------------Brace class

Körbuch des Vereins für
    Deutsche Schäferhunde ----Book of breeding suitability inspection of the S.V.

Körzeichen ----------------Certified as suitable for breeding

Kräftig --------------------Strong

"Kreich" -------------------Crawl! Creep!

Kriegshund ----------------War dog

Kruppe --------------------Croup

Kurz ----------------------Short

Langhaarig ----------------Long-haired

"Lass" ---------------------Let go! Out!

Läufe ---------------------Running gear, legs

"Leg dich" -----------------Lie Down!

"Legen" -------------------Lie Down!

Leine ---------------------Leash

Leistung ------------------Field training

Leistungsbuch -------------Field trial registration book

Leistungsprüfung ----------Field trial

Leistungssieger
    Leistungssiegerin ---------Field trial champion dog and bitch

Leistungswanderpreis
    des S.V. -------------------Field trial trophy of the S.V.

Liebhaber -----------------Fancier

Links ---------------------Left, lefthand

Lobende Erwähnung --------Highly recommended

Mangelhaft ----------------Passable, mediocre

Maske --------------------Mask, face

Melde Hund ---------------Army messenger dog

Meldehundprüfung ---------Messenger dog trial

Meldeschein --------------Registration certificate

Meldung ------------------Entry, registration

Mit ----------------------With

Mit Amme aufgezogen-------Raised with a foster mother

179

Mitglied, Mitglieder _____Member, members
Monatshefte _____Unbound monthly issue of a publication
Monatsschrift _____Monthly magazine

Nachgewiesen _____Indicated
Nase _____Muzzle, nose
Nederland Hundestammbuch _Netherlands stud book (all breeds)
Neulings-Klasse _____Novice class
Nicht nachgewiesen _____Not indicated; not shown on the record
"Nimm" _____Take it!
Nummer _____Number

0 _____Zero; failed
Offeneklasse _____Open Class
Offeneleistungsklasse _____Open Class for dogs with training degrees.
The winner of this class in each sex, if
qualified Excellent (V) wins the Reichs-
sieger title at the anual Reichssieger show,
provided he or she has attained the min-
imum age for the breed, even though de-
feated in another class by a dog not eligible
or not entered in OLK.
Ohne Amme _____Without a foster mother
Ohren _____Ears
Osterreichischer Verein
für deutsche Schäferhunde __Austrian Association for the German Shepherd Dog
Osterreichisches
Hundestammbuch _____Austrian stud book (all breed)
Ortsgruppe _____Local group; local club

Paar _____Pair, brace
"Pass auf" _____Watch out! Alert!
Pfeger und Salz _____Pepper and salt
Pfote, Pfoten _____Paw, foot
"Pfui" _____Shame! No!
Pinscherklub _____Pinscher Club (Köln) founded 1895
Pinscher-Schnauzer-Klub
(P.S.K.) _____Pinscher and Schnauzer Club
Pinscherzuchtbuch (PZ) ____Pinscher Club stud book
Pinscher-Schnauzer-
Zuchtbuch (P.S.Z.) _____Pinscher and Schnauzer Studbook
Platz _____Place (in competition)
"Platz" _____Down!
Prämierung _____Award
Polizei Dienst Hund _____Trained dog in actual police service
Polizei Dienst Hund Prüfung_Test or field trial for working police dogs
Polizeihund _____Police-trained dog (of any breed)
Preis, Preise _____Prize, prizes
Preishüten _____Herding trial
Preishüten Sieger _____Herding champion

Preishüten Siegerin _____Herding champion bitch
Prüfung _____Test, trial, examination
Prüfungsverband der
  Zuchtvereine für Dienst-
  hundrassen in Kartell ____Training competition organization of special-
                            ty clubs for service dog breeds affiliated
                            with the Kartell

Rechts _____Breed
Reichsfachgruppe Deutsches__Breed standard, breed characteristics
Rasse _____Right (righthand)
Rassekennzeichen
  Hundewesen e.V. _____Post-Hitler name for D.K.H.
Reichsobmann _____Chief of a nationwide organization under
                           Hitler
Reichsverband Deutscher
  Kleintierzüchter e.V. _____German Small Anmial Breeders' Organization
                            (inc.) Established under Hitler regime
Reichsverband für das
  Deutscher Hundewesen ____Hitler equivalent of D.K.H.
Reichssieger, Reichssiegerin _Hitler equivalent of Jahressieger and Jah-
                             ressiegerin
Rein _____Pure, entire, solid (of color)
Reinzucht _____Pure bred
Richter _____Judge
Richterbericht _____Judge's report
Riesenschnauzer _____Giant Schnauzer
Rot _____Red
Rücke _____Back
Rude _____Stud dog, male
Rute _____Tail, stern

Salf und Pfeffer _____Salt and pepper color
Sanitätshund (SH) _____Red Cross dog
Sattel _____Saddle
Schäferhund _____Shepherd Dog
Schäferhund Verein (S.V.) __German Shepherd Dog Club
Schau _____Show
Schecken _____Parti-colored
Schnauzer Klub e. V. _____Schnauzer Club, Munich, founded 1907
Schnauzer mittelschlag _____Standard Schnauzer
Schnauzer Zuchtbuch _____Stud book of Schnauzer Club, Munich
Schönheit _____Beauty, bench
Schönheitsieger _____Bench champion
Schokolade _____Chocolate
Schriftleiter _____Editor
Shulhalsband _____Spiked training collar
Schulter _____Shoulder
Schulterhöhe _____Shoulder height
Schutzhundprüfung I _____Formerly Zuchthundprüfung

181

Schutzhundprüfung II _____Formerly Zuchthundprüfung—Guard dog
            trial
Schutzhundprüfung III _____Formerly Polizeihundprüfung or Deinsthund-
            prüfung
Schutzhundhauptprüfung ____Protection dog championship contest
Schutzhundvorprüfung _____Preliminary trial for protection dogs
Schutzhundprüfung _____Trial for protection dogs
Schwarz _____Black
Schwarz mit braunen
   Abzeichen _____Black with brown markings; black and tan
Schwarz mit grauer
   Stichelung _____Black with grey markings; grizzled
Schwarz mit kleinem
   weissen Brustfleck _____Black with small white breast spot
Schwartz mit hellem
   Brustfleck _____Black with light spot on breast
Schwartz mit rostbraun ____Black with rust brown
Schwarzbraun _____Dark brown; black with brown markings
Schwarzbraun mit weisseen
   Brustfleck _____Dark brown with white chest spot
Schwarzgelb _____Tawny; dark yellow
Schwarzgrau _____Black with grey markings
Schwarzrot _____Dark red
Schweitzer Hundestammbuch_Swiss studbook
Schweitzer Sennenhund-
   Verein für Deutschland ____Swiss Sennenhund Club of Germany
Schwester _____Sister
Sehr gut _____Very good (rating next below "excellent")
"Setzen" _____Sit!
Sieger, Siegerin _____Champion dog or bitch
Siegerausstellung _____Championship show
Siegeranwärter,
   Siegeranwärterin _____Certificate winner; prospective champion dog
            or bitch with wins toward the Fachschaft-
            sieger or Klubsieger title
Siegeranwartschaft _____Prospect of a championship
Siegerprüfung _____Championship contest
Silbergrau _____Silver grey
Stattspreis für Zucht oder
   Gebrauchsleistung _____Government prize for obedience or work
            training
Sonderausstellung _____Specialty show
Sonderverein _____Speciality club
Sprungwand _____Hurdle; jump used for training to scale
            fences, etc.
"Such" _____Seek! Trail!
"Such, verloren" _____Seek a lost object!
Suchhund der Polizei
   (SuchH) _____Police tracker
Suchhundprüfung _____Trailing test

Teckel ---------------------Dachshund
Teil ------------------------Part, section, volume
Tiefschwarz ----------------Solid black
Tier ------------------------Animal
Töten ----------------------To destroy (as unwanted puppies in a litter)
Totgeboren -----------------Stillborn

Ubung ----------------------Training exercise
Unbekannt -----------------Unknown
Und -----------------------And
Unterschrift ---------------Signature
Urgrosseltern --------------Great-grandparents
Ungrossenkel,
 Urgrossenkelin -----------Great-great-grandson or granddaughter
Urgrossmutter -------------Great-granddam
Urgrossvater ---------------Great-grandsire
Ururgrosseltern ------------Great-great-grandparents

Vater ----------------------Sire
Verbindung -----------------Mating
Verein ---------------------Club, association
Verein für deutsche
 Schäferhunde e.V. (S.V.)--German Shepherd Dog Association (inc.)
Verein für deutsche
 Schäferhunde in der
 Tschecho-Slowakei --------Czecho-Slovakian German Shepherd Dog As-
                           sociation
Verein für deutsche Spitze___German Spitz Association
Vergebung ------------------Award, bestowal
Vierter --------------------Fourth
Vorderbrust ----------------Forechest
Vorderhand ----------------Forequarters
Vorderpfote ----------------Forepaw
Vorprüfung -----------------Preliminary trial
Vorsitzender ---------------President, chairman
"Vorwärts" -----------------Go ahead!
Vorzüglich (V) ------------Excellent (highest rating)

Wanderpreis ---------------Challenge trophy (best of breed)
Wanderzuchtpreis ----------Breeder's challenge trophy
Wasserhundprüfung --------Water dog trial
Weiss ----------------------White
Weitsprung -----------------Broad jump
Welp, Welpen --------------Young puppy, young puppies
Weltsieger, Weltsiegerin ----World champion dog or bitch
Werfen ---------------------To produce, to whelp
Wesen ----------------------Character, temperament, disposition
Winkelung -----------------Angulation
Wurf ----------------------Litter

Wurfdatum _____Whelping date
Wurfmeldung _____Litter entry, litter registration
Wurfstärke _____Size of litter

Zimmerrein _____House-broken
Zotthaarig _____Shaggy coated
Zucht _____Breeding, rearing, breed, race
Zuchtbuch _____Studbook
Zuchtbuchamt _____Studbook office
Züchter, Züchterin _____Breeder (masculine and feminine)
Zuchtgruppe _____Team
Zuchthündin _____Brood bitch
Zuchtpreis _____Bred by exhibitor prize
Zuchtprüfung
   (Schutzhundprüfung _____Obedience test. (Not exactly corresponding
                            to those given in this country, but required
                            of dogs not having a more advanced train-
                            ing degree in order to be eligible for a
                            championship.)
Zuchtverein _____Speciality club
Zulassung _____Allowed, permitted point or characteristic
"Zur Spur" _____Trail!
"Zur Wache!" _____Watch! On guard!
Zur Zucht nicht zugelassen __Not to be used for breeding
Zur Zucht nur mit Genehmig-
   ung des Zuchtbuchamtes
   zugelassen _____Can be used for breeding only with approval
                            of the Stud Book office
Zweiter _____Second
Zwergpinscher _____Miniature Pinscher
Zwergschnauzer _____Miniature Schnauzer
Zwinger _____Kennel
Zwingerklasse _____Team class
Zwingername _____Kennel name

German Terms and Abbreviations

A. _____Amme
A.D.R.K. _____Allgemeiner Deutscher Rottweilerklub e.V.
Abz. _____Abzeichen
AK _____Altersklasse

B. _____Band. Befriedigend.
B.F.H. _____Blindenführer Hund
BK _____Begrenzte Klasse
Bel. _____Belassen
Bes. _____Besitzer, Besitzerin
Bl. _____Blau
BlHPr._____Blindenführerhundprüfung
Blbr. _____Blau mit braun
Bl. _____Braun
Brgest _____Braungestichelt (elchfarbig)

CAC _____FCI award at smaller shows or to dogs not
                            judged good enough for CACIB
CACIB _____International bench championship awarded
                            by FCI for three firsts with excellent under
                            different judges

D. _____Der, dem, den. Dunkel.
D.H.S. _____Deutsches Hundestammbuch
D.K.H. _____Deutsches Kartells für Hundewesen
D.V. _____Dobermannpinscher-Verein
DSuchH _____Dienstsuchhund
DSuchHPr _____Dienstsuchhundprüfung
Dr. _____Dunkelrot
DrPr _____Dressurprüfung
D.S.V. _____Deutscher Schäferhund Verband

E. _____Eigentümer
E. V. _____Eingetragener Verein
Ep. _____Ehrenpreis

F. _____Fehlerhaft. Führer.
FCI _____Fédération Cynologique Internationale
FS (FSg) _____Fachschaftssieger

G. _____Gut
Gb. _____Gelb
GfH _____Gesellschaft für Hundeforschung
Gen. _____Gennant
Gestr. _____Gestromt
Gew. _____Geworfen. Gewolkt

H. _____Hündin
HPrHt _____Hauptpreishüten
H.G.H. _____Herden Gebrauchs Hund
H.L.E. _____Höchstlobende Erwähnung
Hr. _____Hirschrot

JK _____Jugend-Klasse
JS _____Jahressieger
JSn _____Jahressiegerin
JunghK _____Junghundklasse

185

K. ----------------------------------Kampioen
KB ----------------------------------Körbuch des Vereins für deutsche
Schäferhunde e. V.
KS ----------------------------------Klubsieger
KSn ---------------------------------Klubsiegerin
KoK ---------------------------------Komondor-Klub im Kartell

LE ----------------------------------Lobende Erwähnung
LS or LSg ---------------------------Leistungssieger
LWP ---------------------------------Leistungswanderpreis des S.V.

M. ----------------------------------Maske. Mutter. Mangelhaft.
MA ----------------------------------Mit Amme aufgezogen
MH ----------------------------------Melde Hund
MHPr --------------------------------Meldehundprüfung

NHSB --------------------------------Nederland Hundestammbuch
N. nachgew. -------------------------Nicht nachgewiesen
Nr. ---------------------------------Nummer

O. ----------------------------------Zero (Failed; no good). Ohne.
O. A. -------------------------------Ohne Amme
OK ----------------------------------Offeneklasse
OLK ---------------------------------Offeneleistungsklasse
OSV ---------------------------------Osterreichischer Verein für deutsche
Schäferhunde

P.D.H. ------------------------------Polizei Dienst Hund
P.D.H.Pr ----------------------------Polizeidiensthundprüfung
P.D.Z. ------------------------------Prüfungsverband der Zuchtvereine für
Diensthundrassen im Kartell
P.H. --------------------------------Polizeihund
P. K. -------------------------------Pinscherklub (Köln)
P.S.K. ------------------------------Pinscher-Schnauzer Klub
P.S.Z. ------------------------------Pinscher-Schnauzer-Zuchtbuch
P.Z. --------------------------------Pinscherzuchtbuch
Pfslz. ------------------------------Pfeffer and Salz
P. u. S. ----------------------------Pfeffer und Salz

R. ----------------------------------Rot. Rüde.
R.D.H. ------------------------------Reichsverband für das Deutsche Hundewesen
R.D. Kl. ----------------------------Reichsverband Deutscher Kleintierzüchter

S. ----------------------------------Sieger. Sattel.
Sbgr. -------------------------------Silbergrau
SH ----------------------------------Sanitätshund
SHSB --------------------------------Schweitzer Hundestammbuch
SPr ---------------------------------Siegerprüfung
SSZB/AS -----------------------------Schweitzer Sennenhund Zuchtbuch,
Appenzeller Sennenhund

SSZB/BS -----------------------------Schweitzer Sennenhund Zuchtbuch,
Berner Sennenhund
SV ----------------------------------Verein für deutsche Schäferhunde
SV-TS -------------------------------Verein für deutsche Schäferhunde in der
Tschecho-Slowakei
SZ ----------------------------------Zuchtbuch für deutsche Schäferhunde
SchH I ------------------------------Schutzhundprüfung I (formerly Zuchthund-
prüfung)

186

SchH II _____Schutzhundprüfung (now Schutzhundprü-
                            fung II)
SchH III _____Schutzhundprüfung III (formerly Polizei-
                            hundprüfung and Diensthundprüfung)
SchHHPr. _____Schutzhundhauptprüfung
SchHVPr. _____Schutzhundvorprüfung
SchZ _____Schnauzer Zuchtbuch (München)
Schwz. _____Schwarz
Schwz-B _____Schwarz mit hellem Brustfleck
Schwz. m. rostbr. _____Schwarz mit rostbraun
Schwzbr. _____Schwarzbraun
Schwbrws. _____Schwarz mit weissem Brustfleck
Schwzgb. _____Schwarzgelb
Schwzgr. _____Schwarz mit grauer Stichelung; Schwarzgrau
Sg. _____Sehr gut
StP _____Stattspreis für Zucht oder Gebrauchsleistung
SuchHPr. _____Suchhundprüfung
SuchHHPr. _____Suchhundhauptprüfung
Sn. _____Siegerin

T. _____Teil

U. _____Und

V. _____Vorzüglich. Vater. Verein.

W. _____Weiss. Wurfstärke
WPr. _____Wasserhundprüfung
WS _____Weltsieger
WT _____Wurftag
WZPH _____Wanderzuchtspreis des SV für Hündinnen
WZPR _____Wanderzuchtspreis des SV für Rüden

Z _____Zuchter, Züchterin
ZDS _____Zuchtbuch für Deutsche Spitze
ZK _____Zuchtklasse
ZPr _____Zuchtpreis
ZPr _____Zuchtprüfung (now Schutzhundprüfung I)
ZPr _____Zuchtprüfung
ZPrH _____Zuchtprüfunghund
Zh. _____Zotthaarig
ZwK _____Zwingerklasse

* _____Körzeichen (heisst angekört)

(!) _____Zur Zucht nicht zugelassen

(?) _____Zur Zucht nur mit Genehmigung des Zucht-
                            buchamtes zugelassen

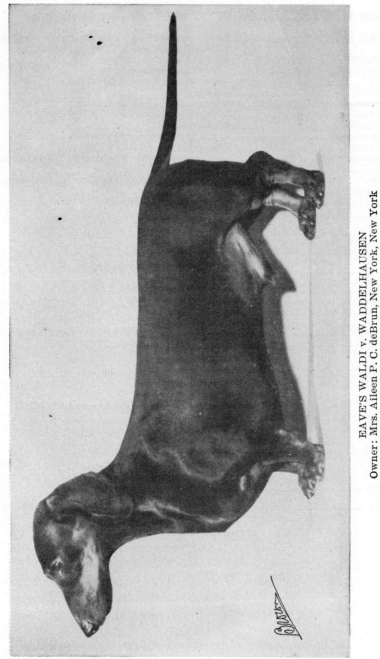

EAVE'S WALDI v. WADDELHAUSEN
Owner: Mrs. Aileen P. C. deBrun, New York, New York

188

Champion Dachshunds and Famous Kennels

By Mildred L. Hill

ROBABLY no other breed owners
enjoy cooperation, harmony, and general good will toward
one another as do the owners of Dachshunds, and no doubt
this all comes about because the Dachshund is so loyal, and
has such a merry and gay disposition combined with a wonderful sense of humor. The Dachshund is an excellent
hunter and fearless in his undertakings, and the popularity
of the breed is definitely on the increase—and why shouldn't
it be, with its intriguing appearance, its devoted companionship, and its vigilance in the protection of its owner's home?
This chapter reflects a spirit of co-operation and sportsman-
ship on the part of many breeders and kennel owners that
makes it possible for me to tell you more about Champion
Dachshunds and famous kennels.

The American breeders, Josef and Maria Mehrer, West
Hempstead, L. I., New York, are responsible for the estab-
lishment of the bloodlines of "Marienlust" which, according
to pedigrees of their stock, show considerable Luitpoldsheim,
Werderhavelstrand, and Flottenberg ancestry. Although
the Mehrers have raised other breeds of dogs, their personal
preference apparently is for the Dachshund. Their strain of
Marienlust has produced and is producing many fine winners, and when show reports are read, the name Marienlust
is almost always among the headliners.

With deep sorrow, Josef and Maria Mehrer informed the Dachshund fancy that their famous stud, Champion Leutnant v. Marienlust, born January 1, 1938, had died July 23, 1950, at their kennels in West Hempstead, at the age of twelve and one-half years.

In 1940, when Leutnant was about two and one-half years old, he won the Dachshund Club of America Specialty at Morris and Essex. It is interesting to note that in past years, winners at this Specialty Show have been from either the first, second, or third generations of his get: Ch. Gunther v. Marienlust was the winner in 1942, 1943, and 1945; Ch. Superman v. Marienlust, in 1944; Ch. Bit O'Black of Tween Hills, in 1946; Ch. Cynthia of Jo-Rene, in 1947; Ch. Cinderella v. Marienlust, in 1949; and Ch. Aristo v. Marienlust, in 1950.

Leutnant's son, Ch. Gunther v. Marienlust, owned by Mrs. John W. Cross, won the Veterans Class at the parent Club's Specialty in a class of five entrants. And to top off his record, he also was the winner of this Club's fortieth anniversary cup for his wins of 1941, 1942, and 1943; he also won the Golden Jubilee Plaque in 1945. Ch. Gunther v. Marienlust was the sire of twenty champions: Ch. Janet of Tenroc, Ch. Marlene of Tenroc, Ch. Donald of Tween Hills, Ch. Little Vicki of Tween Hills, Ch. Black Knight of Tween Hills, Ch. Baron of Tween Hills, Ch. Blackie Dockie, Ch. Gunther Again, Ch. Cornhill Linda, Ch. Hexe v. Waldhof, Ch. Blackbeauty of Tween Hills, Ch. Bit O'Black of Tween Hills, Ch. Bencelia's Candy, Ch. Cinderella v. Sieghofen, Ch. Bavarian Mousi, Ch. Rotcod v. Tenroc, Ch. Guntherette of Earldale, Ch. Donahue of Brentwald, Ch. Derresheim of Brentwald, and Ch. Ballerina v. Marienlust.

It will be of interest to many that the German import, Arri v. Luitpoldsheim bred to Friede v. Marienlust produced Ch. Zep v. Marienlust, and that Ch. Zep v. Marienlust bred to Ch. Senta v. Luitpoldsheim (Hansi v. Holzgarten ex Herta v. Luitpoldsheim) produced Ch. Leutnant v. Marienlust, who truly set the "fashion" and "demand" for top black-and-tan Dachshunds. Leutnant was not shown extensively, but when he was shown, he made top wins. He was retired to stud, and his contribution to the breed has been most invaluable.

190

CH. ARRI v.d. DANIELS
Sire: Int. Ch. Favorite v. Marienlust   Dam: Ebony Maid v.d. Daniels
Breeder: Mr. and Mrs. Dale Daniels of Gilroy, California
Owner: Mrs. Walter D. Monroe, Little Gate Kennels, Lake Forest, Illinois

CH. LADY v. DYCHLAND—Daughter   CH. NODDY V. DYCHLAND—Sire
CH. ITSIT OF STEINHOFF—Grandsire
Three generations of Dychland Kennels Dachshunds
Herman G. Cox, Fort Worth, Texas

He had length of body, correct angulation, elegance of head and neck, and beautiful feet. Without a doubt, many of the good Dachshunds of today owe their qualities to Ch. Leutnant v. Marienlust. The Mehrers used Ch. Leutnant extensively in their own kennels: Leutnant ex Moya v. Marienlust produced Ch. Cavalier v. Marienlust and Ch. Gunther v. Marienlust; Leutnant ex Ch. Herzville v. Marienlust produced Lovely v. Marienlust; Leutnant ex Dottie v. Lindenheim produced Trudi v. Lindenheim; Leutnant ex Moya v. Marienlust also produced Ch. Superman v. Marienlust; Leutnant ex Herzy v. Marienlust produced Hiram of Heying-Teckel and Hercules of Heying-Teckel; Leutnant ex Ch. Guntherette of Earldale produced Commanderette of Earldale; and Leutnant sired many other good Dachshunds including Ch. Lustic v. Marienlust, another son from the breeding of Leutnant to Ch. Herzville v. Marienlust. Ch. Leutnant v. Marienlust bred to Veni v. Marienlust produced Chanter v. Marienlust. Ch. Ego v. Lenzgouen is also a Ch. Leutnant get, and still another son was Ch. Commander of Aycock, owned by Mrs. Scott Wood, Fresno, California. I should like to mention here also, that Ch. Antonia of Little Farm is the full litter sister of Ch. Leutnant v. Marienlust. Ch. Antonia of Little Farm was bred to Sgr. and Am. Ch. Aha v. Lindenbuhl, Willoughby Kennels, Cleveland, Ohio, and this breeding resulted in a line-bred and true Luitpoldsheim litter.

The Mehrers at present are offering another good stud, their Success v. Marienlust, sired by Ch. Sir Joe of Little Gate ex Dirndel v. Marienlust (Sir Joe is a son of Leutnant v. Marienlust ex Adelheid v. Brentwald).

In their kennels the Mehrers have produced many champion Dachshund studs, among them Am. and Can. Ch. Favorite v. Marienlust, owned by the Fred Heyings, Pacoima, California; Ch. Leutnant v. Marienlust and Diplomat v. Marienlust (both sired by Ch. Zep v. Marienlust ex Ch. Senta v. Luitpoldsheim); Ch. Zep v. Marienlust sired by Arri v. Luitpoldsheim ex Friede v. Marienlust; and Ch. Lustic v. Marienlust, sired by Ch. Leutnant v. Marienlust ex Ch. Herzville v. Marienlust (who was one of the most beautiful bitches in the breed). Ch. Cinderella v. Marienlust is another of the Mehrers' outstanding bitches, and is now owned by Mrs. Walter D. Monroe of Little Gate Kennels. Ch. Leutnant v. Marienlust's son Ch. Gunther v. Marienlust, owned by Mrs. John W. Cross, Wilton, Connecticut, has twenty champions to his credit. Ch. Lustic v. Marienlust, a black-and-tan, bred by the Mehrers, completed his championship in five shows, and is now owned by Mrs. Jimmie Dodge, Denver, Colorado, under whose ownership he recently took two Best in Show wins. Ch. Cavalier v. Marienlust and Ch. Gunther are full brothers. Another Marienlust stud of the Mehrers who produced champion sons and daughters was Message v. Marienlust, sired by Ch. Diplomat v. Marienlust ex Melinda v. Marienlust.

Heying-Teckel Kennels, Mr. and Mrs. Fred Heying, Pacoima, California, have been breeders of Dachshunds for twenty years, and their oldest trophy is engraved "1930." Their first Dachshund "happened" to be a good one—and after doing some winning, Mr. and Mrs. Heying became staunch supporters of the breed. In 1941, while attending the Morris and Essex Show, the Heyings purchased two Ch. Herman Rinkton daughters—one, R. Anny of Jonedith, was the dam of Ch. Demitasse of Heying-Teckel, and bred to Ch. Favorite v. Marienlust produced Ch. Dresden of Heying-Teckel. The litter sister of Ch. Demitasse, Dinah of Heying-Teckel, bred to Ch. Favorite v. Marienlust produced Ch. Calidox Daphne, owned by the Heyings; Ch. Calidox Nicholas, owned by Mr. and Mrs. A. C. Spraggins, Walnut Creek, California; and Ch. Calidox Luigi, owned by Raymond S. Hill, Phoenix, Arizona.

Heying-Teckel Kennel's most famous stud is their black-and-tan Am. and Can. Ch. Favorite v. Marienlust. In his get this stud has definitely contributed more to the fancy than any other Dachshund stud. Ch. Favorite was whelped April 21, 1945, sired by Bruce v. Marienlust ex Melinda v. Marienlust, and has sired many champions, including Ch. Cedric of Heying-Teckel (dam, Cobina v. Marienlust); Ch. Calidox Nicholas, Ch. Calidox Luigi, and Ch. Calidox Daphne (dam, Dinah of Heying-Teckel); Ch. Lucifer v. Bergman (dam, Rivenrock Dulcie); Ch. Dresden of Heying-Teckel (dam, R. Anny of Jonedith); Ch. Merry-O's Meru Mist (dam, Bucknam's Merry-O); Ch. Fashion Plate of Ewardale, Ch. Roxy's Rena, Ch. Derbydachs Schatze, Ch. Arri v. d. Daniels; Ch. Jeffrey of Heying-Teckel (dam, Jubilee of Heying-Teckel); Ch. Dulcie v. Bergman; and he has many more offspring that have completed their championships or have nearly completed them. Two young sons of Ch. Favorite v. Marienlust, San Souci's Stardust and Vincent of Heying-Teckel, were recently sent via Pan-American Clipper to Honolulu to the kennels of Dr. Napp Young for show as well as for breeding foundation stock. Vincent is the litter brother of Ch. Valencia of Heying-Teckel, owned by Raymond S. Hill.

Ch. Hershey of Heying-Teckel and Hiram of Heying-Teckel are litter mates sired by Ch. Leutnant v. Marienlust ex Herzy v. Marienlust. Many of the Heying-Teckel Dachshunds have won Hound Groups, Best of Varieties, and have been shown in many parts of the United States. Am. and Can. Ch. Favorite v. Marienlust has two all-breed Best in Show wins to his credit and three Specialty Best in Show wins also. The Specialty Show of the Dachshund Club of California was won three consecutive years by Ch. Favorite. In shows practically all over the country and in Honolulu, Ch. Favorite's get, in many instances, receives top placings.

Complimenting a great stud and sire, The American Dachshund in April 1953 issued a supplement to its publication. The star of this supplement, which is known as "The Favorite Issue," was, of course, Ch. Favorite v. Marienlust. To date he has sired sixty-six champions, and three of his get have made their championships in Canada. They are: Can. Ch. Elena of Gera (owners, Pam-Lin Kennels, dam, Ch. Rebecca of Gera); Can. Ch. Dachsheims Black Berry, and Can. Ch. Dachsheims Tar Baby (owners, Jean and Herbert Fletcher, New Westminister, Canada, dam, Ch. Blackberry v. d. Daniels, whom I own). The dam of Ch. Favorite v. Marienlust's first champion was Rivenrock Dulcie, owned by Mr. and Mrs. Edward F. Hirschman, Sepulveda, California. Up through 1953, according to information I have, Ch. Favorite has sired one hundred thirty-two registered litters. When Ch. Favorite celebrated his ninth birthday on April 21, 1954, he must have had a gleeful time with his proud owners, the Fred Heyings, and his proud breeders, the Josef

AM. and CAN. CH. FAVORITE v. MARIENLUST
The most spectacular and prolific sire of champions and other winners
the breed has ever known.
Sire: Bruce v. Marienlust   Dam: Melinda v. Marienlust
Owner: Heying-Teckel Kennels, Mr. and Mrs. Fred Heying,
Pacoima, California

Mehrers, who had travelled from Long Island to help celebrate the event.

Additional brood bitches at Heying-Teckel Kennels include Ch. Sunkist of Heying-Teckel, Ch. Gloria of Heying-Teckel, and Lana of Gera; the latter is the dam of Falcon of Heying-Teckel, winner of the Dachshund Club of California Eighth Futurity, and was sired by Favorite also. A stud that is making a good name for himself in the show ring is Ch. Lance of Heying-Teckel, also a Favorite son. Ch. Lance of Heying-Teckel took Best of Breed at Westminster in 1952; his dam is Lovely v. Marienlust, and his full litter sister is Ch. Lotus of Heying-Teckel, who has done some very great winning for her owner, Donia Cline. Hainheim Kennels, George C. Spradling, Wichita, are the owners and breeders of Champion Hainheim's Lance, a son of Ch. Lance of Heying-Teckel ex Hainheim's Zaranthaetta, whelped March 17, 1952. This young Lance son has also done some beautiful and outstanding winning.

As owners of Raymihill Kennels, my husband and I have been breeders and exhibitors for more than eighteen years. It is with regret that we inform the fancy that our Ch. Calidox Luigi died of pneumonia on March 11, 1953. Ch. Calidox Luigi bred to our Breezy Lane Pepper Pott (Rivenrock Torpedo ex Breezy Lane Peanuts) produced Lambia of Raymihill, who has ten points toward her championship, and who completed her Canadian championship by taking the Hound Group in Victoria, B. C., and is owned by the Earl Millers, San Diego; and Libby of Raymihill, who has twelve points toward her championship, and is owned by Mrs. Speer, of Indiana. Ch. Calidox Luigi, again bred to Breezy, produced Ch. Alden of Raymihill, owned by Dr. Louis A. Cornet. Ch. Alden of Raymihill, up to this time, has taken two Group wins, eight Group placings, nine Best of Breeds, and completed his championship in five shows. The first time he was shown, he took Best of Variety over Specials in an entry of forty. He is handled in the ring by Alice Marie Cornet. His full litter brother is Ch. Alcott of Raymihill, currently owned by the Myrandy Kennels, Andrew H. Rihl. Ch. Alcott finished his championship very quickly also. At the age of ten and one-half months, Alcott took Best in Match; at another

CH. LOTUS OF HEYING-TECKEL
Sire: Ch. Favorite v. Marienlust   Dam: Lovely v. Marienlust
Owner: Donia Cline, Los Angeles, California

CH. LANCE OF HEYING-TECKEL
Sire: Am. and Can. Ch. Favorite v. Marienlust
Dam: Lovely v. Marienlust
Breeders and Owners: Mr. and Mrs. Fred Heying, Pacoima, Calif.

197

match, he took Best Puppy Dog, all breeds, and from then on he went to higher wins, taking them as did his famous sire, Ch. Calidox Luigi, and even duplicating his sire's wins.

Breezy's next litter was sired by Ch. Standard of Heying-Teckel (Ch. Favorite v. Marienlust ex White Gables Brenda) and produced Ch. Michaela of Raymihill (owned by Mrs. Neville R. Stephens, Tubac, Arizona) and Mario of Raymihill (owned by Mrs. Wm. Olds, San Francisco, California), who has both majors and extras points on his championship. Others in this litter were Mirth of Raymihill and Mentor of Raymihill. Breezy bred to Ch. Favorite v. Marienlust produced Ch. Bright Angel of Raymihill, who took Best in Futurity, Dachshund Club of California, at eleven months of age, and completed her championship with nearly all major shows and one Hound Group. Ch. Bright Angel is owned by Mrs. Fanny Leonpacher, Lafayette, Louisiana. The full litter sister of Ch. Bright Angel is Ch. Blossom of Raymihill, who is currently owned by Raymond S. Hill. Blossom was only shown eleven times and completed her championship in "hot" competition wherever exhibited, including two circuits. Breezy was recently bred to Am. and Can. Ch. Harborvale Aladin and whelped five puppies, but they are still too young to be out of their puppy classes. Breezy Lane has Int. Ch. Dimas Earthstopper as her grandsire, and his influence has been a great factor in the quality of her get.

Other bitches at Raymihill that have contributed to our breeding program have been Trigg's Dunder, who bred to Ch. Calidox Luigi produced Lilibett of Raymihill, owned by Ainslie Walter, Santa Monica, California; and Lucia of Raymihill, owned by Mrs. Wheaton Walter, former editor of the Kennel Crier, now living in Santa Monica too; Ch. Minton of Heying-Teckel, Ch. Blackberry v. d. Daniels, and her daughter, Bebee of Raymihill, sired by Dachsheim's Mardi; Hedvig v. d. Stephens, a Ch. Harborvale Aladin daughter ex Heidi v. d. Stephens (a Ch. Calidox Luigi daughter).

Ch. Valencia of Heying-Teckel (Ch. Favorite v. Marienlust ex White Gables Brenda) completed her championship at Denver, Colorado, September 23, 1949. She was seven-

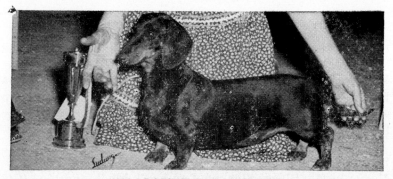

CH. BLOSSOM OF RAYMIHILL
Sire: Am. and Can. Ch. Favorite v. Marienlust
Dam: Breezy Lane Pepper Pott
Owner: Raymond S. Hill, Phoenix, Arizona

CH. BRIGHT ANGEL OF RAYMIHILL
Sire: Am. and Can. Ch. Favorite v. Marienlust
Dam: Breezy Lane Pepper Pott
Owner: Mrs. Fanny Leonpacher, Lafayette, Louisiana

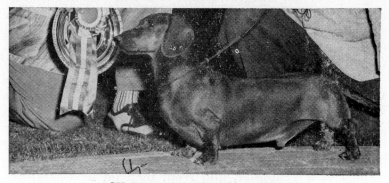

CH. PETERMAN'S CANDIDATE
Sire: Am. and Can. Ch. Aristo v. Marienlust
Dam: Peterman's Juliana

teen months old when she completed her championship and became the fourteenth champion sired by Ch. Favorite. Valencia went on to Tulsa, Oklahoma, where she took the Hound Group, and in 1950, she also took the Hound Group at the Tucson Kennel Club. Valencia is currently owned by Raymond S. Hill.

Raymihill Kennels' studs include Am. and Can. Ch. Harborvale Aladin (Ch. Aristo v. Marienlust ex Sunset v. Marienlust); Black Star of Lambros, black-and-tan (Ch. Bronze v. d. Daniels ex Ch. Miss Ruby Daniels of Pal-Mar); Robin of Raymihill, clear red (Ch. Harborvale Aladin ex Gay Lady v. Cavalier, sired by Ch. Cavalier v. Marienlust ex Little Lady, a Ch. Cavalier granddaughter); Champion Crespi's Thunderbird, black-and-tan (Crespi's Gene Miracle ex Rivenrock Dorothy); Dexter of Marstone, black-and-tan (Ch. Favorite v. Marienlust ex Marta of Gera). Dexter is a litter brother of Ch. Seth of Marstone and of Tinker Bell of Marstone, who is owned by the breeder, Marcella Firestone. Still another stud is Morey of Raymihill (Ch. Calidox Luigi ex Gay Lady v. Cavalier).

Am. and Can. Ch. Harborvale Aladin bred to Ch. Blackberry v. d. Daniels produced Ch. Susie of Raymihill, currently owned by Mrs. Wm. C. Mooney, Dallas, and purchased as foundation stock for her newly established kennel, Bill-Ora. Ch. Susie of Raymihill finished her championship in seven shows, and was then bred to Ch. Allegro of Gera (another son of Ch. Favorite v. Marienlust), and whelped a litter of four; with their second bitch, Hilda v. Hargelroad also bred to Ch. Allegro of Gera, the Bill-Ora Kennels are getting an excellent start in Dachshund breeding! Ch. Susie of Raymihill is a litter sister of Todd of Raymihill, who has also been an excellent winner and is owned by Mrs. Marion Y. Patten, Patmar Kennels, Clearwater, Florida.

Other champion get of Am. and Can. Ch. Harborvale Aladin include Ch. Crespi's Ronnie, clear red, owned by Mrs. Neville R. Stephens, Tubac, Arizona, a Group winner in California, Colorado, and Arizona, and Best of Breed winner also. Ronnie finished his championship in March 1954 under Judge Mrs. David Dodge. He made his debut in the spring of 1953 as a youngster, and from then on he established

TINKER BELL OF MARSTONE
Sire: Am. and Can. Ch. Favorite v. Marienlust   Dam: Marta of Gera
Owner: Mrs. Marcella S. Firestone, North Hollywood, California

CH. ALDEN OF RAYMIHILL
Sire: Ch. Calidox Luigi   Dam: Breezy Lane Pepper Pott
Owner: Dr. Louis A. Cornet, Washington, D. C.

CH. ALCOTT OF RAYMIHILL
Sire: Ch. Calidox Luigi   Dam: Breezy Lane Pepper Pott
Owners: Mr. and Mrs. Andrew H. Rihl, Trappe-Collegeville, Penna.

201

himself in the show ring. Ch. Crespi's Donnie, black-and-tan, owned by Donia Cline, is the full litter brother of Ch. Crespi's Ronnie, and Donia Cline is their breeder. Ch. Donnie, under the expert handling of Mrs. Cline, has Group wins and Group placements, and Best of Breed wins to his credit. Whelped March 5, 1952, both Ch. Donnie and Ch. Ronnie are proven studs. Their dam, Champion Rivenrock Tamale, is also the dam of the outstanding young male, Crespi's Jamboree, who is owned by Donia Cline and in excellent competition, took Best of Winners at the 1954 Sierra Specialty.

Am. and Can. Ch. Aristo v. Marienlust, a clear red, sired by Bruce v. Marienlust ex Freda O'Red Bairn (breeder Kenneth W. Raymond), was whelped March 24, 1946. He completed his championship in six shows, and is owned by Mrs. Lancaster Andrews, West Hempstead, Long Island, New York. Ch. Aristo v. Marienlust has ten Best in Show all-breed wins in the United States to his credit, and one Best in Show in Canada. In addition, he has one hundred twenty Best of Variety wins at all-breed shows, which include Westminster, three times; Morris and Essex, twice; Eastern, twice; and International (Chicago), twice. In 1951, Aristo was selected as the All American Hound of 1950 by the all-breed Judge A. Alfred LePine. It is of interest also, that Aristo's full litter sister is Alice v. Marienlust, owned by Hainheim Kennels, George C. Spradling, Wichita, Kansas.

Aristo has taken Best of Variety (the highest win obtainable at a Specialty) nine times, which includes the Dachshund Club of America, Bay Colony at Boston, twice; New Jersey Specialty, three times; Pennsylvania, twice; St. Louis, once; and others. Aristo has won forty-six Groups in the United States, including Westminster, Philadelphia, Eastern (Boston), Westchester, and International (Chicago); he has won three Groups in Canada, and has, in addition, placed over one hundred times either first, second, third, or fourth in the Group.

Aristo is the leading Dachshund Plaque winner, having won fifteen Dachshund Club of America bronze plaques, one eleven-inch and fourteen eight-inch, for Best of Variety in most severe competition.

AM. and CAN. CH. ARISTO v. MARIENLUST
Sire: Bruce v. Marienlust   Dam: Freda O'Red Bairn

CH. RIVENROCK TAMALE
Sire: Ch. Eric Again v. d. Daniels   Dam: Rivenrock Seal
Owner: Donia Cline, Los Angeles, California

As a stud, Ch. Aristo v. Marienlust has proved his worth also; his get as of the present time includes twelve champions. Aristo bred to Ch. Cornhill Linda (daughter of Ch. Gunther v. Marienlust) produced Ch. Hardway Welcome Stranger, red, whelped January 31, 1949, owned by Mrs. John W. Cross, Jr., Wilton, Connecticut. Ch. Hardway Welcome Stranger has won Best in Show five times. He won Best in Show at the Old Dominion Kennel Club all-breed show where the entry was nearly one thousand, and from May 1953 to June 1953, he won four Best in Show awards, all at major all-breed shows. In addition, Ch. Hardway Welcome Stranger has taken Best of Variety wins at six large Specialty Shows, including St. Louis Dachshund Club, 1952; Bay Colony Dachshund Club, 1953 and 1954; Dachshund Club of New Jersey, 1953; Dachshund Club of America (parent Club), 1953; and the Florida East Coast Dachshund Club, 1954; with these wins, which certainly establish an excellent record, he is quite rightfully following in the footsteps of his all-famous sire, Am. and Can. Ch. Aristo v. Marienlust.

Ch. Peterman's Candidate (another son of Ch. Aristo v. Marienlust ex Peterman's Juliana), a clear red owned by the late Mrs. Miriam Van Court, completed his championship in less than six months in the East. He was presented to the Western Dachshund Fancy at San Mateo Kennel Club Show, where he took Best Smooth in an entry of fifty-one smooths under Judge Laura Delano. He returned to the East for further showing, and in August 1951, took the Hound Group at the Maine Kennel Club. In September 1951, Ch. Peterman's Candidate won the Dachshund Club of California Specialty Show by taking Best in Show over an entry of two hundred and eleven, which was said to be the largest entry in Dachshunds ever recorded in California shows. In February 1952, Candidate took Best Hound at the Eastern Dog Show, Boston, after he had won the Bay Colony Dachshund Specialty in an entry of ninety-eight. In addition, he won the Von Nidda Memorial Trophy for the Dachshund placing highest in the Group, and the Lee Wood Memorial Trophy for Best Smooth; his win is recorded on each trophy, while his illustrious sire has two wins recorded on the latter memorial trophy. Candidate took the Hound Group and

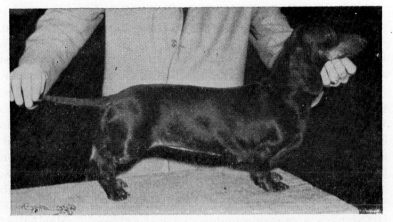

CH. BLACK BEAUTY O'PFEIFER'S
Sire: Can. Ch. Dolf v. d. Daniels   Dam: Black Magic v. Teckelhof
Owner: Carl O. Pfeifer, Oak Grove, Oregon

CH. PFAVORETTA O'PFEIFER'S
Sire: Can. and Am. Ch. Favorite v. Marienlust
Dam: Ch. Black Beauty o'Pfeifer's
Breeder and Owner: Carl O. Pfeifer, Oak Grove, Oregon

Best Smooth wins at the 1952 Morris and Essex Show to top off his grand record.

Am. and Can. Ch. Harborvale Aladin, clear red, is another Ch. Aristo v. Marienlust ex Sunset v. Marienlust son, and his breeders are Harborvale Kennels, on Mobile Bay, Daphne, Alabama. He has established himself in the West and was piloted to his championship by his former owner, Mrs. Anna E. Appelgate, Los Angeles, California. He completed his championship points at three Specialty Shows within one month! At the Dachshund Club of California Specialty Show, entry one hundred and forty-one, he took five points; he was named Best of Variety at the Northern California Dachshund Specialty Show; he was Best in Show, acquiring five more points, at the Dallas Dachshund Club Specialty Show in an entry of ninety-eight Dachshunds. His dam is a granddaughter of Ch. Leutnant v. Marienlust on her sire's side, Ch. Superman v. Marienlust. Aladin won his Canadian championship in three straight Canadian shows. Am. and Can. Ch. Harborvale Aladin is now owned by Raymihill Kennels, and is one of our top studs. Since we acquired him, he has sired three champions.

Quite unusual is the fact that all three of Ch. Aristo v. Marienlust's sons won the same weekend in three different parts of the United States: Ch. Hardway Welcome Stranger won Best in Show at the Old Dominion Kennel Club, Arlington, Virginia; Ch. Peterman's Candidate took Best of Breed, Baltimore, and placed in the Group; and Am. and Can. Ch. Harborvale Aladin took Best of Breed, and placed in the Group at Santa Ana, California.

Ch. Bencelia's Candy v. MacJomin bred to Ch. Aristo v. Marienlust produced Ch. MacJomin's Asa and Ch. MacJomin's Candy Kiss, owned by the MacJomin Kennels (Minnie Mackennan and Josephine Wright), Pawling, New York. Ch. MacJomin's Asa won his first Dachshund Club of America plaque as Best Puppy at this Specialty in 1949; then, in 1950, he took his second win at this Specialty by annexing Best of Winners. Before he had reached the age of two years, he won his championship with wins of Best of Breed, and first in Hound Group at Bryn Mawr; Best of Winners at Morris and Essex; and Winners at Westbury, all in 1950.

CH. DERBYDACHS KANDI STYCK
Sire: Ch. Favorite v. Marienlust   Dam: Ch. Kandi of Badger Hill

CH. ALICE of HEYING-TECKEL
Sire: Ch. Favorite v. Marienlust   Dam: Commanderette of Earldale
Owners: Mr. and Mrs. Charles C. Fernsell, Palm Beach, Florida

Am. and Can. Ch. Derbydachs Kandi Styck, black-and-tan male, was winner of the 1953 Westminster and Morris and Essex Shows. Kandi Styck has thirteen first placements in the Hound Group, has won four Specialty Shows, and has accumulated forty-three Best of Variety wins. One of his daughters is Ch. Chardelines Kandina v. Teckelhof, whose dam is Christiana v. Teckelhof (a daughter of Ch. Omar v. d. Daniels). This excellent bitch, who completed her championship in approximately four months, is owned by Mrs. Charles C. Fernsell, New Philadelphia, Ohio.

The Teckelheim Kennels of Grayce Greenburg, Camarillo, California, have been included among the leading Dachshund kennels for more than thirty years. Grayce Greenburg imported Ch. Kensal Call Boy, whose name appears in many outstanding Dachshund pedigrees. Other champions who have contributed much to the fancy and to Teckelheim include Ch. Prinz Call Boy, Ch. Gretel v. Monchbruch, Ch. Aldar Again of Greenburg, Ch. Her Grace of Greenburg, and Ch. Sally Forth of Greenburg. Commemorating the memory of Ch. Sally Forth of Greenburg, Mrs. Greenburg has donated a very beautiful sterling silver tray as a Challenge Trophy for the Bred by Exhibitor Class at the Los Angeles Specialty Show. The first time it was offered, it was won by Ch. Calidox Daphne, a litter mate of Ch. Calidox Luigi and Ch. Calidox Nicholas, sired by Ch. Favorite v. Marienlust ex Dinah of Heying-Teckel. Another Teckelheim champion is Teckelheim Peggy Moxley, who, together with her son Jeremia of Jonor, is owned by Mary Jane Osha, Minneapolis.

For more than fifteen years, Kay Dore has been the Kennel Manager at Teckelheim, and it was she who imported Kelvindale John, one of the top studs at Teckelheim, from Scotland. He carries excellent foreign bloodlines, including Ch. Fire Black Velvet, Ch. Wolf v. Birkinschloss (a German import), and Rotfink-Schneid.

The kennels at Teckelheim are the most modern that can be had and have many features that are not found in the usual run of kennels—even to treated glass for controlling sun exposure, and a type of lighting that is especially con-

CH. WHITE GABLES FIRE ENGINE

Sire: Ch. White Gables Basil   Dam: White Gables Streamliner
Owner: Eugene H. Shabatura, Duluth, Minnesota

ducive to keeping Teckelheim Dachshunds in the best of health. All feeding and water vessels are stainless steel.

At Chicago, recently, a testimonial dinner, arranged by Mrs. Helen Monroe of Little Gate Kennels, was given as a tribute to Grayce Greenburg for her contributions as a breeder, as an exhibitor, and as publisher of the American Dachshund, the breed magazine for the fancy. More than fifty people attended the dinner party, and an appropriately engraved plaque was presented to Mrs. Greenburg. Mrs. Greenburg has also been honored by the Dachshund Club of America which presented her with an honorary membership. In addition, she was presented with the Dog World Award for outstanding service to dogs.

In 1952, Grayce and Mike Greenburg celebrated their Golden Wedding Anniversary at their home in Camarillo. More than two hundred friends attended and wished them joy and happiness. In addition to the many beautiful gifts presented to them by friends in the United States and foreign countries, Mr. and Mrs. Greenburg were presented with a huge, four-tiered, beautifully decorated wedding cake by the Dachshund Club of California.

Grayce Greenburg has been actively breeding and exhibiting Dachshunds for thirty years, and is greatly admired for her constant faith in our breed. She is the editor of the breed magazine, The American Dachshund, which is the official publication for about twenty Dachshund Clubs throughout the United States. A member of the National Association of Breed Publications, The American Dachshund is published each month by The American Dachshund Publishing Company.

Derbydachs Kennels, owned by Dorothy Derby Fitzgerald, Oconomowoc, Wisconsin, boast not only of several American champions, but also of foreign champion-sired studs, among whom are Ch. Bergman of Gay Galahad, their newest, sired by Ch. White Gables Basil ex Ch. Galatea v. Bergman; Ch. Echo of Badger Hill, sired by Ch. White Gables Scaramouche ex Ch. Albions Own Penelope; Ch. Dachscroft Cid of Little Gate, sired by Ch. Moto's Pride of White Gables ex Little Gate's Honey Bun; and their two English imports, Brambul Benedict (grandson of Ch. Silvae

210

CH. POINCIANNA of OLTERRA
Sire: Ch. Diplomat v. Marienlust   Dam: Cornhill Poppy
Breeder and Owner: Mrs. Frederick H. Olney, Foxboro, Mass.

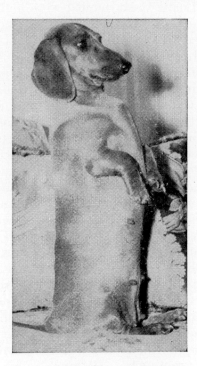

CORNHILL POPPY
Sire: Ch. Meistersinger of Windyriver
Dam: Puppe v. d. Howitt of Windyriver (Imp.)
Owner: Mrs. Frederick H. Olney, Foxboro, Mass.

211

Zebo and Ch. Zeus v. Schwarenberg ex Reanda Golden Morning) purchased from Mr. Barry Restall, England, and Reanda Golden Eve, purchased from Mrs. Elizabeth Meyer, England. Another import at Derbydachs Kennels is Amah of the Moat, who is from the Moat Kennels, England.

Red Locket Kennels, established by Woodrow W. Dorward, Sun Valley, California, have been breeding Dachshunds for many years. Before moving to California, this kennel was located in Illinois. Their Ch. Si of Doxland (Ch. White Gables Scaramouche ex Kay of Badger Hill) finished his championship when he was less than fifteen months old. Ch. Si of Doxland was heavy in Luitpoldsheim breeding. Another stud at Red Locket Kennels is Hercules of Heying-Teckel, whose dam is Herzy v. Marienlust, a sister of the Mehrers' Ch. Herzville v. Marienlust. Hercules of Heying-Teckel and Ch. Lustic v. Marienlust were both sired by Ch. Leutnant v. Marienlust. Hercules, bred to Ebony Maid v. d. Daniels, produced an outstanding puppy, Red Locket Scaramouche. Red Locket Kennels owned Ch. White Gables Scaramouche, who was the son of Piper v. Dachshafen (Ch. Leutnant v. Marienlust ex Ch. White Gables Bavarian Senta). White Gables Bavarian Senta was a daughter of Ch. Senta v. Luitpoldsheim ex Russ v. Luitpoldsheim. Red Locket Kennels bred Ch. Scaramouche to several bitches of Badger Hill breeding owned by Mr. Dorward; Ch. Red Locket Commodore, Ch. Red Locket Commander, Ch. Red Locket Cheri-Py were all produced from similar breedings. This breeding program has been a continuation of line-breeding sons and daughters, along with an occasional outbreeding to heavier Marienlust bloodlines. The get of this program has done very well in the show ring.

Red Locket Kennels have continued their breeding program with their Ch. Badger Hill Nobby, sired by Badger Hill Jackson ex Ch. Derbydachs Schatze. Nobby is a litter brother of Ch. Badger Hill New Deal and Ch. Badger Hill Nox, and is a grandson of Ch. Favorite v. Marienlust, and a double grandson of Ch. Albion's Own Penelope and Ch. White Gables Scaramouche. His puppies are now appearing in the show rings.

The Badger Hill Kennels are owned by Harry and Vivien

CH. CID, JR. OF LAKELANDS, CH. WHITE GABLES GOLDILOCKS,
CH. CORNHILL GOLDIE, CH. ERIC v. STAHLHAUS
White Gables Kennels, Miriam Van Court, Los Angeles, California

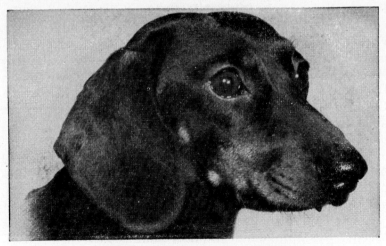

CH. BLACKBERRY v. d. DANIELS
Sire: Ch. Ebony Eric v. d. Daniels   Dam: White Gables Blackberry
Owner: Raymond S. Hill, Phoenix, Arizona

213

Sharpe, Madison, Wisconsin. Their breeding program was originally based on bitches heavy in Asbeck breeding. One of their first good producers was Pflueger's Volga, a daughter of Champion Achat v. Werderhavelstrand ex Ch. Vroni v. Rosenbaum, who bred to Ch. Zep v. Marienlust produced Cleo of Badger Hill. The greatest producer in Badger Hill Kennels has been Ch. Albion's Own Penelope, a daughter of Alsvin v. Isartal and Amber of Badger Hill, who is a descendant of Pflueger's Victor. Ch. Penelope has produced nine champions, which is more than any other living bitch today, and through her daughters she is the granddam of seven others. Ch. Albion's Own Penelope is the dam of the great long-haired Dachshund, Ch. Badger Hill Mr. Chips. Ch. Penelope bred to Ch. White Gables Scaramouche produced three champions from this one mating: Ch. Echo of Badger Hill, Ch. Karen of Badger Hill, and Ch. Kandi of Badger Hill. Subsequent Badger Hill breedings have been bitches of these same bloodlines bred back, in most cases, to Ch. White Gables Scaramouche sons. Ch. Badger Hill Nox is currently owned by Mr. and Mrs. Lester Noel Webb, Perrysburg, Ohio.

White Gables Kennels have also contributed a great deal to the breed with their champion studs and bitches. Practically every registered Dachshund's pedigree will include the names of one or more dogs of White Gables stock. Foremost is Ch. Eric v. Stahlhaus, who sired twelve champions including Ch. Cornhill Goldie v. Dachshafen, bred by Mrs. Delphin Young; other daughters were Ch. Marigold v. Dachshafen, Ch. Cornhill Beska, and Ch. Cornhill Lenska. Ch. Eric v. Stahlhaus also sired Ch. Eric Again v. d. Daniels and Ch. Ebony Eric v. d. Daniels, both sires of many champions.

Ch. Cornhill Goldie v. Dachshafen, who was whelped April 15, 1937, and died in March 1947, produced five champions: Sungold, Goldilocks, Merry-go-Round, Mehitabel, and Moto's Pride of White Gables.

Am. and Can. Ch. Cid Junior of Lakelands, whose breeder was Mrs. Maude Daniels Smith, Malvern, Pennsylvania, was a brother of Ch. Eric v. Stahlhaus, and died on December 12, 1948, at the ripe old age of eleven and one-half years. He was the son of Ch. Cid v. Werderhavelstrand and

214

CH. MINTON OF HEYING-TECKEL
Sire: Am. and Can. Ch. Favorite v. Marienlust
Dam: White Gables Brenda
Owner: Raymond S. Hill, Phoenix, Arizona

FLAIR OF RAYMIHILL
Sire: Ch. Calidox Luigi   Dam: Ch. Valencia of Heying-Teckel
Owner: Mrs. Marian Y. Patten, Clearwater, Florida

CH. CRESPI'S RONNIE
Sire: Am. and Can. Ch. Harborvale Aladin   Dam: Ch. Rivenrock Tamale
Owner: Mrs. Neville R. Stephens, Tubac, Arizona

Ch. Harriet v. Stahlhaus, and sired fifteen champions, of which Ch. Moto's Pride of White Gables and Ch. Omar v. d. Daniels (the latter owned by Mrs. Anna M. Gargett, Michigan) were probably the most renowned. Ch. Cid Junior also sired Ch. White Gables Oliver Twist, now in Honolulu at Twin Seas Kennels. Ch. Cid Junior had two Best in Shows to his credit and was the winner of more than twenty Groups. Another son of Ch. Cid Junior, Ch. Sungold of White Gables, owned by Maude D. Smith, sired her Ch. Cinnamon v. Dachshafen II, who in turn sired Ch. Cinnamon v. Dachshafen III. In addition to this, Ch. Cid Junior sired Ch. White Gables Mehitabel, the dam of seven champions, including Ch. White Gables Basil, still owned by White Gables Kennels, and the Bud Spraggins' Ch. White Gables Gadabout, who in turn sired their Ch. Rock Manor Gold Flash. Ch. White Gables Merry-go-Round, the dam of Ch. Bucknam's Merrymaker, was another daughter of Ch. Cid Junior. The John Redmonds, of Sacramento, have Ch. Redmond's Sir Guy, a Cid Junior son. And the George E. Manzers, of Colorado Springs, own Int. Ch. Manzer's Jack O'Diamonds, another Ch. Cid Junior offspring.

Ch. Cavalier v. Marienlust, bred by the Josef Mehrers and owned by White Gables Kennels, sired thirteen champions, and when bred to Ch. White Gables Mehitabel, produced Ch. Gadabout; Ch. Merrymaker; Ch. Bucknam's Merry Andrew; and Ch. Basil and his three litter sisters, Ch. Marjoram, Ch. Rosemary, and Ch. Thyme. Ch. White Gables Thyme bred to Ch. Calidox Nicholas produced Ch. Black Forest's Diogenes, whose breeder-owner is Mrs. L. Zingler, of the famous Black Forest Kennels, Everett, Washington, which have been registered since 1925. Ch. Cavalier v. Marienlust also sired Ch. Eddie v. Dachshafen and Ch. Kippy v. Dachshafen, of the Maude D. Smith v. Dachshafen Kennels, Malvern, Pennsylvania. Ch. Bucknam's Merrymaker likewise is the sire of many champions. Ch. White Gables Basil, whelped May 18, 1944, sired six champions, among whom are Ch. Max Rossman v. Notfort, whelped October 18, 1945, and owned by Jack and Luci Ward Natteford, North Hollywood, California; Ch. Parker's Vagabond, owned by Roy D. Parker, Napa, California; Ch. Bergmanor Gay Guy,

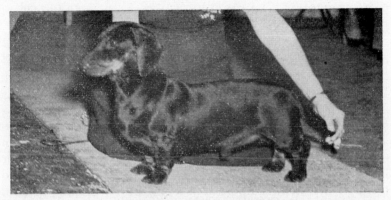

MARIO OF RAYMIHILL
Sire: Ch. Standard of Heying-Teckel   Dam: Breezy Lane Pepper Pot
Owner: Mrs. William Olds, San Francisco, California

CH. DUCHESS OF LAMBROS
Sire: Ch. Favorite v. Marienlust   Dam: Johanna of Lambros
Owners: Mr. and Mrs. Gus J. Lambros, Yuba City, California

owned by the Edward F. Hirschmans, Bergmanor Kennels, Sepulveda, California; Ch. Bergman Gay Galahad, owned by Derbydachs Kennels; Ch. Michele of Hildesheim, at one time also owned by White Gables Kennels, but now with the Richard V. Pells; and Ch. Hallwyre Harpo, owned by Albert Dain, Dallas, Texas.

White Gables Kennels maintain that the bitch is definitely the background of the kennel, and they are proud of their champion bitches, Goldie, Mehitabel, Fussbudget, White Gables Prunes and Prisms, and White Gables Nutmeg.

Much to the regret of the Dachshund fancy, the shining star of White Gables Kennels, Miriam Van Court, passed away quite suddenly on November 11, 1952. Miriam Van Court was an able judge of the breed, an excellent selector in her breeding programs at White Gables Kennels, and through her kennel operations contributed greatly to past and present-day Dachshunds. White Gables is being kept active as a kennel name, and their Dachshunds will always be remembered in any discussion of our present-day pedigrees.

Mrs. Ramona Lancaster Andrews, owner of the famous Am. and Can. Ch. Aristo v. Marienlust, donated the beautiful sterling silver trophy to be awarded at the Sierra Dachshund Breeders Club in memory of Miriam Van Court. For permanent possession, this trophy must be won three times by the same owner, but not necessarily with the same dog. The first time the trophy was offered was June 20, 1953, when it was won by Ch. Hainheim's Lance, owned by Hainheim Kennels, George C. Spradling, Wichita, Kansas. At this same Specialty Show, held June 26, 1954, the Miriam Van Court Trophy was won by Ch. Dandy Dachs Danny, owned by Donia Cline. Danny was whelped March 2, 1952, and made his championship on August 2, 1953, becoming the fifty-ninth champion sired by Ch. Favorite v. Marienlust.

Rock Manor Kennels, Irene and Bud Spraggins, Walnut Creek, California, are the home of six champions: Am. and Can. Ch. White Gables Gadabout, whelped September 22, 1943 (sired by Ch. Cavalier v. Marienlust ex White Gables Mehitabel), winner of many Hound Groups and also a Best in Show; Ch. Rock Manor's Gold Flash, whelped December

CH. SPARLING ADONIS
Sire: Teckelheim Gustava   Dam: Ch. Sparling Sugar Peg of Jonor
Breeder and Owner: Mrs. James L. Sparling, Sr.

CH. ROCK MANOR'S GOLD FLASH
Sire: Am. and Can. Ch. White Gables Gadabout
Dam: Ch. White Gables Mehitabel
Breeders and Owners: Mr. and Mrs. A. C. Spraggins, Walnut Creek, Calif.

219

1, 1945 (sired by Ch. White Gables Gadabout ex Ch. White Gables Prunes and Prisms), a home-bred dog who completed his championship on his first birthday; Ch. Calidox Nicholas, whelped September 21, 1947 (sired by Ch. Favorite v. Marienlust ex Dinah of Heying-Teckel), who also completed his championship well under two years of age and is credited with a Best in Show at the Cascade Specialty in 1949 under Judge Anna Gargett. Rock Manor Kennels' brood bitches are Ch. White Gables Prunes and Prisms, Am. and Can. Ch. Ship's Mascot Miss Peaches, and Am. and Can. Ch. White Gables Tansy, sired by Ch. Bucknam's Merrymaker ex Ch. Fussbudget of White Gables.

Rock Manor Kennels, formerly of Alderwood, Washington, have been breeders for many years, and their get is prominent in Pacific Northwest regions, as well as in the San Francisco Bay region where this kennel is somewhat newly established.

Little Gate Kennels, registered since 1942, and owned by Mrs. Walter D. Monroe, Lake Forest, Illinois, began their breeding program more than twelve years ago, and have not spared effort, ambition or expense in developing finer and better Dachshunds. Little Gate bred Ch. Merryman of Little Gate; Ch. DeSha of Little Gate (deceased); Ch. Peter Pan of Little Gate; Can. Ch. Little Gates Melochrino; Ch. Alva of Little Gate; Ch. Little Gates Letty (deceased), who in retirement became the house pet of Mrs. Huck, Creekside Kennels; Ch. Lawrence of Little Gate; Ch. Sheba of Little Gate; Ch. Robin Hood of Little Gate; Ch. Sir Joe of Little Gate; and Ch. Stradivari of Little Gate.

Little Gate Kennels also purchased many fine Dachshunds and completed their championships, including Ch. White Gables Rosemary, Ch. Zanzibar of White Gables, Ch. Nutmeg of White Gables, Ch. White Gables Fuchsia, Ch. Zep v. d. Daniels, Ch. Arri v. d. Daniels, Ch. Cynthia v. Jo-Rene (deceased), and Ch. Cinderella v. Marienlust.

One of the top studs at Little Gate was Ch. Moto's Pride of White Gables, who died in 1953 at the age of fourteen years. Moto, greatly loved by his owner, is truly missed. During his life he sired twenty champions. He was the son

CAN. and AM. CH. RED JADE v. REDMOND
Sire: Ch. Eric Again v. d. Daniels   Dam: Ch. Redmond's Star Dust
Owners: Virgilio and Isabella Cheda

CAN. and AM. CH. BERGMANOR BOYBOY
Sire: Ch. Lucifer v. Bergman   Dam. Riverbottom Tinklegirl
Owner: Mrs. Lester Noel Webb, Perrysburg, Ohio

of Am. and Can. Ch. Cid Junior of Lakelands, and many pedigrees carry Ch. Moto's name as sire.

Other studs at this kennel include Ch. Merryman of Little Gate, sired by Ch. Ducknam's Merrymaker; Ch. Arri v. d. Daniels, sired by Ch. Favorite v. Marienlust; Ch. Stradivari of Little Gate; and Ch. Sir Joe of Little Gate, sired by Ch. Leutnant v. Marienlust ex Adelhide v. Brentwald.

Little Gate's newest stud is Ch. Bronze v. d. Daniels, bred by the D. D. Daniels, whelped January 3, 1949, sired by Bobolink v. d. Daniels ex Sweet Sue v. d. Daniels. Handled by the late Nicky Finn under Judge Mervin Rosenbaum, Ch. Bronze v. d. Daniels completed his championship at Reno, Nevada, where he took Best in Show, going over all other breeds. Since that time, he has had many wins, including eleven Hound Groups, two more Best in Show wins at Portland, Oregon, and Olympia, Washington, plus one Best in Specialty Show at the Dachshund Club of Portland. Ch. Bronze v. d. Daniels is a glorious red, who possesses a beautiful topline, good bone and feet, and has an excellent gait. His litter mates are Scarlet v. d. Daniels, Copper v. d. Daniels (currently owned by the Marlong Kennels, Fort Smith, Arkansas), and Amber v. d. Daniels. Ch. Little Gate Nicholay is a son of Ch. Bronze v. d. Daniels ex Ch. Cinderella v. Marienlust; Black Star of Lambros is a black-and-tan son of Ch. Bronze v. d. Daniels ex Miss Ruby Daniels of Pal-Mar, and is owned by Raymond S. Hill.

Outstanding bitches at Little Gate include Ch. Cinderella v. Marienlust (sired by Ch. Leutnant v. Marienlust ex Veni v. Marienlust) who has to her credit two Best in Show wins, and Best Dachshund at the Parent Club Specialty Show, Rye, New York, September 1949, under Judge Grace Hirschman, of California, in an entry of one hundred and eighty-four Dachshunds. Ch. Cinderella was bred by the Josef Mehrers.

Bunnell Dachshunds, the kennels of Mrs. Donald Bunnell (a sister of Mrs. Helen D. Monroe of Little Gate Kennels) pride themselves on the fact that their dogs are so strong in Werderhavelstrand and Bavarian Russ stock. Their newest champion stud is Ch. Little Gate Jackson, sired by Ch. Black Jack v. Bergman. Another Bunnell Kennels' male that is

BUNNELL BERTRAND
Sire: Hercules of Heying-Teckel   Dam: Bunnell Denora
Owner: Mrs. Donald Bunnell, Los Angeles, California

CH. LITTLE GATE JACKSON
Sire: Ch. Black Jack v. Bergman   Dam: Gretchen v. Jaegerhaus III
Owner: Mrs. Donald Bunnell, Los Angeles, California

proving his worth is Ch. Bunnell Borus, dark red, owned and campaigned to his championship by Robert K. Maiden, Kansas City, Missouri. The Bunnell Kennels have recently moved to their Clearwater address, and they are planning an expanded program of breeding and showing. Ch. DeSha of Little Gate, now deceased, was another top dog at Bunnell Kennels. Bunnell Bertrand, sired by Hercules of Heying-Teckel ex Bunnell Denora, is currently working on his championship.

Tubac Kennels, Mr. and Mrs. Neville R. Stephens, Tubac, Arizona, are also breeders of smooth-coated Dachshunds, and have finished the championships of several top dogs, including Ch. Michaela of Raymihill (sired by Ch. Standard of Heying-Teckel ex Breezy Lane Pepper Pott, whelped November 29, 1950). Her first win was in March 1952 when she took Best of Breed, and from then on she accumulated her points rapidly, often placing in the Hound Group, and also winning the Group. She is a very good black-and-tan bitch, with good bone, temperament, and topline, who possesses beautiful feet and has an excellent gait. Another young champion at Tubac Kennels is their flashy, clear red male, Ch. Crespi's Ronnie, sired by Am. and Can. Ch. Harborvale Aladin ex Ch. Rivenrock Tamale. He has taken Best of Breed many times, and also has a few Hound Groups to his credit. Tubac Kennels have several fine bitches which head their breeding program, including, among others: April Again v. d. Daniels, Heidi v. d. Stephens (Ch. Calidox Luigi's daughter), Ch. Michaela of Raymihill, and Rhetta of Raymihill. This kennel is currently campaigning some good bitches to head their breeding program, which includes Alma of Bill-O, whelped July 7, 1953, sired by Ch. Allegro of Gera ex Hilda v. Hargelroad.

Rivenrock Kennels is presided over and owned by Mrs. Anne Smith Wenden, North Hollywood, California. Mrs. Anne Smith Wenden was President of the Sierra Dachshund Breeders Association when this group held its first Specialty Show in September 1945 at Ontario, California, to celebrate the Dachshund Golden Anniversary Year. The Secretary of the Association was Donia Bussey (now Mrs. Charles D. Cline). This Club was organized in 1944, and Anne Smith

CH. LEUTNANT'S HANNAH BONNY O'DOUD
Sire: Ch. Leutnant v. Marienlust   Dam: Easter's Hannah O'Doud
Breeder and Owner: Francis J. Doody, Dayton, Ohio

CH. ERDA v. NESBITTENHOF
Sire: Casanova v. Nesbittenhof   Dam: Albion's Own Doris Ellenbert
Owner: Mrs. Francis J. Doody, Dayton, Ohio

CH. LEUTNANT'S HANNAH BEAU O'DOUD
Sire: Ch. Leutnant v. Marienlust   Dam: Easter's Hannah O'Doud
Breeder and Owner: Francis J. Doody, Dayton, Ohio

Wenden was chosen President because of the extreme interest in Dachshunds which she had acquired while residing in England. She has owned and bred Dachshunds since about 1940. Ch. Rivenrock Dorcas, a black-and-tan daughter of Ch. Dimas Earthstopper was a beautiful bitch, and bred to Ch. Eric Again v. d. Daniels produced Rivenrock Doric and Rivenrock Dormouse. Ch. Rivenrock Manhattan was also bred by Rivenrock Kennels and was sired by Ch. Eric Again v. d. Daniels ex Rivenrock Leda, who is a half sister of Mrs. Donia Cline's Ch. Chadwick of Crespi Street. Ch. Rivenrock Manhattan is also now owned by Mrs. Donia Cline, as are Ch. Rivenrock Tamale (sired by Ch. Eric Again v. d. Daniels ex Rivenrock Seal), and Rivenrock Dorothy (sired by Ch. Chadwick of Crespi Street).

In 1947, Rivenrock Kennels moved to Carmel, California, and reduced their stock considerably. They are no longer actively engaged in breeding and showing, but Anne Smith Wenden is enjoying life with her most devoted Dachshunds.

Crespi Street Kennels, Los Angeles, California, are owned and presided over by Mrs. Charles D. Cline, and the Dachshunds of her daughter, Nancy Ann, are likewise kennelled there. Smooth-haired dogs include Ch. Chadwick of Crespi Street, bred and owned by Donia Cline, as well as other top dogs that are champions, one of whom is Ch. Rivenrock Manhattan, affectionately called "Hattie," bred by Rivenrock Kennels. At the age of fifteen months, she went Best of Winners at Madison Square Garden. Another champion is Nancy Ann Oberg's Rivenrock Teak, who has made sensational wins, including the Award in Memory of Ch. Cid Jr. of Lakelands offered by the A. E. Van Courts for Best of Variety at the Sierra Specialty Show, Los Angeles. Ch. Rivenrock Teak's picture appears in the new *Encyclopedia on Dogs* as the model Dachshund bitch.

Crespi Street Kennels are pursuing a splendid breeding program with excellent results. Their new stud, Ch. Dandy Dachs Danny, is becoming famous for his get. Ch. Dandy Dachs Danny bred to Ch. Rivenrock Tamale produced the sensational youngster, Crespi's Jamboree, a magnificent clear red male, who took such beautiful wins as Best of

CH. LUDWIG v. SIGMARINGEN II
Sire: Ch. Eden of Gera   Dam: Hilda v. Sigmaringen II
Owner: G. A. Plummer, Dallas, Texas

CH. EDEN OF GERA
Sire: Ch. Favorite v. Marienlust   Dam: Ch. Rebecca of Gera
Owner: G. A. Plummer, Dallas, Texas

CH. RED SULTAN v. REDMOND
Sire: Ch. Eric Again v. d. Daniels   Dam: Ch. Redmond's Star Dust
Owner: G. A. Plummer, Dallas, Texas

Winners, five points, at the 1954 Specialty Show, Long
Beach. Danny is a Group as well as a Best of Breed winner.
Ch. Rivenrock Tamale bred to Am. and Can. Ch. Harborvale
Aladin produced two champions in one litter: Ch. Crespi's
Ronnie, owned by Mrs. Neville R. Stephens, Tubac, Arizona,
and Ch. Crespi's Donnie, owned by Mrs. Donia Cline, the
breeder. The litter was whelped March 5, 1952. Ronnie is
clear red, whereas Donnie is black-and-tan. Ch. Rivenrock
Tamale, their dam, is the fourth dog sired by Ch. Eric Again
v. d. Daniels that Mrs. Cline has finished to championship.
Rivenrock Dorothy, sired by Ch. Chadwick of Crespi Street
ex Ch. White Gables Philadelphia, is working on her championship also. Ch. Lotus of Heying-Teckel is another top
bitch that has made grand wins and has produced quality
puppies for Crespi Street Kennels.

Gene and Ray Shultis, with their Dachshunds of Gera,
Van Nuys, California, have been breeders since 1941. Their
top stud is Ch. Black Jack v. Bergman, another winning son
of Ch. Favorite v. Marienlust. When the Shultises purchased
their first Dachshund in 1941, the seller "talked" them into
going to their first dog show, and from then on, they were
interested! After going to more shows and studying pedigrees, they realized that they did not have just what they
wanted for breeding and foundation stock, so decided to go
forth and purchase the best they could. Describing their
experiences, the Shultises state:

"The Marienlust and Rivenrock bloodlines seemed to
be just what we wanted. We particularly liked the offspring
of Ch. Dimas Earthstopper, the English import owned by
Anne Wenden of Rivenrock fame. Ch. Rivenrock Dorcas, a
black-and-tan daughter of Earthstopper was, in our opinion,
the most beautiful bitch it has been our pleasure to see. We
tried to buy this bitch from Anne Wenden, but were unsuccessful.

"Ch. Rivenrock Dorcas bred to Ch. Eric Again v. d.
Daniels produced two red bitches, Rivenrock Doric and
Rivenrock Dormouse; unfortunately, Rivenrock Dormouse
did not reach maturity. We finally were successful in the
purchase of Rivenrock Doric from Anne Wenden. We attempted to purchase a black-and-tan bitch of Marienlust

CH. BADGER HILL NOX
Sire: Badger Hill Jackson   Dam: Ch. Derbydachs Schatz
Owner: Mrs. Lester Noel Webb, Perrysville, Ohio

CH. WEBB'S TORRID v. TECKELHOF
Sire: Ch. Omar v. d. Daniels   Dam: Renate v. Teckelhof
Owner: Lester Noel Webb, Perrysburg, Ohio

bloodlines, but unfortunately, none were available at that time. Our Rivenrock Doric was bred to Ch. White Gables Basil, producing our Ch. Rebecca of Gera and Roxane of Gera, who have both been wonderful producers. Doric was bred back to Basil at a later date, but died of a caesarean operation. However, we give full credit to her and her sire for our predominantly good toplines, heads, and necks. Our Ch. Rebecca of Gera bred to Ch. Favorite v. Marienlust produced Ch. Allegro of Gera, and Ch. Agilita of Gera, both Best in Show winners, and Aria of Gera, whom we consider to be our very best producing brood bitch. Aria bred to Ch. Badger Hill Nobby produced Ch. Oliver of Gera and Octava of Gera (eight points). Then Aria bred to Admiral v. Marienlust (Ch. Leutnant v. Marienlust ex Ch. Herzville v. Marienlust) produced our lovely Ch. Annette of Gera. Aria's youngest litter is sired by Calvert v. Marienlust, and the puppies are just under one year of age at this time. We are very optimistic about several of these youngsters.

"Ch. Rebecca of Gera's litter sister, Roxane of Gera, bred to Ch. Trojan of Heying-Teckel produced Ch. Cara of Gera and Can. Ch. Caesar of Gera, and Roxane bred to Hercules of Heying-Teckel produced Ch. Arlinda of Gera.

"A repeat breeding of Ch. Rebecca and Ch. Favorite produced four: Ch. Eden of Gera, Ch. Eve of Gera, Can. Ch. Elena of Gera, and Electra of Gera (seven points).

"We are very grateful to Anne Wenden for selling us Rivenrock Doric, our foundation bitch, and thankful for being lucky enough to have bred twelve American champions and three Canadian champions in the relatively short period we have been breeding, about ten years."

It is of interest to note that Ch. Allegro of Gera, owned by J. C. Walters, Dallas, has made a great show record for his owner and breeders. In 1952, Allegro was classed as the top winner in Dachshunds for that year. He received the Quaker Oats Company award for the most Hound Group wins in 1952 in the Southern Division—one of four annual awards made by this company. Allegro has taken Best in Show three times. Ch. Eden of Gera, now owned by G. A. Plummer, Dallas, is also a top winner.

George E. and Rena R. Manzer, Colorado Springs, Colo-

CH. BADGER HILL QUICK FIRE
Sire: Ch. Badger Hill New Deal   Dam: Ch. Wynne of Ringold
Owners: Mrs. W. M. Orcutt and Mrs. Gary Gerber

CH. EVE OF GERA
Sire: Ch. Favorite v. Marienlust   Dam: Ch. Rebecca of Gera
Owner: Valera M. Malloy, Columbus, Ohio

231

rado, have several top dogs in their kennels, among whom are Am. and Can. Ch. Manzer's Jack O'Diamonds, sired by Ch. Cid Jr. of Lakelands ex Ch. Bucknam's Queen Bee; he is an excellent red male and, undefeated, completed his Canadian championship in four successive shows. Another excellent Dachshund from this kennel is Ch. Manzer's Tristai (Int. Ch. Herman Rinkton ex Bucknam's Queen Bee), a black-and-tan stud.

Dachscroft Kennels, owned by Mrs. David B. Doggett, Lake Geneva, Wisconsin, are the home of many fine Dachshunds who carry the famous Asbeck, Marienlust, Plater Schulhaus, and Werderhavelstrand bloodlines. Dachscroft Kennels are the breeders of Ch. Dachscroft's Playboy, sired by Ch. Moto's Pride of White Gables ex Little Gate Honey Bun; Dachscroft's Moonplay; and also Ch. Dachscroft's Tuffet, an up-and-coming dog sired by Dachscroft's Moonplay ex Little Gate Honey Bun. The sire of Little Gate Honey Bun is Falk v. Plater Schulhaus ex White Gables Red Riding Hood.

At Sigmarigen Kennels, G. A. Plummer, Dallas, are three outstanding champions: Ch. Red Sultan v. Redmond, whelped February 26, 1947, sired by Ch. Eric Again v. d. Daniels ex Ch. Redmond's Star Dust; Ch. Far Star's Sirius, whelped March 17, 1947, sired by Ch. Leutnant v. Marienlust ex Furstin v. Zauberberg; and Ch. Eden of Gera, a clear red and a top winner, sired by Ch. Favorite v. Marienlust ex Ch. Rebecca of Gera. All three of these dogs are contributing much to the breed.

The Sparling and Louhelen Dachshund Kennels, owned and operated by Eva Sparling and Helen Grugette, Moweaqua, Illinois, have kennelled Ch. Alexander v. Jo-Rene as their stud, and Ch. Eric Carl v. Luen v. d. Daniels (Ch. Eric v. Stahlhaus ex Rote Sally v. d. Daniels), Ch. Sparling's Adonis, and Ch. Harborvale Circe, a black-and-tan Ch. Superman daughter, together with seven brood bitches.

The Dychland Kennels, owned by Mr. and Mrs. Herman G. Cox, Fort Worth, Texas, take pride in their champions: Ch. Itsit of Steinhoff, Ch. Noddy v. Dychland, Ch. Lady v. Dychland, and Ch. Carbon of Heying-Teckel. Another of their outstanding dogs was the late Ch. Feri Ellenbert,

232

CH. SPARLING LOUHELEN AURORO
Sire: Ch. Alexander of Jo-Rene   Dam: Ch. Harborvale Circe
Owner: Eva Sparling, Moweaqua, Illinois

CH. SPARLING LOUHELEN FAVOR-RITA
Sire: Ch. Favorite v. Marienlust   Dam: Ch. Harborvale Circe
Owner: Eva Sparling, Moweaqua, Illinois

whelped April 10, 1934, and sired by Ch. Feri Flottenberg ex Ch. Heka Flottenberg. He was very strong in Flottenberg and Luitpoldsheim bloodlines, and was the product of careful and highly selective breeding of Germany's and America's finest specimens and winners. Ch. Feri Ellenbert, a clear red, excelled in head, correct ear setting, chest, and topline, which he passed on to his get. His record of wins included Morris and Essex Shows, 1934, 1935, and 1936, and Westminster, 1935, and 1936.

Ch. Noddy v. Dychland, clear red, whelped August 2, 1945, sired by Ch. Itsit of Steinhoff ex Steinhoff's Lela, will be remembered as the young dog that made such a sensational record in 1946 and 1947 by taking Best in Show, all breeds, at the age of eight months—the first time he was shown. He completed his championship in three shows. He has been shown eleven times, has two Best in Show wins to his credit and eight Groups. His sire, Ch. Itsit of Steinhoff, clear red, whelped February 28, 1941, was sired by Ch. Zep v. Marienlust ex Burzel v. Doerfler, and completed his championship in 1946. He is very strong in Luitpoldsheim bloodlines.

Ch. Lady v. Dychland, clear red, is a home-bred dog sired by Ch. Noddy v. Dychland ex Krukiels Anna Christina, and was whelped March 10, 1948. She has gone Best in Show and taken Best of Variety ten times. Ch. Noddy v. Dychland is also the sire of two home-bred dogs, Citation v. Dychland, whelped June 2, 1948, and Annette v. Dychland, whelped October 27, 1946. Annette is on the border line of completing her championship, and Citation took the puppy class at Westminster in 1948, the only time she was shown.

In practically all pedigrees of the finer smooth-haired Dachshunds, the Werderhavelstrand bloodlines will appear, and Ch. Schalk v. Werderhavelstrand is another stud of that strain that contributed much to the breed. Ch. Schalk v. Werderhavelstrand was whelped in Werder-a-Havel, Germany, July 17, 1932. His sire was Lenz Assmannscheim, a great Dachshund stud in Germany (Rotfink-Schneid ex Elifchen v. Ammersee), and his dam was Sascha v. Werderhavelstrand (Rotfink-Schneid ex Katerl v. Werderhavelstrand). This strain is still very prominent in Dachshund

234

Ch. Tressie Huettner Gardner
with seven puppies sired by Ch. Premier of Starkrest.

CH. MILRDACHS JEFFERSON
Sire: Ch. White Gables Basil   Dam: Bergmanor Praline
Breeder and Owner: Inez C. Miller, Gardena, California

235

pedigrees. Other imported smooth-haired Dachshund studs that did much for the breed in America were those of Flottenberg bloodlines.

Upon the death of Herbert Bertrand, Ellenbert Farm Kennels, Greenwich, Connecticut, some of his Flottenberg stock was sent to the kennels of Florence Keller, Blue Key Kennels, Newbury, Ohio. This kennel now is considered to have the most concentrated Flottenberg bloodlines in the world. Flottenberg stock which was at Herbert Bertrand's kennels include Ch. Helmar Ellenberg, Ch. Hanko Flottenberg, and Ch. Heimo Flottenberg. Another German imported male was Ch. Hasso-Flottenberg, owned by Dr. Everett W. Johnson, Wichita, Kansas. Speaking of this fine bloodline, I owned a daughter of Ch. Hasso-Flottenberg, and even to the age of eleven years, she had the most beautiful level topline that one could ask for. She was Joyous of Wayston, Wayston Kennels, Lake Forest, Illinois.

Another champion that contributed much to the breed in days gone by at Ellenbert Farm Kennels and elsewhere, was the Eng. and Am. Ch. Dimas Earthstopper. Earthstopper was imported from England by Mr. Bertrand and later sent to Mrs. Anne Smith Wenden, Rivenrock Kennels, California. Earthstopper enjoyed many top wins in the East before his shipment West. He was not kennelled at Rivenrock for any length of time when he sickened and died. The influence of Earthstopper is strongly pronounced in many of our Dachshunds of today—even to the third generation, and among dogs that show this influence are Rivenrock Teak, Rivenrock Dulcie, Ch. Black Jack v. Bergman, and Ch. Lucifer v. Bergman.

Of the foreign Dachshunds which have arrived recently in this country, two are at the kennels of Josef and Maria Mehrer: Odo vom Eschbachta, black-and-tan, sired by Egon v. d. Fuchslunte ex Kathi vom Eschbachtal; and Ado vom Tannenberg, red, sired by Stups vom Werderhavelstrand ex Blonda vom Burgermoos; the latter dog, Ado vom Tannenberg, is quite heavily bred in Werderhavelstrand bloodlines. Another German Dachshund imported recently is owned by Mrs. Laurence E. Speces, Canton, Ohio; this Werderhavelstrand stud, purchased from Frau Stroh,

Frankfurt/Main, Germany, was whelped July 30, 1950, and is known as Isegrim vom Werderhavelstrand. The sire of this import is Hanno vom Werderhavelstrand ex Molly vom Werderhavelstrand. I should like to make mention here that Frau Stroh is the originator of the famous Fallator bloodlines, and her kennels are known as Fallator Kennels.

Speaking of German imported Dachshunds, the American Kennel Club now recognizes a three-generation pedigree of the Teckelklub of Germany so that these imports may be given their American Kennel Club individual registration.

From England comes Eng. Ch. Ashdown Starshine, A. K. C. No. 283101, sired by Ch. Silvae Sailors Quest ex Ashdown Russian Polka. This black-and-tan smooth-haired male was purchased from R. W. Pilkington, England, in 1952, and should be a valuable addition to the breed in the United States. He is owned by Mr. and Mrs. Lawrence H. Cook, Atherton, California. Here in America, Eng. Ch. Ashdown Starshine is affectionately called "Tommy." He is a full brother of Eng. Ch. Ashdown Skipper, who has fifteen Challenge Certificates to his credit. The sire of "Tommy" and Skipper was the holder of seventeen English Challenge Certificates.

From the kennels of Dr. Louis A. Cornet, Washington, D. C., comes Ch. Rotcod v. Tenroc (sired by Ch. Gunther v. Marienlust ex Streamlined Miss of Earldale), who is a leading Dachshund Group winner, taking eleven Groups; placing first and second in the Group thirteen times each; third in the Group three times; and fourth in the Group three times; Best of Variety, thirty-three times; and Best in Show, once. Ch. Karl v. Tenroc II, sired by Karl v. Tenroc ex Streamlined Miss of Earldale, has likewise secured his niche in Dr. Cornet's kennels. Another up-and-coming young champion here is Ch. Alden of Raymihill, sired by Ch. Calidox Luigi ex Breezy Lane Pepper Pott, who is making a name for himself in the show ring under the able handling of Alice Marie Cornet, and is making a name for himself as a stud too. Alden is a Best of Breed and Group winner of note.

Norman C. Sharp, Sacramento, California, is the proud owner of Ch. Top Dox Eric, sired by Ch. White Gables Basil

237

ex San Souci Sorceress (a Ch. Favorite v. Marienlust daughter), and whelped March 11, 1950 (breeder, Thomas Pringle, Jr., Claremont, California). Top Dox Eric weighs approximately twenty-six pounds and is a clear red. In about forty-one showings, Eric has taken Best of Breed thirty-five times, and has won eighteen Hound Groups. Eric won his championship in six straight show wins. As a puppy, he was shown at the Dachshund Club of California Futurity show, and was purchased by Nicky Finn, professional handler, and later sold to Mr. Norman Sharp, under whose ownership he was campaigned to victory.

A champion who contributed a great deal to the breed and whose name appears many times in pedigrees is Int. Ch. Herman Rinkton, owned by Mrs. Annis A. Jones, New Jersey. Ch. Herman Rinkton's show record is outstanding. He was whelped November 22, 1935, sired by Ch. Achat v. Werderhavelstrand ex Ch. Anni Rinkton, and was bred by Victor Moench, Buffalo, New York. Ch. Herman Rinkton completed his championship in 1937. In 1938, he was purchased by C. Hyland Jones but was shown with Mrs. Annis A. Jones listed as owner. He had one hundred Best of Breed wins, placed ninety-six times in the Hound Group, and had fourteen Best in Show wins. He won his Canadian championship in 1939, and in Canada he also took the "spotlight" by being awarded Best of Breed six times; winning Groups four times; and being Best of All Breeds several times. In 1947, this excellent master of the show ring came out of retirement and won the Veteran Class at the Dachshund Club of New Jersey Specialty Show. In his days of retirement, Ch. Herman Rinkton stayed with Rosalie Scheurich, Tween Hills Kennels, Matawan, New Jersey, and it was there that he passed on to his happy hunting grounds at the age of fourteen years.

Teckel-Haven Kennels, Albuquerque, New Mexico, is being run by Stella Goodrich since the death of her husband, O. O. Goodrich. Ch. Ruepel of Hickory Hill is there at stud. In addition to standard long-haired Dachshunds, Teckel-Haven also has Miniature long-haired Dachshunds. The English imported bitch Grunwald Lotus produced a litter sired by the Irish Ch. Zickvon Grunpark. Teckel-Haven

238

AM. and CAN. CH. DIRECT von MARIENLUST
Sire: Am. and Can. Ch. Favorite von Marienlust
Dam: Ch. Herzville von Marienlust
Owner: T. J. McNaughton, Elkins Park, Pennsylvania

CH. SPARLING'S JEFFREY
Sire: Ch. Alexander of Jo-Rene
Dam: Ch. Sparling's Sugar Peg of Jonor
Owner: Everett E. Thorn, Ft. Wayne, Indiana

purchased Dachshunds from G. A. Lloyd Kennels, Chesterfield, England. The Dachshund that was in the film "The Huckster" with Clark Gable was owned by the late Mr. O. O. Goodrich.

Mrs. Jessie Bucknam, Sacramento, California, is the breeder of the famous Ch. Bucknam's Merrymaker, who has returned to his breeder after a most successful show career with Mrs. Walter D. Monroe, Little Gate Kennels, Lake Forest, Illinois. Ch. Merrymaker, whelped in December 1942, completed his championship when he was less than two years of age—truly a sensational winner, he took several Best in Show wins as well as many Best Hound Group wins. Ch. Bucknam's Merrymaker bred to Ch. Fussbudget of White Gables produced Ch. White Gables Nutmeg; Ch. Merrymaker bred to Ch. White Gables Fuchsia produced Ch. Merryman of Little Gate (both these dogs are owned by Mrs. Walter D. Monroe); and Ch. Merrymaker bred to Ch. Asbury's Jewel produced Ch. Buckskin of Etiwanda, owned by Mrs. Mary Asbury Bladin, Sacramento.

The D. D. Daniels, Aptos, California, are the owners of the kennels whose Dachshunds always carry "v. d. Daniels" in their registered names, and they are the breeders of that famous stud, Ch. Omar v. d. Daniels, who was a top sire in 1947, having produced many champions in that year. He was sired by Ch. Cid Junior of Lakelands ex Rote Sally v. d. Daniels, and this dam, in turn, was sired by Ch. Eric v. d. Daniels ex Sally Wartburg v. d. Schroth. Ch. Omar v. d. Daniels is a deep clear red, and is truly a beautiful specimen of the breed. He is owned by Mrs. Anna M. Gargett, of Michigan.

Another prominent "v. d. Daniels" champion is Ch. Blackberry v. d. Daniels, sired by Ch. Ebony Eric v. d. Daniels (Ch. Eric v. Stahlhaus ex Vicki v. d. Daniels). Vicki v. d. Daniels is the litter sister of Ch. Omar v. d. Daniels. The dam of Ch. Blackberry v. d. Daniels is White Gables Blackberry. Ch. Blackberry, currently owned by Raymond S. Hill, is one of the litter of four bitches from this mating; the second one to become a champion is Ch. Berry v. d. Daniels. The other two bitches in this litter are Miss Ebony v. d. Daniels and Ebony Maid v. d. Daniels, who in turn is

240

FISSELHOF EBONY PRIDE
Sire: Ch. Black Lustre v. d. Daniels   Dam: Fisselhof Cavell
Owner: Mrs. Walter Monroe, Lake Forest, Illinois

CH. BLACK LUSTRE v. d. DANIELS
Sire: Ch. Zep v. d. Daniels   Dam: Dachsheims Black Baby
Owner: Mrs. Robert Fissell, Golf, Illinois

the dam of Ch. Arri v. d. Daniels owned by Mrs. Helen Monroe, Little Gate Kennels. Ch. Blackberry v. d. Daniels also has two half brothers who completed their championships: Ch. Zep v. d. Daniels and Ch. Danny v. d. Daniels. Ch. Eric Again v. d. Daniels bred to Cornhill Crickett produced Ch. Ricki v. d. Daniels, and Ch. Omar v. d. Daniels bred to Duchess Schatzi v. d. Daniels produced Can. Ch. Neta v. d. Daniels. Ch. Eric Again v. d. Daniels bred to Redmond's Star Dust produced Ch. Red Honey v. Redmond, who completed her championship at the tender age of thirteen months. She was recently sold and flown to her new owner, Dr. Napp Young, Honolulu, but was bred to Ch. Favorite v. Marienlust before shipment. Another v. d. Daniels champion sired by Ch. Omar v. d. Daniels ex Ch. Donna v. d. Daniels is Ch. Forever Don Omar v. d. Daniels.

The D. D. Daniels and their kennels have won National recognition for the many fine Dachshunds they have produced. Their newest champion is Duane v. d. Daniels, whelped May 31, 1952 (sired by Gary v. d. Daniels ex Dachsheim's Black Baby), who completed his championship in June 1954 by taking four major shows. Ch. Blackberry v. d. Daniels is the granddam of Ch. Duane v. d. Daniels, a black-and-tan Dachshund.

The D. D. Daniels are also the breeders of Ch. Bronze v. d. Daniels, owned by Mrs. Helen Monroe, Little Gate Kennels, and of Ch. Miss Ruby Daniels of Pal-Mar, owned now by Mrs. Evelyn Lambros. Ch. Bronze bred to Ch. Miss Ruby Daniels produced a litter of three males, two black-and-tan, and one red. Black Star of Lambros, now owned by Raymond S. Hill, is from this litter and has points toward his championship. Other studs that have won recognition are Black Treasure v. d. Daniels, sired by Am. and Can. Ch. Zep v. d. Daniels. Black Treasure is now owned by Mrs. Lynn George, Phoenix, Arizona, and the son of Black Treasure, Teufel v. d. Daniels is currently owned by the D. D. Daniels.

Another well-known Dachshund breeder was Mrs. Gilbert L. Stewart, who owned the famous Windyriver Kennels at which resided Ch. Tenchen of Windyriver, Ch. Meistersinger of Windyriver, whose name appears in so many pedigrees of Dachshunds of Marienlust breeding, and last but

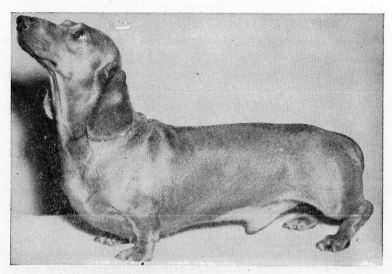

CH. SPARLING LOUHELEN ALDEN
Sire: Ch. Alexander of Jo-Rene   Dam: Ch. Harborvale Circe
Owner: Eva Sparling, Moweaqua, Illinois

CH. SPARLING LOUHELEN RACI
Sire: Ch. Alexander of Jo-Rene   Dam: Sparling Louhelen Ora
Owner: Eva Sparling, Moweaqua, Illinois

not least, Ch. Hertzrumpf of Windyriver. This kennel was located at Hamilton, Massachusetts.

Elbow Bend Kennels, Jane Lenier, have moved from their former location in Chula Vista, California, to Zionsville, Indiana, and are breeders of long-haired Dachshunds as well as smooth-haired dogs. A breeder since 1934, Jane Lenier first owned a black-and-tan imported bitch. This Dachshund lived to the ripe old age of thirteen years, but was never bred. Elbow Bend Kennels purchased foundation breeding stock from Mrs. William F. Ascher, Ascherhoff Kennels, California.

The background of Elbow Bend stock is Am. and Can. Ch. Cid Junior of Lakelands and his ancestors. White Gables Kitty Fisher is the only living daughter out of the litter of Ch. Cid Junior of Lakelands ex Ch. White Gables Marjoram, and she, bred to Ch. Favorite v. Marienlust, produced a litter of six. Others at Elbow Bend include Rock Manor Lustre, sired by Ch. White Gables Gadabout ex Ch. Ship's Mascot Miss Peaches, whose breeder is Rock Manor Kennels; and Crespi's Chad-Anne, sired by Ch. Chadwick of Crespi Street ex Ch. Rivenrock Manhattan. Rivenrock Roderick is one of the studs at Elbow Bend.

Hildesheim Kennels, Mr. and Mrs. Richard V. Pell, were located for many years in Darien, Connecticut, but for the past several years have been located at Thousand Oaks, California. A Best in Show Winner in the West is their Champion Michele of Hildesheim, a Ch. White Gables Basil son. Not long ago, Ch. Arno v. Hildesheim, now over twelve years of age, won the Veteran Class at the Dachshund Club of California Specialty Show, still performing as he did when he was a "gay young blade in Dachshund-dom!" Mrs. Pell also used to breed and show wire-haired Dachshunds in the East, and one of her favorites was Ch. Veroni v. Hildesheim. Hildesheim Kennels are no longer so actively engaged in breeding or showing, but rather, are enjoying their laurels.

Mr. and Mrs. Andrew E. Propper, Boston, Massachusetts, are proud of their dark-red smooth-coated Dachshund dog, Ch. Bart v. Teckelhof, sired by Ch. Omar v. d. Daniels ex Black Widow v. Teckelhof. Bart was nineteen months old when he embarked upon his show career and completed

244

CH. DACHSBERRY'S PACEMAKER
Sire: Ch. Favorite v. Marienlust   Dam: Dachsberry's Roberta
Breeders and Owners: Mr. and Mrs. Elmer E. Berry, Santa Ana, Calif.

CH. DACHSBERRY'S REBECCA
Sire: Jonathan of Heying-Teckel   Dam: Merry-O's Glory Song
Breeders and Owners: Mr. and Mrs. Elmer E. Berry, Santa Ana, Calif.

245

his championship in five straight shows. Bart, who weighs approximately twenty-two pounds, is a Group winner, and has many Best of Variety wins to his credit also. He won his Canadian championship promptly and has his Cuban championship in addition to two Best in Show awards.

Because so many famous kennels and Dachshund breeders exhibit at the Morris and Essex Show, it may be of interest to tell something about this annual spring event. Morris and Essex is one dog show that every dog exhibitor should attend. It is an outdoor show held on the M. Hartley Dodge Estate, Madison, New Jersey, known as Giralda Farms, and comprising some twenty-five acres of beautiful grounds. Breeds are invited to exhibit at this spectacular show, and of course, Dachshunds have always been invited although some breeds are not invited and therefore do not participate. The show is generally held the latter part of May, and "Special American Bred Dogs and Bitches Classes" are held in addition to the regular American Kennel Club classes. To the winner of the Special American Bred Dogs and Bitches Class is awarded the M. Hartley Dodge, Jr., Memorial Trophy. This show has been held for approximately twenty-five years, and is sponsored by Mrs. M. Hartley Dodge. Judges for this show come from many parts of the United States and even from foreign countries to pass judgment on the entries. To win or even be in the "ribbons" at Morris and Essex—or "M and E" as the fancy calls it— is truly an accomplishment to be proud of. A one-day show, judging is done in some forty rings, and it is expertly managed for the comfort of all who exhibit there.

The Dachshund Club of America is the parent Club for Dachshund owners and became affiliated with the American Kennel Club in 1895. The Club's governing body consists of a President, Vice-President, Secretary, Treasurer, Board of Directors, and a Delegate to the American Kennel Club. The Club has a Regional Committee which serves the parent Club in various areas in the United States. Other committees are charged with the responsibility for performing certain specific duties with a view to serving the Club's members.

The comparatively new breed magazine that is serving the Dachshund fancy so well, especially those interested in

CH. KORPORAL JOHNN GARDNER
Sire: Ch. Captain Johnn   Dam: Schnapps XIX
Breeder and owner: Leone G. Hanratty, Mound, Minnesota

CH. TRESSIE HUETTNER GARDNER
Sire: Ch. Captain John   Dam: Schnapps XIX
Breeder and owner: Leone G. Hanratty, Mound, Minnesota

247

breeding, is *The Dachshund Digest*, published at East Rochester, New York, and edited by Mrs. Stanley A. Davis. In addition to editing *The Dachshund Digest*, Mrs. Davis does a great deal of pedigree work, for she has one of the most valuable reference collections relating to Dachshunds that is to be found in America.

Mrs. Davis first became interested in Dachshunds while she was in high school. Then, following her marriage, she attended the San Mateo Show where the large Dachshund entry intensified her desire to become a Dachshund owner. Following World War II, when she and her husband returned to the East Coast, Mrs. Davis began doing research on the breed and building her library on Dachshunds, for she was determined that even her first dog would be a good specimen.

The first Dachshund purchased by Mr. and Mrs. Davis was Hugo of Bel-Clar. When they acquired Hugo, Mrs. Davis started on her first pedigree work. Mrs. Davis' interest in tracing pedigrees has increased until today it involves tracing all major smooth lines to their origin, and also tracing all smooth champions to common denominators. The extensive records she has compiled have been the source of the *Digest* page "Great Dogs of Old."

Of her pedigree work, Mrs. Davis says:

"I am fortunate to have in my library both the Woodiwiss and Allen books on the English pedigrees. These, as you may know, were compiled before 1900 and include every dog, registered or not, that there was any information on from the origin of the breed in England. They are rare, only about one hundred copies were printed, and I was very lucky to get the copies owned by one of the most successful early English breeders, Major Hayward of the famous Honey Kennel, which includes notes which he added from his personal knowledge concerning dogs he brought from Germany, etc. I also have his copies of the English Dachshund Club handbooks, with his notes, etc., in them. He was the first Secretary of that Club, as you perhaps know, and so his notes and records are very fascinating to anyone interested in pedigree work. From these and Miss Dixon's records, I have been able to find and record information

CINNAMON OF OLTERRA
Sire: Ch. Cinnamon v. Dachshafen II
Dam: Ch. Poincianna of Olterra
Breeder and Owner: Mrs. Frederick H. Olney, Foxboro, Mass.

CH. MERRY-KAY v. BELLEAU
Sire: Ch. Favorite v. Marienlust   Dam: Bucknam's Merry-o
Owner: Donia Cline, Los Angeles, California

CH. FIDDLERS HILL TUPPENCE
Sire: Ch. Showboy of Smith   Dam: Fiddlers Hill Tiffany
Breeders and Owners: Joe and Catherine Dardis, Portland, Oregon

which otherwise might become lost. As you know, their Kennel Club does not record dogs as ours does, and many dogs there were unregistered years ago—dogs that were widely used as breeders or studs.

"Among some of these early English breeders whose Kennel Names will appear often in our present dogs if one goes back far enough (all started breeding before 1900) are Major P. C. G. Hayward, the Honey strain, including his great Champion, Ch. Honeystone, black-and-tan, June 25, 1912. Honeystone was the winner of eighteen Challenge Certificates, and was considered the outstanding dog produced in England prior to World War I, and he figures very prominently in the pedigrees of our American dogs. Major Hayward owned many other outstanding winners, but to name just one dog, it would have to be Honeystone.

"Harry Jones was another early English breeder who bred or owned many of the dogs that we find in the pedigrees of American dogs. While he used no particular kennel name, most of his dogs' names began with the letter 'J,' such as his Champion Joan of Arc.

"Claude Woodhead used for his dogs the name 'Brandesburton.' This was formerly a German kennel name. He not only brought into England dogs of the 'Brandesburton' prefix, such as Brandesburton Filius, bred by Forester Weber in Germany, but used the prefix himself. Many of his breeding, as well as the German 'Brandesburton' appear in our pedigrees.

"Mr. M. Wooten bred a number of English champions prior to 1900 that appear in our pedigrees, among them Champions Zigzag, Zadkiel, Zulette, and Zeyn.

"Mr. W. Arkwright is another breeder who produced any number of dogs that appear in our records. Again, he used no particular kennel name to distinguish his dogs. Among his famous early champions, was English Champion Maximus, born in 1881.

"With the Germans, it is hard to know where to stop or start—there are so many that should be mentioned. Among the earlier ones are E. Pohlmey, whose Schneid Kennels in Cossebaude, Germany, were started in 1889.

AM. and CAN. CH. FIDDLERS HILL POLKA
Sire: Ch. White Gables Basil   Dam: Hexe v. Verrueckten Hause
Breeders and Owners: Joe and Catherine Dardis, Portland, Oregon

AM. and CAN. CH. FIDDLERS HILL SCHOTTISCHE
Sire: Ch. White Gables Basil   Dam: Hexe v. Verrueckten Hause
Breeders and Owners: Joe and Catherine Dardis, Portland, Oregon

Champion Florette Schneid was imported to the U. S. A., and finished her American championship in 1906.

"The Asbeck Kennels in Hamm, Germany, are among the most widely known in this country. Started by Augustus Asbeck about 1887, it was later carried on by Karl Asbeck. Their breeding stock carries the Asbeck name. Among the early imports to this country was American Champion Asbeck's Drickes who finished his championship in 1912. The Asbeck Kennels supplied one of the most successful of the English sires in Asbeck's Teo (Teo v. Numarkt). Teo also appears often in the breeding of the American dogs. In going through the imported dogs, Asbeck dogs would be among the top in numbers brought to this country.

"Dr. Fritz Engelmann was among the early breeders. He bred many of the very early recorded German dogs, using the kennel name of 'v. Sonnenstein.' He was one of the very early breeders of longhairs and lightweight smooths. His book, *The Dachshund*, is still widely quoted.

"Wilhelm v. Daacke, another early breeder, started in 1868, used no particular kennel name for his breeding, and further during the early days of the breed, it was common practice for a dog's name to be changed as it went from owner to owner, which makes it difficult for the historian to find the source of the dog. Among 'v. Daacke's' breeding are a number of dogs who have left their mark on our dogs of today. Chief among them, perhaps, is Monsieur Schneidig, a red, born in 1890.

"The Berolina Kennels of G. Barnewitz, Berlin, produced prior to 1900, as well as after, many dogs who appear often in our pedigrees. Berolina Casper, born in 1896, is perhaps best known.

"Gib Hals Kennel of Paul Selchow was founded about 1906, and was based largely on the red, Sieger Gib Hals Schrimm.

"Hermann Schaller's Lamboywald Kennels produced a number of dogs that influenced our present dogs. Among them was Sgr. Niggel v. Lamboywald, born about 1905.

"Also, in this period was the start of the Lichtenstein Kennels of F. Widmann, Laufamholz, plus the 'v. d. Haide' breeding of Heinrich Salzer.

252

AM. and CAN. CH. WHITE GABLES TANSY
Sire: Ch. Bucknam's Merrymaker (C.D.)
Dam: Ch. Fussbudget of White Gables
Owners: Mr. and Mrs. A. C. Spraggins, Walnut Creek, California

ROCK MANOR DIANA
Sire: Ch. Calidox Nicholas   Dam: Rock Manor Daris
Owners and Breeders: Mr. and Mrs. A. C. Spraggins, Walnut Creek, Calif.

ROCK MANOR SUPREME
Sire: Am. and Can. Ch. Favorite v. Marienlust
Dam: Rock Manor Lorna v. Miller
Breeders and Owners: Mr. and Mrs. A. C. Spraggins, Walnut Creek, Calif.

253

"The Flottenberg Kennels of G. F. Muller were founded about 1911. A number of Flottenberg dogs were imported to this country by Herbert Bertrand of the Ellenburt Farm Kennels.

"Emil Sensenbrenner's 'Luitpoldsheim' kennels were founded in 1913. A number of successful show winners and sires were imported, among them, Champion Arno v. Luitpoldsheim, owned by Victor Moench, and Champion Ingo v. Luitpoldsheim, owned by Governor Earle.

"Von Werderhavelstrand Kennels of Margarete Erb produced some very well-known American sires: the great Champion Cid v. Werderhavelstrand owned by H. H. Sachers, and Champion Achat v. Werderhavelstrand, owned by Victor Moench.

"Other names that should be mentioned are 'v. Fallator' — Frau Stroh, Frankfurt/Main, Germany; 'Lindenbuhl' — Simon Barthel; 'Plater Schulhaus' — Melanie Warnecke; 'Erdmannsheim'—Emil Ilgner.

"In Austria, two kennels should be named: St. Huberty (breeder Anton Bauer) which produced Peterl in St. Huberty, who is found in both American and English pedigrees. It is interesting to note that Peterl's grandsire, Alarich v. Wienerwald was imported into the United States, and made his championship in 1905, yet most of the breeding from him is found in Germany, Austria, and England, and in later dogs brought to the U. S. A.

"The von Fehmarn Kennels of O. Uchilles also produced a number of dogs found in our breeding.

"Among the early American breeders were: William Bradley, Allendale Kennels; Dr. Herbert Sanborn, Isartal; Mrs. Beatrice Tainter, Voewood Kennels; Mrs. Harriet Preede, Jaegerhaus Kennels; George Semler, West End; Mrs. Marie Fuchs, Astarte; and Teckelheim, first owned by Fanny Erhardt, later by Grayce Greenburg."

Because you have, by this time, a better acquaintance with famous kennels and famous champions, it is befitting to quote the following comments of a great and worthy breeder of Dachshunds, Albert E. Van Court, of White Gables Kennels, as set forth in an article he wrote which was published in 1951 in *Popular Dogs*:

254

AM. and CAN. CH. WHITE GABLES GADABOUT
Sire: Ch. Cavalier v. Marienlust   Dam: Ch. White Gables Mehitabel
Owners: Mr. and Mrs. A. C. Spraggins, Walnut Creek, Calif.

'FOUR FUNDAMENTALS'

by

ALBERT E. VAN COURT

(Reprinted through the courtesy of *Popular Dogs* Magazine)

"In the thirteen years of our activities in Dachshunds, my wife and I have observed and judges emphasize and re-emphasize certain attributes of the breed—particularly size and color—but in spite of changing tastes the Dachshund has, through his own virtues, won a deep-rooted place in the hearts of the public.

"During these thirteen years, breeders have changed the emphasis from red to black, from medium-sized to large dogs and back again several times. Personally, I think it makes no difference if he be red or black, large or small, as long as he is a good specimen conforming to the Standard. But I do feel that four basic fundamentals are sometimes lost sight of in the endeavor of some to produce super shoulder placement, super running gear, or super whatnot. Some attain their desired goal in improving one particular part of the dog but lose, in so doing, basic fundamentals— namely: type, balance, temperament, and condition. If a Dachshund has not good type, balance, and sound temperament, he is not a real Dachshund.

"Now type is an attribute hard to define exactly, just as the words beauty and elegance are hard to define. For a Dachshund to have type he must be endowed with head, neck, backline, body, and outline, which classifies him immediately as the correct example of what the experienced breeder demands as a correct specimen.

"If the head is not elegant, if the neck is not long and graceful, if the backline is not level, if the body is not developed and of sufficient length, if angulation—front and aft— is lacking, then the whole dog loses that eye-filling appeal which perfect type demands.

"Usually the judge starts his examination at the head, and a non-typical head and expression, although no more important than other attributes, is a great handicap and often quickly relegates the specimen to that great middle

CH. CHARDELINE'S KANDINA v. TECKELHOF
Sire: Ch. Derbydachs Kandi Styck   Dam: Christiana v. Teckelhof
Owners: Mr. and Mrs. Charles E. Fernsell, Palm Beach, Florida

CRESPI'S DONNIE
Sire: Ch. Harborvale Aladin   Dam: Ch. Rivenrock Tamale
Breeder and Owner: Donia Cline, Los Angeles, California

class of common or mediocre dogs. It is hard for a Dachshund to have good type without a good head and a true Dachshund expression. A short neck, or shelly middlepiece, or improper angulation also removes the dog from being classed as typical.

"If type is satisfactory, the dog must also be well balanced. One part should not be over-developed to a point where the symmetry of the whole is destroyed. A welldeveloped forechest with properly angulated shoulders is much to be desired but if not in proportion to the hindquarters, the desired balance is lost. All should form a symmetrical whole.

"Next we must have good temperament. A Dachshund which is cross, timid, or which is not alert should be discarded. That line in the Standard which says a Dachshund should be clever, lively, and courageous to the point of rashness is too often forgotten. The real Dachshund is gay, happy, and alert and is not a plodder or a dullard.

"Condition is also important. A dog in full bloom is in good health, and the dog's nobility and elegance are emphasized if exhibited with shiny, well-conditioned, radiant coat covering firm muscles and flesh.

"Movement is a great exposer of virtues and faults. Bad angulation prevents good movement. If improperly angulated in front, the dog cannot reach forward properly, and is inclined to paddle. If improperly angulated in the rear, the dog drags himself along the ground instead of propelling himself by a rear-end drive and follow-through which lets the pads of the hind feet be seen as the dog goes away from you. Many dogs may gait in a straight line, but they have little power of propulsion if not properly angulated.

"I prefer to study a Dachshund more from the viewpoint of virtues than faults. By this I do not mean that serious faults should be overlooked. Most dogs have a few faults, but some have so much type and quality that the virtues overshadow the faults. Conversely, a dog with only negligible faults may never be a top dog because it lacks type, balance, or elegance. The dogs which reach the top of the ladder all have some fault, but they attain their top rating by showing *type, balance,* and *elegance.* The dog which does not rise above mediocrity can blame his plight not so much on his faults but more on his lack of virtues.

"The perfect dog does not exist, but a great dog, if shown fearlessly under many judges, will find his proper place at the top and you will always find this great dog having type, balance, and sound temperament."

ELSA of ELWOOD
Sire : Chota's Major Mite   Dam: Heidi of Homecrest
Owner: Mrs. Dorothy Ferdinand, Huntington, L. I., N. Y.

Long-haired Dachshunds, three months old
Left to right: Ch. Trouble Shooter of Barcedor, Ch. Miss Troublesome of Barcedor, Double Trouble of Barcedor, Ch. Trouble-son of Barcedor
Breeder and Owner: Dorothy W. Barberis, Bethlehem, Pa.

LONG-HAIRED DACHSHUNDS

Int. Ch. Mira-Erlenmark of Seton, sired by Michael v. Walder ex Mona Lisa v. Walder, is owned by John Pollard, England, and is the winner of seven Champion Certificates under seven different judges in England. She was gone Best of Breed six times; Best of All Coats at the Scottish Dachshund Club's Champion Show in June 1946; Best in Show, Longhair Dachshund Club's Specialty in July 1946; and won a Champion Certificate and Best of Breed at Leicester in August 1948. Ch. Mira-Erlenmark is the dam of Ch. Okauna Loa-Erlenmark, Laurits-Erlenmark, and Ingrid-Erlenmark.

Seton Dachshunds Kennels are owned by Miss Peggy Seton-Buckley, Little Farm, Highmoor near Henley on Thames, England, and included in her kennels in longhaired Dachshunds is Grisbeech Director of Seton, a Best in Show winner by Dominant of Seton.

Gipsy Barn Kennels, Mrs. Max W. Zabel, Wilmette, Illinois, are proud indeed of Ch. Tommy Tucker of Riverbank, who is the founder of the strain of Gipsy Barn long-haired Dachshunds, and in the several years that Ch. Tommy Tucker of Riverbank has been under the ownership of Mrs. Zabel, he has sired the following champions of record: Ch. Abner of Gipsy Barn, Ch. Antonio of Gipsy Barn, Ch. Carlo of Gipsy Barn, Ch. King Cole of Drake Manor, Ch. Loki Boy of Drake Manor, Ch. Sari of Gipsy Barn, Ch. Tytucker of Gipsy Barn, Ch. Steven of Gipsy Barn, Ch. Tyka of Gipsy Barn, Ch. Zandy of Gipsy Barn, and Ch. Zarky of Gipsy Barn; and, in addition to this, he is also the grandsire of Ch. Gipsy Barn's Hillary, Ch. Sienfenjagenheim Adam, Ch. Pantaloons of Hickory, Ch. Lenz v. Zarky of Hafts Acres, Ch. Kelle of Gipsy Barn, whose sire is Ch. Zarky of Gipsy Barn, and who also has the distinction of producing four champions in one litter. Ch. Steven of Gipsy Barn sired Ch. Mr. Morry of Gipsy Barn and Ch. Miss Bessie of Gipsy Barn.

Ch. Antonio of Gipsy Barn, a black-and-tan, is owned by Mrs. Charlotte Sibley, Forever Kennels, San Francisco, and was bred by Mrs. Max Zabel.

Gipsy Barn foundation stock includes Giegerl v. Rauhen

261

Kamm (imported), Ch. Tommy Tucker of Riverbank, Ch. Veto of Riverbank, and Ch. Zarky of Gipsy Barn in their stud ranks. In bitches, Ch. Gisela v. Teckelhof, Ch. Gretchen v. d. Waldhuette, Clarissa of Riverbank, Tiana v. Teckelhof, Ch. Fair Lady of Gipsy Barn, Lezah of Gipsy Barn, Lotte of Gipsy Barn, Priscilla Prim of Gipsy Barn, Audry of Gipsy Barn, and Misstucky of Gipsy Barn are included.

Gipsy Barn Kennels are managed by Mr. and Mrs. Fred Beyer at Crab Orchard, Kentucky, and their dogs are farm-raised. Gipsy Barn Kennels state: "The long-haired Dachshunds are a variety of the Dachshund noted for their elegance; are affectionate pets, good companions, watch dogs, and true Hounds. They are ideal in the home, are naturally clean, and may be safely trusted with children because of small stature and gentleness. In addition, they are easily trained for home and field and are very intelligent. They possess unique beauty and elegance in appearance. Fully grown, the longhair will weigh about eighteen pounds, and as to color, the reds vary from a golden red to a deep mahogany, frequently with black markings. Longhairs also are black-and-tan, and they are just as attractive as the reds." Gipsy Barn also makes the statement: "Best available research discloses that the long-haired Dachshund is a separate species, and while not well-known in this country, is one of the oldest varieties of the breed."

There are, in reality, three officially approved Standards for longhairs: *i.e.,* the German Standard, the English Standard, and the American Standard, but apparently all three agree that the coat should resemble that of the Irish Setter— flat and slightly wavy, shiny on body, with feathering at the points given in the Standards, and reaching its greatest length, as it does with the Irish Setter, on the under side of the tail, forming, so to speak, "a flag."

Another Gipsy Barn champion that is bringing home laurels to his proud owner, Jane Lenier, Elbow Bend Kennels, Zionsville, Indiana, is Ch. Kelle of Gipsy Barn, a red male sired by Ch. Zarky of Gipsy Barn ex Ch. Fair Lady of Gipsy Barn. Ch. Kelle was purchased in January 1949 from Mrs. Max Zabel, and his wins have been most impressive both before and since his ownership by Jane Lenier. Shown

CH. WILLIAM DE SANGPUR
Best Longhair, Westminster, 1948
Best Longhair, Dachshund Club of America, 1946 and 1948
Best Longhair, Morris and Essex, 1946, 1947 and 1948
Owner: Hills' Kennels, Mr. and Mrs. Wm. B. Hill, Jr.
Hicksville, L. I., N. Y.

CH. HEINDRICH vom KLEINE BEINE
Sire: Ivalo v. Nesbittenhof   Dam: Brunhilde XII
Breeder and Owner: Carl Focht, Dayton, Ohio

263

nineteen times, he has taken fifteen Best of Variety wins and one Hound Group; he had seven Best of Variety wins when acquired by Mrs. Lenier, and his show record includes wins at Westminster in 1948. June of Gipsy Barn, a long-haired black-and-tan bitch, now owned by Elbow Bend Kennels, was sired by Ch. Tommy Tucker of Riverbank ex. Ch. Gretchen v. d. Waldhuette, and is a sister of the famous Ch. Antonio of Gipsy Barn, but out of a different litter; she is younger than Ch. Antonio. A litter of five puppies sired by Ch. Kelle of Gipsy Barn ex June of Gipsy Barn, three dogs and two bitches, comprise the first family of this mating at Elbow Bend Kennels. Elbow Bend Kennels also added an import to their long-haired Dachshunds, Anka v. Eulersdorf, a red standard bitch, originally purchased by Grayce Greenburg of Teckelheim Kennels from Wilhelm Gerd-Dietrich, Germany, which will bring new bloodlines to the breeding program in longhairs at Elbow Bend.

The Forever Kennels, Charlotte Sibley, have been located in San Francisco, California, for more than twenty years, and are most prominent as breeders and exhibitors of longhairs because of their outstanding black-and-tan long-haired stud, Am. and Can. Ch. Antonio of Gipsy Barn. Antonio was whelped September 28, 1944, and was bred by Mrs. Max Zabel, of the famous Gipsy Barn Kennels. Antonio is an outstanding long-haired stud and has contributed many fine specimens to the longhair fancy. He was the surprise longhair of 1945, winning his championship points at the age of thirteen months. He was a Best of Variety winner at the St. Louis Specialty Show in 1945, and Best of Winners at the Dachshund Club of America Specialty Show in 1945. Many other wins have been amassed by Ch. Antonio of Gipsy Barn since then, including Best of Shows. His sire was Ch. Tommy Tucker of Riverbank (sire of nineteen champions) ex Ch. Gretchen v. d. Waldhuette (dam of six champions). Ch. Antonio of Gipsy Barn is still alive and being used at stud. His eyesight is somewhat impaired now, and he has had several of his teeth extracted too, but he acts and feels like a youngster.

Charlotte Sibley, the owner of Am. and Can. Ch. Antonio of Gipsy Barn, is very proud of his many champion and

THE PRIDE OF MARIN
Sire: Ch. Forever Golden Antonio   Dam: Ch. Gold Brocade of Marin
Owner: Carl O. Pfeifer, Oak Grove, Oregon

CH. ANTONIO v. BARCEDOR
Sire: Int. Ch. Antonio of Gipsy Barn   Dam: Ch. Heidi vom Friedenswald
Breeder and Owner: Dorothy W. Barberis, Bethlehem, Pa.

near-champion get, which include, among others: Ch. Forever Beloved Belinda, owned by Henrietta Kieran, San Francisco; Ch. Forever Giondoni's Antonio and Ch. Forever Langesk Mercurio, owned by Mollie Weatherstone, San Francisco; Ch. Plume v. d. Bush and Ch. Golden Flirt v. Bush, owned by Dave and Libby Bush, San Leandro, California; Ch. Forever Amber v. Grant and Ch. Merry Antonette v. Barcedor, owned by Mrs. Scott Wood, Fresno, California; Ch. Christine of Marin, owned by the Virgilio Chedas; Ch. Antonio v. Barcedor, Ch. Comtesse Amnamirl v. Barcedor, and his grandsons, Ch. Forever Golden Nugget, and Ch. Forever Golden Antonio; and his granddaughter, Ch. Forever Golden Opportunity; also the following youngsters who are nearing their championships: Forever Tony Dame Annette of Marin, Juliane of Marin, owned by Mary Young, Forever Tristin Langesk's, owned by James Clinton, Forever Langesk's Tawnee, Forever Bewitched, Black Mantilla v. Bush, Langesk's Antonia, and Forever Behold, owned by Mrs. Evan.

Am. and Can. Ch. Antonio of Gipsy Barn is truly a magnificent specimen and a great showman—even to this date, he loves the show ring!

Another longhair kennel of quality is presided over by Virgilio and Isabella Cheda, San Rafael, California, and is known as "Dachshunds of Marin, The Hallmark of Quality." Their great producer and stud is Int. Ch. Gold Ransom v. Teckelhof, a beautiful red longhair, whelped February 23, 1948, sired by Frankel v. Teckelhof ex Gretchen of Detroit, bred by Anna M. Gargett, Rochester, Michigan, of the Teckelhof Kennels fame.

Int. Ch. Gold Ransom v. Teckelhof is the sire of many champions also, including Ch. Gold Brocade of Marin; Ch. Gold Lace of Marin; Ch. Gold Sensation of Marin; Ch. Gold Rush of Valgo; Ch. Forever Golden Nuggett; Ch. Forever Golden Antonio; Ch. Forever Golden Opportunity; Ch. Forever Golden Star; Ch. Count Nikki v. Allen; and the grandsire of Ch. Gold Christine of Marin, Ch. Plume O'v. d. Busch; Ch. The Pride of Marin; Ch. Gold Valiant of Marin; Ch. Princess Peggy of Marin; and Antoniette of Marin, who has thirteen points, including both majors, towards her

266

CH. MICHAELA OF RAYMIHILL
Sire: Ch. Standard of Heying-Teckel   Dam: Breezy Lane Pepper Pott
Owner: Mrs. Neville R. Stephens, Tubac, Arizona

GRETA'S CARLO von KRALC
Sire: Ch. Karl v. Spies   Dam: Ch. Greta von Kralc
Breeder and Owner: Margaret C. Smith, Chillicothe, Ohio

267

championship.

Approximately seventeen years ago, the Chedas owned their first long-haired Dachshund, a black-and-tan bitch out of German stock. However, this bitch was not the starter of their long-haired foundation stock—which is from "all-American" stock. Annie Lore v. Grant, a Gipsy Barn-Northmont bitch, was the beginning of their foundation stock, and bred to their Am. and Can. Ch. Gold Ransom v. Teckelhof produced three champions in one litter—Ch. Gold Sensation of Marin, Ch. Gold Lace of Marin, and Ch. Gold Brocade of Marin. For this, she also received the long-haired Dachshund Dog World Award of Canine Distinction in 1952. A bitch from this mating, Ch. Gold Lace of Marin, bred to her litter brother, Ch. Gold Sensation of Marin, produced Ch. Princess Peggy of Marin, owned by the Wm. Olds, of San Francisco. This second bitch from their first breeding, Ch. Gold Brocade of Marin, bred to Ch. Antonio of Gipsy Barn, produced Ch. Gold Christine of Marin and Ch. Julianne of Marin. Ch. Gold Brocade bred to the Ch. Gold Ransom son, Ch. Forever Golden Antonio, produced two top dogs: The Pride of Marin, currently owned by Carl Pfeifer, Oak Grove, Oregon, and the other male, The Toast of Marin, currently owned by Frank McHugh, San Francisco. Gold Ruffles of Marin, bred to Ch. Antonio of Gipsy Barn, produced two champions in her first litter; Gold Ruffles is owned by the Dave Busches of San Leandro, California. This kennel, Dachshunds of Marin, is now in its fourth generation out of their original stock, and by following a program of selective breeding, is gradually getting Dachshunds with correct fronts and dark eyes—dogs that are good movers and have beautiful temperaments. Coats are correct—long and silky, and free from any trace of "a curly coat." This kennel emphasizes good conformation, good temperament, and good coats.

The Robert E. Hendersons, San Francisco, only recently acquired from Virgilio and Isabella Cheda a beautiful long-haired red male, Ch. Gold Valiant of Marin, sired by Ch. Forever Golden Antonio ex Sheezadaisy of Marin.

In speaking of long-haired Dachshunds of Northern California, Isabella Cheda states:

Long-haired Dachshunds owned by Mildred Sias, Arcadia, California
Upper: CH. RUDY v. HAPSBURG
Lower: CH. CLAUDIA OF RED HILL

269

"About the time of the retirement of Ch. Antonio of
Gipsy Barn from the show ring, we started showing Gold
Ransom v. Teckelhof. He was purchased from Anna M.
Gargett, the breeder, and is a beautiful clear red. He too
finished his American and Canadian Championships and
has sired many champions. One of his most outstanding
sons, Ch. Forever Golden Antonio (owned by Margaret F.
Taylorson, residing at The Cedars, Ross, California), out
of a Ch. Antonio of Gipsy Barn daughter, was Best of Variety
at the great Westminster Show in 1953 and 1954, and was
voted the Most Outstanding Longhair of 1953, with ten
Group firsts, and four Best in All Breeds show wins. This
dog has produced to date two sons of outstanding quality,
Ch. Gold Valiant of Marin and Ch. Pride of Marin.

"Many German imports have found their way into this
area. Brought into this country by service men and their
families, they carry such well-known kennel names as
Habichtshof, Mospring, Lechtenstein, Zinnowitz, Rando-
bruch, Waldenau, Baudenhard, Wolfsanzgel, von Fels, and
many others. Occasionally, these imports have been shown,
but few have been used for breeding due to the fact that so
much "red tape" and confusion have denied the dogs' being
recognized for American Kennel Club registration; and then
again, many of them had no three-generation certified pedigree. Some of these dogs were quite outstanding; some, of
course, showed the effects of the war-torn years in mal-nu-
trition and rickets, and many were definitely poor specimens
in every way.

"Besides Charlotte Sibley, the Don Grants, and the
Chedas of Marin, in Northern California, we have other
breeders of note in longhairs: the D. V. Bushes, Peter
Josephs, and the George Weatherstones. They are using
the same combination of bloodlines with slight out-crosses
to well-known *smooths,* and unrelated longhairs, and have
produced some excellent stock also.

"The increased demand for good show specimens has
been most pronounced, and better long-haired Dachshunds
being shown are now the rule, rather than the exception.
The future looks bright for this beautiful variety of the
breed, and with careful and selective breeding by longhair

270

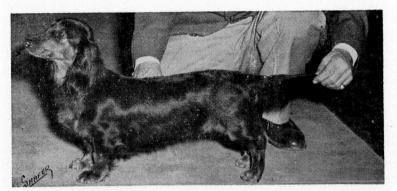

CH. MISS TROUBLESOME OF BARCEDOR
Sire: Ch. Morna's Mr. Trouble   Dam: Ch. Heidi vom Friedenswald
Breeder and Owner: Dorothy W. Barberis, Bethlehem, Pa.

CH. KARL v. SPIES
Sire: Ch. Carlo of Gipsy Barn   Dam: Massey's Penelope
Owner: Margaret C. Smith, Chillicothe, Ohio

fanciers, the time will come when these lovely creatures will be in still greater demand.

"Only by showing in competition will we be able to prove the quality of our dogs, and then only can we see for ourselves if our breeding program is sound. Make it a rule never to breed to or from a dog carrying the faults you are trying to eliminate. A good-moving, flashy, long-haired Dachshund is a joy to behold, the same as it is with a smooth."

Mrs. William Burr Hill, Hicksville, L. I., New York, whose dogs carry the name "De Sangpur" as a part of their registered names, has been a breeder of long-haired Dachshunds for many years, and one of considerable note. This kennel has a red long-haired stud, Ch. William de Sangpur, who, although now approximately eleven years of age, is still going strong as a stud. Ch. William was sired by Ch. Achat v. Walleck ex Ruby de Sangpur and was whelped on April 27, 1943. He holds the record, attested to by the National Breeders Registry, for siring long-haired champions, which now total twenty-two. Ch. William de Sangpur took Best of Variety at Morris and Essex three times; at the Dachshund Club of America, Rye, New York (the parent Club's annual Specialty Show), twice; and at Westminster (1948) once, giving him a total of some sixty-five Best of Variety wins. One of his outstanding sons, Ch. Saqui de Sangpur, whose dam is Ch. Penny Ante of Northmont, is owned by Mrs. Donia Cline, Crespi Street Kennels, Los Angeles.

Crespi Street Kennels purchased this fine, red, long-haired dog from his breeder immediately following his fine win at the 1949 Madison Square Garden Show, where he took Best of Variety, competing with six long-haired Specials, all top dogs in the breed. Ch. Saqui de Sangpur has been a consistent winner at Western shows since making his debut under the ownership of the Clines, and recently took Best in Show at Ogden, Utah. Ch. Saqui de Sangpur, bred to Steinwinter's Nikki, produced Ch. Crespi's Zilly and Ch. Crespi's Malachi. Malachi is currently owned by the Running Creek Kennels, Dallas, Texas. Ch. Crespi's Zilly, an excellent bitch and a show winner of record, bred to Ch.

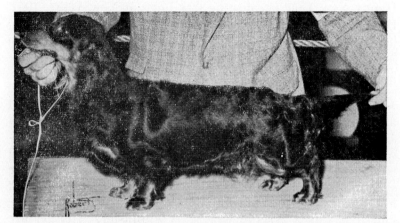

CH. TROUBLE SHOOTER OF BARCEDOR
Sire: Ch. Morna's Mr. Trouble   Dam: Ch. Heidi vom Friedenswald
Breeder and Owner: Dorothy W. Barberis, Bethlehem, Pa.

CH. HEIDI VOM FRIEDENSWALD
Sire: Cerno von Wallerdorf   Dam: Lieserl von Kleinhesselohe
Breeder: Maria Burkhard, Germany
Owner: Dorothy W. Barberis, Bethlehem, Pa.

Antonio of Gipsy Barn, has produced a very beautiful and outstanding youngster, a black-and-tan dog christened Happy New Year because he was born at New Years, 1954. He'll surely be "a surprise" just like his famous sire was, because he has what it takes to really go forth and win, so watch the show reports for a new rising star on the horizon of the longhair fancy.

Brentwald Kennels, the Harold Patricks, Manchester, Missouri, are also breeders of long-haired Dachshunds and are enthusiastic about their Ch. Brentwald Quest, born July 27, 1950, sired by Ch. William de Sangpur ex. Ch. Brentwald of Le-Ann of Deepwoods. This long-haired Dachshund is a brilliant clear red, has excellent coat and is a terrific showman, both in and out of the show ring. He was defeated but once while being campaigned for his championship, and that was a reserve win at Westminster. His get are also proving their worth: Brentwald Illa, owned by Carolyn Straus, has annexed twelve points on her championship; Brentwald William II, owned by Joan Ettman, has a major show; at the age of ten months, Brentwald Quest II was a winner, acquiring four points toward his championship, and placed third in the Puppy Sweepstakes at the St. Louis Specialty. He is owned by J. R. Randle; and Brentwald Viscount has four points, major, towards his championship, and is owned by the Harold Patricks, Brentwald Kennels. Ch. Brentwald Quest is noted for passing on to his get excellent temperaments, good coats and bone, and feet par excellence!

The late Thassilo Krug von Nidda was a pillar in the breed and an excellent breeder and exhibitor of long-haired Dachshunds. Mr. Krug von Nidda's father owned Dachshunds in Germany, and his interest in them never waned. In 1938, Mr. and Mrs. Thassilo Krug von Nidda imported three red long-haired Dachshunds from the Primrosepatch Kennels in England. Two were bitches, Priscilla and Polly, and the other, a male, was Rose Brocade of Primrosepatch. Rose Brocade of Primrosepatch had to his credit two of the three Certificates required for his English championship, and quickly annexed his American championship under the American Kennel Club rating.

CH. TROUBLE-SON OF BARCEDOR

Sire: Ch. Morna's Mr. Trouble   Dam: Ch. Heidi vom Friedenswald
Breeder and Owner: Dorothy W. Barberis, Bethlehem, Pa.

PLUME d'OR v. d. BUSCH

Sire: Am. and Can. Ch. Antonio of Gipsy Barn
Dam: Gold Ruffles of Marin
Breeders and owners: Dave and Libby Bush, Irvington, Calif.

The first litter to be produced under the Von der Nidda Kennel banner was bred in 1939 and included two champions, Ch. Carlo von der Nidda and Ch. Vicki von der Nidda. Vicki took a good win at the Golden Jubilee Specialty Show of the Dachshund Club of America in 1945. Another litter, whelped July 30, 1947, produced Uhlan, Marlene, Morna, Maedchen, and Hussar, all of whom made their championships. Hussar took Best Longhair at the Rye Specialty Show. This litter was sired by Ch. Primrosepatch Gay Lancer ex. Ch. Vicki von der Nidda.

Mr. and Mrs. Andrew E. Propper, Boston, have an outstanding winner in their black-and-tan stud, Ch. Black Prince von der Nidda, who took Best of Variety at six consecutive shows. Black Prince's sire is Ch. Rose Brocade of Primrosepatch ex Primrosepatch Black Satin.

Mrs. Donia Cline owns Ch. Carla von der Nidda, whom Mrs. Cline finished to her championship with Carla taking three consecutive wins as Best Longhair at all-breed shows. Ch. Carla was whelped June 2, 1948, sired by Ch. Rose Brocade of Primrosepatch ex Primrosepatch Gold Walda.

Mrs. Dorothy W. Barberis, of Barcedor Kennel fame, Bethlehem, Pennsylvania, together with her husband, Major Barberis, purchased a long-haired Dachshund from a Bavarian Kennel for a pet and companion, only, during their stay in Europe. Upon returning to the United States, the Barberises decided to show this dog, who was known to them as "Tessie." By this time, Tessie had grown into an adult bitch, and when she went into the show ring with her owner, Mrs. Barberis, she won! Nicky Finn, the professional handler, saw Tessie, liked her, and completed her championship.

After a good deal of correspondence with the American Kennel Club and the kennel powers in Germany, Mrs. Barberis finally got Tessie's papers, only to learn that her little long-haired Dachshund whom she had fondly called Tessie, was living incognito, and in reality was Heidi vom Friedenswald, sired by Cerno v. Wallerdorf ex Lieserl v. Kleinhesselohe, breeder, Maria Burkhard, Augsburg, Bavaria. With papers all cleared, Ch. Heidi vom Friedenswald (Tessie) was bred to Ch. Antonio of Gipsy Barn, and this mating produced Ch. Antonio v. Barcedor, owned by Mrs. Barberis, and Ch. Merry Antonette of Barcedor, owned by Mrs. Scott Wood, Fresno, California. Another youngster from this litter was Tony's Dark Victory.

Another kennel that has done some long-haired Dachshund breeding recently is the Red Locket Kennels, Sun Valley, California, operated by W. W. Dorward, who bred two daughters of Ch. Badger Hill Mr. Chips to Ch. Badger Hill Nobby, a smooth-haired dog who has the longhair genes. Several litters of long-haired Dachshunds have been produced recently, although this kennel is active primarily in the breeding of the smooth-haired variety.

From Badger Hill Kennels, Harry and Vivien Sharp, Madison, Wisconsin, came a Best in Show winner when Ch. Raphael of Calyla took this top win at the Dallas Specialty Show in November 1953. Ch. Raphael's sire is Ch. Badger Hill Mr. Chips ex Resi v. Nesbittenhof. The dam of Ch. Badger Hill Mr. Chips is the smooth-haired bitch, Ch. Albion's Own Penelope, and the sire is Alsvin v. Isartal. J. C. Walters, Dallas, Texas, the owner of Ch. Raphael of Calyla, informed me recently that this beautiful long-haired dog died a short time ago from a kidney disorder. Ch. Raphael of Calyla was whelped May 18, 1951.

Another long-haired daughter of Ch. Badger Hill Mr. Chips is Ch. Badger Hill Boots, a black-and-tan, whose dam is Badger Hill Serta. Ch. Badger Hill Boots is owned by Lucile Brophy who is extremely proud of this dog's wins.

Miss Laura F. Delano, who presides over Knocknagree Kennels, Rhinebeck, New York, is an Eastern breeder of long-haired Dachshunds of note. Miss Delano's two home-bred long-haired dogs, Ch. Samson of Knocknagree and Ch. Josephine of Knocknagree, sired by Ch. Jo Jo Edson ex Ch. Fair Lady of Gipsy Barn, give Miss Delano many hours of pleasure. A litter mate of these two champions is Gizelle of Knocknagree. Ch. Fair Lady of Gipsy Barn, sired by Ch. Beto of Riverbank ex. Ch. Grisella v. Teckelhof, has proved her worth as a foundation bitch for Knocknagree Kennels. This kennel has long been known too for the excellent Irish Setters bred there, and incidentally, had Best Team in Show of Irish Setters at Chicago International, 1951, so this kennel

CH. DeSHA OF LITTLE GATE (d)
Owner: Mrs. Donald Bunnell, Los Angeles, Calif.

can boast of the "tall" (Irish Setters) and of the "small" (long-haired Dachshunds), for their long-haired Dachshunds rightfully have the quality and type of coat that the Irish Setters display.

Deepwood Kennels, Mr. and Mrs. C. J. Leander, Excelsior, Minnesota, have as one of their studs the imported longhair, Peter v. Gelsenkirchen, and as another, his son, Ch. Dandy of Deepwoods.

Seldom does a breed have a devotee like Mrs. William F. Ascher, Ascherhoff Kennels, Arcadia, California, who passed away recently. She acquired her first Dachshund more than fifty years ago and raised smooth-haired as well as long-haired Dachshunds. She undoubtedly was one of the earliest Dachshund breeders in the United States, and her Ascherhoff Kennel stock still appears in the pedigrees of many fine long-haired and smooth-coated Dachshunds today.

CH. CALIDOX NICHOLAS
Sire: Am. and Can. Ch. Favorite v. Marienlust
Dam: Dinah of Heying-Teckel
Owners: Mr. and Mrs. A. C. Spraggins, Walnut Creek, Calif.

NESTOR VON STROMBERG

Imported chocolate dapple Dachshund

First chocolate dapple in this country and responsible for most
of the present-day dapples in America.

Owner: Justine Cellarius, Belmont, California

DAPPLED DACHSHUNDS

Mrs. Justine Cellarius, Belmont, California, is the foremost breeder of dappled Dachshunds in the United States. A number of years ago, when the Cellariuses went to Germany, they purchased and imported a chocolate dappled Dachshund known as "Nestor v. Stromberg." This dog, which is now dead, was the first chocolate dapple in this country and is responsible for most of the present-day dapples in America—there are still very few of this color.

The best-known dapple stud at Cellarius is a black-and-tan, Ch. Uhlan v. Cellarius. This dog took his best win at a Specialty Show of one hundred ten Dachshunds, and went Best of Breed. He is very low, very sturdy, with excellent bone, and he sires grand pups. His sire, Niggel v. Falltor, and his dam, Urschl v. Falltor, are both imports from Germany. Niggel v. Falltor is out of Hansi v. Holzgarten, a famous German dog, and his dam is Renzi v. Falltor. Urschl v. Falltor's sire was Erwin v. Luitpoldsheim ex Hexl-Weidmannsfreud. Another chocolate dapple stud at Cellarius is Fillip Cellarius, who has exceptional bone and is beautifully marked. His sire was the imported dapple Nestor v. Stromberg ex Olga's Bonnie Sue, a bitch who in turn was sired by Ch. Pretzel of Widbrook ex Getigert v. Evwajoheim. Still another stud is a small but fine chocolate-and-tan male, Baby Hansi Cellarius, sired by Hansi v. Stromberg Cellarius ex Widbrook Onyx, a black dappled Dachshund imported from Canada. Another stud at Cellarius is Teckelheim John Cellarius, sired by the import Kelvindale John ex Toumey's Teckelheim Penelope, who was out of an import when Mrs. Cellarius brought over to America Niggel v. Falltor, the famous Brilliant v. Falltor, later acquired by Grayce Greenburg.

Over a period of years, Justine Cellarius imported thirteen smooth-haired Dachshunds and one long-haired Dachshund before the war. One of the most outstanding was a red bitch, Ch. Pia v. Plater Schulhaus. Mrs. Cellarius has been raising Dachshunds for more than a quarter of a century, and has been most intrigued by the breed. She has a collection of about seven hundred Dachshund models, all different and of every conceivable material, which are said to be the most interesting collection of such models ever assembled.

Small's Dachshunds Kennels, Brookfield, Illinois, have dapples also, and have offered a gray dappled male Dachshund of excellent bloodlines to the fancy. Mrs. Marie Nesenger has done some breeding of dapples, and her Nesenger's Allspice, owned by David U. Langaker, is a black-and-silver dappled Dachshund.

Hollyhill Kennels, Miss Wendy A. Riley, England, several years ago had a pair of silver dappled Miniature wirehaired Dachshunds.

Dapples are rarely shown, and apparently there are so few of them that they just do not get to the show rings.

DAPPLE FILLIP CELLARIUS AND A PLAYMATE
Sire: Imp. Dapple Nestor von Stromberg
Dam: Olga's Bonnie Sue (Sired by Ch. Pretzel of Widbrook)
Owner: Fred Cellarius, Jr., Belmont, California

CH. PRIMROSEPATCH DIAMOND   TINYTECKEL PIXIE
Miniature Dachshunds
Tinyteckel Kennel, Miss Avis Earle, North Hollywood, California

SMOKYHOLE ROLFI
Miniature Dachshund
Owner: Tinyteckel Kennel, Avis Mary Earle, North Hollywood, Calif.

283

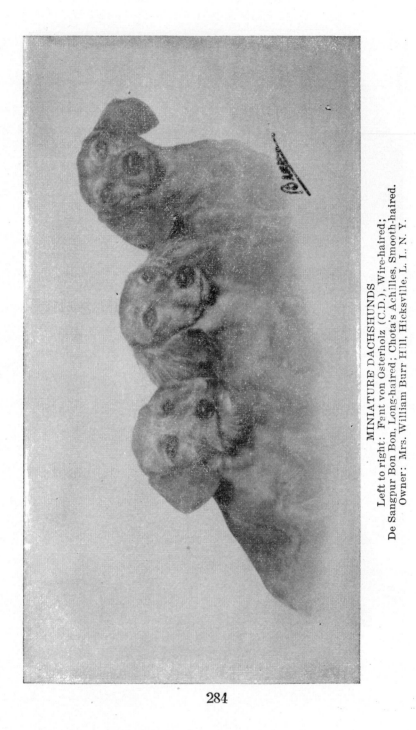

MINIATURE DACHSHUNDS

Left to right: Fant von Osterholz (C.D.), Wire-haired;
De Sangpur Bon Bon, Long-haired; Chota's Achilles, Smooth-haired.
Owner: Mrs. William Burr Hill, Hicksville, L. I., N. Y.

MINIATURE DACHSHUNDS

Contrary to thought and belief, the long-haired Miniatures are definitely not toys, or "toyish" in any sense of the word. A Miniature is every bit as much a Hound as the standard Dachshund and can readily compete with the standards, not only in the show ring, but in field trial work. Long-haired Miniatures are winning in show ring competition with standards and even completing their championships!

Tinyteckel Kennels, whose owner is Miss Avis Mary Earle, Beverly Hills, California, were established several years ago. Miss Earle came to the United States from England and brought with her five long-haired English Miniature Dachshunds: Primrosepatch Zinia, Gracechurch Fairy Dream, Smokyhole Mimi, Smokyhole Rolfi, and Ch. Primrosepatch Diamond. Ch. Primrosepatch Diamond made his American championship in competition with long-haired standard Dachshunds in California and has the distinction of being the first long-haired Miniature Dachshund champion in America. He completed his championship late in the summer of 1949.

When Miss Earle left England in 1948, she chose to purchase from the best English kennels, the best Miniature Dachshunds available, regardless of price, to start her Tinyteckel Kennels In America. Much to her credit, Miss Earle has succeeded with her long-haired Miniatures in open competition with long-haired standard Dachshunds. Not only has Miss Earle accomplished this, but she is having the pleasure of seeing puppies of her own breeding develop and go forth for show-ring honors. Her Tinyteckel Ever Ready is the holder of an Obedience Title.

Out of twenty-two well-trained motion picture dogs, Tinyteckel Ever Ready was chosen for the leading dog part with Bob Hope in his picture "Fancy Pants." This sturdy little Miniature takes everything in his stride—lights, cameras and general confusion at the studio, and is completely undisturbed! There is nothing "toyish" about him, or about other Miniatures. They are real Dachshunds both in type and temperament and can hunt in the field with the best of them. They live in outdoor unheated kennels at Tinyteckel, just as they did in England, even when the snow was thick on the ground.

Ch. Primrosepatch Diamond, whelped January 10, 1946, is a black-and-tan, and was bred by Mrs. O. Smith-Rewes, England, and imported in January 1948. His sire was Ch. Marcus of Mornyvarna, the first English champion in Miniatures. His owners, Mr. and Mrs. Portman Graham, England, were saddened by the death of Ch. Marcus Mornyvarna about a year ago. Ch. Primrosepatch Diamond is the only Miniature Dachshund ever to sire a Best Dog in Show. Jeffrey of Paddenswick, sired by Ch. Primrosepatch Diamond before he was exported to America, made this outstanding win at the London City and Suburban Show, May 1948.

What is believed to be the largest litter of Miniatures on record was whelped four days following Miss Earle's arrival in California. This litter, five bitches and three dogs, was sired by Ch. Diamond ex Primrosepatch Zinia. Ch. Diamond can also claim the distinction of having sired the first long-haired Miniature film star, as well as having been the first Miniature to sire an obedience title holder, Tinyteckel Ever Ready, C. D. It can well be said, without fear of contradiction, that Ch. Diamond has the best head ever seen on any long-haired Miniature Dachshund, either in England or America, and he passes this magnificent head on to his offspring.

Ch. Smokyhole Rolfi was bred by Mrs. H. L. Waddington, Smoky Hole, Uplyme, Lyne Regis, England, and imported by Miss Earle in 1948. He is the smallest black-and-tan stud at Tinyteckel, weighing six pounds and two ounces. Ch. Smokyhole Rolfi has sired several litters of beautiful puppies, including several that weigh less than five pounds when fully grown. His pedigree, like that of Ch. Primrosepatch Diamond, contains names of many of the most famous Miniatures, from Karl Fleesen of Brenevil to Black Watchof Primrosepatch. Ch. Rolfi bred to Tinyteckel Elfin produced Tinyteckel Cricket, whelped July 20, 1952, and Ch. Rolfi bred to Tinyteckel Miss Mouse produced Tinyteckel Buttercup, whelped May 26, 1952. Tinyteckel Buttercup is the famous little star of the Dennis Day television show. Butter-

Miss Avis Earle and her five English Imported dogs
GRACECHURCH FAIRY DREAM
PRIMROSEPATCH ZINIA, SMOKYHOLE ROLFI, SMOKYHOLE MIMI,
CH. PRIMROSEPATCH DIAMOND
Tinyteckel Kennels, North Hollywood, California

cup has a complete wardrobe, including raincoats, sweaters, hats, lace dresses, and even a "Mink Coat," which the studio made up for her. She is a little showman, and gets her share of wins in the show ring too. This little television star, Tinyteckel Buttercup, weighs four pounds!

Ch. Smokyhole Rolfi is also the sire of Tinyteckel Gretal, whelped November 10, 1950, dam, Primrosepatch Zinia, and Tinyteckel Cricri, whelped July 20, 1952, dam, Tinyteckel Elfin, all owned and bred by Miss Earle. Ch. Rolfi is also the sire of Tinyteckel Millicent, whelped June 3, 1951, dam, Tinyteckel Dinah, owned by the Belleau Kennels of Cordelia Skapinsky. De Sangpur Juliette is another daughter of Ch. Smokyhole Rolfi. Owned by Mrs. William Burr Hill, Hicksville, New York, De Sangpur Juliette's dam is Tinyteckel Titania.

Primrosepatch Zinia, breeder Mrs. O. Smith-Rewes, England, was imported with Ch. Diamond and was in whelp to him and produced the litter of eight puppies. This litter of Miniatures was adjudged Best Litter, Dachshund Puppy Match, North Hollywood, and has been shown four times on television and pictured many times in Coast papers as a record litter for Miniatures. Primrosepatch Zinia was a pure red long-haired Miniature. Her show career started in England, and she had completed thirteen of the required fifteen points on her American championship when she passed on to her happy hunting grounds. Her wins were made against long-haired standard Dachshunds. Primrosepatch Zinia's dam, English Primrosepatch Miss Mouse, has the distinction of being the first Miniature to win a Challenge Certificate in open competition with standard Dachshunds. Three Challenge Certificates are needed to become an English champion.

Gracechurch Fairy Dream is another English import at Tinyteckel Kennels. She is a beautiful golden-coated long-haired Miniature bitch, with perfect feathering, a very dark nose, and dark eyes. She too has taken three wins of Best of Variety of Breed in excellent competition against long-haired standards. Smokyhole Mimi, a very tiny golden Miniature, was imported from England in 1948 and also has done excellent winning in the American show rings. Tiny-

288

SEVERAL OF WEBB'S WEE MINIATURE DACHSHUNDS
ON OLD ORGAN
Breeder and Owner: Mrs. Lester Noel Webb, Perrysburg, Ohio

teckel Pixie, sired by Ch. Primrosepatch Diamond ex Primrosepatch Zinia, is one of the puppies that comprised the litter of eight. Pixie is now a fine red stud at Tinyteckel Kennels, weighs seven pounds, and is completely typical of the breed in every way.

Another Tinyteckel Miniature is the clear red stud, Tinyteckel Robin Hood, whelped May 18, 1952, sired by Tinyteckel Domino ex Tinyteckel Amber.

Very recently, Miss Earle returned to England for a visit and to call upon English breeders of Miniatures and see their stock. She purchased and imported a smooth-coated clear red Miniature dog, Tinyteckel Magical of Seale, bred by Mrs. M. Howard, England. Magical of Seale was whelped August 3, 1952, and was sired by Minivale Magical ex Marvelous of Seale. The Minivale Kennels are the breeders of Minivale Magical. Magical of Seale is the sire of Tinyteckel Cuddles of the Ray Bolger television shows that so many television devotees enjoy.

The Osterholz Kennels, Ida and Fritz Kroeff, are located at 4271 Boston Road, New York, New York. These kennels were established many years ago and are leaders in Miniature Dachshunds. Kennelled here we find a German import, Kasko v. d. Jeetzel, whelped April 27, 1948, sired by Daxel v. d. Jeetzel ex Irmchen v. d. Jeetzel, breeder Wilhelm v. Daacke; Kaeti v. d. Jeetzel, litter sister of Kasko, is also kennelled here. Other dogs at the Osterholz Kennels are Traumchen v. Osterholz, whelped June 11, 1948, sired by Kibitz v. Osterholz ex Maerchen v. Osterholz, and Osta v. Osterholz, sired by Kibitz v. Osterholz ex Minnie v. Osterholz.

When Mrs. Aleta Conner, Conner Kennels, Odessa, Texas, passed away recently, the Miniature Dachshund ranks lost an excellent breeder and friend.

Belleau Kennels, Harbor City, California, are owned by Mrs. Cordelia Skapinsky, and it is there that she has kennelled her Miniature stud, Belleau's Kleine Mahn (nine and one-half pounds), whelped August 22, 1947, sired by Eric v. Hixl ex Skapinsky's Red Girl; until recently, she also had kennelled there her Kaynels Drummer Boy, a six and one-half pound Miniature Stud. Mrs. Skapinsky, quite active in the breeding of Miniatures, is the breeder of Trudy Too

Miniature Dachshunds on What-Not
Breeder and Owner: Mrs. Lester Noel Webb, Perrysburg, Ohio

291

of Belleau, owned by Mrs. Neville R. Stephens, Tubac, Arizona.

Mr. and Mrs. Charles L. Strouss, Phoenix, Arizona, have a black-and-tan smooth-coated Miniature stud, Kummel v. Souzenstagger, whose sire is Liebreich Richard v. Sis Q ex Heidi die Bachstelzen, breeder Charles A. H. Rekerdress, Orangeburg, New York. Kummel weighs nine pounds and is excellent in bone, topline, general conformation, and temperament. His pedigree reflects Lieutenant Baldwin Giandoni, and he is very heavily bred in Kargollheim stock. His get in the Western states have done very well.

Mrs. Dwight Garner, owner of Garner's Kennels, Ida Grove, Iowa, is most enthusiastic about Miniatures, and has kennelled her Freias Tena of Garner, eight pounds, and Starkrest's Might Cheer, who has made excellent wins among Miniatures. Garner's Kennels' top Miniature stud is Lusty Wind's little Knick-Knack, seven pounds, who likewise is a top winner among the Miniatures.

Mrs. Earl Pringle, Albany, Oregon, has recently acquired Beau Brummell III, a six and one-half pound, red smooth-coated Miniature stud, from Lavine T. Littlejohn, North Hollywood, California. Beau Brummell III is a valuable addition to the Miniature fancy in the Pacific-Northwest area.

Doxie Dynasty's Kennels, owned by Mr. and Mrs. W. W. Giles, North Port, New York, have many fine Miniatures, and among them we find Doxie Dynasty's Blinken and Doxie Dynasty's Bambi, both smooth-coated Miniatures. Doxie Dynasty's Kringle was sold recently to a Northern California breeder, Mrs. William Rubke, Willellen's Kennels, San Francisco.

New York State can boast of two top kennels that breed Miniatures: Limelight Kennels, Reg., Dachshunds in Miniature, owned by Dr. Lyman R. Fisher, Sun Downs, Ithaca, New York, an established breeder since 1937. Mrs. Wm. Burr Hill, Hicksville, Long Island, New York, is a breeder of note and is very proud of her long-haired Miniature Dachshund, Ch. De Sangpur wee Allene, whelped in April 1952. This Miniature made all of her championship points in competition with standards.

292

WEBB'S PINK LADY WITH LITTER OF PUPPIES IN A TOP HAT

Mr. and Mrs. Lester Noel Webb, Perrysburg, Ohio, are also breeders of Miniature Dachshunds and have at stud, Dunder of Donde, whose sire is Gnome v. Daustin ex Gretel v. Dunenbruch. Dunder's pedigree includes the names of several imported Miniatures. His breeders are Mr. and Mrs. Don Diessner.

Mr. and Mrs. Jack Beard's kennels, known as The Dachs' Den, are located at Lincoln, Nebraska. In addition to many other top Miniature Dachshunds, a Dunder of Donde's daughter, Jinny Jinx of Dachs' Den, is kennelled there.

The Miniature Dachshund breeders in the United States have formed their own organization, known as the American Miniature Dachshund Association, with National headquarters at Northport, Long Island, New York. This group is devoted exclusively to the advancement and improvement of the Miniature Dachshund, and seeks to secure a separate Standard and point rating for Miniatures. The founder of this association is W. W. Giles, and the Founders' Committee was composed of Mrs. Don Diessner, Mrs. Grayce Greenburg, Mrs. Elizabeth Kargoll, Mrs. William Sias, and Mrs. Lester Noel Webb. The American Miniature Dachshund Association maintains a service for its members and for those interested in Miniature Dachshunds by furnishing free literature and membership applications, and maintains a Nation-wide directory of kennels, puppies, and stud service.

The popularity of the Miniature Dachshund is increasing rapidly, and Miniature breeders hope and expect to establish Miniature show classes separate from the standard Dachshund classes, and to have separate championship status for their Miniatures. In the open classes at shows held under the rules and regulations of the American Kennel Club, Miniature Dachshunds may be entered in the Open Dogs Class, under nine pounds, Miniature (if twelve months of age, or over) ; and in the Open Bitches Class, under nine pounds, Miniature (if twelve months of age, or over). In other regular classes of the American Kennel Club, this division is not made. In England, classes are divided for standards and Miniatures. In Germany also, the Miniature Dachshund has been recognized, and is shown in classes for

Miniatures. Here in America, the German Standard is followed, and the weight for dogs is placed at nine pounds (no more), and for bitches, eight pounds.

The development of the American Miniature Dachshund commenced as early as 1930, but in reality, the American Miniature Dachshund is in its infancy, and its breeders seek to make it a separate variety. The Miniature Dachshund is bred in all three coats, *i.e.*, smooth coat, longhair, and wirehair, the same as the standard size Dachshund. It should be understood that a Miniature Dachshund is not to be mistaken for a "small or undersized" standard Dachshund, but is specifically bred as a Miniature Dachshund. The same general features and temperament found in the standard Dachshund likewise are found in the Miniature Dachshund, and by the same yardstick, the same general faults found in the standard Dachshund also are found in the Miniature Dachshund.

WEBB'S PINK LADY
Smooth-haired Miniature
Sire: Hansi of Starcrest   Dam: Fraulein Liebchen
Breeder and owner: Mrs. Lester Noel Webb, Perrysburg, Ohio

SIR KAY OF HOHENBURG (1½ years old)
Wire-haired Dachshund
Sire: Ch. Burschle of Hohenburg   Dam: Dachshafen Astarte Meridith
Owner: Hohenburg Kennels, Mrs. David L. Wall, Worcester, Mass.

CH. MAX VON HOHENBURG
Wire-haired Dachshund
Sire: Ch. Franklin of Hohenburg   Dam: Marline of Hohenburg
Owner: Hohenburg Kennels, Mrs. David L. Wall, Worcester, Mass.

WIRE-HAIRED DACHSHUNDS

As nearly as I can determine, the smooth-coated Dachshund was interbred to the English Dandie Dinmont Terrier in the beginning of the eighties, and thus came into being the wire-haired, or as the Germans describe this variety of the breed, the "rauhhaar," which, translated, means "rough hair" or "rough coat."

I have seen the wire-haired Dachshund in four colors: brindle (salt-and-pepper); reddish brown (cinnamon-and-salt); black with tan markings; and, recently, the "wheaten," or a light golden blonde shade. All are beautiful. The wire-haired Dachshund should have a harsh wirey coat with an undercoat. If they are to have the proper coat, wire-haired Dachshunds should not be "single coated," like the smooth-haired Dachshunds. The proper coat requires very little stripping or grooming, but the soft-coated or woolly type necessarily requires coat attention. In many instances, the breeding of the smooth-coated Dachshund to the wire-haired Dachshund gives harsher coats to the wire-haired offspring. In such a mating, smooth-coated puppies as well as wire-coated puppies may result.

Except for the jaw, eyebrows, and ears, the entire body should be covered with an even, harsh coat. The eyebrows should be bushy, the ear coverage almost smooth. The following is an excerpt of the Standard which was adopted by the parent Club, The Dachshund Club of America, and approved by the Board of Directors of the American Kennel Club on July 9, 1935, as the official breed Standard for Dachshunds as applies to the wire-haired Dachshund:

"(B) WIRE - HAIRED DACHSHUND — The general appearance is the same as that of the short-haired, but without being long in the legs, it is permissible for the body to be somewhat higher off the ground.

"HAIR—With the exception of jaw, eyebrows, and ears, the whole body is covered with a perfectly uniform, tight, short, thick, rough, hard coat, but with finer, shorter hairs (undercoat) everywhere distributed between the coarser hairs resembling the coat of the German Spiky-Haired Pointer. There should be a beard on the chin.

"The eyebrows are bushy; on the ears, the hair is shorter than on the body; almost smooth, but in any case conforming to the rest of the coat. The general arrangement of the hair should be such that the wire-haired Dachshund, when seen from a distance should resemble the smooth-haired.

"Any sort of soft hair in the coat is faulty, whether short or long, or wherever found on the body; the same is true of long, curly, or wavy hair, or hair that sticks out irregularly in all directions; a flag tail is also objectionable.

"TAIL—Robust, as thickly haired as possible, gradually coming to a point, and without a tuft.

"COLOR OF HAIR, NOSE, AND NAILS—All colors are admissible. White patches on the chest, though allowable, are not desirable."

The popularity of the wire-haired Dachshund is steadily improving as will be noted from the following tabulation of entries at Westminster Kennel Club Shows, which many exhibitors refer to as Madison Square Garden, or "The Garden," shows:

Year	Wirehair Entry
1945	17
1946	9
1947	7
1948	17
1949	21
1950	19
1951	28
1952	24
1953	25

I have no information as to the wire-haired entry for 1954.

The consensus of opinion is that wire-haired Dachshunds are very obedient, and that they are often more obedient than the other two varieties of the breed—the smooth-haired and the long-haired. The wire-haired Dachshund is perhaps slower, but is reliable, and will face all undergrowth and water fearlessly, qualities which in some degree may be due to their denser coats. They are tenacious as hunters, also.

298

Mr. and Mrs. Harold Patrick, Manchester, Missouri, are to be heartily congratulated on their contribution to the wire-haired Dachshund. They have the famous "Brentwald Kennels," and it was at this kennel that Am. and Can. Ch. Brentwald Joshua W. first saw the light of day on October 21, 1946. His sire is Ch. Lumpacius Hubertus (brindle) ex Ch. Jerry Hubertus (brindle). Practically all of the stock behind Joshua is German, but there are, of course, some Swedish bloodlines in his pedigree. Joshua's grandsire on his sire's side was the Swedish import, Sports Buster. This wire-haired Dachshund, Sports Buster, was imported by Mrs. Richard V. Pell, Hildesheim Kennels, when he was a puppy, and was purchased from Mrs. Veroni Sandstrom, Sports Kennels, Sweden. Sports Buster completed his championship in the United States under Mrs. Pell's ownership. Joshua's show record is terrific, and includes five Best in Show wins, sixty-one first placements in Hound Groups, and one hundred fifty-three Best of Variety wins! As of June 1954, he was the sire or grandsire of thirty-five champions. Champions he sired are as follows: Ch. York W. Murlake, Int. Ch. Youvonne W. Murlake, Ch. Valencia W. Murlake, Ch. Yo-Ellen W. Murlake, Ch. The Witch's Brat, Ch. Brentwald Destiny, Ch. Brentwald Caprice, Ch. Brentwald Brigadier, Ch. Brentwald Copyright, Ch. Fabian of Lelou, Ch. Frolic of Lelou, Ch. Salty Wire of Heying-Teckel, Ch. Black Wire of Heying-Teckel, Ch. Sissy von Lindenau, and Ch. Briarcliff v. Klingsor.

Ch. Joshua is the grandsire of the following: Ch. Starkrest's Vagabond, Ch. Starkrest's Nanette, Ch. Starkrest's Lotti, Ch. Starkrest's Souvenir, Ch. Brentwald Warbonnet, Ch. Red Locket Hexe, Ch. Teckelow's Gretchen, Ch. Teckelow's Penny, Ch. Livewire of Heying-Teckel, Ch. Pinocchio W. of Raymihill, Ch. Bergmanor Euchre, Ch. Prinzessin Millie v. Stephens, Ch. Hush yo' Mouf Liza v. d. Stephens, Ch. Prinz Maxmillian v. Stephens, and Ch. Albrecht v. d. Stephens.

Ch. Joshua is the great-grandsire of Ch. Hainheim's Nancy, Ch. Starkrest's Dictator, Ch. Calyla Topsy, and Ch. Calyla Turvy.

Ch. Brentwald Joshua W. was piloted to fame by William R. Ake, professional handler, Dallas, Texas, who purchased "Buzz" (as he was called by the Akes) from his breeders on June 10, 1947, at the age of seven months and nineteen days. On January 11, 1948, "Buzz" was taken on a whirlwind campaign, and in fifteen shows in eleven states, he took Best of Variety thirteen times, and Best Opposite Sex at the other two shows, and topped off this amazing record with two Hound Group wins. He completed his championship when fourteen months of age, for this show campaign was completed in about five months. On November 29, 1948, "Buzz" took Best Dog in Show at Louisville, Kentucky, and was also awarded the Dog World Award of Canine Distinction for the following:

1948—Won American Championship Undefeated in Sex, plus two Group wins.
Won Canadian Championship in four successive shows in four successive days, and Best of Variety at each.
Won Best of Variety thirty-three times in thirty-five shows.

1949 Won Best of Variety, Westminster, Madison Square Garden, defeating seven dogs, nine bitches, and six Specials.
Won B. V. B., Ottumwa, Iowa; St. Petersburg; Detroit; Des Moines; Oklahoma City; and Clearwater. In addition, annexed five Hound Groups, making a total of eleven Group wins in his show career thus far.

"Buzz" was handled exclusively throughout his show career by "Bill" Ake, handler-owner. After much negotiating, "Buzz" was sold in 1949 to Herman G. Cox, Fort Worth, Texas, who is not only a breeder-exhibitor of Dachshunds, but a licensed A. K. C. Judge. Here, at the Dychland Kennels, Ch. Brentwald Joshua W. headed the list of worthy studs. He made his debut under the Dychland banner at Daytona Beach, Florida, and took Best in Show. He was Best of Variety at Westminster in 1949 and 1950, at the Rye, New York, Specialty Show in 1948 and 1949, and at Morris

300

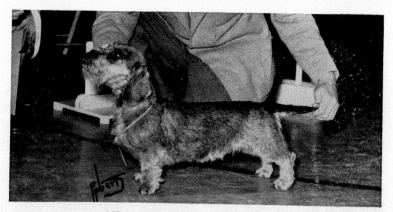

CH. HUSH-HUSH v. d. STEPHENS
Wire-haired Dachshund
Sire: Ch. The Witch's Brat   Dam: Brentwald Toni
Owner: Stanley Orne, Kirkland, Washington

CH. STARKREST'S SOUVENIR
Sire: Ch. Brentwald Destiny   Dam: Starkrest's Top Tune
Owner: Mrs. Anne E. Appelgate, Los Angeles, California

CH. PINOCCHIO W. OF RAYMIHILL
Wire-haired Dachshund
Sire: Ch. The Witch's Brat   Dam: Brentwald Toni
Owner: Mrs. Anne E. Appelgate, Los Angeles, California

301

and Essex in 1949. In 1950, the Quaker Oats Award for the Southern Division was presented to Ch. Brentwald Joshua W. and Mr. Herman G. Cox, his owner at that time, for having won more Group firsts than any other dog of any breed in that Division. Only four Quaker Oats Awards are presented annually, so Joshua was one of the four winners in the United States.

He was defeated only once in the breed, and that was by his famous mother, Ch. Jerry Hubertus, and at this show, he took Best of Opposite Sex! Joshua's remarkable record is to be commended. His showmanship is superb, and he has certainly contributed more than any other one dog to the popularity of the wire-haired Dachshund of today.

Other top wirehairs at Brentwald Kennels include Ch. Brentwald Traci, Ch. Brentwald Jo-Ellyn W., Ch. Jerry Hubertus, Ch. Brentwald Destiny, Brentwald Theodora, and Brentwald Thaddeus.

Tubac Kennels are the result of a hobby that has grown into a business, and have been in operation for several years under the management of the owners, Mr. and Mrs. Neville R. Stephens, Tubac, Arizona. The Stephens formerly resided in Pasadena, California. Tubac, Arizona, is located between Tucson and Nogales at the foot of the Santa Rita Mountains. There is ample barking and "screaming" room, the nearest neighbors being one mile away. At Tubac Kennels, the temperature of all kennel buildings is regulated with thermostatic heat controls. The kennels are constructed of brick-burned adobes, twelve inches wide, eighteen inches long, and four inches thick, which retain warmth in winter and retard heat absorption in summer. A majority of the runs are separated by adobe walls.

The number of dogs kennelled here ranges from eighty to over one hundred dogs and puppies, and as of June 1954 included fifteen champions. Tubac Kennels has Dachshunds of all three coat varieties. Through me, they became interested in wire-haired Dachshunds, and purchased from Raymihill Kennels one-half interest in Brentwald Toni, the full litter sister of Brentwald Traci, who is now a champion.

When Ch. Brentwald Joshua W. was being retired from the show ring, he was purchased by Mr. and Mrs. Stephens,

302

CH. FAY-DACHS MINDORA
Sire: Strolch vom Holzgarten   Dam: Ch. Minton of Heying-Teckel
Owner: Raymond S. Hill, Phoenix, Arizona

JOSHUETTA W. OF RAYMIHILL
Sire: Ch. Brentwald Joshua W.   Dam: Brentwald Toni
Owner: Raymond S. Hill, Phoenix, Arizona

DACHSCROFT'S TWEED JACKET
Sire: Hollyhill Petrouka (Eng.)   Dam: Ch. Hollyhill Silvershell
Owner: Margaret C. Smith, Chillicothe, Ohio

who are his present owners. By them, he has been presented to the wirehair fancy as a top wire-haired stud. Other wire-haired Dachshunds kennelled at Tubac include a granddaughter of Joshua, Ch. Hainheim's Nancy, sired by Ch. Brentwald Destiny ex Ch. Starkrest's Nanette. Ch. Hainheim's Nancy's career has been most spectacular, for shortly after she was six months of age, she started and finished her championship in six days by winning three five-point shows, and coming up from the Junior Puppy Bitch Class at each event. Since confirmation of her championship, she has been shown in Specials, and has nearly always gone Best of Variety, and usually has won a spot in the Hound Group. She is light wheaten in color, with black nose and black eyes. Ch. Tubac's Jeritza W. is a daughter of Joshua ex Ch. Hush yo' Mouf Liza v. d. Stephens (and Liza is the daughter of Ch. The Witch's Brat). Jeritza started her show career by winning a Sanctioned Match as Best in Match at the age of nine months, then took second Best Wire-haired at the Southern California Puppy Futurity, and completed her championship by making all her points at major shows. Ch. Tubac's Christoph is another Joshua-sired winner ex Brentwald Toni, and is the latest of the Joshua sons to complete his championship. "Bill" Ake states that Christoph is more like his sire than any wire-haired dog or bitch he has ever seen. Christoph was also a Futurity puppy winner, and completed his championship at the age of twelve months with all major show points.

Ch. Brentwald Warbonnet, whelped June 22, 1950, and sired by Ch. York of Murlake ex Starkrest's Cookie, completed her championship quickly and has been a top brood bitch at Tubac Kennels.

Ch. Albrecht v. d. Stephens, whelped April 2, 1952, sired by Ch. Brentwald Copyright ex Black Magic Zipper, is a double grandson of Joshua. Albrecht won his first points as a puppy in November 1952, and completed his championship by the following October. Litter mates of Albrecht are Adolph v. d. Stephens, owned by Ruth M. Sarko, Phoenix, who is working on his championship too; Anton v. d. Stephens; and Axel v. d. Stephens. This entire litter was comprised of males. Their beautiful wire-haired dam gave her

304

life having her family, and the litter was raised by a foster mother, Betty v. Hoellental, a black-and-tan smooth-haired bitch owned by Mr. and Mrs. Lynn George, Phoenix.

Joshua bred to Ch. Brentwald Warbonnet produced Tubac's Abednego W.; Joshua bred to Ch. Hush yo' Mouf Liza v. d. Stephens produced Tubac's Johanna W., and Ch. Tubac's Jeritza W.; and Joshua bred to Brentwald Virginia produced Ch. Sauci of Murlake; incidentally, Ch. Sauci of Murlake was bred back to a son of Joshua, Ch. Tubac's Christoph, and has a litter of three bitches and two males. Ch. Sauci is now owned by Gwen Nedbalek and June Nichols of Oklahoma City. Joshua bred to Amelia Murlake produced Frolic of Lelou and Fabian of Lelou, both now champions. Bred by Leon Warren, Santa Ana, California, Frolic is owned by the Neville R. Stephens, while Fabian is owned by Mrs. Helen T. Noble, Santa Ana, California.

Joshua bred to Ch. Brentwald Caprice produced Ch. Sissy W. von Lindenau, and she too was finished to her championship by the Stephens. Ch. Prinz Maximillian v. d. Stephens and Ch. Prinzessin Millie v. d. Stephens are litter mates sired by a Joshua son, Ch. Brentwald Destiny ex Ch. Brentwald Warbonnet.

Because of their extensive traveling and their exhibiting and attendance at so many dog shows, Mr. and Mrs. Neville R. Stephens and Tubac Kennels have in reality done more to popularize wire-haired Dachshunds than any other persons or kennels in the United States. During the past three years, they have started and completed the championships of fifteen dogs and bitches, and in so doing, have traveled a total of 125,000 miles. Occasionally, one of their dogs will go on a circuit with a professional handler, but nearly always the Stephens are following right behind with Mr. Stephens doing a great deal of the handling in the show ring himself. A great amount of credit is due this fine couple for the interest, time, money, and effort that they have so generously given to further the wire-haired Dachshund.

Stanley Orne, Fir Trees Kennels, Kirkland, Washington, is also a wirehair breeder whose interest stemmed from his two Irish wire-haired imports, Greygates Prima Donna, bitch, and Greygates Intermezzo, dog, which he purchased from the Greygates Kennels in Ireland. Mr. Orne also purchased a wire-haired youngster sired by Ch. The Witch's Brat ex Brentwald Toni from Tubac Kennels. This dog, Ch. Hush Hush v. d. Stephens, made his championship very quickly. Since that time, Mr. Orne has bred his Greygates Prima Donna twice to Joshua, and only recently completed the championship of his first home-bred dog, Ch. Fir Trees Coco. On their way to championships are other wire-haired Dachshunds, including Fir Trees Sharon W. (a litter sister of Ch. Fir Trees Coco), currently owned by Mrs. Neville R. Stephens. Fir Trees Bridget is also working on her championship.

Here at Raymihill Kennels, our interest in wire-haired Dachshunds started with the purchase of Brentwald Toni from the Brentwald Kennels in March 1951. In June 1951, at the Harbor Cities Show, Long Beach, Raymond S. Hill and Anne E. Appelgate, together, purchased The Witch's Brat, from Jerry Rigdon, the handler and breeder of this extremely good wire-haired dog. At this same show, Black Magic Zipper, the full litter sister of The Witch's Brat, was purchased from Mr. Rigden by Mrs. Neville R. Stephens. These two dogs, whelped March 16, 1950, were sired by Ch. Brentwald Joshua W. ex Zipper of Badger Hill.

The Witch's Brat entered into his show career as a wee youngster, and in February 1951, won his puppy dog class at Westminster; then, at Morris and Essex in 1951, he took Winners Male, five points; in 1952, again at Westminster, he went Winners Dog, Best of Winners, and Best of Opposite Sex for five points, and also won the George G. Frelinghuysen, Jr., Challenge Sterling Silver Trophy for Best of Winners in wire-haired Dachshunds, bringing this award to the West for the first time. Again in 1952, he continued his wins at Detroit, Santa Ana, Beverly Rivera Kennel Club at Santa Monica, California, and at the 1952 Morris and Essex Show where he finished his championship and won the Hartley M. Dodge, Jr., Memorial Trophy, a sterling silver bowl, for Best in Special American Bred Dogs and Bitches Class, Wire-haired. To win this, he had to win over both dogs and bitches coming together in the same class. Thus,

306

Ch. The Witch's Brat started his show career at Westminster and finished at Morris and Essex, repeating his wins for two consecutive years at the largest all-breed shows in the United States.

In the summer of 1953, he took two Hound Groups in the Pacific Northwest at Vancouver, Washington, and again at Portland, Oregon, where he took another Challenge Trophy for the Hound Group win.

Ch. The Witch's Brat has an excellent harsh wire coat, and excellent temperament and conformation. As a wirehaired stud and showman, and an outstanding specimen of this variety of the breed, Ch. The Witch's Brat is rated highly. He sired three champions from one litter: Ch. Pinocchio W. of Raymihill, owned by Anne E. Appelgate, Los Angeles; Ch. Hush yo' Mouf Liza v. d. Stephens, owned by the Neville R. Stephens, and Ch. Hush Hush v. d. Stephens, owned by Stanley Orne, Kirkland, Washington. Ch. The Witch's Brat bred to the German import, Quelle vom Eifatal, owned by the Alfons Westrichs, Flushing, New York, produced three bitches and two males. We purchased the three bitches, naming them as follows: Sanchia W. of Raymihill, Senta W. of Raymihill, and Schelee W. of Raymihill. Later, Mrs. Ellen M. Conant, Omaha, purchased Sanchia. After owning Sanchia several months, Mrs. Conant reported that the dog had died and immediately purchased the litter sister, Senta W. of Raymihill, of whom she is very proud.

Another Joshua offspring at Raymihill Kennels is our Joshuetta W. of Raymihill, who, although but a youngster, boasts of both major show wins toward her championship. A full litter sister of Ch. Tubac's Christoph, Joshuetta is "cinnamon-and-salt" in color, and her dam is Brentwald Toni.

Our newest wire-haired champion is the black-and-tan bitch, Ch. Fay-Dachs Mindora, who completed her championship in June 1954 at the Harbor Cities Show. She was sired by the German imported wire-haired stud, Strolch vom Holzgarten (currently owned by the Fay-Dachs Kennels) ex Ch. Minton of Heying-Teckel. This imported wire-haired Dachshund is from the famous Holzgarten Kennels, Dachau,

307

Germany, whose stock appears in almost every pedigree of Dachshunds, regardless of coat. Mindora completed her championship in five shows; all points were majors and were won in close competition always; in fact, she was only shown five times in her entire show career. Her full litter brother, Fay-Dachs MacTavish Mint, whom we also own, is likewise working on his championship. A litter sister, Fay-Dachs Margot, who has many points on her championship, is currently owned by Mrs. Scott Wood, Fresno, California. This litter was whelped December 30, 1952, and their beautiful dam, Ch. Minton of Heying-Teckel, died in the whelping.

Ch. Brentwald Joshua W., bred to Ch. Starkrest's Souvenir, produced a litter of five whelped October 16, 1953. The one bitch in the litter is Souvianne W. of Raymihill, who won her puppy bitch class at the recent Harbor Cities Show, and who will be piloted to her championship by her new owner, Donald F. Hickey, Oklahoma City.

Starkrest's Kennels, Elmhurst, Illinois, owned by Bill and Mildred Stark, are also breeders of quality wirehairs, including Ch. Starkrest's Vagabond, Ch. Starkrest's Lotti, Ch. Starkrest's Nanette, Ch. Starkrest's Echo, Ch. Starkrest's Souvenir, and Ch. Starkrest's Dictator. The dam of Ch. Starkrest's Souvenir is Starkrest's Top Tune (the dam of four champions), and the sire of Souvenir is Ch. Brentwald Destiny, who is the sire of four champion get. Ch. Starkrest's Souvenir bred to the German imported wirehair, Strolch vom Holzgarten, produced a litter of three bitches and two males whelped May 21, 1954, which look most promising.

J. C. Walters, Calyla Kennels, Dallas, Texas, owns Ch. Starkrest's Lotti, a wire-haired bitch that has not only been a top winner, but has been an excellent producer. Bred to Mr. Walters' smooth-haired stud, Ch. Allegro of Gera, Lotti has produced Ch. Calyla Topsy, owned by Mr. Walters, and Ch. Calyla's Turvy, owned by the Wearytime Kennels of Mr. and Mrs. Guy Meyer, Dallas. Mr. and Mrs. Hutt Fife, Running Creek Kennels, Dallas, are breeders and owners of wirehairs who piloted Ch. Starkrest's Vagabond to many wins. Vagabond's sire is Ch. York of Murlake ex Ch. Starkrest's Top Tune. Ch. Starkrest's Vagabond's youngsters,

TUBAC'S JERITZA W.
Sire: Ch. Brentwald Joshua W.
Dam: Ch. Hush yo' Mouf Liza v. d. Stephens
Owner: Mrs. Neville R. Stephens, Tubac, Arizona

CRESPI'S AHME
Owner: Mrs. Neville R. Stephens, Tubac, Arizona

CH. ALBRECHT v. d. STEPHENS
Sire: Ch. Brentwald Copyright   Dam: Black Magic Zipper
Owner: Mrs. Neville R. Stephens, Tubac, Arizona

Running Creek's Flashywire and Running Creek's Steel Wire, are currently being shown.

While Heying-Teckel Kennels, Pacoima, California, are primarily known for smooth-coated Dachshunds, they also breed wire-haired Dachshunds. The start of their wirehair breeding program is based on Ch. Barb Wire, whelped March 12, 1950, sired by Ch. Favorite v. Marienlust (smooth) ex Cerka z Drasky, an imported dog owned by Katherine Knapp. A bitch, Ch. Live Wire of Heying-Teckel, whelped March 13, 1951, resulted from the breeding of Ch. Barb Wire of Heying-Teckel to Ch. Brentwald Copyright, a son of Ch. Brentwald Joshua W. Heying-Teckel's current wire-haired stud, Ch. Salty Wire of Heying-Teckel, is the son of Ch. Brentwald Joshua W. ex Ch. Barb Wire of Heying-Teckel. Ch. Live Wire of Heying-Teckel has done some remarkable winning. She has also been a good brood bitch at Heying-Teckel Kennels.

Ch. Brentwald Joshua W. bred to Ch. Barb Wire of Heying-Teckel produced Blackwire of Heying-Teckel, owned by Mr. and Mrs. George E. Spencer, Portland. Blackwire completed his championship recently and shortly thereafter became ill and died. Whelped September 30, 1951, Blackwire was bred to Leach's Merry Cissy and Produced Casa Del Dox Corsair, whelped October 12, 1952, and owned by his breeder, Burgess M. Leach, Portland. Ch. Valencia Murlake, currently owned by Mr. and Mrs. Alex Keenan, San Francisco, was purchased from the Heying-Teckel Kennels as a champion. Her sire is Ch. Brentwald Joshua W. ex Rashua Murlake. Ch. Valencia was whelped January 28, 1950, and completed her championship in December of the same year.

Another breeder in the Pacific Northwest area is Lorheim Kennels, which recently completed the championship of Ch. Bergmanor Euchre. The breeders of Euchre are Bergmanor Kennels (E. F. Hirschmans), and the sire of Euchre is Ch. Brentwald Copyright (a Ch. Brentwald Joshua W. son) ex Bergmanor Teaser. The Bergmanor Kennels have Dachshunds of all three coat varieties, and have been exhibiting Dachshunds since 1932.

Hainheim Kennels, Mr. and Mrs. George C. Spradling,

Wichita, Kansas, are also breeders of good wire-haired Dachshunds and have kennelled Ch. Starkrest's Nannette, who bred to Ch. Brentwald Destiny, produced Ch. Hainheim's Nancy, the beautiful wheaten wire-haired bitch that has done so much winning for her present owners, the Neville R. Stephens.

A new wire-haired Dachshund is owned by Fay-Dachs Kennels, Gene and Pat Nesbitt, Tracy, California. In offering to the wirehair breeders the stud services of their German import, Strolch vom Holzgarten, A. K. C. No. H-395968, whose sire is Lenz-Olympia (rauhhaar-rot) ex Bessi vom Holzgarten (rauhhaar-schwarzrot), Fay-Dachs Kennels' prime interest is to provide complete and true wirehair outbreeding to the American fancy. According to his detailed German pedigree and registration, Strolch vom Holzgarten is a product of true wirehair breeding. Practically all American wirehairs stem from Am. and Can. Ch. Brentwald Joshua W., and there is great need for a good, true, wirehair to provide for out-breeding. The youngsters of Strolch vom Holzgarten are just now appearing in the show rings, and are taking their share of the wins, whenever and wherever they are shown, confirming his worth. Gene and Pat Nesbitt are very enthusiastic about wire-haired Dachshunds, and have several excellent wire-haired youngsters that will be shown to their championships soon. Their first home-bred dog to win her championship is the black-and-tan wire-haired bitch, Ch. Fay-Dachs Mindora, who is a Strolch vom Holzgarten daughter ex Ch. Minton of Heying-Teckel (a smooth-coated bitch).

The Hollyhill Kennels, Wendy A. Riley, Minehead, Somerset, England, run a pack of Dachshunds as hunters of badgers, foxes, rabbits, otters, and squirrels. Hollyhill Kennels' stock is quite well represented in the United States, and they breed for courage, constitution, and conformation. They train their hunting Dachshunds on a "dragged skin," never on an artificial bait, and they never permit their Dachshunds to go hunting on their own. The dogs must be good tempered and get along well together. Also, they must possess courage and drive.

Mrs. David B. Doggett, Dachscroft Kennels, Lake Geneva, Wisconsin, not only has wire-haired Dachshunds from leading breeders in the United States, but also has some very good imported dogs, most of which are from Hollyhill Kennels. Mrs. Doggett has imported six English wirehairs (four bitches and two dogs), including Hollyhill Silvershell (in whelp to Hollyhill Petrouka, an outstanding English wirehair), who, approximately a month later, whelped a litter of five puppies. Ch. Hollyhill Piper-Piper, who was bred to Hollyhill Gisella, produced a litter of two at Dachscroft. Dachscroft Kennels formerly owned also the excellent English wire-haired bloodlines bitch, Dachscroft Hapence, which was sold to the Neville R. Stephens.

Other English wire-haired imported Dachshunds have been sent to J. A. R. Irving, Vancouver, and include Ch. Georg of Wytchend, a top show winner, and a promising young bitch from the Wytchend Kennels of Major T. Ellis-Hughes. Thomas Ladd, New York, acquired Gretchen of Wytchend, sired by Mercury of Seton ex Gretl of Wytchend.

Mr. and Mrs. F. J. Doody, Dayton, Ohio, have a German imported wire-haired bitch, Wonne von Kniephof, who recently whelped a litter of two, a dog and a bitch, sired by Ch. York W. of Murlake, whose owner is Mrs. Merton Farlow, Indianapolis.

The Laurence E. Speces, Canton, Ohio, recently imported two wire-haired Dachshunds from Germany, a dog and a bitch, sired by the German stud, Arras v. d. Ranhen Bergen.

Other wire-haired imports include the German salt-and-pepper bitch, Toni (Baucke) and her litter of three dogs and one bitch, sired by Sieggold's Boris, son of the famous Sieger Pitt v. Fogler, owned by Mrs. Gertrude Baumgartner, Portland, Oregon. This litter is registered with the German Teckel Club of Duisburg, and was bred in the excellent traditions of the formerly well-known East German Rauhhaar Teckel Kennel, von Frange.

Martin Shallenberger, Ashbourne, Harrods Creek, Kentucky, has an imported wirehair, Klausner v. Mentor Line, which he advertised extensively.

Mrs. Maude Daniels Smith formerly had her wirehair, Ch. Ergo vom Knull of Dachshafen, kennelled at her Dachshafen Kennels, but I have no recent information on this dog. Mrs. Smith's interest in wirehairs has been re-kindled with her wire-haired bitch, Dearest v. Dachshafen, sired by Prejudice of Edgemere ex Menschenfreund's Dear, and whelped November 4, 1951.

Another wire-haired Dachshund exhibitor of note is Stanley Todd, Reading, Pennsylvania, whose Ch. Thomanel's Lola is the first wire-haired Dachshund to win a Westminster Kennel Club Hound Group (1952), and she took Best Wire-haired at the Dachshund Club of America Specialty Show, Rye, New York, in 1951. Mr. Todd's Eng. and Am. Ch. Wylde Surmise has taken Best of Variety twice at the large Devon, Pennsylvania, Specialty Shows, and is also a Challenge Certificate winner at the Crufts, England, Show. Her wins also include in 1953, Best of Variety at Westminster, Harbor Cities, and International (Chicago) Shows. Other wirehairs include Mr. Todd's Ch. Grunwald Melody, an English import whose sire is Eagle of Dunkurque, owned by Mrs. J. Littmoden, England. Still another English import is Ch. Patiola of Aissela. In former years, another top wire-haired dog at this kennel was Ch. Prejudice of Edgemere, a magnificent dog, purchased from Charlotte Sibley, Forever Kennels, San Francisco, who affectionately called the dog "Dice."

Bred by Miss Emilie S. Bromley, Philadelphia, Ch. Prejudice of Edgemere won the George G. Frelinghuysen, Jr., Challenge Trophy for wire-haired Dachshunds at Westminster three times, and he also took Best Wirehair at Westminster during his show career.

An outstanding established breeder of wire-haired Dachshunds is Miss Emilie S. Bromley, Edgemere Kennels, Philadelphia. In addition to Ch. Prejudice of Edgemere, exceptional dogs from her kennels include Ch. Duplicate of Edgemere, Second Edition of Edgemere, and many others. She owns two imported dogs, Ch. Ajax of Ouborough of Edgemere and Greygates Prelude of Edgemere. The latter is imported from Ireland's Greygates Kennels.

The John Chaffes, Waldbach Kennels, Malvern, Pennsylvania, who offer the sterling silver challenge bowl in memory of their Ch. Sonia v. Hildesheim, are pillars in the

313

breeding, showing, and exhibiting of wire-haired Dachshunds. Among the many top wirehairs found at this kennel
are Ch. Sonia v. Waldbach, Magda v. Waldbach, and Swartz
v. Waldbach.

Teckelow Kennels are owned by Mrs. Merton Farlow,
Indianapolis, and her wire-haired Dachshund, Ch. York of
Murlake, a son of Ch. Brentwald Joshua W. ex Sascha v.
Murlake, heads her wire-haired stock. Another top dog
here is Am. and Can. Ch. Youvonne W. Murlake, sired by
Ch. Brentwald Joshua W. and bred by W. R. Ake. This dog
completed her championship at the age of seventeen months.
Ch. Teckelow's Penny, sired by Ch. Brentwald Destiny ex
Ch. Youvonne W. Murlake, is another excellent wirehair
here. A litter sister of Ch. Youvonne W. Murlake is Ch.
Yo-Ellen W. Murlake, currently owned by Mr. and Mrs.
Walter R. Tobler, New Jersey, who made her championship
under the age of nineteen months. Teckelow's Hans II is
another top wirehair at this kennel, which is contributing
so much to the popularity and breeding of good Dachshunds
of this coat variety.

More and more breeders are becoming interested in the
wire-haired Dachshund, adding this coat variety to their
kennels. Exhibits at the shows are increasing, and the
public, seeing these wiry little clowns in the show rings, is
becoming more and more conscious of the attributes of
this variety.

☆　☆　☆　☆

I gratefully acknowledge the co-operation and courtesy
of the many breeders and kennels who have so kindly supplied material and photographs used in this chapter.

MILDRED L. HILL.

314

CH. TUBAC'S CHRISTOPH
Sire: Ch. Brentwald Joshua W.   Dam: Brentwald Toni
Owner: Mrs. Neville R. Stephens, Tubac, Arizona

CH. THE WITCH'S BRAT
Sire: Am. and Can. Ch. Brentwald Joshua W.   Dam: Zipper of Badger Hill
Owners: Raymond S. Hill, Phoenix, Arizona, and Anne E. Appelgate,
Los Angeles, California

CH. RUMPUS RIDGE MERRY NICHOLI
Sire: Sambo v. Bergman   Dam: Ch. Bucknam's Merry Jane
Owner: Micaelia F. Randolph, San Francisco, California

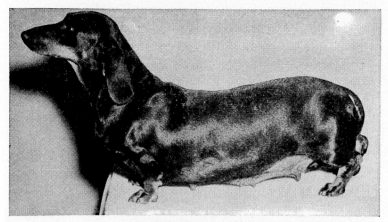

CH. HARBORVALE CIRCE
Sire: Ch. Superman v. Marienlust   Dam: Dhyrral v. Dachsholme
Owner: Eva Sparling, Moweaqua, Illinois

316

List of Champions

For each dog the following data are given in order: registered name, registration number, owner at time of completion of championship, and breeder.

1910
Felman of Dalmore, 111130____H. A. Dalrymple_____Dalmore Kennels
Hinda of Dalmore, 107639_____A. B. Wright_____H. A. Dalmore
Lady of Pumpernickel, 117491__Mrs. D. Hutchinson_____B. Hunt
Largo, (not reg.)_____Mrs. W. W. Burnett_____
Plum West End, 124004_____Mrs. C. Davies Tainter_____George Semler
The Doctor, 114347_____Mrs. P. M. Wand_____G. Muss-Arnolt
Windholme's Wallace, 134544___Karl Bjurman_____W. Stuber
Windholme's Zefora, 138134____Karl Bjurman _____W. Stuber

1911
Helga M., 150597_____Karl Bjurman_____Dr. C. Motschenbacher
Liesel, 140699_____Miss Gertrude Locke_____Dr. Wendland
Seppel v. Lichtenstein West
   End, 108549_____Cox and Wilson_____Geo. G. Rummel
Tante West End, 103091_____L. H. Graeber_____Geo. Semler
The Princess, 128481_____Mrs. E. A. McClure_____J. Bergman

1912
Antje v. Lichtenstein, 160290___Mrs. A. Hungerford_____M. Widman
Boni v. Lichtenstein West End,
   108546_____Mrs. A. Hungerford_____Geo. Semler
Drickes, 130563_____Mrs. A. Hungerford_____K. Asbeck

1913
Erna, 159079_____Mrs. A. Hungerford_____Geo. Semler
Fritz Forst, 148186_____John Sinnott_____C. O. Folkens
Rosette II West End, 146638___Mrs. A. Hungerford_____G. Semler
Seppel vom Harz, 158605_____Mrs. E. A. McClure_____Not Recorded

1914
Bitte South Shore, 144162_____Mrs. A. Hungerford_____Mrs. A. Hungerford
Boni South Shore, 159365_____Mrs. A. Hungerford_____H. T. Peters
El Sur Deutschland, 164203____El Sur Kennels_____A. J. Molera
El Sur Young Lady, 164206____El Sur Kennels_____A. J. Molera
Felix v. Lichtenstein, 156457___Mrs. A. Hungerford_____M. Widmann

317

1914 (cont'd)

Grand Lady, 158918_____A. J. Molera_____El Sur Kennels
Johann v. Niederlang, 159467__John Sinnott_____H. Jessen
Jupla South Shore, 159370_____Mrs. A. Hungerford_____Mrs. A. Hungerford
Lulu Frankonia Jaegerslust,
   152660_____Rosemont Kennels_____Fr. Klein
Myra South Shore, 159078_____Mrs. A. Hungerford_____Geo. Semler
Otto v. Blacktoft, 154567_____Blacktoft Kennels_____H. S. Reichenheim
Rosa v. Niederlang, 159469_____H. Jessen_____H. Jessen
Voewood Frieda, 145805_____Mrs. A. Rubino_____Mrs. C. Davies Tainter

1915

Fritzi S., 159091 _____A. J. Schulte_____Norwood Kennels
Kamerad South Shore, 176314___Mrs. A. Hungerford_____Mrs. A. Hungerford
Nonne South Shore, 168615_____Mrs. A. Hungerford_____Mrs. A. Hungerford
Schlupferle v. Esslingen, 174045_G. E. Heise_____Carl Reinhold
Teckelheim Tenor, 185196_____Mrs. F. D. Erhardt_____Mrs. F. D. Erdhardt
Tenor v. d. Haide, 167955_____Dr. Herbert Sanborn_____Heinrich Saelzer
Voewood Erda v. Boris, 191254_Mrs. C. D. Tainter_____Mrs. M. Fuchs

1916

Blacktoft Topsi, 166685_____Mrs. F. D. Erhardt_____Mrs. C. H. Lester
El Sur Diana, 204438_____Miss E. A. Flowers_____El Sur Kennels
El Sur Tannhauser, 204437_____El Sur Kennels_____El Sur Kennels
Erna v. d. Haide, 184771_____Mrs. F. D. Erhardt_____H. Salzer
Raufbold Jaegerslust, 161445___M. B. Fitzpatrick_____Fr. Wendland
Teckelheim Traum, 185197 _____Mrs. F. D. Erhardt_____Mrs. F. D. Erhardt
Verbena, 187595_____Mrs. X. R. Meyer_____Lord Wrottesby

1917

Irpa vom Isartal, 197893_____D. R. Smith_____M. Bransford

1920

Lulu K., 241839_____J. M. Tienken_____Frank Koenig

1921

Nona v. Boris, 229280_____John Sinnott_____Mrs. Mary Fuchs

1922

Freki v. Isartal, 209277_____Dr. Herbert Sanborn_____Mrs. E. R. Newhauser
Rosemont Kamerad II v. Fern
   Felsen, 304359_____Rosemont Kennels_____Fern Rock Kennels
Rosy T., 296225_____J. Sinnott_____John M. Tienken

1923

Blue Blood Erika, II, 272256_____Blue Blood Kennels_____Blue Blood Kennels

1924

Hansel v. Boris, 278738_____Mrs. Marie Fuchs_____Mrs. Marie Fuchs
Korb's Gretchen, 396183_____Louis F. Korb_____Mrs. Marie Jamal

1925

Aladar v. Boris, 389721_____Grayce Greenburg_____Martin Grimm
Rottraut v. Boris, 307061_____Grayce and Mike Greenburg___Mrs. Marie Fuchs

1926

Baxter's Patz, 462184_____J. M. and R. T. Campbell_____K. S. Connell
Pauline vom Jaegerhaus, 444405_Jaegerhaus Kennels_____Harriet McC. Preede

1927

Gretchen v. Moruth, 712861_____J. M. and R. T. Campbell_____J. M. Campbell
Katrina v. Moruth, 553455_____J. M. and Ruth T. Campbell___J. M. Campbell
Teckelheim Kasperl of
   Voewood, 449054_____Mrs. C. D. Tainter_____Mrs. F. D. Erhardt

1928

Yolanda v. Boris, 398717_____Astarte Kennels_____Mrs. Marie Fuchs

1929

Dottie, 693316_____Mr. and Mrs. John F. Rohde __Nicholas Hansen
Elfe v. Sollingerwald, 599590___Mrs. Gussie Held _____Gussie Held
Ingo v. Luitpoldsheim, 695146__George H. Earle, IV_____E. Senssenbrenner
Kensal Call Boy, 679081_____M. and G. Greenburg_____E. W. Ricks
Rex v. Sollinge, 702341_____Mrs. Gussie Held_____Mrs. Gussie Held

1930

Fenia of Allendale, 305783_____Anthony G. Alt_____Allendale Farm Kennels
Fritz v. Nielsen, 355927_____Anthony G. Alt_____Albert Nielsen
Gretchen Kasperl, 751726 _____Charles F. Speidell, Jr._____Chas. F. Speidell, Jr.
Linda v. Boris, 752515_____Mrs. Peter King_____Chas. F. Speidell, Jr.
Racker v. Luitpoldsheim, 742415_Mrs. D. K. Jay_____Emil Senssenbrenner
Redrust of Greenburg, 735967__Mike and Grayce Greenburg____Grayce and Mike Greenburg
Rhoda Jagerlust, 736457_____Mrs. Peter King_____Mrs. Nora Perkins
Wussa Dassel v. Greenburg,
    732309_____James Walker Trullinger_____Grayce and Mike Greenburg
Wuza v. Greenburg, 703739_____Jessie I. Bucknam_____Grayce Greenburg

1931

Aladar Again of Greenburg,
    706293_____ Mike and Grayce Greenburg____Grayce Greenburg
Bolventor of Greenburg, 730208_William B. Cornish_____Grayce Greenburg
Dack'l II, 763775_____Edmund B. and M. Katie Lang_M. Katie Lang
Dora of Taviston, 788893_____Emefar Kennels_____C. E. Rattee
Fritzi v. Buxtehude, 598643____John F. Rohde_____John F. Rohde
Heddy of Voewood, 781680____Anton Kappelmeir_____Anton Kappelmeir
Kensal Vincel of Greenburg,
    730590_____Jessie I. Bucknam_____Mike and Grayce Greenburg
Krabbe Assmannsheim, 790143_Hanns P. Kniepkamp_____Dr. and Mrs. E. Assmann
Ratzmann-Muck of Voewood,
    694164_____Mrs. C. Davies Tainter_____Mr. Tackmann
Rudy v. Wittelbach, 781681____Anton Kappelmeir_____Anton Kappelmeir
Susie v. Wittelbach, 776096____Anton Kappelmeir_____Mrs. H. Herrmann

1932

Astarte Nino v. Boris, 794611__Mrs. David C. Dodge_____Astarte Kennels
Edel v. Wittelbach, 767367_____Anton Kappelmeir_____Mrs. C. Davies Tainter
Ego Assmannsheim of
    Voewood, 802932_____Mrs. C. Davies Tainter_____Dr. E. Assmann
Emefar Skoal, 785969_____Emefar Kennels_____Ivar Karlson
Graf v. Luitpoldsheim, 770737__Belle Terre Kennels_____William Horvay
Gretel of Benfield of Emefar,
    810997 _____Emefar Kennels_____Countess of Erroll
Heini Flottenberg, 846421_____Ellenbert Farm _____G. F. Muller
Hilde of Greenburg, 763502_____Alois F. Strehle_____Millie Vogel
Ida M., 791028_____Mr. and Mrs. Peter King_____Anton Kappelmeir
Prinz Call Boy v. Parks, 757573_Mike and Grayce Greenburg___Mrs. E. B. Parks
Voewood Kasperl, 783535_____Mrs. C. Davies Tainter_____Mrs. C. Davies Tainter

1933

Berta v. Bucknam, 843917_____Jessie I. Bucknam_____Jessie I. Bucknam
Blackey Walck, 810605_____Walck Kennels_____Julius T. Walck
Christine Assmannsheim,
    886176_____Ellenbert Farm_____Dr. and Mrs. Erich Assmann
Dago v. Westhof, 825394_____D. Schaefer_____Mrs. J. Heubach
Liesel v. Moruth, 717763_____J. M. Campbell_____J. M. Campbell
Elfe v. Luitpoldsheim, 742414__George H. Earle, IV_____Emil Sensenbrenner
Elsa Cinders, 879614_____James Walker Trullinger_____James Walker Trullinger

1933 (cont'd)

Faraway Stahlhaus Bowser,
  856797 _____G. F. Steele_____Miss Jean Walker
Gretchen of Little Farm, 865602_Mrs. David C. Dodge_____Mrs. Catherine Cannon
Heka Flottenberg, 871972_____Ellenbert Farm_____G. F. Muller
Held v. Erlbachtal, 856232_____Mrs. Gussie Held_____Franz Weidemann
Hirschmann's Bergman, 839886_Edward F. Hirschman_____Mrs. Martha Marchetti
Jacob of Postlip, 803439_____Babel Kennels_____Mrs. D. Mitchell
Nazi v. Fels, 756435_____Felice Gunther_____A. Stephan
Nazi v. Fels' Liesel, 868927____M. Ethel Ash_____Max Gellert
Olla v. d. Erkaburg, 781265_____Mary E. Fryling_____Max Muller
Stecher's Adam v. d. Aal,
  880246_____S. A. Stecher_____S. A. Stecher
Vodegel's Raecher, 888944_____Mrs. Maude Daniels Smith_____Mrs. Frida Vodegel
Zeb of White Gate, 821026_____Mary E. Fryling_____Mary E. Fryling

1934

Adda-Graues Kloster, 994709____Mrs. Ruth J. Dodge_____Kurt Bernhard
Amalia Schneid, 959407_____Mrs. E. Russell Duggan_____Mrs. E. Russell Duggan
Apollo of Emefar, 830111_____Emefar Kennels_____Emefar Kennels
Arno v. Luitpoldsheim, 925890__Victor Moench_____Emil Sensenbrenner
Axel v. d. Aal, 880245_____E. Horner and S. A. Stecher_____S. A. Stecher
Boris Call Boy v. Bucknam,
  802055_____A. J. Schoendorf_____Jessie I. Bucknam
Bums v. Sonnenhang, 809525_____S. A. Stecher_____Franz Weiner
Burschle v. d. Aal, 953934_____Aal Kennels_____S. A. Stecher
Cid's Teufel, 914444_____Abigail S. Vare_____H. H. Sachers
Cid v. Werderhavelstrand,
  831578 _____H. H. Sachers_____Mrs. Margarete Erb
Danni-Scheid, 906441_____Mrs. Richard C. Bondy, Jr._____Edouard Pohlmey
Eroica Ditmarsia, 871162_____Babel Kennels _____Theodor Wittmaack
Esel Horst, 920984_____Mr. and Mrs. Frank Morgan___Warren R. Gibbs
Felix v. Wittelbach, 932200_____Mrs. Anton Kappelmeir_____Mrs. Anton Kappelmeir
Feri Flottenberg, 893657_____Ellenbert Farm_____G. F. Muller
Figaro Schneid, 959406_____Mrs. E. Russell Duggan_____Mrs. E. Russell Duggan
Flora v. Biebrich, 920524_____Ellenbert Farm_____Adam Land
Fricka aus der Neidhohle,
  948785_____Ellenbert Farm _____Axel Straube
Fritz-Loui II of Greenburg,
  789250_____John G. Levison_____Mrs. E. B. Park
Fuerst v. Donnersmark, 899702__LaFayette Lentz_____M. K. Salen
Gretel v. Monchbruch, 885038___Grayce Greenburg_____Ernsts Frohlich
Her Grace of Greenburg, 804122_Mike and Grayce Greenburg___Glenn E. Martin
Madchen, 798215_____Mrs. Maude Daniels Smith_____Anton Kappelmeir
Sally-Forth of Greenburg,
  953315_____Grayce Greenburg_____Grayce Greenburg
Sascha v. Hildesheim, 929021___Mrs. L. C. Du Bois_____Anton Kappelmeir
Schalk v. Werderhavelstrand,
  901637_____Mrs. H. D. Sims_____Margarete Erb
Sports-Sascha, 751227_____M. Katie Lang_____Frau Rittmeister v. Sanstrom
Stella v. Wittelbach, 902530____Mrs. Maude Daniels Smith_____Anton Kappelmeir
Swartpick Schneid, 856231_____Mrs. Russell Duggan_____Edouard Pohlmey
Teo v. Lindenbuhl of Ren Lak,
  930581_____Mrs. Joseph J. O'Donohue, III_Simon Barthel
Trudie of Greenburg, 752816___Mr. and Mrs. George Schroth__Grayce Greenburg
Voewood H'sin, 818228_____Mr. and Mrs. C. W. Greenough_Mrs. C. Davies Tainter
Waldiff Ellenbert, 931683_____Ellenbert Farm_____Ellenbert Farm
Waldmann v. Sollingbrook,
  874381_____Mrs. H. D. Sims_____Ludwig E. Baumann
Yvonne v. Werderhavelstrand,
  901636 _____Mrs. H. D. Sims_____Margarete Erb

1935

Acta of White Gate, 957825____Mary E. Fryling_____Mary E. Fryling
Ash's Waldman Schneid, 964961_Mrs. Tom E. Ash_____Mrs. E. Russell Duggan
Atilla v. d. Howitt, 954995_____Mr. and Mrs. P. A. B. Widener__Mrs. P. P. Rikovsky
Barli-Assmannsheim, 933353____Falcon Heights Kennels_____Dr. and Mrs. Erich Assmann
Bartonbury Vex, 912368_____Miss Pam Johnston_____Mrs. V. Rycroft
Bona of Little Farm, 969014____Mrs. David C. Dodge_____Mrs. David C. Dodge
Christabel Ellenbert, 964299____Ellenbert Farm_____Ellenbert Farm
Cid's Cinnamon v. Dachshafen,
    972105_____Mrs. Maude Daniels Smith_____Mrs. C. Davies Tainter
Emefar Sox Double, 939644_____Mrs. Chas. W. Rosenbaum, Jr._D. T. Carlisle
Ergo v. Knull of Dachshafen,
    A-9909 _____Mrs. Maude Daniels Smith_____Carl Horle
Evchen v. d. Aal, 913479_____Mrs. L. C. DuBois_____S. A. Stecher
Fells v. Falkenturm, 992779____Mrs. George Ludford Harvey___Mrs. L. L. Romine
Feri v. Belle Terre, 974610_____Miss Dorothea Mathes_____William Horvay
Frau Aggie of Little Farm,
    895460_____Mrs. David C. Dodge_____Mrs. David C. Dodge
Fritz Munchausen, 965559_____Charles Boettcher, II_____Charles Boettcher, II
Haschi-Flottenberg, 996239_____Ellenbert Farm_____G. F. Mueller
Hestia Ellenbert, 964304_____Ellenbert Farm_____Ellenbert Farm
Hexe v. Knype, 776658_____Redledge Kennels_____Hanns P. Kniepkamp
Hilda of White Gate, 913151____Mary E. Fryling_____Mary E. Fryling
Liebermann of Greenburg,   Mr. and Mrs. Bertram
    951910_____   Millhauser _____Mrs. Grayce Greenburg
Lot v. Falltor, 977750_____Mrs. Tristan C. Colket_____Heinrich Stroh
Machle's Garbo, 880049_____Mrs. Willard F. Machle_____Mrs. William F. Ascher
Maerchen v. Dachshafen, 959447_Mrs. Maude Daniels Smith____Mrs. Annette S. Stewart
Mia v. d. Schroth, 947345_____Valentine V. Milde_____Mr. and Mrs. Geo. Schroth
Midge v. Wittelbach, 936644____Mr. and Mrs. Wm. E. Schmidt_Anton Kappelmeir
Mona of Sycamore, A-25408___Mrs. L. L. White_____Mrs. John R. Meeker
Mops of Featherhill, 964293____Mrs. William H. Coleman_____Mr. and Mrs. C. R. Holmes
Moritz v. Wittelbach, 936642___Mrs. Anton Kappelmeir_____Mrs. Anton Kappelmeir
Oto v. Bucknam, 947084_____Mrs. Jessie I. Bucknam_____Mrs. Jessie I. Bucknam
Otto v. Lichtenstein, 827848____Hulburd Johnston_____Albert Nielsen
Parchman's Komerad, 983644__William H. Parchman_____Wm. H. Parchman
Quilp, 896217_____Mrs. Peter King_____Charles F. Speidell, Jr.
Ren-Lak Cilly, 841953_____Mrs. C. Davies Tainter and
                                Mrs. J. J. O'Donohue, III____Mrs. Jos. O'Donohue, III
Roti v. Lichtenstein, 925011____Hulburd Johnston_____Hulburd Johnston
Ruth v. Rosentor, 921221_____Mrs. C. O'D. Macpherson_____Richard Knopp
Saschas Mentor, 815666_____M. Katie Lang_____Edmund B. and M. Katie Lang
Schwarz v. Hildesheim, 933887__Mrs. L. C. Du Bois_____Mrs. L. C. Du Bois
Sports Buster, 955001_____Mrs. L. C. Du Bois_____Mrs. Veroni Sandstrom
Sporty's Madele, 958339_____John M. Maris_____John M. Maris
Susi v. Rodelstein, 909422_____Victor Moench _____Leo Kohler
Tess of Tynewydd, A-8627_____George G. Frelinghuysen, Jr._Miss F. T. Watts
The Princess of Greenburg,
    862455_____Mrs. L. R. Goetsch_____Laura Wallace
Tristan v. Sollinge, 954501_____Mrs. Gussie Held_____Mrs. Gussie Held
Waldines Letzter Waldmann
    v. d. Windburg, 949867_____Mrs. Lawrence Zimmerman_____Carl Thieme
Widbrook Zieta, 969472_____Black Forest Kennels_____Mrs. A. K. Hedley-Peek
Zilly v. Leitschenstein, 947582_Windyriver Kennels_____Otto Markart

1936

Achat v. Werderhavelstrand,
    A-47136 _____Victor Moench_____Margarete Erb
Adah of Babel, 946625_____Babel Kennels_____Babel Kennels

1936 (cont'd)

Allsworth Gerda v. Sollinge,
926487 _____ _____ Mrs. Fred Hicks _____ Mrs. Gussie Held
Apollo of Dunkerque, A-8626 ____ George G. Frelinghuysen, Jr. ___ Charles L. Lambe
Asbecks-Hinnerk, 958710 _____ Mr. and Mrs. George Schroth ___ Karl Asbeck
Asbecks-Sabine, A-49082 _____ Mrs. Tristan C. Colket _____ Karl Asbeck
Beta v. Bergwald, 960126 _____ Miss Pam Johnson _____ Fritz Buchhard
Blatz of Little Farm, 969017 ___ Mrs. David C. Dodge _____ Mrs. David C. Dodge
Cheerio of Emefar, A-6499 ____ Emefar Kennels _____ Emefar Kennels
Christopher Ellenbert, A-308 ___ Mrs. Albert Loest _____ Ellenbert Farm
Cid's Ginger v. Dachshafen,
972106 _____ _____ Walter T. Stern _____ Mrs. C. Davies Tainter
Cid's Gretel of Lakelands,
939798 _____ Mrs. Carroll G. Stewart, Jr. _____ H. H. Sachers
Cid's Stein Song, 977231 _____ Edith M. Groves _____ J. Russell Smith
Cynara of Little Farm, 998923 __ Mrs. F. E. De Vinay _____ Mrs. David C. Dodge
DeLou's Schalk II, A-49899 ____ Mrs. H. D. Sims _____ Mrs. H. D. Sims
DeLou's Rea, A-70693 _____ Mrs. H. D. Sims _____ Mrs. H. D. Sims
Diana v. Kniepkampsheim,
963691 _____ Mrs. Laurence A. Horswell ____ Hanns P. Kniepkamp
Fax v. Teckelhof, A-96838 _____ Llieno Kennels _____ Mrs. Lawrence Zimmerman
Feri Ellenbert, 964302 _____ Ellenbert Farm _____ Ellenbert Farm
Franklin of Hohenburg, 941193 _ Mr. and Mrs. David L. Wall ____ Mr. and Mrs. David L. Wall
Greenoway H'sin Greta, A-15345 _ Mr. and Mrs. C. W. Greenough _ Mr. and Mrs. C. W. Greenough
Gretchell v. d. Schroth, 977573 _ Mr. and Mrs. Harold L. Mack,
                              Jr. _____ Grayce Greenburg
Hanka-Flottenberg, 916632 _____ Ellenbert Farm _____ G. F. Muller
Hans v. Ardolin, 893669 _____ Dr. Louis A. Cornet _____ Stuart Winch
Hansel v. Lindenbuhl, A-24704 _ Dr. E. H. Marquardt _____ Simon Barthel
Hansel v. d. Schroth, 977572 ___ Mr. and Mrs. Harold L. Mack,
                              Jr. _____ Grayce Greenburg
Hazel of Sunstorm, A-138104 ___ G. G. Frelinghuysen, Jr. _____ Mrs. T. H. Gaspari
Hederl v. Holzgarten, 995298 ___ Mrs. Albert J. Beveridge _____ Karl Botz
Inge, v. d. Aal, 910610 _____ Aal Kennels _____ Mr. and Mrs. Emil Hempel
Kobold v. Fuchsenstein, A-65550 _ Mr. and Mrs. Howard Eric ____ August Kessler
Liesel v. Fels-Berg, A-23304 ___ Mrs. Maude Daniels Smith ____ Mrs. M. Ethel Ash
Long Eagle of Sycamore,
A-25409 _____ _____ Mrs. L. L. White _____ Mrs. L. L. White
Lotte v. Falkenturm, A-20135 __ Willoughby Kennels _____ Gussie Held
Maritza v. Wittelbach, 932201 __ Mrs. C. B. Ward _____ Anton Kappelmeir
Maxl v. Dachshafen, 944801 ____ Mrs. Maude Daniels Smith ____ Mrs. L. C. Du Bois
Natchen v. Hildesheim, A-25365 _ Mrs. L. C. Du Bois _____ Mrs. L. C. Du Bois
Pamheim Pumpkin, 880180 ____ Miss Pam Johnston _____ Miss Pam Johnston
Penny Wayston, 977457 _____ Hulburd Johnston _____ John H. Schlomer
Peter Assmannsheim, 896481 ___ Mrs. Maude Daniels Smith ____ Erich Assmann
Prince of Littleton, 997146 ____ Mr. and Mrs. Howard Eric ____ Mrs. F. J. Parsons
Raecher's Dunder v. Erlenheim,
A-3238 _____ Mrs. Earline G. Clegg _____ John F. Clegg
Raecher's Rogue Song, A-111332 _ Edith M. Groves _____ Edith M. Groves
Raecher's Stolz, 985685 _____ Round Hill Kennels _____ Mrs. Maude Daniels Smith
Sari v. Belle Terre, 975959 _____ William Horvay _____ William Horvay
Saschas Bismarck, 895512 _____ Teufelseck Kennels _____ Edmund B. and M. Katie Lang
Schoendorf's Red Rogue, 971836 _ Albert J. Schoendorf _____ Grayce Greenburg
Scotsward Gretchen, A-17554 ___ Mrs. C. B. Ward _____ Mrs. Charles B. Ward
Suwana Waldmeister, 956961 __ Mr. and Mrs. Wm. H. Coleman _ W. E. McMunn
Tenchen of Windyriver, A-66784 Windyriver Kennels _____ Mrs. Fred Hicks
Veroni v. Hildesheim, A-25367 __ Mrs. Maude Daniels Smith _____ Mrs. L. C. Du Bois
Veto v. Teufelsstern, A-48431 __ Mr. and Mrs. Howard Eric ____ Albert Brill
Voewood's Cid's Schalk, 972107 _ Mrs. C. Davies Tainter _____ Mrs. C. Davies Tainter
Vroni v. Rosenbaum, A-52804 __ Mrs. Wallace Pflueger _____ Wilhelm Bellenber

1936 (cont'd)

Yvonne v. Plater Schulhaus,
    A-7460 _____Blue Key Kennels_____Mrs. Melanie Warnecke

1937

Alma v. d. Dychland, A-41375__Herman Cox, Jr._____Idlewood Kennels
Anna v. d. Adlerstein, A-71847_Mrs. Jerome Landfield_____Miss U. Still
Anny Rinkton, 932422_____Victor Moench_____Victor Moench
Antonia of Little Farm,
    A-126044 _____Mrs. David C. Dodge_____Mr. and Mrs. J. Mehrer
Argo v. Lindenbuhl, A-142284__Mrs. Lynde Selden_____Simon Barthel
Benji v. Hildesheim, A-87161__Mrs. Richard V. Pell_____Mrs. A. H. Gilkison
Bergman der Zweite of G.,
    A-29892 _____Mr. and Mrs. Ed. F. Hirschman_Grayce Greenburg
Berta of Little Farm, 969012___Mr. and Mrs. R. W. Pringle_____Mrs. David C. Dodge
Biene of Sycamore, A-55233____Mrs. L. L. White_____Mrs. L. L. White
Burschle of Lakelands, 937852__Mrs. Alfred N. Beadleston_____H. H. Sachers
Cara of Fair Acres, A-70496____Mr. and Mrs. Sidney A. Moss__Mr. and Mrs. Wm. H. Coleman
Cilli V. Zinnowitz, A-92043_____Mrs. Ruth J. Dodge_____K. W. Thaden
David of Tynewydd A-8628_____Sunstorm Kennels _____S. Foxwell
Dinkelspiel of Little Farm,
    A-10147 _____Mrs. David C. Dodge_____Mrs. David C. Dodge
Edgebrook Schatzie v.
    Bucknam, 949984_____Mrs. Jerome Landfield_____Mrs. Jessie I. Bucknam
Eric-Falcon Heights
    O'Voewood, 907827 _____Maude Daniels Smith_____Falko W. Schilling
Eric v. Stahlhaus, A-67706_____Maude Daniels Smith_____George F. Steele
Etzel v. Plater Schulhaus,
    A-147734 _____Blue Key Kennels_____Mrs. Melanie Warnecke
Fanni v. Werderhavelstrand,
    A-137857 _____Pommel Rock Kennels_____Margarete Erb
Forseti v. Isartal, A-13046_____Mrs. H. D. Sims_____Dr. Herbert C. Sanborn
Frankie of Riverbank, A-141639_Mr. and Mrs. Howard Eric_____Mr. and Mrs. Howard Eric
Fricka Ellenbert, A-6953_____Mrs. Russell Openshaw_____Ellenbert Farm
Gundel v. Elfentann, A-50646__Mrs. Mary Bary and
                                Saddlerock Kennels_____Wilhelm Matthes
Halloh v. Muchtsborn, 184110___Joan Blair _____Kathe Westhoff
Heidi-Flottenberg, A-110956____Ellenbert Farm_____G. F. Mueller
Heimo-Flottenberg, A-110957___Ellenbert Farm_____G. F. Mueller
Helmi-Flottenberg, A-147144. ___Willoughby Kennels_____G. F. Mueller
Herman Rinkton, A-96033_____Richard S. Heller_____Victor Moench
Herzi-Flottenberg, A-176849____Ellenbert Farm_____G. F. Mueller
Hugo v. Lindenwood, A-162006_Dr. E. H. Marquardt_____Dr. E. H. Marquardt
Jacobsen's Rock v. Bremen,
    991369 _____Mrs. Julius F. Jacobsen_____Mrs. Lydia M. Wittrock
Kissel v. Fels-Berg, A-23303_____Maude Daniels Smith_____Mrs. M. Ethel Ash
Koboldina v. Dachshafen,
    A-154128 _____Maude Daniels Smith_____Maude Daniels Smith
Kurt v. Stahlhaus, A-67705_____Mrs. Geo. Schroth and
                                Melvin F. Rosenbaum_____George F. Steele
Lady Sandra v. Peyton, 983787_Mr. and Mrs. R. W. Peyton_____Grayce Greenburg
Liebchen v. Fleinfeld, A-57402_Mr. and Mrs. Everett E.
                                Littlefield_____Mrs. Fred Hicks
Loni v. Fuchsenstein, A-65549__Mr. and Mrs. Howard Eric_____August Kessler
Lore v. d. Buchhorst, A-42185__John Amann_____John Amann
Maenne v. Wulff Kunult,
    A-10956 _____Mrs. Marilla Wood Holland_____Mrs. M. Ethel Ash
Maudie of Riverbank, A-146115_Mr. and Mrs. Howard Eric_____Mrs. Maude Daniels Smith
Midge v. Edelhof, A-97522_____Mr. and Mrs. W. E. Schmidt__Mr. and Mrs. W. E. Schmidt
Mops of Fair Acres, A-110459__Mr. and Mrs. Wm. H. Coleman_Mr. and Mrs. Wm. H. Coleman

1937 (cont'd)

Munn's Walkure of Fair
Acres, A-30360_____W. Earl McMunn_____Mrs. Wm. H. Coleman
Pia v. Plater Schulhaus, 957576__Mrs. Justine Cellarius_____Mrs. Melanie Warnecke
Piccolo aus der Neidhohle,
A-201090 _____Maude Daniels Smith_____Axel Straube
Redledge Alexander, A-8975____Alverna Stark _____Redledge Kennels
Senta v. Luitpoldsheim, A-27967_Emma Flecher_____Emil Sensenbrenner
Sophie v. Weichfeldstrand,
A-27595 _____Edith M. Groves_____John H. Schlomer
Sports Ruffian of Lakelands,
A-41155 _____H. H. Sachers_____Hans H. Sachers
Teckelheim Friedo, A-743_____Grayce Greenburg_____Clifford M. Adam
Vici v. Seeblick, 973932_____Mr. and Mrs. Bert Ramsey____Harold R. Fredericks
Victoria v. Ascherhof, A-97214_Mrs. W. F. Ascher_____Mrs. William F. Ascher
Vincel's Knabe v. Bucknam,
A-57531 _____Jessie I. Bucknam_____Mrs. Jessie I. Bucknam
Vips v. Schwarenberg, A-172603_C. Hyland Jones_____Emil Schray
Waldfried v. Walder, A-71848__Mrs. James Park Bradley_____Mrs. L. S. Bellamy
Waldmeister v. Hester, A-57522_Mrs. Marie Mitchell_____John P. Walkup
Zep v. Marienlust, A-146166____Mr. and Mrs. J. Mehrer_____Mr. and Mrs. J. Mehrer

1938

Adelina of Riverbank, A-173323_Mr. and Mrs. Howard Eric____Mr. and Mrs. Eric
Allsworth Linda v. Strelitz,
980698_____Marion V. Burchard_____Mrs. Fred Hicks
Aneita v. Llieno, A-259301____Llieno Kennels_____Llieno Kennels
Arri v. Marienlust, A-180912___Mr. and Mrs. J. Mehrer_____Mr. and Mrs. J. Mehrer
Axel of Jonedith, A-173505 ___George C. Spradling_____John H. Schlomer
Bernd v. Plater Schulhaus,
A-34306 _____Hulburd Johnston_____Melanie Warnecke
Beska v. d. Trapp, A-206583____Llieno Kennels_____El Jacoby
Braun O'Stone Hut, A-299074__Mr. and Mrs. Samuel C. Disbrow_Mrs. Maude Daniels Smith
Christel v. Schutzenstein,
A-184109 _____Joan Blair_____Carl Schutz
Cid's Lone Ace v. Dachshafen,
A-103101 _____Miss Ruth Grant Jones_____Mrs. Maude Daniels Smith
Cilly v. Plater Schulhaus,
A-77504 _____Willoughby Kennels_____Melanie Warnecke
Cornhill Goldie v. Dachshafen,
A-206304 _____Maude Daniels Smith_____Mrs. Delphin F. Young
Dolf v. Mimosa, A-149120_____Mr. and Mrs. J. L. vonGlahn__Mr. and Mrs. J. J. vonGlahn
Drauf Hunter's Luck, A-222634_Carl Heimbuch _____Carl Heimbuch
Falk v. Walder, A-119353_____Mr. and Mrs. Howard Eric____Mrs. L. T. Bellamy
Faust of Blue Key, A-187216___George C. Spradling _____Blue Key Kennels
Firs Black Berry, A-30710_____Daleswell Kennels_____Mrs. B. Huggins
Freda v. Stahlhaus, A-67703____Mrs. Abbott Kimball_____George F. Steele
Gold Standard v. Teckelhof,
A-127243 _____Willoughby Kennels_____Mrs. Lawrence Zimmerman
Groucho of Little Farm, A-93731_Mrs. David C. Dodge_____Mrs. David C. Dodge
Hanko-Flottenberg, A-110958___Ellenbert Farm_____G. F. Mueller
Hanni-Flottenberg, A-240346___Ellenbert Farm_____G. F. Mueller
Hans v. Friedrichshof, A-104187_Mr. and Mrs. Hugh C. Friedrich_Mrs. William F. Ascher
Harriet v. Stahlhaus, 970210__Mrs. Maude Daniels Smith_____George F. Steele
Hasso-Flottenberg, A-179031___Mrs. Owen A. West_____G. F. Muller
Heini v. Hester, 918324_____Mrs. Marie Mitchell _____Mrs. Marie Mitchell
Hermine v. Ascherhof, A-134568_Mr. and Mrs. Hugh C. Friedrich_Mrs. Wm. F. Ascher
Jean of Wayston, A-153961_____Hulburd Johnston_____Hulburd Johnston
Juwel v. Waldberg, A-220916___Mrs. Philip S. Dickinson_____Fritz Buchard

Kobold's Loni of Blue Key,
  A-177789 _____Florence K. Trullinger_____Maude Daniels Smith
Krup-in's Schnick, A-52805_____Mrs. Wallace Pflueger_____Wilhelm Bellenberg
Kupfer v. d. Windburg,
  A-220914 _____Mrs. Philip S. Dickinson_____Carl Thieme
Kurt v. Dachshafen, A-172852__Maude Daniels Smith_____Maude Daniels Smith
Mansi v. Landeck, A-42571_____Conrad Schneider_____Conrad Schneider
Micky v. Teckelhof, A-29928_____Mrs. Lawrence Zimmerman___Mrs. Lawrence Zimmerman
Mimosa v. Hildesheim, A-44500_Mrs. Richard V. Pell_____Mr. and Mrs. J. L. vonGlahn
Otto v. Achat, A-156975_____Mrs. Donald Cutler_____Victor Moench
Pamheim Pamchen, 979317____Grassmere Kennels_____Pam Johnston
Penny v. d. Schroth, A-213721__Mrs. David C. Dodge_____Mr. and Mrs. Geo. E. Schroth
Prinz v. Stalhaus, A-53011_____Edith M. Groves_____George F. Steele
Raecher's Trine v. Erlenheim,
  A-3239 _____Mrs. Earline G. Clegg_____John F. Clegg
Redledge Edeltrud, A-8978_____Redledge Kennels_____Redledge Kennels
Serena v. Dachshafen, A-174620_Marion V. Burchard_____Round Hill Kennels
Steuben v. Teckelhof, A-104233_Mrs. H. T. McCormick_____Mrs. Lawrence Zimmerman
Sunstorm Seven of Diamonds,
  A-149348 _____G. G. Frelinghuysen, Jr._____G. G. Frelinghuysen, Jr.
Tanya of Fair Acres, A-70498__Mr. and Mrs. Wm. H. Coleman_Mr. and Mrs. Wm. H. Coleman
Teck v. Falltor, 999359_____Hulburd Johnston_____Heinrich Stroh
Theo v. Holzgarten, A-228532_Alexander Herman Lynch_____Karl Botz
Varna v. Waldberg, A-220919__Mrs. Philip S. Dickinson_____Mrs. F. Franklyn
Veronika Goseneck, A-229094__Mrs. George Strawbridge_____Dr. Heinrich Benecke
Voewood's Dago v.
  Dachshafen, A-190205_____Maude Daniels Smith_____Mrs. C. Davies Tainter
Wooton's Wilma, A-225963_____Capt. Garza A. Wooton_____Capt. Garza A. Wooton

Aachen v. Hildesheim, A-253008_Mr. and Mrs. John C. Chaffe___Mrs. Richard V. Pell
Anni of Craig Oaks, A-223676_Henry F. Tiedemann_____Henry F. Tiedemann
Arra v. Hildesheim, A-258005__Mrs. Richard V. Pell_____Mrs. Richard V. Pell
Barcwyn Alma, A-325693_____Mrs. Winifred E. Crabtree_____Winifred E. Crabtree
Bee v. Steuben of Windyriver,
  A-311742 _____Windyriver Kennels _____Hiram G. Hines
Berolina v. Rotschafen, A-216821_Mrs. H. D. Sims_____F. G. Stivers and Cecil Rotsch
Bogus, A-105069_____Mrs. Donald F. Cutler, Jr._____Mrs. Fred Hicks
Brutus v. Smolhaus, A-322655__Mrs. Paul J. Atkinson_____Mr. and Mrs. Paul J. Atkinson
Chico v. Zinnowitz, A-92044___Ruth J. Dodge_____Ruth J. Dodge
Cid Junior of Lakelands,
  A-253475 _____Miriam Van Court_____Maude Daniels Smith
Conrad v. Rotschafen, A-272145_Mrs. H. D. Sims_____F. G. Stivers and Cecil Rotsch
Copper v. d. Schroth, A-215940_Capt. and Mrs. R. J. Melanphy_Mr. and Mrs. Geo. E. Schroth
Cornhill Beska, A-284202_____White Gables Kennels_____Mrs. Delphin F. Young
Count Heinrich v. Culmara,
  A-198501 _____Mr. and Mrs. E. S. Cullenward_Mr. and Mrs. E. S. Cullenward
Drollig v. Llieno, A-260091_____Llieno Kennels_____Llieno Kennels
Edith Rinkton, A-257278_____Ramona L. Andrews_____Edith M. Groves
Esruma Marta, A-234639_____C. Hyland Jones_____C. Hyland Jones
Evechen v. Dachshafen,
  A-156227 _____Grassmere Kennels_____Maude Daniels Smith
Firs Taviseha, A-30711_____Daleswell Kennels_____C. A. Faland
Fraulein of Hohenburg,
  A-134625 _____Mr. and Mrs. David L. Wall___Mr. and Mrs. David L. Wall
Frech v. Hildesheim, A-258001__Maude Daniels Smith_____Greenoway Kennels
Grassmere Fritzl, A-50228_____Grassmere Kennels_____Mrs. Carl Lichtenberg
Greenoway Adolph, A-86387____Mrs. Clark Miller_____George Fries
Hade Ja v. d. Schroth, A-134256_Mr. and Mrs. George Schroth__Mr. and Mrs. Geo. Schroth

Heinrich of Willoughby,
  A-192838 _____Willoughby Kennels_____Willoughby Kennels
Heka of Little Farm, A-158315__Mrs. David C. Dodge_____Mrs. David C. Dodge
Helmar-Flottenberg, A-240347__Ellenbert Farm_____G. F. Mueller
Hoka Ellenbert, A-287955_____Ellenbert Farm_____Ellenbert Farm
Honey v. Dachshafen, A-75987__Thomas B. Moor_____Mrs. Alice B. Fisher
Kobold v. Plater Schulhaus,
  A-263175 _____Mrs. Carl H. Hanna_____Melanie Warnecke
Ledah of Babel, A-220472_____Mrs. R. E. Danielson_____Babel Kennels
Llieno's Marko v. Teckelhof,
  A-215436 _____Jimmie H. Sullivan_____Mrs. Lawrence Zimmerman
Marigold v. Dachshafen,
  A-251502 ____ _____Miriam Van Court_____Maude Daniels Smith
Mops of Fair Acres II, A-110466_H. Rathbun Hees_____Mr. and Mrs. Wm. H. Coleman
Nudel v. Teipelskrug, A-312458_Pommel Rock Kennels_____Karl Blank
Pflueger's Freier, A-199179____M. s. Wallace Pflueger_____Mrs. Wallace Pflueger
Pflueger's Lisa, A-192511_____M.s. Wallace Pflueger_____Mrs. Wallace Pflueger
Rauh v. Hildesheim, A-312827__M's H. G. Fownes_____Mrs. Everett E. Littlefield
Redledge Denker of Grotonia,
  A-21499 __ _____Katharine Winthrop_____Redledge Kennels
Redledge Vagabond, A-183671__Katharine Winthrop_____Redledge Kennels
Scarlett of Riverbank, A-248815_Mr. and Mrs. Howard Eric_____Mr. and Mrs. Howard Eric
Schwarze Perle v. Teckelholf,
  A-250121 __ _____Romona L. Andrews_____Mrs. Lawrence Zimmerman
Sonja v. Hildesheim, A-236391__John C. Chaffe_____Mr. and Mrs. Richard V. Pell
Sox v. Bucknam, A-94264_____Mr. and Mrs. A. P. Macdonald_Jessie I. Bucknam
Tanya of Jonedith, A-29322____Capt. Garza Wooton_____James W. Trullinger
Tavia Hainheim, A-193455_____Charles W. Summers_____George C. Spradling
Teckelheim Steppin Forth,
  A-297652 _____Paul David Foreman_____Grayce Greenburg
Trina v. Eichwald, A-233477___Roberta Woodson_____Roberta Woodson
Vagabund v. Paulinenberg,
  A-284031 _____George C. White_____Albert Fuchs
Vincel's Flare of Westmore,
  A-30631 _____Mr. and Mrs. R. W. Peyton__Mrs. Jessie I. Bucknam
Yvonne v. Pommel Rock,
  A-244670 _____Mrs. L. Selden_____Mrs. Lynde Selden

1940

Aha v. Lindenbuhl, A-305929____Willoughby Kennels_____Simon Barthel
Aha of Willoughby, A-355597__Willoughby Kennels_____Willoughby Kennels
Anita (Kamphausen), A-30.939_Willoughby Kennels_____Peter Kamphausen
Annie Van O, A-330879_____ __Marion V. Burchard_____Marion V. Burchard
Arno v. Hildesheim, A-284705 Mrs. Richard V. Pell_____Mrs. Richard V. Pell
Bavarian Hansl, A-284398_____Emma Flecher_____Emma Flecher
Bavarian Lump, A-284397_____John C. Chaffe_____Emma Flecher
Bismarck v. Kimmelhof,
  A-260606 _____Marion G. Kimball_____Marion G. Kimball
Burschle v. Habichtshof,
  A-48402 _____Herbert Campbell_____Hans Hank
Burschle of Hohenburg,
  A-280371 _____Mr. and Mrs. David L. Wall___Mr. and Mrs. David L. Wall
Christel v. d. Bunslauer Heide-
  Limelight, A-220961_____Dr. Lyman R. Fisher_____Gertrud Kucza
Cid's Amber v. Dachshafen,
  A-214204 _____Maude Daniels Smith_____Maude Daniels Smith
Cornhill Lenzska, A-209164____Delphin F. Young_____Mrs. Delphin F. Young
Dammerig v. Llieno, A-260093__Mildred Tebeau_____Llieno Kennels

Deine Freude Hainheim,
   A-283630 _____George C. Spradling_____Mrs. M. Katie Lang
De Lou's Sammy, A-349005____Mrs. H. D. Sims_____Mrs. H. D. Sims
Dimas Earthstopper, A-422591__Ellenbert Farm_____G. Petty
Dinglespiel v. Munn, A-251334__Mr. and Mrs. W. Earl McMunn_W. Earl McMunn
Eric v. Achat, A-342647_____Harry J. Hill_____Victor Moench
Etzel's Hansel v. d. Buchhorst,
   A-258567 _____John Amann_____John Amann
Gisela v. Teckelhof, A-281102__Mr. and Mrs. Howard Eric____Llieno Kennels
Goldilocks of White Gables,
   A-306883 _____White Gables Kennels_____Miriam Van Court
Grassmere Johann, A-215405____Grassmere Kennels_____Grassmere Kennels
Grisolda v. Teckelhof, A-310760_Mrs. Lawrence Zimmerman____Llieno Kennels
Grotonia Doru v. Cram,
   A-300803 _____Katharine Winthrop_____Katharine Winthrop
Gunther v. Marienlust, A-353348_Jeannette S. Gillies_____Mr. and Mrs. J. Mehrer
Gypsy of Riverbank, A-400785__Mr. and Mrs. Howard Eric____Mr. and Mrs. Howard Eric
Hanni-Lore v. d. Waldhuette,
   A-306910 _____Mr. and Mrs. Howard Eric____Mr. and Mrs. Henry Riemann
Harpo of Little Farm, A-158314_Hallwyre Kennels_____Mrs. David C. Dodge
Helmar Ellenbert, A-337985____Ellenbert Farm_____Ellenbert Farm
Helmi's Held v. Werdenfels,
   A-270416 _____Emil Amann_____Scott L. Koch
Hero of Dunkerque of
   Sunstorm, A-216534_____G. G. Frelinghuysen, Jr._____Sir Charles L. Lambe
Hielia Ellenbert, A-179784_____Florence S. Keller_____Ellenbert Farm
Hylah Ellenbert, A-337982_____Ellenbert Farm_____Ellenbert Farm
Igo-Forth of Greenburg II,
   A-252066 _____Mr. and Mrs. Laurence J. Stock_Grayce Greenburg
Illo v. Plater Schulhaus,
   A-341672 _____Charles E. Holden_____Melanie Warnecke
Laban of Babel, A-220470_____Babel Kennels_____Babel Kennels
Larsen's Sonnenlicht, A-449996_Jennie Larsen_____Ruth H. Potter
Leutnant v. Marienlust,
   A-302029 _____Mr. and Mrs. J. Mehrer_____Mr. and Mrs. J. Mehrer
Liebchen v. Perkath, A-233543_Mrs. P. W. Carr_____Mrs. Dick Kirschbaum
Liesel of Black Forest, A-143823_Black Forest Kennels_____Black Forest Kennels
Linda v. Edelhof, A-360627____Mrs. Wm. E. Schmidt_____Mr. and Mrs. Wm. E. Schmidt
Linda of Mayndale, A-397065__Mrs. Carl H. Hanna_____Charles F. Schaefer
Little Annis, A-380887_____Rosalia A. Scheurich_____Rosalia A. Scheurich
Marie of Hohenburg, A-343279__Mr. and Mrs. David L. Wall___Mr. and Mrs. David L. Wall
Meander's Brainstorm, A-237612_Charles B. Tovell, Jr._____Mr. and Mrs. J. Mehrer
Meistersinger of Windyriver,
   A-273696 _____Windyriver Kennels_____Windyriver Kennels
Menschenfreund's Dusty,
   A-404026 _____Mrs. Henry G. Fownes_____Paul P. Britsch
Nico of Little Farm, A-257595__Mrs. David C. Dodge_____Mrs. David C. Dodge
Nino of Little Farm, A-257596__Mrs. David C. Dodge_____Mrs. David C. Dodge
Obed of Babel, A-308585_____Babel Kennels_____Babel Kennels
Pamheim Velvet, A-248635_____Mrs. Pam Johnston Patterson_Mrs. Pam Johnston Patterson
Pretzel of Widbrook, A-399412__Dr. Everett W. Johnson_____Mrs. A. K. Hedley-Peek
Robbe v. Anjon, A-307375_____Anne Bowman_____Mr. and Mrs. J. Mehrer
Siebert of Wooton's, A-407149__Capt. and Mrs. Garza A. Wooton_Capt. and Mrs. G. A. Wooton
Sungold of White Gables,
   A-306884 _____Maude Daniels Smith_____Miriam Van Court
Teckelheim Fehr-Lieb, A-321283_Grayce Greenburg _____Grayce Greenburg
Watersport v. Dachshausen,
   A-300273 _____W. Frank Hardy_____Irmgard Hackney
Wooton's Brenda Sue, A-261950_Capt. and Mrs. Garza A. Wooton_Capt. Garza A. Wooton

Achat v. d. Walleck, A-415702__**Dr. Marie H. Karger**_____Bruno Lopp

Aliel v. Hildesheim, A-258007__Mrs. A. J. Brosseau_____Mrs. Richard V. Pell

Amsel v. Erlenheim, A-219826__S. C. Hopkins_____Mrs. Earline G. Clegg

Asbury's Sally of Greenburg,

  A-321096 _____Mr. and Mrs. A. Bruce Asbury_Grayce Greenburg

Bertra v. Hildesheim, A-396486_Mr. and Mrs. Richard V. Pell__Mrs. Richard V. Pell

Brockett's Griselda, A-388279__Robert M. Brockett_____Robert M. Brockett

Dago Junior v. Dachshafen,

  A-412720 _____Maude Daniels Smith_____Maude Daniels Smith

Degen v. Llieno, A-260094_____Llieno Kennels_____Llieno Kennels

Dunder's Ditto v.

  Waldmaenchen, A-353722_____Mr. and Mrs. G. F. Eward_____Mr. and Mrs. G. F. Eward

Evechen v. Hildesheim A-333117_Mrs. Richard V. Pell_____Grassmere Kennels

Far Away Schlifferlin, A-255556_Maude Daniels Smith_____Jean Walker

Gilt of Willoughby, A-358530__Mrs. Robert Newman_____Willoughby Kennels

Hansel III, A-174140_____Gunnar Swalgren_____Hulburd Johnston

Harras Ellenbert, A-443130____Ellenbert Farm _____Ellenbert Farm

Helka Ellenbert, A-416296____Ellenbert Farm_____Ellenbert Farm

Hexe v. Hoellental, A-370600__Mrs. Natalie Webster_____August Schuhmann

Ingo v. Plater Schulhaus,

  A-396555 _____White Gables Kennels_____Melanie Warnecke

Johannes Rinktonberg, A-384336_Mrs. Raymond P. Brandt_____Rosalia A. Scheurich

Limelight Berlinerlicht,

  A-378984 _____Limelight Kennels_____Limelight Kennels

Limelight Breslauerlicht,

  A-378985 _____Limelight Kennels_____Limelight Kennels

Little Farm Jada v. d.

  Schroth, A-194800_____Mr. and Mrs. George Schroth__Mrs. David C. Dodge

Max v. d. Daniels, A-311425___Mr. and Mrs. D. D. Daniels____Mr. and Mrs. D. D. Daniels

Max of Hohenburg, A-415926__Mr. and Mrs. David L. Wall____Mr. and Mrs. David L. Wall

Midge's Madchen v. Edelhof,

  A-384689 _____William E. Schmidt_____Mr. and Mrs. Wm. E. Schmidt

Miss Muffett v. Walder,

  A-420006 _____Mr. and Mrs. Howard Eric____Mrs. L. S. Bellamy

Moto's Pride of White Gables,

  A-379271 ____ _____Mr. and Mrs. Walter D. Monroe_White Gables Kennels

Nadia of Little Farm, A-257592_Henry W. Norton_____Mrs. David C. Dodge

Omar v. Hildesheim, A-374295__Mrs. Richard V. Pell_____Mrs. Everett E. Littlefield

Oscar of Little Farm, A-311098__Mrs. John B. Hayden_____Mrs. David C. Dodge

Otilder, A-457530_____Mrs. Chester A. Braman, Jr.__Mrs. Chester A. Braman, **Jr.**

Pall Mall of Little Farm,

  A-311094 _____Mr. and Mrs. Geo. Schroth_____Mrs. David C. Dodge

Pflueger's Malta, A-292762_____Mrs. Wallace Pflueger_____Mrs. Wallace Pflueger

Pumpernickel of Blue Key,

  A-385644 _____ _____Florence S. Keller_____Florence S. Keller

Pumpkin of Blue Key, A-522801_Florence S. Keller_____Florence S. Keller

Ragazza v. Hildesheim, A-258002_Mrs. John C. Chaffe_____Greenoway Kennels

Ramsay's Talisman, A-380087__Norton S. Parker_____Mr. and Mrs. Bert Ramsay

Ricke of Ballyteckel, A-435355_E. S. Bromley_____Miss Delphine Peard

Roadside Peter, A-398538_____Mrs. Carl H. Hanna_____Gertrude L. Hanna

Robin of Riverbank, A-400784_Mr. and Mrs. Howard Eric____Mr. and Mrs. Howard Eric

Schnapps aus der Neidhohle,

  A-414127 _____Mrs. Barclay K. Douglas_____Josephine H. Douglas

Sheba of Babel, A-451435_____Babel Kennels_____John C. Chaffe

Swartze v. Walbach, A-410985_John C. Chaffe_____Babel Kennels

Trinket of Windvriver, A-434660_Windvriver Kennels_____Windvriver Kennels

Trudie v. Heinenputz, A-440737_Ruth H. Potter_____Ruth H. Potter

Vega v. Erlenheim, A-297880__Frank C. Wilson_____Mrs. Earline G. Clegg

Vickie Baum, A-380888_____Rosalia A. Scheurich_____Rosalia A. Scheurich

Victoria Valhalla, A-394293____George C. White_____Paul P. Britsch
We-Coll-Em Susan, A-453421___Mr. and Mrs. Charles D. Coll__Mrs. Charles D. Coll

1942

Ajax of Albion, A-408914_____Harry Sharpe_____Charles Edward Holden
Anny Ondra, A-466934_____R. A. Scheurich_____Rosalia A. Scheurich
Anton, A-466933_____R. A. Scheurich_____Rosalia A. Scheurich
Barcwyn Winston, A-486400____William E. Schmidt_____Winifred E. Crabtree
Bavarian Russ, A-405914_____Charles E. Holden_____Emma Flecher
Brenda of Blue Key, A-522304__Florence S. Keller_____Florence S. Keller
Dignity of Edgemere, A-551346_E. S. Bromley_____Emilie S. Bromley
Esruma Eva, A-399714_____C. Hyland Jones_____C. Hyland Jones
Fraulein Fido of Alema,
   A-433988 _____Mrs. Albert Loest_____Mrs. Albert Loest
Freifrau Hainheim, A-483409__Mr. and Mrs. Charles Kellogg__George C. Spradling
Fussbudget of White Gables,
   A-374294 _____White Gables Kennels_____Tom Stevenson
Galatea v. Bergman, A-430986__Mr. and Mrs. Edw. F.Hirschman_Lorane M. Newman
Gretel of Brandenburg Farm,
   A-344059 _____Dr. L. Willis Strong, Jr._____Magdalena Brandenburg
Hertzrumpf v. Teckelhof,
   A-356088 _____Windyriver Kennels_____Mrs. Lawrence Zimmerman
Hugo v. Waldbach, A-470202___Mrs. John C. Chaffe_____Mrs. Gaze E. Lukas
Impudence of Edgemere,
   A-551342 _____E. S. Bromley_____Emilie S. Bromley
Janet of Tenroc, A-543554_____Rose Mary Cornet_____Dr. Louis A. Cornet
Lorelei v. Edelhof, A-360625____William E. Schmidt_____Mr. and Mrs. Wm. E. Schmidt
Lucy Lockett of White Gables, Dr. H. W. Vanlandingham
   A-306880 _____ and W. W. Dorward_____Miriam Van Court
Lumpacious Hubertus, A-647990_Frank Hardy_____Irmgard Hackney
Mitzie of Blue Key, A-526712__George E. Brown, Jr._____Florence S. Keller
Mitzi v. Konkapot, A-499253___Beatrice M. Andel_____Irmgard Hackney
My Girl of Edgemere, A-551343_Mrs. E. S. Bromley_____Emilie S. Bromley
Myra v. Dachshafen, A-396488_Mr. and Mrs. Kenneth T.
                          Phillips _____Maude Daniels Smith
Penny of Lednem, A-511030____Spiro M. Mendel_____Capt. Garza A. Wooton
Queen of My Heart, A-436931__Mr. and Mrs. Henry S. Bussey_Mr. and Mrs. Harry S. Bussey
Rikki v. Dachshafen, A-513665_Dr. R. vonDecken-Luers_____Maude Daniels Smith
Rinkie v. Rinchen, A-494387___John F. Bowne_____Kathryn S. Carr
R. Lou of Jonedith, A-454695__Mrs. Annis A. Jones_____Edith M. Graves
Sascha v. Dychland, A-416036__Herman G. Cox_____Mrs. Marie S. Piper
Siren of Homehouse, A-357072__Mrs. Raymond M. Bell_____John M. Maris
Tommy Tucker of Riverbank,
   A-400781 _____Mrs. Max W. Zabel_____Mr. and Mrs. Howard Eric
Trooper of Homehouse, A-357074_J. O. Barnes_____John M. Maris
Uhlan v. Cellarius, A-289804__Mrs. Justine Cellarius_____Justine Cellarius
We-Coll-Em Annabell, A-465394_Mrs. Charles D. Coll_____Mrs. Charles D. Coll

1943

Arnette v. Dachshafen, A-509202_Maude Daniels Smith_____Maude Daniels Smith
Bavarian Mousi, A-546670_____Emma Flecher_____Emma Flecher
Bencelia's John, A-583425_____Bencelia Kennels_____William B. Klimkiewicz
Carrot of Blue Key, A-664928__Florence S. Keller_____Florence S. Keller
Cossack Prince of Leonca,
   A-445154 _____Wm. W. Bexson_____Mrs. Leon C. Johnson
Diplomat v. Marienlust,
   A-514697 _____Mr. and Mrs. J. Mehrer_____Emma Flecher
Donald of Tween Hills, A-536466_John F. Bowne_____Rosalia A. Scheurich
Dougmel Dodo of Little Farm,
   A-462940 _____Mrs. David C. Dodge_____Melvie Clubb

1943 (cont'd)

Gretchen v. d. Waldhuette,
    A-680158 _____Mrs. Max W. Zabel_____Mr. and Mrs. Henry Riemann
Hopfen's Venus, A-584807_____S. C. Hopkins_____S. C. Hopkins
Loki Boy of Drake Manor,
    A-652788 _____Mrs. L. Willis Strong, Jr._____L. Willis Strong, Jr.
Marlene v. Tenroc, A-543553___Dr. Louis A. Cornet_____Dr. Louis A. Cornet
Menschenfreund's Sable,
    A-613946 _____Maude Daniels Smith_____Mary Martin Travis
Omar v. d. Daniels, A-582021__Mr. and Mrs. D. D. Daniels_____Mr. and Mrs. D. D. Daniels
Prinz v. Blachtan, A-825089____George E. Brown, Jr._____Cecilia Newman
Quirk of Little Farm, A-389761_Mrs. David C. Dodge_____Mrs. David C. Dodge
Teckelheim Royal Amber,
    A-464610 _____Grayce Greenburg_____Grayce Greenburg
Veto of Riverbank, A-671151___Mrs. M. W. Zabel_____Mrs. Howard Eric
White Gables Mehitabel,
    A-474943 _____White Gables Kennels_____White Gables Kennels

1944

Aida Ellenbert, A-592785_____Maude Daniels Smith_____Ellenbert Farm
Alwin v. Brentwald, A-579423__H. and May R. Patrick_____H. and May R. Patrick
Asbury's Jewel, A-421957_____Mr. and Mrs. A. Bruce Asbury_Mr. and Mrs. A. Bruce Asbury
Bencelia's Hansi, A-723241_____Bencelia Kennels_____Bencelia Kennels
Black Knight of Tween Hills,
    A-586464 _____Lt. R. A. Scheurich, A.N.C.___Rosalia A. Scheurich
Bucknam's Merrymaker,
    A-690590 _____Jessie I. Bucknam_____Jessie I. Bucknam
Cassandra of Lindakin, A-604545_Mr. and Mrs. K. Philips_____Mr. and Mrs. Kenneth Philips
Cinnamon v. Dachshafen II,
    A-485071 _____Mrs. Maude Daniels Smith_____Maude Daniels Smith
Cinnamon v. Dachshafen III,
    A-682286 _____Maude Daniels Smith_____Maude Daniels Smith
Dark Rosleen v. Dachshafen,
    A-172856 _____Herbert Campbell_____Maude Daniels Smith
Dora Ellenbert, A-530174_____Mrs. Mary W. Geibel_____Ellenbert Farm
Elmerich of Alema, A-524584__Mrs. Albert Loest_____Mrs. Albert Loest
Eric Again v. d. Daniels,
    A-670739 _____Anne Smith Wenden_____Mr. and Mrs. D. D. Daniels
Ester v. Eichwald, A-561718___W. H. Holt_____Roberta Woodson
Franzl v. d. Stark-Garten,
    A-505951 _____Mrs. Max W. Zabel_____L. Willis Strong, Jr.
Fritz of Lindakin, A-348262_____Mr. and Mrs. Kenneth T. Philips_Mrs. Hans H. Sachers
Goelin's Moto Mitz' Fritzie,
    A-684575 _____W. J. Wilkins_____George E. Brown, Jr.
Gremlin of Edgemere, A-665445_Mrs. E. S. Bromley_____Emilie S. Bromley
Gunther Again, A-586467_____Mrs. Reginald Wainwright_____Rosalia A. Scheurich
Haidee v. Rotschafen, A-408926_Mr. and Mrs. Cecil C. Rotsch_Mr. and Mrs. Cecil C. Rotsch
Hallwyre Harpo's Hildchen,
    A-661220 _____Hallwyre Kennels_____Hallwyre Kennels
Hecka v. Waldbach, A-578417___Mrs. John C. Chaffe_____Mrs. John C. Chaffe
Ingaborg Hainheim, A-483410___Mrs. Paul Atkinson_____George C. Spradling
King Cole of Drake Manor,
    A-652791 _____Wm. D. Cox_____L. Willis Strong, Jr.
Little Vickie of Tween Hills,
    A-586468 _____C. Weier_____Rosalia A. Scheurich
Luna of Willoughby, A-463886__Harkness Edwards_____Willoughby Kennels
Mark Anthony of Northmont,
    A-519191 _____Northmont Kennels_____Herbert Campbell
Mister Tom Mato of Blue Key,
    A-664931 _____Florence S. Keller_____Florence S. Keller

Persimmon of Blue Key,
A-664932 _____Florence S. Keller_____Florence S. Keller
Rose Brocade of Primrosepatch,
A-356570 _____Mrs. E. K. von Nidda_____Mrs. O. Smith-Rewse
Sandra of Banksville, A-485299_Mrs. Richard V. Pell_____Eagen J. Zygmont
Sassy Lassy v. Bergman,
A-580091 _____Mr. and Mrs. Edw. F.
                            Hirschman _____Mr. and Mrs. Edw. F. Hirschman
Superman v. Marienlust,
A-640366 _____Mr. and Mrs. D. Gregory Volkert_Mr. and Mrs. J. Mehrer
Traviata of Edgemere, A-675182_E. S. Bromley_____Emilie S. Bromley
Vagabond Hubertus, A-720930__Felicia Coleman_____Frank W. Hardy
We-Coll-Em Polliana, A-573940_Mr. and Mrs. Charles D. Coll__Mrs. Charles D. Coll
White Gables Bavarian Senta,
A-405915 _____White Gables Kennels_____Emma Flecher
White Gables Merry-Go-Round,
A-474941 _____Jessie I. Bucknam_____White Gables Kennels
White Gables Scaramouche,   Woodrow Dorward and
A-595316 _____ Dr. H. W. Vanlandingham__White Gables Kennels
White Gables Zanzibar,
A-449458 _____Little Gate Kennels_____Tom Stevenson
Zarky of Gipsy Barn, A-703851__Hazel J. Zabel_____Hazel J. Zabel

1945

Bit O'Black of Tween Hills,
A-759952 _____John F. Bowne_____Rosalia Scheurich
Blacky Dockie, A-723909_____Fred C. Reeb_____Charles W. Walter
Cavalier v. Marienlust, A-521022_White Gables Kennels_____Mr. and Mrs. J. Mehrer
Ebony Eric v. d. Daniels,
A-725204 _____Charlotte R. Sibley_____Mr. and Mrs. D. D. Daniels
Goelin's Moto Mitz' Mitzie,
A-684579 _____W. J. Wilkins_____George E. Brown, Jr.
Happy Daze of Blue Key,
A-664930 _____Ivycroft Kennels_____Florence S. Keller
Little Gate's Letty, A-692762___Mrs. Walter D. Monroe_____Mrs. Walter D. Monroe
Premier of Starcrest, A-766496_Mildred E. Stark_____Mildred E. Stark
Rinky of Heying-Teckel,
A-618054 _____Caroline Weir_____Norton S. Parker
Riven Rock Dorcas, A-703171__Rivenrock Kennels_____Anne Smith Wenden
Staff Sergeant v. Marienlust,
A-818236 _____Mr. and Mrs. D. Gregory Volkert_Mr. and Mrs. J. Mehrer
Tonkahof Lano, A-476943_____Henry W. Norton_____Henry W. Norton
Vicki v. d. Nidda, A-768590_____Mr. and Mrs. Krug von Nidda__John F. Kelley
White Gables Prunes an'
Prisms, A-662682_____Mr. and Mrs. A. C. Spragging__White Gables Kennels

1946

Bucknam's Queen Bee, A-764105_Jessie I. Bucknam_____Jessie I. Bucknam
Herzville v. Marienlust,
A-712597 _____Mr. and Mrs. J. Mehrer_____Mr. and Mrs. J. Mehrer
Sergeant Ed, A-661866_____Joseph K. Hearne_____Marie M. Hearne
Freia of Leonca, A-566548_____Fred E. Lawrence_____Victor Moench
Antonio of Gipsy Barn, A-884426_Mrs. Max W. Zable_____Mrs. Max Zable
Black Forest Regin v.
Holzarten, A-491315_____Mrs. L. Zingler_____Miss Agnes S. Westinghouse
Rufus Hainheim, A-536548_____George C. Sprading_____George C. Sprading

Ship's Mascot Miss Peaches,

    A-895012 _____Allan C. Spraggins_____Lois S. Shipp

White Gables Gadabout,

    A-746650 _____White Gables Kennels_____White Gables Kennels

Zomara of Little Farm,

    A-831063 _____Mrs. David C. Dodge_____Mrs. David C. Dodge

Bavarian Goldie, A-803525_____Louis Flecher_____Louis Flecher

Black Forest's Herzbube,

    A-750971 _____ __ _____Black Forest Kennels_____Black Forest Kennels

Etzel v. Waldbach, A-666246___Mrs. John C. Chaffe_____George Roschmann

Ricky v. Marienlust, A-691869_Mr. and Mrs. J. Mehrer_____Mr. and Mrs. J. Mehrer

Roger v. Marienlust, A-691872___Mr. and Mrs. J. Mehrer_____Mr. and Mrs. J. Mehrer

White Gables Nutmeg, A-799533_White Gables Kennels_____White Gables Kennels

Andy v. Nesbittenhof, A-877633_Mr. and Mrs. G. A. Nesbitt_____Mr. and Mrs. G. A. Nesbitt

Attila of Towaco, A-430792____Julia Beyer_____Julia Beyer

Black Beauty of Tween Hills,

    A-759953 _____A. Scheurich_____A. Scheurich

Corvette v. Dachshafen,

    A-794979 _____Maude Daniels Smith_____Maude Daniels Smith

Queen Lady's Loretta, A-564301_Mr. and Mrs. H. Bussey_____Mr. and Mrs. H. Bussey

Rudy v. Hapsburg, A-720933___Mrs. William F. Ascher_____Mrs. M. Brandenburg

White Gables Basil, A-799528__White Gables Kennels_____White Gables Kennels

William de Sangpur, A-726233_Berthold J. D'Alexandre_____Berthold J. D'Alexandre

Zandy of Gipsy Barn, A-703850_Hazel J. Zable_____Hazel J. Zable

Little Orchard's Gretel,

    A-800499 _____Willis J. Wilkins_____Willis J. Wilkins

White Gables Philadelphia,

    A-797597 _____White Gables Kennels_____Mr. and Mrs. L. R. Robinson

White Gables Rosemary,

    A-799539 _____White Gables Kennels_____White Gables Kennels

Baron Scipp v. d.

    Buchhorst, A-831074_____John Amann_____John Amann

Cynara's Dark Knight, A-570824_Mrs. Forest E. DeVinay_____Mrs. Forest E. DeVinay

Fair Lady of Gipsy Barn,

    A-900737 _____Mrs. Max W. Zable_____Mrs. Max W. Zable

Gipsy Barn's Jennifer, A-823410_Hazel J. Zable_____Mrs. Ernest V. Wright

Itsit of Steinhoff, A-608454____Dorothy S. Pickett_____Homer Steinhoff

Kurt v. Sigmaringen, A-836901_S. C. Hopkins_____G. A. Plummer

Redmond's Star Dust, A-832249_Mrs. Josephine Brumbaugh_____Phyllis M. Redmond

Vermilion of Little Farm,

    A-560318 _____Phyllis M. Redmond_____Mrs. David C. Dodge

White Gables Fuchsia, A-603613_Mrs. Edna R. Steinhoff_____White Gables Kennels

Hertha's Gypsie, A-693718_____G. A. Plummer_____Dorothy S. Pickett

Hopfen's Pierre, A-874811_____S. C. Hopkins_____S. C. Hopkins

Brumbaugh's Teckelheim

    Tanya, A-935683_____Dr. Hans Lehfeldt_____Grayce Greenburg

Bucknam's Busy Bee, A-764102_Mrs. David C. Dodge_____Jessie Bucknam

Chadwick of Crespie Street,

    A-874941 _____White Gables Kennels_____Donia Bussey

Mikosz v. Teckeldorf, H-1407__Jessie I. Bucknam_____Dr. Hans Lehfeldt

Pride of Edgemere, A-814568__Emilie S. Bromley _____Emilie S. Bromley

Trooper v. Waldbach, A-898306_Mrs. John C. Chaffe_____Mrs. John C. Chaffe

Wal-Ora's Dusky of Leonca,

    A-769537 _____Ora Belle McCollom_____Mrs. Leon C. Johnson

Bosko aus Muspellsheim,

    A-373106 _____ _____Miss Verna Riemann_____Mrs. Toni Herwig

Carlo of Gipsy Barn, A-831963_Mrs. Max W. Zable_____Mrs. Max W. Zable

Favorite v. Marienlust,

    A-880407 _____Mr. and Mrs. J. Mehrer_____Mr. and Mrs. J. Mehrer

Gipsy Barn's Hillary, A-947568_Hazel J. Zable_____Harry J. Hill
Hexe v. Waldhof, A-809107____Kurt Wehrhagen_____Kurt Wehrhagen
Meteor v. Marienlust, A-580125_Mr. and Mrs. J. Mehrer_____Mr. and Mrs. J. Mehrer
Rocket of Hildesheim, A-791778_Mrs. Richard V. Pell_____Mrs. Richard V. Pell
Si of Doxland, A-937305_____Woodrow W. Dorword
                             and Howard J. Kaiser_____Howard J. Kaiser
White Gables Marjoram,
    A-799529 _____White Gables Kennels_____White Gables Kennels
Diann v. Sollinge, A-915636___Anna A. Wassermeyer_____Anna A. Wassermeyer
Gayrobyn Derek, A-900251_____Edmund W. Druman_____Mary G. Cobb
Elfi of Arundel, A-874532_____Sara A. Thayer_____Mr. and Mrs. Henry F. Cate, Jr.
Guntherette of Earldale,
    A-911067 _____Aubria E. Bywaters_____Aubria E. Bywaters
Salute v. Dachshafen, A-794076_Maude Daniels Smith_____Maude Daniels Smith
Seppl v. d. Trausnitz, H-24161_Miss Frances A. Anthofer_____
Super-Red v. Marienlust,
    A-896660 _____Mrs. Gregory Volkert_____Mr. and Mrs. J. Mehrer
Albion's Own Penelope,
    A-801455 _____Charles E. Holden_____Charles E. Holden
Banjie v. Marienlust, A-803812__Mr. and Mrs. J. Mehrer_____Mr. and Mrs. J. Mehrer
Carlo v. d. Nidda, A-449451____John Heard_____Baron Krug von Nidda
Cynthia v. Jo-Rene, A-832947__Irene Marshall_____Joe B. Marshall
Ego v. Lenzgruen, A-649576___Roland Lehr _____Roland Lehr
Erich Hubertus, H-2795_____Frank W. Hardy_____Frank W. Hardy
Ingo of Hickory Hill, A-844156_Harry J. Hill_____Harry J. Hill
Ruepel of Hickory Hill,
    A-844158 _____Harry J. Hill_____Harry J. Hill
Sari of Gipsy Barn, H-2755____Mrs. Max W. Zable_____Mrs. Max W. Zable
Amber of Black Hole Hollow,
    A-908509 _____Josephine H. Douglas_____Josephine H. Douglas
Baron of Tween Hills, A-759951_Rosalia A. Scheurich_____Rosalia A. Scheurich
Bavarian Ola, A-849592_____Marie M. Hearne_____Marie M. Hearne
Demitasse of Heying Teckel,
    A-911345 _____Mrs. Fred Heying_____Mrs. Fred Heying
DeSha of Little Gate, A-740897_Mrs. Walter D. Monroe_____Mrs. Walter D. Monroe
Hill's Katrinka, A-796634_____Mrs. Frank F. Hill, Jr._____Mrs. J. Galloway
Leutnant's Hannah Beau
    O'Doud, A-887432_____Francis J. Doody_____Francis J. Doody
Noddy v. Dychland, A-995180__Mary Lynn Cox_____Herman G. Cox
Rotcod v. Tenroc, A-876651____Dr. Louis A. Cornet_____Aubria B. Bywaters
Adel v. Marienlust, A-831058__Mr. and Mrs. J. Mehrer_____Mr. and Mrs. J. Mehrer
Rock Manor's Gold Flash,
    A-995983 _____Mr. and Mrs. A. C. Spraggins__Mr. and Mrs. A. C. Spraggins
Sindi of Etiwanda, A-773527___Mr. and Mrs. A. Bruce Asbury_Mr. and Mrs. A. Bruce Asbury
Abner of Gipsy Barn, A-884427_Mrs. Max W. Zabel_____Mrs. Max W. Zabel
Axel Hainheim, A-536546_____George C. Spradling_____George C. Spradling
Cornhill Linda, H-1388_____Delphin F. Young_____Delphin F. Young
Crickett II of Badger Hill,
    H-3921 _____Harry R. Sharpe_____Harry R. Sharpe
Donna v. d. Daniels, A-848908_Mrs. D. D. Daniels_____Mr. and Mrs. D. D. Daniels
Karl v. Tenroc II, A-793871___Dr. Louis A. Cornet_____Aubria E. Bywaters
Ricki v. d. Daniels, A-818456____Mr. and Mrs. D. D. Daniels____Fred B. Pulling, Jr.
Waverly v. Marienlust,
    A-737625 _____Mr. and Mrs. J. Mehrer_____Carlton Bedell
White Gables Tansy, A-799534_Jessie I. Bucknam_____White Gables Kennels

1947
Bavarian Apollo, A-893282____Emma Flecher _____ ___Emma Flecher
Jo Jo Edson, A-912487_____Mrs. William Burr Hill, Jr.____Cecelia M. Grossman

1947 (cont'd)

Tiz Liz v. Bergman, A-947841__Mr. and Mrs. Edw. F.
Hirschman ____ _____Virginia I. and Oral D. Lavely
Barcwyn Success, A-797515____Winifred E. Crabtree_____Winifred E. Crabtree
Bavarian Joy, A-726945_____Louis Flecher_____Louis Flecher
Captain Johnn, H-20727_____Starkrest Kennels_____Amanda DeMaster
Dockie's Duchess of Calrene,
 A-968257 _____Mr. and Mrs. F. C. Reeb_____Mrs. Fred C. Reeb
Laurence of Little Gate,
 A-740398 _____Mrs. Walter D. Monroe_____Mrs. Walter D. Monroe
Oro Fino of Louhelen, A-812537_Louie R. Grugette_____Louie R. Grugette
Poincianna of Olterra, A-874082_Frederick H. Olney_____Mrs. Frederick H. Olney
Raccoon of Edgemere, A-814569_Emilie S. Bromley_____Emilie S. Bromley
Cleopatra of Northmont,
 A-510194 _____Northmont Kennels_____Herbert Campbell
Ed-El-Fra's Anise, H-8717_____Edwin and Eleanor S. Kivela__Edwin and Eleanor S. Kivela
Eric Carl v. Luen v. d. Daniels,
 A-633015 __ _____Robert F. Shaffer_____Mr. and Mrs. D. D. Daniels
Little Orchard's Pitti Pat,
 A-860001 _____Little Orchard Kennels_____Little Orchard Kennels
Nick Katine of Blue Key,
 A-980946 _____ _____Florence S. Keller_____Florence S. Keller
Bucknam's Merry Daze,
 A-800279 _____Jessie I. Bucknam_____Jessie I. Bucknam
Cheltenham's Liebschen, H-7336_Casimir I. Geibel_____Mrs. Marie M. Hearne
Siefen Jagenheim Adam, H-78__John F. Siefen_____Harry J. Hill
Alva of Little Gate, A-740896_Mrs. Walter D. Monroe_____Mrs. Walter D. Monroe
Banshee of Edgemere, A-948425_Emilie S. Bromley_____Emilie S. Bromley
Barcwyn Skill, A-797514_____Winifred E. Crabtree_____Winifred E. Crabtree
Blackberry v. d. Daniels,
 A-859984 _____Mr. and Mrs. D. D. Daniels_____Mr. and Mrs. D. D. Daniels
Exclusive of Edgemere,
 A-814563 _____Emilie S. Bromley_____Emilie S. Bromley
Falstaff v. Teckeldorf, H-11642_Katharina Lehfeldt_____Katharina Lehfeldt
Knockout of Edgemere,
 A-814564 _____Emilie S. Bromley_____Emilie S. Bromley
Ramsay's Guardsman, A-967466_Mr. and Mrs. Bert Ramsay_____Mr. and Mrs. Bert Ramsay
Rivenrock Manhattan, A-964757_Anne S. Wenden_____Anne S. Wenden
V-Jay of Crespi, A-912474_____Donia Bussey_____Donia Bussey
Whirlaway's Amaze Me,
 H-12474 _____Leon F. Warren_____Mrs. Wm. M. Thomas
Buckskin of Eliwanda, A-937763_Mr. and Mrs. A. Bruce Asbury_Mr. and Mrs. A. Bruce Asbury
Charlotte of Crespi Street,
 A-874942 _____Donia Bussey_____Donia Bussey
Goldenen Julia v. Sunset View,
 A-902090 _____Mrs. Elsa M. Worthington_____Mrs. Elsa M. Worthington
Max Rossman v. Notfort,
 A-955948 _____Luci Ward Natteford_____Luci Ward Natteford
Primrosepatch Gay Lancer,
 H-22003 _____Mrs. Osborne Howes_____Mrs. Evans
Tytucker of Gipsy Barn,
 H-26020 _____Mrs. Max W. Zabel_____Mrs. Max W. Zabel
Debbie LaFlamme, A-935929___Dorothy G. La Flamme_____Mrs. Wm. Burr Hill, Jr.
Debutante of Rosalona,
 A-972343 ___ _____Solon P. Clickner_____Solon P. Clickner
Gauner v. Hoellental, A-742882_August Schuhmann_____August Schuhmann
Jerry Hubertus, H-2797_____Frank W. Hardy__ _____Frank W. Hardy
Rivenrock Stinger, A-964758__Anne Smith Wenden_____Anne Smith Wenden
Teckelow's Amos, H-8520_____Merton O. Farlow_____Mrs. Robert M. Koonth

Wanda of Northmont, H-4649__Northmont Kennels_____Northmont Kennels
Webb's Tempest, A-976571_____Mrs. Lester Noel Webb_____Mrs. Lester Noel Webb
Bavarian Tempo, A-922842_____Louis Flecher_____Louis Flecher
Diana v. Waldbach, H-2657_____Mrs. John C. Chaffe_____Mrs. John C. Chaffe
Gay Cavalier v. Dachshafen,
    A-937362 _____ Maude Daniels Smith_____Maude Daniels Smith
Midge of Fre-Delsa, H-6235____Frederick Pearson_____Frederick Pearson
Omaranna of Teckelhof,
    A-994747 _____Nicholay Finn_____Anna M. Gargett
Pantaloons of Hickory Hill,
    H-2623 _____Mrs. Carl H. Hanna_____Harry J. Hill
Steven of Gipsy Barn, H-2674__Mrs. Max W. Zabel_____Mrs. Max W. Zabel
Sunset of Hohenburg, H-8388__Mr. and Mrs. David L. Wall___Mr. and Mrs. David L. Wall
Aristo v. Marienlust, H-5469___Mr. and Mrs. J. Mehrer_____Kenneth W. Raymond
Aurgelmir v. Isartal, A-691219_Dr. Herbert C. Sanborn_____Dr. Herbert C. Sanborn
Gus v. Sigmaringen, A-867518_G. A. Plummer_____G. A. Plummer
Mona Lisa v. Tegernsee, H-20531_Frances Anthofer_____Frances Anthofer

Donahue of Brentwald, A-976597_Mrs. Harold Patrick_____Mrs. Harold Patrick
Dulcie v. Bergman, H-42819___Alberta Schafer and Grace   Alberta Schafer and Grace
                              Hirschman _____   Hirschman
Kandi of Badger Hill, H-14755_Harry R. Sharpe_____Harry R. Sharpe
Tessa v. Sollinge, H-38198_____Anna A. Wassermeyer_____Anna A. Wassermeyer
Zasu of Little Farm, A-831059_Mrs. David C. Dodge_____Mrs. David C. Dodge
Dachscroft Cid of Little Gate,
    H-14597 _____Dachscroft Kennels_____Dachscroft Kennels
Hu-Kay Arabella, H-12917_____Hu-Kay Kennels_____Hu-Kay Kennels
Saqui de Sangpur, H-33221____Mrs. William Burr Hill, Jr.____Mrs. William Burr Hill, Jr.
White Gables Oliver Twist,
    A-860428 _____White Gables Kennels_____White Gables Kennels
Bucknam's Merry Andrew,
    A-690588 _____Jessie I. Bucknam_____Jessie I. Bucknam
Kelle of Gipsy Barn, H-25704__Mrs. Max W. Zabel_____Mrs. Max W. Zabel
Whirlaway of Northmount,
    A-519193 _____Northmont Kennels_____Herbert Campbell
Brentwald Joshua W., H-27136_Mrs. Harold Patrick_____Mrs. Harold Patrick
Derresheim of Brentwald,
    A-976596 _____Mrs. Harold Patrick_____Mrs. Harold Patrick
Forever Don Omar, H-37604_____Charlotte R. Sibley_____Charlotte R. Sibley
Karen of Badger Hill, H-14754_Harry R. Sharpe_____Harry R. Sharpe
Lorelei of Fre Delsa, H-12927__Frederick Pearson_____Frederick Pearson
Miss Bessie of Gipsy Barn,
    H-29289 _____Mrs. Max W. Zabel_____Mrs. Max W. Zabel
Prejudice of Edgemere,
    A-814567 _____Emilie S. Bromley_____Emilie S. Bromley
Zep v. d. Daniels, A-955953_____Mr. and Mrs. D. D. Daniels____Mr. and Mrs. D. D. Daniels
Cinderella v. Marienlust,
    H-15175 _____Mr. and Mrs. J. Mehrer_____Mr. and Mrs. J. Mehrer
Gay of Waldbach, H-31018_____Alma R. Dietrich_____Mrs. John C. Chaffe
Redmond's Sir Guy, H-22007___Phyllis M. Redmond_____Phyllis M. Redmond
Black Rose of Hidden Acres,
    H-18365 _____John F. Bowne_____John F. Bowne
Calidox Daphne, H-27949_____Mrs. Jay Retzlaff_____Mrs. Jay Retzlaff
Lady v. Dychland, H-56820____Herman G. Cox_____Mr. and Mrs. F. E. Chambers
Mellow Hill Andrew, H-40303__Rock Manor Kennels_____S. L. Mellows
Red Honey v. Redmond, H-36680_Mrs. John Redmond_____Mrs. John Redmond
Seppel v. Tarau, A-982842_____Mrs. William G. Goodwin_____Mrs. William G. Goodwin

1948 (cont'd)

Teckelheim Peggy Moxley,
H-2932 _____ _____Grayce Greenburg_____E. D. Moxley
Tyka of Gipsy Barn, H-25626__Mrs. Max W. Zabel_____Mrs. Max Zabel
We-Coll-Em Charlie, H-532____Mr. and Mrs. Charles D. Coll__Mr. and Mrs. Eugene R. Luitz
Wild Fire of Blue Key, H-25673_Florence K. Brainard_____Florence K. Brainard
Bencelia's Candy, H-45949_____Bencelia Kennels_____Bencelia Kennels
Berry v. d. Daniels, A-859981__Mr. and Mrs. D. D. Daniels____Mr. and Mrs. D. D. Daniels
Cinderella v. Sieghofen,
A-806174 _____Gean M. Champion_____Gean M. Champion
Don Quixote of Teckeldorf,
H-11641 _____Katharina Lehfeldt_____Katharina Lehfeldt
Dresden of Heying Teckel,
H-42823 _____Mr. and Mrs. Fred Heying_____Mrs. Fred Heying
Echo of Badger Hill, H-14759__Harry R. Sharpe_____Harry R. Sharpe
Ed-El-Fra's Willie Wee Wee,
H-65978 _____:__Eleanor S. Kivela_____Eleanor S. Kivela
Erda v. Nesbittenhof, H-15562_Mr. and Mrs. Gordon A. Nesbitt_Gordon A. Nesbitt
Lena v. Zarky of Haft's Acres,
A-979639 _____Mary Lee Haft_____Harry J. Hill
Leutnant's Hannah Bonny
O'Doud, A-887434_____Francis J. Doody_____Francis J. Doody
Manzer's Jack o' Diamonds,
A-993087 _____White Gables Kennels_____White Gables Kennels
Menschenfreund's Dandy,
H-14598 _____Marie Martin Travis_____Marian J. Young
Menschenfreund's Dusty II,
A-693251 _____Marie Martin Travis_____Marie Martin Travis
Eddie v. Dachshafen, H-19073__Maude Daniels Smith_____Maude Daniels Smith
Flick v. Wilhelms, A-818540____Flo G. Baum_____Marjorie, Jacquelyn and
Loraine Trepagnier

Penny Ante of Northmount,
A-821193 _____Northmont Kennels_____Northmont Kennels
Roddy de Sangpur, H-37307____Mrs. William Burr Hill, Jr._____Mrs. William Burr Hill, Jr.
White Gables Onyx, H-18937___White Gables Kennels_____White Gables Kennels
Cragrobyn Isadora, H-19429____Mrs. Percy W. Cobb_____Mrs. Percy W. Cobb
Little Annis of Tween Hills,
H-7882 _____Clara Weier_____Clara Weier
Lustic v. Marienlust, H-5615____Mr. and Mrs. J. Mehrer_____Mr. and Mrs. J. Mehrer
Dandy of Deepwoods, H-70314__Mary G. Lenander_____Mary G. Lenander
Golden Glow of Rosolona,
A-843246 _____Solon P. Clickner_____Solon P. Clickner
Manzer's Tristan, H-14157_____George E. and Rena Ray Manzer_George E. and Rena Ray Manzer
Merryman of Little Gate,
H-13332 _____Mrs. Walter D. Monroe_____Mrs. Walter D. Monroe
Rivenrock Teak_____Anne Smith Wenden_____Anne Smith Wenden
Manzer's Rebecca, H-60409____George E. and Rena Ray Manzer_George E. and Rena Ray Manzer
Sparling's Hugo of Louhelen,
H-18859 _____Mrs. Louie R. Grugette_____Mrs. Louie R. Grugette
We-Coll-Em Mary, H-23753_____Mr. and Mrs. Charles D. Coll__Audrey B. Divvens
Willie v. Waldbach, H-31902__Stanley F. Todd_____Mrs. John C. Chaffe
Lucifer v. Bergman, H-42820___Alberta Schafer and Grace   Alberta Schafer and Grace
Hirschman _____ Hirschman

1949

Annie v. Teckelhof, H-31257___Anna M. Gargett_____Anna M. Gargett
Calidox Nicholas, H-53999_____Mrs. Jay Retzlaff_____Mrs. Jay Retzlaff
Dachscroft's Playboy, H-2921__Dachscroft Kennels_____Dachscroft Kennels
Dachsheim's Dale Ebony,   H. E. and Winifred M. Wash-H. E. and Winifred M. Wash-
H-53466 _____burn _____burn
Far Star's Sirius, H-39644_____Mr. and Mrs. Francis K. Allan_Mr. and Mrs. Francis K. Allan

Gayladd of Edalma, H-26340___Ed. W. Drumm_____Ed. W. Drumm
Misery v. Teckeldorf, H-18673__Katharina Lehfeldt_____Katharina Lehfeldt
Peterman's Georgina, H-32054_Sara E. Peterman_____Sara E. Peterman
Sonia v. Waldbach, H-57218_____Mrs. John C. Chaffe_____Mrs. John C. Chaffe
White Gables Colette, A-945999_White Gables Kennels_____White Gables Kennels
White Gables Thyme, A-799531_White Gables Kennels_____White Gables Kennels
Ballerina v. Marienlust, H-9514_Mr. and Mrs. J. Mehrer_____Mr. and Mrs. J. Mehrer
Harborvale Circe, H-5603_____Mr. and Mrs. D. Gregory Volkert_Mr. and Mrs. D. Gregory Volkert
Parker's Vagabond, H-6859____Esther C. Parker_____Esther C. Parker
Vee-J of Crespi, A-912476_____Donia Bussey_____Donia Bussey
Alicia of Edlidge, H-50946_____Caroline C. Anthony_____Caroline C. Anthony
Burian's Pretty Penny, H-17185_Clifford J. and Grace Burian___Clifford J. and Grace Burian
Danny v. d. Daniels, A-955950_Mr. and Mrs. D. D. Daniels_____Mr. and Mrs. D. D. Daniels
Gaylady of Edalma, H-26345___Ed. W. Drumm_____Ed. W. Drumm
Kippy v. Dachshafen, H-19072__Maude Daniels Smith_____Maude Daniels Smith
Lieutenant Commander of
   Aycock, H-47656_____Mrs. Allan G. Aycock, Jr._____Mrs. Allan G. Aycock, Jr.
Manzer's Brown Betty (CD),
   H-35813 _____George E. and Rena Ray Manzer_George E. and Rena Ray Manzer
Marleen v. d. Nidda, H-56010__Mr. and Mrs. Krug von Nidda__Mr. and Mrs. Krug von Nidda
Miss Ruby Daniels of Pal-Mar,
   H-18110 _____Paul Frederick Young_____Paul Frederick Young
Olen v. Eichwald, H-4706_____Roberta Woodson_____Roberta Woodson
Sparling's Sugar Peg of Jonor,
   H-32289 _____Eva H. Sparling_____Grayce Greenburg
Arri v. d. Daniels, H-28170_____Mr. and Mrs. D. D. Daniels_____Mr. and Mrs. D. D. Daniels
Badger Hill Ginger, H-35587__Harry R. Sharpe_____Harry R. Sharpe
Cedric of Heying-Teckel,
   H-46031 _____Mr. and Mrs. Fred Heying_____Mr. and Mrs. Fred Heying
Dinah of Deepwoods, H-70313_Mary C. Lenander_____Mary C. Lenander
Gustof v. Waddelhausen, H-8924_Mr. and Mrs. Robert Sweet_____Theresa S. Sweet
Hussar v. d. Nidda, H-56013____Mr. and Mrs. Krug von Nidda__Mr. and Mrs. Krug von Nidda
Mr. Morry of Gipsy Barn,
   H-29288 _____Mrs. Max W. Zabel_____Mrs. Max W. Zabel
Tyanah of Gipsy Barn, H-25267_Mrs. Max W. Zabel_____Mrs. Max W. Zabel
Uhlan, v. d. Nidda, H-56020____Mr. and Mrs. Krug von Nidda__Mr. and Mrs. Krug von Nidda
Von Purtnem's Miss Missile,
   H-63498 _____H. W. Mentrup_____H. W. Mentrup
Alexander of Jo-Rene, H-17202_Joe B. Marshall, Jr._____Joe B. Marshall, Jr.
Atlas v. Sieghofen, H-56506_____Gean M. Champion_____Gean M. Champion
Marjo's Rudolph, H-47231_____Marie M. Hearne_____Marie M. Hearne
Melba v. Bel-Clar, H-59630_____Belle D. Clark_____Belle D. Clark
Merry-o's Morn Mist, H-51019_Cordelia Skapinsky_____White Gables Kennels
Peter Pan of Little Gate,
   A-797453 _____Mrs. Walter D. Monroe_____Mrs. Walter D. Monroe
Red Jade v. Redmond, H-36677_Isabella Cheda _____Mrs. John Redmond
Red Sultan v. Redmond, H-36676_Mrs. John Redmond _____Mrs. John Redmond
Rosolona's Jasper, H-47883_____Solon P. Clickner_____Solon P. Clickner
Zetta of Badger Hill, H-24764__Harry R. Sharpe_____Harry R. Sharpe
Schotzy Babe, H-65396_____Betty W. Ingram_____Norma Cummings
Ali v. Herrenwald (Ger.),
   H-107576 _____Francis Elliott Madd_____Albert Boesser
Bencelia's Beliebt, H-35824_____Peter G. Monks_____Bencelia Kennels
Bergmanor Gay Galahad,
   H-58106 _____Bergmanor Kennels_____Bergmanor Kennels
Briarcliffe v. Klingson (not
   registered)
   Calidox Luigi, H-54000_____Mrs. Jay Retzlaff_____Mrs. Jay Retzlaff

1949 (cont'd)

Ellen v. Hoellental, H-16834____August Schuhmann_____August Schuhmann
Hallwyre Harpo, H-31221_____Albert A. Dains_____Hallwyre Kennels
Harborvale Constellation,
    H-5604 _____Mr. and Mrs. D. Gregory Volkert_Mr. and Mrs. D. Gregory Volkert
Lori II of Leonca, H-18485____Loretta S. Makley_____Mrs. Leon C. Johnson
Morna v. d. Nidda, H-56012____Mr. and Mrs. Krug von Nidda__Mr. and Mrs. Krug von Nidda
Peterman's Hugh III, H-32053_Sara E. Peterman_____Sara E. Peterman
Roxy's Rena, H-39521_____Etta V. Harkness_____Etta V. Harkness
Shetuker of Willoughby,
    H-24082 _____Willoughby Kennels _____Willoughby Kennels
Youvonne v. Murlake, H-69357_William and Alice R. Ake_____William and Alice R. Ake
Gayteck of Edalma, H-26342___Ed. W. Drumm_____Ed. W. Drumm
Kleetal's Arvis, H-67276_____Kleetal Kennels_____Kleetal Kennels
Maxine of Gipsy Barn H-52929_Mrs. M. Zabel_____Mrs. M. Zabel
Primrosepatch Diamond (Eng.),
    H-66255 _____Avis Mary Earle_____Mrs. O. Smith Rewse
Priscilla's Andy, H-21661_____Priscilla S. Stormont_____Priscilla S. Stormont
Smoky of Lindell, H-67148_____Jack W. Lindell_____Jack W. Lindell
Sparling's Adonis, H-63910____Mrs. James L. Sparling, Sr.__Mrs. James L. Sparling, Sr.
Starkrest's Handy Fashion,
    H-72644 _____Starkrest Kennels_____Starkrest Kennels
Victor of Gipsy Barn, H-53528_Mrs. Max W. Zabel_____Mrs. Max W. Zabel
Bergmanor Gay Guy, H-72119__Bergmanor Kennels_____Bergmanor Kennels
Cavalier v. d. Nidda, H-86552__Mr. and Mrs. Krug von Nidda__Mr. and Mrs. Krug von Nidda
Derbydachs Schatze, H-97918__Harry R. Sharpe_____Dorothy B. Derby
Erica v. d. Daniels, H-3953____Mr. asd Mrs. D. D. Daniels____Dr. L. A. Gerber
Fashion Plate of Ewardale,
    H-92457 _____Mr. and Mrs. G. F. Eward____Mr. and Mrs. G. F. Eward
Gold Ransom v. Teckelhof,
    H-113178 _____Virgilio and Isabella Cheda____Anna M. Gargett
Honey Pride v. d. Buchhorst,
    H-67014 _____John Amann_____Marilyn E. Amann
Madchen v. d. Nidda, H-56935__Mildred C. Howes_____Mr. and Mrs. Krug von Nidda
Priscilla Prim of Gipsy Barn,
    A-886693 _____Mrs. Max W. Zabel_____Mrs. Max W. Zabel
Schnitzi of Gipsy Barn, H-6339_Mrs. Maurice Weimer_____Mrs. Max W. Zabel
Yo-Ellyn W. Murlake, H-69358_W. R. Tabler_____Wm. R. and Alice M. Ake
Alex v. Nesbittenhof, A-951971_H. R. Kolp_____Gordon A. Nesbitt
Camelia v. d. Isar, H-72417____Frances A. Anthofer_____Frances A. Anthofer
Debutante of Fre Delsa, H-72309_Frederick Pearson_____Frederick Pearson
Ed-El-Fra's Doll Face, H-63011_Gilbert M. Brachofen_____Eleanor S. Kivela
Jato Ace, H-53531_____Paul H. Dane_____Paul H. Dane
Kleetal's Betka, H-26566_____Kleetal Kennels_____Kleetal Kennels
Kurt of Rose Arbors, H-60211__Muriel M. Welsford_____Muriel M. Welsford
Olga of Dachau, H-41623_____Dr. and Mrs. Olen E. Brown__Dr. and Mrs. Olen E. Brown
Priscilla's Bella, H-39838_____Priscilla Stirling Stormont_____Priscille Stirling Stormont
Edloham's Alice, H-78328_____Edith L. and Helen A. Haman___Edith L. and Helen A. Haman
Heidesta's Frika, H-110604_____Heidesta Kennels_____Louie F. Hoffman
Lacey of Gipsy Barn, H-38339_Mrs. Max W. Zabel_____Mrs. Max W. Zabel
Marquetta of Northmont,
    A-821192 _____Northmont Kennels_____Northmont Kennels
Ron-Dachs Red Rogue, H-53967_Bernard J. Beck_____Bernard J. Beck
Valencia of Heying-Teckel,
    H-72404 _____Mr. and Mrs. Fred Heying_____Mr. and Mrs. Fred Heying

1950

Badger Hill Lady, H-62673 ____Harry R. Sharpe_____Harry R. Sharpe
                            Alberta Schafer and Grace
Black Jack v. Bergman, H-42818_ Hirschman _____A. Schafer and G. Hirschman

Butz vom Gritgluck (Ger.),

    H-137146 _____Mrs. C. D. Bevis_____W. Dingel

Claudia of Red Hill, H-71508__Mrs. Mildred Sias_____Mrs William F. Ascher

Dachskell's Nordlicht, H-12911__Charles F. Kellogg_____Charles F. Kellogg

Derbydachs Kandi Too, H-94541_Dorothy B. Derby_____Dorothy B. Derby

June of Gipsy Barn, H-66158__Mrs. Max W. Zabel_____Mrs. Max W. Zabel

Sheba of Little Gate, H-43480__Mrs. Walter D. Monroe_____Mrs. Walter D. Monroe

Black Prince v. d. Nidda,

    H-82313 _____Mr. and Mrs. Krug von Nidda_Mr. and Mrs. Krug von Nidda

Ebony Eric v. d. Daniels, Jr.,

    H-3954 _____Mr. and Mrs. D. D. Daniels____Dr. L. A. Gerber

Smokyhole Rolfi (Eng.),

    H-66257 _____Avis Mary Earle_____Mrs. H. L. Waddington

Tuckerose of Gipsy Barn,

    H-58179 _____Mrs. Max W. Zabel_____Mrs. Max W. Zabel

Cindi of Heying-Teckel,

    H-24062 _____ ___Dr. Lucille Nye Schober_____Dr. Lucille Nye Schober

Gaypat of Edalma, H-47187____Ed. W. Drumm_____Ed. W. Drumm

Mitzi v. Schwarzwald Hof,

    H-21672 _____Schwarzwald Hof Kennels_____Schwarzwald Hof Kennels

Sparling's Louhelen Cito,   Eva Sparling and Helen

    H-73778 _____ Grugette _____E. Sparling and H. Grugette

Sparling's Louhelen Clio,   Eva Sparling and Helen

    H-73779 _____ Grugette _____E. Sparling and H. Grugette

Victoria of Gipsy Barn,

    H-53527 _____Mrs. Max W. Zabel_____Mrs. Max W. Zabel

Alida v. Marienlust, H-60796__Mr. and Mrs. J. Mehrer_____Mr. and Mrs. J. Mehrer

Bart v. Teckelhof, H-96503____Anna M. Gargett_____Anna M. Gargett

Otto XX, H-21556_____Leone G. Hanratty_____Leone G. Hanratty

Robin Hood of Little Gate,

    H-63847 _____Mrs. Walter D. Monroe_____Mrs. Walter D. Monroe

Ruff-Ruff, H-104433_____Alma R. Dietrich_____Alma R. Dietrich

Brentwald Pedro, H-76978_____Mrs. Harold Patrick_____Mrs. Harold Patrick

Fiddlers Hill Polka, H-65543__Fiddlers Hill Kennels_____Catherine Johnson Dardis

Gipsy Lizz of Gipsy Barn,

    H-91761 _____Edward Emmers_____Mrs. Max W. Zabel

        Mr. and Mrs. James G. Long,

Dachsgarten Serenade, H-66690_ Jr. _____Mr. and Mrs. J. G. Long, Jr.

Dalton's Favorite Starlet,

    H-73412 _____Mrs. Ella A. Dalton_____Mrs. Ella A. Dalton

Elbow Bend's Vandal, H-107095_Elbow Bend Kennels_____Elbow Bend Kennels

Midas de Sangpur, H-32580____Mrs. Wm. Burr Hill, Jr._____Mrs. Wm. Burr Hill, Jr.

Rock Manor Priscilla, H-63138_Rock Manor Kennels_____Rock Manor Kennels

Annette v. Dychland, H-22172__Herman G. Cox___ _____R. H. Coffman

Carla v. d. Nidda, H-86553____Mr. and Mrs. Krug von Nidda_Mr. and Mrs. Krug von Nidda

Dachscroft's Moonplay, H-68508_Dachscroft Kennels_____Carl and Janet Hertzberg

Debby of Deepwoods, H-70311__Mary G. Lenander_____Mary G. Lenander

Derbydachs Kandi Styck,

    H-94542 _____Dorothy B. Derby_____Dorothy B. Derby

Edloham's Abner, H-78330_____Edith L. and Helen A. Haman_Edith L. and Helen A. Haman

Effri v. d. Wurm (Ger.),

    H-151155 _____John F. Siefen_____Friedrich Hochmuth

Elbow Bend's Vixen, H-107092_Elbow Bend Kennels_____Elbow Bend Kennels

Fiddlers Hill Schottische,

    H-65541 _____Fiddlers Hill Kennels_____Catherine Johnson Dardis

Hainheim's Zarantha, H-69661_Hainheim Kennels _____Hainheim Kennels

Rebecca of Gera, H-37741_____Gene M. Shultis_____Gene M. Shultis

Rivenrock Rust, H-69304_____Donia Bussey_____Anne Smith Wenden

Tiz Derek v. d. Wolf, H-54243__Elizabeth Q. Wolf_____Elizabeth Q. Wolf

Trojan of Heying-Teckel,

    H-63752 _____Mr. and Mrs. Fred Heying____Mr. and Mrs. Fred Heying

1950 (cont'd)

Damon v. Talheim, H-86618____Maude Daniels Smith_____Jane R. Purse

Duplicate of Edgemere, H-84300_Emilie S. Bromley_____Emilie S. Bromley

Edloham's Ajax, H-78332_____Edith L. and Helen A. Haman__Edith L. and Helen A. Haman

Patiola of Aissela (Eng.),
    H-132721 _____Stanley F. Todd_____Mrs. S. Whittey

Peter of Black Hole Hollow,
    H-125192 _____Josephine Hartford Douglas___Josephine Hartford Douglas

Sir Kay of Hohenburg, H-80184_Herthwood Kennels_____Herthwood Kennels

Tessie v. Biburg, not registered_

Ed-El-Fra's Tarbaby, H-97513__Kathleen M. Hale_____Eleanor S. Kivela

Gipsy Barn's Tedder, H-103973_Mrs. Max W. Zabel_____Emmet J. O'Connell

Kleetal's Boadicea, H-129854____Kleetal Kennels_____Kleetal Kennels

Kleetal's Enchantress, H-115548_Kleetal Kennels_____Kleetal Kennels

Kleetal's Rhapsody, H-94792___Kleetal Kennels_____Kleetal Kennels

Sebastian of Red Locket,
    H-70208 _____Mr. and Mrs. W. W. Dorward_Mr. and Mrs. Henry C. Rublee

Von Purtnem's Ring Leader,
    H-72643 _____H. W. Mentrup_____Mr. and Mrs. Richard C. Dusse

Schnapsie v. Hunstein (Ger.),
    H-172424 _____Jack E. Milner_____Ludwig Niederhofer IV

Stellou's Heidi of K. J. Kastle,
    H-36964 _____James W. Miller_____Louis K. Zimmer

Tressie Huettner Gardner,
    H-93580 _____Leone G. Hanratty_____Leone G. Hanratty

Badger Hill Mr. Chips, H-84970_Harry R. Sharpe_____Harry R. Sharpe

Herman v. Tenroc, H-37911____Dr. and Mrs. Louis A. Cornet__Dr. and Mrs. Louis A. Cornet

Ramona of Greenly Hall,
    H-59036 _____Mrs. Harold Fogleson_____Mrs. Harold Fogleson

York W. Murlake, H-69356____Wm. R. and Alice M. Ake_____Wm. R. and Alice M. Ake

Black Knight v. d. Nidda,
    H-82312 _____Mr. and Mrs. Krug von Nidda__Mr. and Mrs. Krug von Nidda

Bronze v. d. Daniels, H-102463_Mr. and Mrs. D. D. Daniels___Mr. and Mrs. D. D. Daniels

Don Juan v. Teckeldorf,
    H-82499 _____Katharina Lehfeldt_____Katharina Lehfeldt

Hendrick's Royal Flush,
    H-36800 _____Wm. J. Hendrick_____Casimir I. Geibel

Macjomin's Asa, H-94753_____Minnie MacKennan_____Minnie MacKennan

Mary Ann v. Sigmaringen,
    H-70631 _____G. A. Plummer_____Mr. and Mrs. Francis K. Allan

Minton of Heying-Teckel,
    H-53461 _____Mr. and Mrs. Fred Heying____Mr. and Mrs. Fred Heying

Siefenjagenheim Hermann,
    H-137301 _____Siefenjagenheim Kennels_____John F. Siefen

Starkrest's Cadet, H-72660_____Starkrest Kennels_____Starkrest Kennels

1951

Bergmanor Bon Bon, H-83170__Bergmanor Kennels_____Bergmanor Kennels

Brentwald Destiny, H-122257___Mrs. Harold Patrick_____Mrs. Harold Patrick

Chota's Pretzel, H-88290_____Muriel M. Glenz_____Muriel M. Glenz

Creekside's Ludwig, H-72649___Mildred A. Huck_____Mildred A. Huck

Desire v. Marienlust, H-91370__Mr. and Mrs. J. Mehrer_____Mr. and Mrs. J. Mehrer

Eugenia of Gipsy Barn,
    H-119871 _____Mrs. Max W. Zabel_____Mrs. Max W. Zabel

Gari v. Spies, H-63892_____Mr. and Mrs. Lawrence E. Spece_Mr. and Mrs. Lawrence E. Spece

Harborvale Aladin, H-78672____Harborvale Kennels_____Harborvale Kennels

Jandelo's Ebony, H-104569_____Jandelo Kennels_____Elizabeth D. Derteen

Nick A Time of Blue Key,
    H-68541 _____Ted Farrell_____Florence K. Brainard

Samson of Knocknagree,
    H-106019 _____Laura F. Delano_____Laura F. Delano

Siefenjagenheim Broff,
   H-137305 _____Siefenjagenheim Kennels_____John F. Siefen
Siefenjagenheim Susabelle,
   H-137306 _____Siefenjagenheim Kennels_____John F. Siefen
Sparling's Louhelen Myra,   Eva Sparling and Helen
   H-118009 _____ Grugette _____Bergmanor Kennels
Antonia of Edlidge, H-50942__Caroline C. Anthony_____Caroline C. Anthony
Forever Revelier, H-134971____Maxmal Kennels_____Charlotte R. Sibley
Jet King of Gipsy Barn,
   H-114002 _____Mrs. Max W. Zabel_____Mrs. Max W. Zabel
Kleetal's Delight, H-115546____Kleetal Kennels_____Kleetal Kennels
Letty of Leonca, H-153779_____Mrs. Leon C. Johnson_____Mrs. Leon C. Johnson
Red Velvet of Fre Delsa,
   H-72311 _____Frederick Pearson_____Frederick Pearson
San Souci's San Pedro,
   H-94793 _____Mrs. Alice L. Thompson_____R. S. Thompson
Stropp v. Drackenheim,
   H-95804 _____William H. Jolly_____William H. Jolly
Valencia Murlake, H-172555____Wm. R. and Alice M. Ake_____Wm. R. and Alice M. Ake
Webb's Torrid v. Teckelhof,
   H-65365 _____Lester N. Webb_____Anna M. Gargett
Hekka v. Freia, H-107478_____Victor Moench_____Victor Moench
Jandelo's Kobold, H-114258____Jandelo Kennels_____Jandelo Kennels
Koboldsheim Lothar, H-71643___Koboldsheim Kennels _____Joseph E. Sperling
Brentwald Caprice, H-122281__Mrs. Harold Patrick_____Mrs. Harold Patrick
Bucknam's Merry Jane, H-68118_Mr. and Mrs. Chas. S. Ingalls__Jessie I. Bucknam
Crespi's Zilly, H-143848_____Donia Cline_____Mrs. Howard G. Steinwinter
The Duchess of Lambros,
   H-80211 _____Mrs. Evelyn Lambros_____Mrs. Evelyn Lambros
The Duke of Red Hill, H-107538_Mrs. Mildred Sias_____Jean T. Knowles
Thomanel's Lola, H-113939_____C. Owen and J. Westbrook____C. Owen and J. Westbrook
Bestor of Gipsy Barn, H-131429_Mrs. Max W. Zabel_____Mrs. Max W. Zabel
Brentwald Jo-Ellyn W., H-27139_Mrs. Harold Patrick_____Mrs. Harold Patrick
Cara of Gera, H-121895_____Mr. and Mrs. Ray E. Shultis__Gene M. Shultis
Challis of Crespi Street, H-78913_Donia Bussey_____Donia Bussey
Cinnamon of Norbourne,
   H-102257 _____Ernest L. Floore, Jr._____Ernest L. Floore, Jr.
Dyna-Mite of Northmont,
   H-104796 _____Northmont Kennels_____Mrs. Wm. Burr Hill, Jr.
Inka v. Nesbittenhof, H-25387__Mr. and Mrs. Gordon A. Nesbitt_Gordon A. Nesbitt
Maximilian v. Notfort, H-83991_Luci Ward Natteford_____L. W. and J. Natteford
Paprika of Norbourne, H-102258_Ernest L. Floore, Jr._____Ernest L. Floore, Jr.
Sir Joe of Little Gate, H-43477_Mrs. Walter D. Monroe_____Mrs. Walter D. Monroe
Sparling-Louhelen Favor-Rita, Eva Sparling and Helen
   H-122158 _____ Grugette _____E. Sparling and H. Grugette
Bencelia's Cavalier, H-31292___Alice M. Harper_____Bencelia Kennels
Black Brocade v. d. Nidda,
   H-56009 _____Mr. and Mrs. Krug von Nidda_Mr. and Mrs. Krug von Nidda
Brentwald O'Keefe, H-55288_____Mrs. Harold Patrick_____Mrs. Harold Patrick
Carbon of Heying-Teckel,
   H-161854 _____Mr. and Mrs. Fred Heying____Mr. and Mrs. Fred Heying
Caru Kanda, H-149214_____Ruth J. Slade_____Ruth J. Slade
Eian of Gipsy Barn, H-119867___Mrs. Max W. Zabel_____Mrs. Max W. Zabel
McDowell's Anni-ver-sary,
   H-110234 _____Mrs. Marjorie A. McDowell____Roberta B. Jones
Pansy de Sangpur, H-32581_____Mrs. Wm. Burr Hill, Jr._____Mrs. Wm. Burr Hill, Jr.
Rivenrock Tamale, H-90813____Anne S. Wenden_____Anne S. Wenden
Showboy of Smith, H-102337___Mr. and Mrs. Ed. L. Smith_____Mrs. Allan G. Aycock, Jr.

Split Rock's Ember, H-112920__Howard A. Rumpf_____Howard A. Rumpf
The Lieutenant of Earldale,
    H-23953 _____Aubria E. Bywaters_____Aubria E. Bywaters
Bonny of Calrene, H-142534_____Mr. and Mrs. Fred C. Reeb_____Mrs. Fred C. Reeb
Brentwald Copyright, H-122278_Mrs. Harold Patrick_____Mrs. Harold Patrick
Dachsberry's Rebecca, H-129010_Mr. and Mrs. Elmer E. Berry__Mr. and Mrs. Elmer E. Berry
Edlcham's Amy, H-78326_____Edith L. and Helen A. Haman__Edith L. and Helen A. Haman
Favorite of Norbourne,
    H-139894 _____Ernest L. Floore, Jr._____Ernest L. Floore, Jr.
Forever Basilotte, H-9421_____Charlotte R. Sibley_____Charlotte R. Sibley
Hardway Welcome Stranger,
    H-110609 _____ _____Mrs. John W. Cross, Jr._____Jeannette W. Gillies
Herzig v. Teckelhof, H-47663___Anna M. Gargett_____Waldbach Kennels
Liebling v. d. Nidda, H-128820_Mrs. Thassilo K. von Nidda_____Mr. and Mrs. Krug von Nidda
Morna's Mr. Trouble, H-166355_Mrs. Andrew E. Propper_____Mrs. Andrew E. Propper
Pandora of Bertmar, H-134199__Herbert H. Berresheim_____Harold F. Harmer
Schnapps v. Haar (Ger.),
    H-82202 _____Charles W. Wachtell_____Anton Franz Muller
Siefenjagenheim Liesel,
    H-137308 _____Siefenjagenheim Kennels_____John F. Siefen
Siefenjagenheim Vesta,
    H-137307 _____Siefenjagenheim Kennels_____John F. Siefen
Bergmanor Black Bart, H-95060_Alberta Schafer and Grace
                                Hirschman _____A. Schafer and G. Hirschman
Celloyd Rouge, H-116954_____Lloyd M. Case_____Dr. Robert S. Buol
Creekside's Lelia, H-133896____Mildred A. Huck_____Mildred A. Huck
Derbydachs Kandi Kain,
    H-94544 _____Dorothy B. Derby _____Dorothy B. Derby
De Sangpur Dice, H-139646____Mrs. Wm. Burr Hill, Jr._____H. H. Tiffany and Mrs. W. B.
                                                            Hill, Jr.
De Sangpur Judy, H-139650____Mrs. Wm. Burr Hill, Jr._____H. H. Tiffany and Mrs. W. B.
                                                            Hill, Jr.

Ed-El-Fra's Paha Poika,
    H-101795 _____Eleanor S. Kivela_____Eleanor S. Kivela
Elbow Bend's Raggedy Ann,
    H-133912 _____Elbow Bend Kennels_____Elbow Bend Kennels
Ivanhill's Whirlaway, H-83821_Mildred Tebeau_____Mildred Tebeau
Kleetal's Corrinne, H-144167___Kleetal Kennels_____Kleetal Kennels
Peterman's Candidate, H-112434_Sara E. Peterman_____Sara E. Peterman
Rotfuch's v. Sollinge, H-140666_Anna A. Wassermeyer_____Anna A. Wassermeyer
Schmeichler, H-105136_____Margie L. Beckenbaugh_____Margie L. Beckenbaugh
Thomanel's Maude, H-113941___C. Owen and J. Westbrook_____C. Owen and J. Westbrook
Black Forest's Diogenes,
    H-105375 _____Mrs. L. Zingler_____Mrs. L. Zingler
Brentwald Brigadier, H-122270_Mrs. Harold Patrick_____Mrs. Harold Patrick
Brentwald Lee-Ann of
    Deepwoods, H-127124_____Mrs. Harold Patrick_____Mary G. Lenander
Carla v. Sunset View, H-76322_Mrs. Flsa M. Worthington_____Mrs. Elsa M. Worthington
Hale Kai's Clover, H-96666____Hale Kai Kennels_____Hale Kai Kennels
Kleetal's Fantasy, H-144177___Kleetal Kennels_____Kleetal Kennels
Kur-Und-Lang Favorite Girl,
    H-124214 _____Mrs. Harold K. Shawan_____Mrs. Harold K. Shawan
Merry Christmas v.
    Dychland, H-140142_____Mrs. Herman G. Cox_____Mary G. Lenander
Sparling's Phil, H-116331_____Eva H. Sparling_____Eva H. Sparling
Tempo v. Teckelhof, H-70032___Richard A. Zimmerman_____Anna M. Gargett
Black Knight of Heying-Teckel,
    H-125377 _____ _____Bertha E. Deakin_____Mr. and Mrs. Fred Heying
Chota's Wendy, H-88292_____Muriel M. Glenz_____Muriel M. Glenz

1951 (cont'd)

Edloham's Alexa, H-78329_____Edith L. and Helen A. Haman_Edith L. and Helen A. Haman

Gold Lace of Marin, H-121184__Virgilio and Isabella Cheda___Virgilio and Isabella Cheda

Sparling's Louhelen Clancy,   Eva Sparling and Helen

   H-123402 _____ Grugette _____E. Sparling and H. Grugette

Split Rock's Eric, H-112916___Howard A. Rumpf_____Howard A. Rumpf

The Duke of Lambros, H-80212_Mrs. Evelyn Lambros_____Mrs. Evelyn Lambros

Hollyhill Piper Piper (Eng.),

   H-166810 _____Dachscroft Kennels_____Miss W. A. Riley

Barcwyn Donald, H-89572_____Winifred E. Crabtree_____Winifred E. Crabtree

Brentwald Valeria, H-117432___Harold Patrick_____Harold Patrick

Cragrobyn Quicksilver, H-109286_Mrs. Percy W. Cobb_____Mrs. Percy W. Cobb

Henni v. Schoberhaus, H-131170_Dr. Lucile Nye Schober_____Dr. Lucile Nye Schober

Lustigkeit's Kurt, H-103140___J. Oscar Schneider_____J. Oscar Schneider

MacJomin's Duke, H-136850____Minnie MacKennan_____Minnie MacKennan

Sans Souci's Santa Rosa,

   H-94797 _____Mrs. Alice L. Thompson_____R. S. Thompson

Starkrest's Caramac, H-183909_Starkrest Kennels_____Otto C. Borchardt

Sunkist of Heying-Teckel,

   H-116702 _____Mr. and Mrs. Fred Heying____Mr. and Mrs. Fred Heying

Wanda's Merry Vicki, H-108060_Wanda L. Jalmasco_____Wanda L. Jalmasco

Barb Wire of Heying-Teckel,

   H-182177 _____Mr. and Mrs. Fred Heying____Catherine I. Knapp

Teckelow's Penny, H-190159____Mrs. Merton A. Farlow_____Mrs. Merton A. Farlow

Ferro de Sangpur, H-32578____Mrs. Wm. Burr Hill, Jr._____Mrs. Wm. Burr Hill, Jr.

Herr Gottleib de Bungay,

   H-181839 _____Evelyn J. Guion_____Evelyn J. Guion

Zeedel Juliette, H-115921_____Zelie de L. Ely_____Zelie de L. Ely

Zeke of Gipsy Barn, H-131427__Mrs. Max W. Zabel_____Mrs. Max W. Zabel

Zinia v. Teckelhof, H-99817___Anna M. Gargett_____Anna M. Gargett

Egyptian Moe of Joyce (Can.),

   H-181169 _____Joy Osterdahl _____Joy Osterdahl

Pfavoretta o' Pfeifer's, H-90807_Carl O. Pfeifer_____Carl O. Pfeifer

Schwiekie v. Hoffmeister,

   H-74311 _____C. R. Hoffmeister_____C. R. Hoffmeister

Silver Oaks of Monty-Ayr,

   H-110580 _____E. S. Montgomery_____John Amann

1952

Crespi's Malachi, H-143849_____Donia Cline_____Mrs. Howard G. Steinwinter

Elbow Bend's Encore, H-107093_Elbow Bend Kennels_____Elbow Bend Kennels

Halfway Otto, H-169634_____Mrs. Theodora A. Randolph____Mrs. Theodora A. Randolph

Huebsche Jungfrau de Bungay,

   H-181837 _____Evelyn J. Guion_____Evelyn J. Guion

Jandelo's Carlo, H-114259_____Jandelo Kennels_____Jandelo Kennels

Black Treasure of Myrandy,

   H-126690 _____Andrew H. Rihl_____Edwin G. Glover

Creekside's Fanfare, H-122687__Mildred A. Huck_____Mildred A. Huck

Lance of Heying-Teckel,

   H-159369 _____Mr. and Mrs. Fred Heying_____Mr. and Mrs. Fred Heying

Rastus of Heying-Teckel,

   H-88173 _____Mr. and Mrs. Fred Heying_____Mr. and Mrs. Fred Heying

Roxy's Reuben, H-39519_____Etta W. Harkness_____Etta W. Harkness

Wynne of Ringold, H-116298___Mrs. Howard J. Kaiser_____Mrs. Howard J. Kaiser

Grimr v. Isartal, H-104489____Herbert C. Sanborn_____Herbert C. Sanborn

Josephine of Knocknagree,

   H-106018 _____Laura F. Delano_____Laura F. Delano

Ultra-Mend Gold Rush of

   Valgo, H-211960_____Frank W. McHugh_____Steward H. Schoonover

Zeedel Jon, H-115920_____Zelie de L. Ely_____Zelie de L. Ely

Crespi's Thunderbird, H-117493_Donia Cline _____Donia Cline
Dokjan's D'Artagnan, H-121063_Dokjan Kennels_____Dokjan Kennels
Kleetal's Congenial, H-173315__Kleetal Kennels_____Kleetal Kennels
Kleetal's Missie, H-172751_____Kleetal Kennels_____Kleetal Kennels
Sparling's Brill, H-152934_____Eva H. Sparling_____Eva H. Sparling
Golden Sensation of Marin,
  H-121181 _____Virgilio and Isabella Cheda___Virgilio and Isabella Cheda
Rhett v. Hildburghausen,
  H-197537 _____Marjorie P. and Leonard L.
                             Dennard _____M. P. and B. L. Dennard
Morna's Mr. Six, H-166353____Mrs. Andrew E. Propper_____Mrs. Andrew E. Propper
Siefenjagenheim Guido,
  H-200159 _____Siefenjagenheim Kennels _____John F. Siefen
Siefenjagenheim Marta,
  H-201596 _____Jandelo Kennels_____John F. Siefen
Allegro of Gera, H-180902____Mr. and Mrs. Ray E. Shultis__Gene M. Shultis
Comtesse Annamirl, H-249814__Bertha E. Deakin_____Dorothy W. Barberis
Casanova v. Teckeldorf,
  H-148126 _____Katharina Lehfeldt_____Katharina Lehfeldt
Dixie Doxie's Ego, H-126989___Dixie Doxie Kennels_____Dixie Doxie Kennels
Little Farm Amelia, H-9414___Mrs. David C. Dodge _____Mrs. David C. Dodge
Playful of Bertmar, H-171470__Herbert H. Berresheim _____H. H. and Rosemary Berresheim
Topdox Eric, H-152852_____Thomas Pringle, Jr._____Thomas Pringle, Jr.
Dachscroft's Hapence, H-168761_Dachscroft Kennels_____Dachscroft Kennels
Maedchen of East Earl,
  H-127883 _____Stanley F. Todd_____Stanley F. Todd
Gold Brocade of Marin,
  H-121185 _____Virgilio and Isabella Cheda____Virgilio and Isabella Cheda
Albion's Own Forester,
  H-100041 _____Chas. E. Holden_____Chas. E. Holden
Buol's Topaz, H-208489_____Robert S. Buol_____Robert S. Buol
Kleetal's Larch, H-145637_____Ruth T. Earle_____Kleetal Kennels
Rochester of Heying-Teckel,
  H-88172 _____Mr. and Mrs. Fred Heying_____Mr. and Mrs. Fred Heying
Starkrest's Helga, H-133534____Starkrest Kennels_____Starkrest Kennels
Reprint of Edgemere, H-84299__Emilie S. Bromley_____Emilie S. Bromley
Wylde Surmise (Eng.),
  H-198036 _____Stanley F. Todd_____Miss S. N. Evans
Brentwald Quest, H-169696_____Mrs. Harold Patrick_____Mrs. Harold Patrick
Forever Golden Nugget,   J. E. Clinton and S. G.
  H-233078 _____ Canavera _____Charlotte R. Sibley
Wearytime's Victoria, H-177188_Mr. and Mrs. Gus H. Meyer _Mr. and Mrs. Gus H. Meyer
Chardeline's Kandina v.
  Teckelhof, H-220131 _____Mr. and Mrs. C. C. Fernsell____Anna M. Gargett
Kleetal's Clementine, H-196255__Kleetal Kennels_____Kleetal Kennels
Red Locket Shamrock, H-170192_Mr. and Mrs. Woodrow W.
                             Dorward _____Mr. and Mrs. W. W. Dorward
Hollyhill Silvershell (Eng.),
  H-161757 _____Dachscroft Kennels_____Miss W. A. Riley
Starkrest's Lotti, H-187698_____Starkrest Kennels_____Starkrest Kennels
Heindrich vom Kleine Beine,
  H-193946 _____Carl Focht_____ ____Carl Focht
Lancer v. d. Nidda, H-128819__Mrs. Thassilo K. von Nidda__Mr. and Mrs. Krug von Nidda
Sambornedach's Edith, H-202724_Eugene D. Sullivan_____Eugene D. Sullivan
Agilita of Gera, H-180905_____Mr. and Mrs. Ray E. Shultis__Gene M. Shultis
Bunnell Boruss, H-102220_____Mr. and Mrs. Donald W. Bunnell_Mr. and Mrs. D. W. Bunnell
Cline-Dach's Katinka, H-179213_Albert W. Cline_____Albert W. Cline
Cyclon v. Marienlust, H-133324__Mr. and Mrs. J. Mehrer_____Mr. and Mrs. J. Mehrer

Gay Demon of Edalma, H-140432_Ed W. Drumm_____Chas. E. Holden
Kleetal's Wonder, H-196297____Kleetal Kennels_____Kleetal Kennels
Peterman's Gay Lothario,
    H-130003 _____Sara E. Peterman_____Sara E. Peterman
Til Eulenspiegel, H-121173_____Duska L. Carman_____Duska L. Carman
Starkrest's Nanette, H-183930__Starkrest Kennels_____Starkrest Kennels
The Witch's Brat, H-226053____R. S. Hill and A. E. Applegate_Jerry Rigden
Forever Golden Antonio,
    H-233079 _____Isabella Cheda_____Charlotte R. Sibley
Jandelo's Hexe, H-114255_____Jandelo Kennels _____Jandelo Kennels
Merry Antonette of Barcedor,
    H-242500 _____Mrs. Scott K. Wood_____Dorothy W. Barberis
Siefenjagenheim Stoff, H-137304_Siefenjagenheim Kennels_____John F. Siefen
Alden of Raymihill, H-149351__Raymond S. Hill_____Raymond S. Hill
Badger Hill Nox, H-183531_____Harry R. Sharpe_____Harry R. Sharpe
Bandit of Indian Hills, H-100697_Mary Jane Osha_____Mary Jane Osha
Chloe's Posey v. Lindwehr,
    H-194833 _____Ada B. Lindsey_____Ada B. Lindsey
Emmy Lou v. Waddelhausen,
    H-222376 _____Mr. and Mrs. Robert H. Sweet__Mr. and Mrs. Robert H. Sweet
Hainheim's Tresilda, H-180128__Hainheim Kennels_____Hainheim Kennels
Kleetal's Reynolds, H-144151__Kleetal Kennels_____Kleetal Kennels
MacJomin's Onyx, H-174352____Minnie MacKennan _____Minnie MacKennan
Parker's Angelica, H-121556____Esther C. Parker_____Esther C. Parker
Red Locket Commander,   Mr. and Mrs. Woodrow W.
    H-177961 _____Dorward _____Mr. and Mrs. W. W. Dorward
Chandon Badger, H-133277_____Natica J. Bates_____Natica J. Bates
Hohenburg Fraulein, H-180194_Hohenburg Kennels_____Hohenburg Kennels
Show Boy of Hohenburg,
    H-154138 _____Hohenburg Kennels _____Hohenburg Kennels
Thomanel's Anka, not registered_E. Thomas and L. Magary_____
Connie de Sangpur, H-52986___Mrs. Wm. Burr Hill, Jr._____Mrs. Wm. Burr Hill, Jr.
Terry de Sangpur, H-53579____Mrs. Wm. Burr Hill, Jr._____Mrs. Wm. Burr Hill, Jr.
Alexander's Rot Schatten,
    H-181480 _____Leslie J. Howell_____Eva Sparling and Helen Grugette
Bit of Bronze, H-236787_____Bertha E. Deakin_____Bertha E. Deakin
Black Beauty o' Pfeifer's,
    H-64882 _____Carl O. Pfeifer_____Mrs. M. E. Eckroth
Chips v. Bel-Clar, H-106522_____Belle D. Clark_____Belle D. Clark
Cracker Jack of Tween Hills,
    H-157377 _____Clara Weier_____Clara Weier
Danhauer's Koenig, H-131752__Mr. and Mrs. M. Danhauer_____Mr. and Mrs. M. Danhauer
Fascination of Earldale,
    H-181368 _____Aubria E. Bywaters_____Aubria E. Bywaters
Lotus of Heying-Teckel,
    H-159368 _____Mr. and Mrs. Fred Heying____Mr. and Mrs. Fred Heying
Brentwald Warbonnet, H-195139_Mrs. Harold Patrick_____Elsie Olin Sang
Giselle of Knocknagree,
    H-106974 _____Laura F. Delano_____Laura F. Delano
Teena v. Sollinge, H-38199____Anna A. Wassermeyer_____Anna A. Wassermeyer
Virginia's Mi-Jo, H-158537____Harley W. Smith_____Harley W. Smith
Bergmanor Boyoboy, H-190539__Bergmanor Kennels_____Mrs. June Ferrell
Dachsgarten Casino, H-137352__Mr. and Mrs. James G. Long, Jr._Mr. and Mrs. James G. Long, Jr.
Diamond Lil of Marin, H-174584_Mrs. L. J. Zander _____Anne F. Murphy
Webb's Torreodora, H-111865___Mrs. Lester Noel Webb_____Mary L. Potter
Live Wire of Heying-Teckel,
    H-200358 _____Mr. and Mrs. Fred Heying ____Mr. and Mrs. Fred Heying
Prinzessin Millie v. Stephens,
    H-256924 _____Mrs. N. R. Stephens_____Mrs. Harold Patrick

1952 (cont'd)

Sissy W von Lindenau, H-202463_Mr. and Mrs. H. C. Leach, Jr._Mr. and Mrs. H. C. Leach, Jr.
Antonio von Barcedor, H-242497_Dorothy W. Barberis_____Dorothy W. Barberis
De Sangpur Traveling Man,
   H-202630 _____Mrs. Wm. Burr Hill, Jr._____Mrs. Wm. Burr Hill, Jr.
Elbow Bend's Forget-Me-Not,
   H-166728 _____Elbow Bend Kennels_____Elbow Bend Kennels
Karl v. Spies, H-23632_____Mr. and Mrs. Laurence E. Spece_Mr. and Mrs. L. E. Spece
Plume d'Or v. d. Busch,
   H-189812 _____David and Libby Bush_____David and Libby Bush
Primrosepatch Pretzel Bit,
   H-153804 _____Leona M. M. Goodspeed_____Leona M. M. Goodspeed
Raphael of Calyla, H-231849____J. C. Walters_____Harry R. Sharpe
Badger Hill New Deal, H-183529_Harry R. Sharpe_____Harry R. Sharpe
Charmaine v. Marienlust,
   H-176627 _____Mr. and Mrs. J. Mehrer_____Mr. and Mrs. J. Mehrer
Danhauer's Witzbold, H-185314_Mr. and Mrs. M. Danhauer____Mr. and Mrs. M. Danhauer
Direct v. Marienlust, H-91369__Mr. and Mrs. J. Mehrer_____Mr. and Mrs. J. Mehrer
Hainheim's Gunilda, H-115060__Hainheim Kennels_____Hainheim Kennels
Kleetal's Maid Marian, H-173307_Kleetal Kennels _____Kleetal Kennels
Lisa v. Sigmaringen, H-238579_G. A. Plummer_____Mr. and Mrs. Clyde S. Driscoll
Seth of Marstone, H-198936____Mrs. Marcella S. Firestone____Mrs. Marcella S. Firestone
Dearest v. Dachshafen,
   H-237050 _____Maude D. Smith_____Maude D. Smith
Wylde Cantata (Eng.),
   H-233509 _____Stanley F. Todd_____Miss S. N. Evans

1953

Forever Beloved Belinda,
   H-187079 _____Henrietta S. Keiran_____Henrietta S. Keiran
Bob's Jill of Ray-Mill, H-183921_Mrs. M. N. Wardall_____Mrs. M. N. Wardall
Hohenburg's Aristo, H-193806__Hohenburg Kennels_____Hohenburg Kennels
Kleetal's Magi, H-145626_____Kleetal Kennels_____Kleetal Kennels
Russ v. Schneid, H-169362_____A. R. Colvin_____A. R. Colvin
Starkrest's Royal Jester,
   H-114237 _____Starkrest Kennels_____Starkrest Kennels
Zeedel Adelaide, H-173640_____Mrs. Hiram B. Ely_____Mrs. Hiram B. Ely
Starkrest's Vagabond, H-183929_Starkrest Kennels_____Starkrest Kennels
Brentwald Story, H-177803_____Mrs. Harold Patrick_____Mrs. Harold Patrick
Hilda v. Sollinge II, H-140667__Anna A. Wassermeyer_____Anna A. Wassermeyer
Buster v. Sigmaringen, H-134247_A. Murl Ake_____G. A. Plummer
Eden of Gera, H-200988_____Mr. and Mrs. Ray E. Shultis___Gene M. Shultis
Rosolona's Dinah, H-187649____Solon P. Clickner_____Solon P. Clickner
Standard of Heying-Teckel,
   H-116701 _____Mr. and Mrs. Fred Heying_____Mr. and Mrs. Fred Heying
Badger Hill Boots, H-237705____Harry R. Sharpe_____Harry R. Sharpe
Forever Giandoni's Antonio,
   H-171088 _____Wm. L. Giandoni_____Charlotte R. Sibley
Queenie v. Sunset View, H-54109_Elsa M. Worthington_____Elsa M. Worthington
Sambornedach's Caesar,
   H-202726 _____Eugene D. Sullivan_____Eugene D. Sullivan
Debutante's Deirdre, H-146185_Nancy F. Onthank_____Nancy F. Onthank
Harborvale Bonnie Charles,
   H-104126 _____Harborvale Kennels_____Harborvale Kennels
Kim of Lildon, H-167605_____Donald E. Frazier_____Donald E. Frazier
MacJomin's Candykiss.
   H-174354 _____Minnie MacKennan_____Minnie MacKennan
Wylde Boomps A Daisy (Eng.),
   H-233508 _____Stanley F. Todd_____Miss S. N. Evans

Agne of Gipsy Barn, H-199122_Mrs. Max W. Zabel_____Mrs. Max W. Zabel
Jandelo's Perro Largo,
   H-166616 _____Jandelo Kennels_____Jandelo Kennels
Rasti vom Borghill, H-241897__Johanna Hedenborg_____Johanna Hedenborg
Alcott of Raymihill, H-149352__Raymond S. Hill_____Raymond S. Hill
Alice of Heying-Teckel,
   H-176835 _____Mr. and Mrs. Fred Heying_____Ray S. Thompson
Merry Kay v. Belleau, H-161517_Cordelia Skapinsky _____Cordelia Skapinsky
Dina v. Amrum, not registered_I. Kroef_____
Josh v. Teckeldorf, H-216531__Katharina Lehfeldt_____Katharina Lehfeldt
Bachofen's Darklis v. Klingsor,
   H-184855 _____Mrs. Walter F. Hildebrand_____Gilbert M. Bachofen
Bencelia's Hill Prince,
   H-222164 _____Bencelia Kennels _____Bencelia Kennels
Ace of Gipsy Barn, H-199120__Mrs. Max W. Zabel_____Mrs. Max W. Zabel
Bergmanor Tizeenie, H-193080_Bergmanor Kennels_____Bergmanor Kennels
Bro Bark's Patti Cake, H-189258_Lucile L. Brophy_____Eva Sparling and Helen
                                                                                                   Grugette
Dachsberry's Pacemaker,
   H-203836 _____Mr. and Mrs. Elmer E. Berry__Mr. and Mrs. Elmer E. Berry
Elbow Bend's Troubles,
   H-114826 _____Elbow Bend Kennels_____Elbow Bend Kennels
Gloria of Heying-Teckel,
   H-189178 _____Mr. and Mrs. Fred Heying_____Mr. and Mrs. Fred Heying
Hibner's Belinda, H-180030____Mrs. Don T. Hibner_____Mrs. Don T. Hibner
Michaela of Raymihill,
   H-178786 _____Raymond S. Hill_____Raymond S. Hill
Reinwald of Edlidge, H-210769_Caroline C. Anthony_____Caroline C. Anthony
Red Locket Hexe, H-187402____Mr. and Mrs. Woodrow W.
                                                 Dorward _____Mr. and Mrs. Woodrow W.
                                                                                                   Dorward
Clipp v. Nesbittenhof, H-214153_Mr. and Mrs. Gordon A. Nesbitt_Mr. and Mrs. Gordon A. Nesbitt
Dachsgarten Cardinal, H-273478_Bud and Marie Lough_____Mr. and Mrs. J. G. Long, Jr.
Elbow Bend's Chatter-Box,
   H-133910 _____Elbow Bend Kennels_____Elbow Bend Kennels
Dolores of Dachau, H-138521___Dr. and Mrs. Olen E. Brown___Dr. and Mrs. Olen E. Brown
Don Juan of Heying-Teckel,
   H-180711 _____Mr. and Mrs. Fred Heying_____Mr. and Mrs. Fred Heying
Hainheim's Lance, H-258131___ _Hainheim Kennels_____Hainheim Kennels
Harborvale Valiant, H-257353__Mrs. Lancaster Andrews_____Harborvale Kennels
Hekka's Siegfried, H-218615___Victor Moench_____Victor Moench
Kleetal's Ingulf, H-222757_____Kleetal Kennels_____Kleetal Kennels
Sparling Louhelen Alden,   Eva Sparling and Helen   Eva Sparling and Helen
   H-206538 _____ Grugette _____ Grugette
Sparling Louhelen Auroro,
   H-206540 _____Eva Sparling and Helen
                                                 Grugette _____Eva Sparling and Helen
                                                                                                   Grugette
Susie of Raymihill, H-168704__Raymond S. Hill_____Raymond S. Hill
Prinz Maximillian v. Stephens,
   H-256923 _____ ___N. R. Stephens__ _____
De Sangpur Eileen, H-234717__Mrs. Wm. Burr Hill, Jr._____Mrs. Wm. Burr Hill, Jr.
De Sangpur Flapper, H-144859_Mrs. Wm. Burr Hill, Jr._____Mrs. Wm. Burr Hill, Jr.
Forever Amber v. Grant,
   H-91376 _____Don L. Grant_____Don L. Grant
Gold Christine of Marin,
   H-193405 _____Virgilio and Isabella Cheda_____Virgilio and Isabella Cheda
Gold Flirt v. d. Busch,
   H-189814 _____David and Libby Bush_____David and Libby Bush

Gold Valiant of Marin,
 H-246570 _____Virgilio and Isabella Cheda_____Virgilio and Isabella Cheda
Princess Peggy of Marin,
 H-158329 _____Virgilio and Isabella Cheda_____Virgilio and Isabella Cheda
Siefenjagenheim Weebor,
 H-137303 _____Siefenjagenheim Kennels_____John F. Siefen
Trouble Shooter of Barcedor,
 H-281555 _____D. W. Barberis_____D. W. Barberis
Badger Hill Nobby, H-183532__Harry R. Sharpe_____Harry R. Sharpe
Bencelia's Real Delight,
 H-257358 _____Bencelia Kennels_____
Clark's Pursuit, H-207571_____Mrs. Geoffrey Clark_____Mrs. Geoffrey Clark
Fritz von Ranger Schmidt,
 H-275263 _____Mr. and Mrs. W. W. Smith_____
Manzer's Red Rogue, H-253260_Caru Kennels_____G. C. and R. R. Manzer
Poppaea von Hohenstauffen,
 H-258514 _____A. W. Stover_____
Sparling's Louhelen Raci,
 H-150829 _____Eva Sparling and Helen   Eva Sparling and Helen
                            Grugette _____ Grugette
Venus von Hohenstauffen,
 H-189475 _____Alberta W. Stover_____Alberta W. Stover
Wee-nee Haven's Darby,
 H-184531 _____John F. Jones_____...John F. Jones
Pinocchio W. of Raymihill,
 H-241714 _____Raymond S. Hill_____Raymond S. Hill and Mrs. N. R.
                                                                   Stephens
Starkrest's Souvenir, H-290472_A. E. Applegate_____
Angell of Gipsy Barn, H-199125_Mrs. Max W. Zabel_____Mrs. Max W. Zabel
De Sangpur Jeffrey, H-144857__Mrs. Wm. Burr Hill, Jr._____Mrs. Wm. Burr Hill, Jr.
Trouble-Son of Barcedor,
 H-281556 _____D. W. Barberis_____D. W. Barberis
Annette of Gera, H-227766_____Mr. and Mrs. Ray E. Shultis__Mr. and Mrs. Ray E. Shultis
Black Lustre v. d. Daniels,
 H-174021 _____Mr. and Mrs. D. D. Daniels___Mr. and Mrs. D. D. Daniels
Kelmah's Christinia, H-289925__Kelmahs Kennels_____
Kleetal's Duncan Phyfe,
 H-145630 _____Kleetal Kennels_____Kleetal Kennels
Kleetal's Rembrandt, H-144155_Kleetal Kennels_____Kleetal Kennels
Rhetta v. Hildburghausen,   Marjorie P. and Bennie L.
 H-197538 _____ Dennard _____M. P. and B. L. Dennard
Zeedel Aladdin, H-149697_____Mrs. Hiram B. Ely_____Mrs. Hiram B. Ely
Fabian of LeLou, H-270037_____Mrs. L. E. Warren_____
Frolic of LeLou, H-270036_____Mrs. N. R. Stephens_____
Hush yo' mouf Liza v. d.   R. S. Hill and Mrs. N. R.
 Stephens, H-241717_____Mrs. Neville R. Stephens_____ Stephens
Iodine W of Heying Teckel,
 H-219229 _____Mr. and Mrs. Fred Heying_____Mr. and Mrs. Fred Heying
Tweed v. Waldbach, H-212226__John C. Chaffe_____John C. Chaffe
De Sangpur Melissa, H-202632__Mrs. Wm. Burr Hill, Jr._____Mrs. Wm. Burr Hill, Jr.
Herr Volkman de Bungay,
 H-181841 _____Evelyn J. Guion_____Evelyn J. Guion
Jandelo's Don Juan, H-60728__Mrs. Louis Derteen, Jr._____Mrs. Louis Derteen, Jr.
Bergmanor Tallula, H-241855___Bergmanor Kennels_____Mr. and Mrs. Ray E. Shultis
Dandy Dachs Danny, H-250417__Mr. and Mrs. Robert E. Hunter__Mr. and Mrs. Robert E. Hunter
Southdown's Adona, H-271533__K. Merrill_____
Black Wire of Heying-Teckel,
 H-236533 _____Mr. and Mrs. Fred Heying____Mr. and Mrs. Fred Heying

1953 (cont'd)

Teckelow's Gretchen, H-266725_Mrs. M. A. Farlow_____

Dea-Dox Pak O-Trouble,.
  H-314009 _____B. E. Deakin_____

Fo ever Langesk's Mercurio, Mr. and Mrs. G. D. Weather-
  H-270296 _____ stone _____

Hansel of Northmont, H-82943_Northmont Kennels_____ ____Northmont Kennels

Badger Hill Quick Fire,   Mrs. W. M. Orcutt and Mrs.
  H-268929 _____ G. Gerber_____Harry R. Sharpe

Blossom of Raymihill, H-236278_Raymond S. Hill_____Raymond S. Hill

Hainheim's Eva, H-210772_____Hainheim Kennels_____Hainheim Kennels

Milrdachs Jefferson, H-150508__Inez C. Miller_____Inez C. Miller

Rhea v. Erricson, H-123736____J. Erricson Worden_____. Erricson Worden

Rosolona's Perfidia, H-259953__Solon P. Clickner_____Solon P. Clickner

Twin Seas Juno, H-201855_____Twin Seas Kennels_____Twin Seas Kennels

Bergmanor Euchre, H-266259__Lorheim Kennels_____Bergmanor Kennels

Salty Wire of Heying-Teckel,
  H-236531 _____Mr. and Mrs. Fred Heying____Mr. and Mrs. Fred Heying

Ed-El-Fra's Sh' Was, H-277038_3iefenjagenheim Kennels _____

Forever Golden Opportunity,
  H-233081 _____Charlotte R. Sibley_____Charlotte R. Sibley

Glenn Valley's Perfedius,
  H-294989 _____G. D. Dimon_____

Greta v. Kralc, H-134153_____Margaret C. Smith_____Anna M. Gargett

Karl Hans von Ritter Bayard,
  not registered_____H. E. Howell_____

Mink von Mecklenburg,
  not registered _____L. W. Thurber_____

Burian's Red Rouf, H-203076__Clifford and Grace Burian_____Clifford and Grace Burian

Cita von Marienlust, H-231815_Mr. and Mrs. J. Mehrer_____Mr. and Mrs. J. Mehrer

Kleetal's Lear, H-248515_____Kleetal Kennels_____Kleetal Kennels

Luigi v. Hildburghausen,
  H-237408 _____Marjorie P. Dennard_____Marjorie P. Dennard

Top Notch of Berbea, H-246558_Bertha E. Deakin and Beryl B. E. Deakin and B. H.
                          H. Zimmerman_____ Zimmerman

Ajax of Ouborough (Eng.),
  H-177199 _____Emilie S. Bromley_____J. V. Rank

Albrecht von der Stephens W.,
  H-263749 _____Mrs. N. R. Stephens_____

Hush-hush von der Stephens,   R. S. Hill and Mrs. N. R.
  H-241712 _____Mrs. Neville R. Stephens_____ Stephens

Split Rock's Irleen, H-242626__Howard A. Rumpf_____Howard A. Rumpf

Ursel von Osterholz, H-347204_I. Kroeff_____

1954

Brigadier v. Sieghofen, H-161506_Elizabeth Krug von Nidda____Mr. and Mrs. Bradford A.
                                              Champion

Louisa von der Nidda, H-242000_Mrs. Philip W. Emery_____Mrs. Philip W. Emery

Primrose Patch Tinyteckle
  (Eng.), H-315364_____Primrose Patch Kennels_____

Chardeline's Corsair, H-253111_C. C. and M. L. Fernsell_____

Dachsberry's Pacemaker,
  H-203835 _____Mr. and Mrs. Elmer E. Berry__Mr. and Mrs. Elmer E. Berry

Kleetal's Morgain, H-263356____Kleetal Kennels_____

Kleetal's Tamara, H-263352____Mr. and Mrs. R. H. Sweet_____

Manhattan of Earldale, H-197941_Aubria E. Bywaters_____Aubria E. Bywaters

Sherwood of Balmoral, H-239079_Alice M. Gromer_____Alice M. Gromer

Sparling's Jeffrey, H-259469___E. E. Thorn_____

White Gables Fire Engine,
  H-150160 _____White Gables Kennels_____White Gables Kennels

Moat Arab (Eng.), H-270740__Mrs. C. E. O'Hara_____

Split Rock's Electra, H-112921__Howard A. Rumpf_____Howard A. Rumpf

Traveler's Rapunzel, H-280156_M. Becker and J. Fitzgerald___

Virginia's Trinka, H-158543___Harley W. Smith_____Harley W. Smith

Arlinda of Gera, H-138847____Mr. and Mrs. Ray E. Shultis__Gene M. Shultis

Badger Hill Perk, H-221446____Harry R. Sharpe_____Harry R. Sharpe

Bon Fire of Blue Key, H-191904_Dorothy Gatelee Davis_____Florence S. Keller

Eve of Gera, H-200985_____Mr. and Mrs. Ray E. Shultis__Gene M. Shultis

Hainheim's Melinda, H-218120__Hainheim Kennels_____Mr. and Mrs. Lynn George

Honey of Bertmar, H-283969___H. H. Berresheim_____

Lisl of Gera, H-240083 _____Mr. and Mrs. Ray E. Shultis__Mr. and Mrs. Ray E. Shultis

Strutter of Heying-Teckel,
  H-296441 _____Mrs. Joe F. Nedbalek_____J. R. Purse and L. F. Ward

Tigertown Toccata, H-242493___Anne J. and Henry P. Tomlinson_A. J. and H. P. Tomlinson

Hainheim's Nancy, H-330368___Mrs. N. R. Stephens_____

Starkrest's Dictator, H-274985__Bro-Bark Kennels_____Starkrest Kennels

De Sangpur Little Professor,
  H-202629 _____Mrs. Wm. Burr Hill, Jr._____Mrs. Wm. Burr Hill, Jr.

De Sangpur Wee Allene,
  H-323688 _____Mrs. W. B. Hill_____

Guyman's Long Deal, H-311832_J. Rigden_____

Fafnir v. Schwanfurst, H-289897_J. D. Willmott_____

Kittri v. Schoberhaus, H-273804_J. D. Willmott_____

Oliver of Gera, H-303671_____Mrs. J. P. Miller_____

Dachsgarten Flamingo,
  H-273480 _____Mrs. L. Miller_____

Badger Hill Argo, H-36953____W. E. Spardley_____

Calyla's Urslina, H-279317____Mrs. J. R. Wess_____

Eaves's Waldi x Waddelhausen,
  H-248880 _____Frederick A. Eaves_____Frederick A. Eaves

Ludwig v. Sigmaringen II,
  H-294468 _____G. A. Plummer_____Edwin D. Hubbard

Rumpus Ridge Merry Nicholi,
  H-293937 _____Micaelia F. Randolph_____Rumpus Ridge Kennels

Brentwald Traci, H-180898____Mrs. Harold Patrick_____Mrs. Harold Patrick

Calyla Topsy, H-275511_____J. C. Walters_____

Oklahoma of Shennis (Eng-
  land), H-309706_____Stanley F. Todd_____Mrs. H. Pead

Herr Volkman's Wunderbar,
  H-314904 _____R. S. Becker_____

Crespi's Ronnie, H-254010_____Mrs. Neville R. Stephens____Donia Cline

Darice of Gera, H-268367_____Mr. and Mrs. J. E. Lloyd_____Edith E. Norton

Favorite Sis of Heying-Teckel,
  H-241828 _____Mr. and Mrs. Fred Heying_____Mr. and Mrs. Fred Heying

Kleetal's Banjo, H-248510_____Kleetal Kennels_____Kleetal Kennels

Kleetal's Sheba, H-263353_____Kleetal Kennels_____

Red Locket Cheri-py, H-266792_Mrs. James P. Miller_____Mr. and Mrs. W. W. Dorward

Rumpus Ridge Gustav v.
  Schlitz, H-327724_____J. E. Chloupek_____

Fir Trees Coco, H-327195_____S. Orne_____

Von Der Bush Zipper, H-309869_D. and L. Bush_____

Miss Troublesome of Barcedor,
  H-281558 _____D. W. Barberis_____D. W. Barberis

Shep-Peke's Karla, H-259459___Vernon E. Greaver_____Margaret C. Smith

The Pride of Marin, H-312368_C. O. Pfeifer_____

Brentwald Udet, H-194031____A. W. Taylor_____Harold Patrick

Bright Angel of Raymihill,
  H-236277 _____Raymond S. Hill_____Raymond S. Hill

Duane v. d. Daniels, H-270680_Mr. and Mrs. D. D. Daniels_____Mr. and Mrs. D. D. Daniels
Favorite Pal of Heying-Teckel,
    H-241829 _____Mr. and Mrs. Fred Heying____Mr. and Mrs. Fred Heying
Fiddlers Hill Tuppence,
    H-277010 _____Fiddlers Hill Kennels_____
Mirzl von Hohenstauffen,
    H-273735 _____M. E. Ryan_____
Shadrach of Calyla, H-249646__B. M. Womack_____J. C. Walters
Sparling Louhelen Delight,   Eva Sparling and Helen
    H-206535 _____ Grugette _____E. Sparling and H. Grugette
Bruno v. Hain, H-230508_____Willard F. Bond_____Willard F. Bond
Calyla Turvy, H-275510_____Mr. and Mrs. J. H. Meyer_____

CH. SAQUI DE SANGPUR
Sire: Ch. William de Sangpur   Dam: Ch. Penny Ante of Northmont
Owner: Crespi Street Kennels, Mr. and Mrs. Charles D. Cline,
Los Angeles, Calif.

CH. REINWALD OF EDLIDGE
Sire: Ch. Bart v. Teckelhof   Dam: Bruenhilde of Edlidge
Breeder and owner: Mrs. Edward A. Anthony, Whitman, Mass.

CH. DANDY DACHS DANNY
Sire: Ch. Favorite v. Marienlust   Dam: Red Locket Jinx
Owner: Donia Cline, Los Angeles, California

The Complete

DACHSHUND

———

PART
II

FROM STYRIA

Styria is the Dachshund's native land. Here is a Styrian lad, in national costume, with his smooth and long-haired "Dackrels."

Preliminary General Training

H OFFENSTHAL wrote: "Every animal has something in common with us; is related to us, and, like us, has his good and his bad days."

No one can hope to be a successful trainer if he does not recognize the truth of the above words. There are very, very few "born" trainers, and those few will not need to read this book. There is a "green hand" with animals as well as with plants, and the "natural trainer" is gifted with the power at birth. He will be able to teach any animal without resorting to the rules which must govern the actions of ordinary mortals. He can go further. He can break all rules; he can put the cart before the horse and the horse will draw it perfectly. He will teach an animal to perform any given exercise without seeming to take any trouble. If you ask him how he managed it, he would not be able to tell you, because the power flows from him. Strangely, it does not always follow that the gifted person is a great animal lover, and, conversely, an animal lover may not make a good trainer.

Quite apart from any special gift, there are many people who can never learn to train a dog. They try very hard, they are patient, they do not lose their temper, but although they

1

persevere, the dog is never trained. In the end they do more harm than good, and my advice to them is to stop trying and either send the dog away to be trained or else give up the idea.

As a rule it is the trainer who is to blame for failure, but, of course, there are untrainable dogs, because, remembering Hoffensthal, "Every animal has something in common with us," and there are plenty of human morons and human criminals. In any case, I should never advise an amateur to try to cure an adult dog of bad ways. A reasonable and intelligent adult dog can be taught what is known as "police training" by which I mean the exercises performed in obedience classes, which are seen at most shows. There are also Working Trials at which various breeds of dogs can compete.

To teach your dog successfully you must know at what you are aiming. It is hopeless to collect a number of exercises which you intend to teach your dog without realizing in what way they will be useful and why they originated. All the exercises in the Trials schedules are not useful and some are calculated to intimidate and depress a dog, and you will be wise to omit them.

Remember that animals have their good and bad days. We may not realize it, but a dog may be feeling languid and off color, just as we do. Any polo pony trainer will tell you the same thing. If this happens, cut short the lesson directly the dog has obeyed your order. That is to say, supposing a dog, which can retrieve well, seems adverse to retrieving on that day. You can't let him refuse to retrieve entirely, but once he has brought you the object you can make a fuss over him and end the lesson.

One word more before I come to the subject of individual exercises. There is always the risk of destroying a dog's initiative and making him too dependent upon his owner. While you are giving a lesson a dog must be interested in you alone and must think of nothing else, but for the rest of time avoid interfering with him at all. Encourage him to look after himself. If a puppy gets into a field through a hole in the hedge, he must find his own way out. He will yell and be in a fine state when he thinks he has lost you, but at any rate give him

2

the chance of getting out himself. You can hide and watch what goes on. If he is really distressed and seems to be losing his head, go back, but don't lift him over the hedge; make him come back to the hole and come through. You are only doing what his own mother would do, and you are being fair to him.

The "Sit"

I do not think puppies should be "schooled" before they are six months old, but the "SIT" is an exception to the rule. It is so easily taught that you can teach a puppy at three months old. It is also one of the most useful of all the accepted exercises, because it enables you to exercise control at any given moment.

To teach the puppy, lay your hand on its neck (your left hand) and gently push down its hind quarters with your right hand. Say "SIT" firmly and loudly. I do not mean that you should shout—that is always to be avoided—but a command must be given in a tone of voice which compels attention. You must keep the puppy in a sitting position and keep on saying "SIT," but, don't forget, do not add any other words. After a moment or two, keep the puppy down with one hand, and give it a really tasty tidbit with the other. Now let it go, pat it, and make a fuss over it. You can repeat the lesson twice more, using exactly the same procedure each time, and that is sufficient for the day. Don't become so enthusiastic that you go on too long. You only do harm. Also, resist the temptation to show off to your friends. You have not done anything very remarkable.

Repeat the lesson next day. You must be regular in your instruction or it will be wasted. The tidbit is an integral part of the proceedings. An ordinarily intelligent puppy will have learned to sit at the word of command in a few days, and very soon it will sit when it wants something to eat. This is as far as you should go with a puppy. It is sufficient for it to sit when commanded to do so. There is much more to the exercise than this, for eventually it will have to "stay put" for an indefinite length of time, but you cannot expect a puppy's brain to absorb more than the elemental part of the exercise. The reason why I advocate teaching it at an early

3

age is because this exercise does not tax its brain and it also avoids the use of force, especially with a big dog. An experienced trainer will make even an adult dog "sit" with the minimum of pressure, but it is a knack, and force should never be used, if possible. Teaching it when young obviates this.

"Heel" On and Off Lead

Although the "SIT" is one of the recognized exercises, I have treated it in the foregoing chapter purely from the point of view of a puppy accomplishment, which will lay the foundation for future development. Its full aspect will be reviewed later on.

There is no doubt that walking at heel both on and off the lead is the first exercise to teach a young dog, and one which is the basis of all work. If you have brought up your puppy properly there should be no need to teach the young dog to walk quietly on the lead, for it will have been accustomed to do so from the time it first went in a collar.

There is no point in telling a novice how to deal with an adult dog which has been allowed to develop the trick of pulling, because it is extremely difficult to cure. It is better to send it to a recognized trainer.

If you intend to compete in obedience classes you will have to train your dog to keep close to your knee when you turn right or left, or if you should "right about turn." Now you are almost sure to find that your first difficulty will be that the dog will lag behind and become bored, particularly when there is a lot of turning and twisting. *Never* listen to anyone who advises you to use a spiked collar. If you can't train without a spiked collar, you had better take to raising white mice.

Strictly speaking (at the moment, at any rate) there are two types of "heel." There is the competition "heel" and the ordinary "follow," which is quite sufficient for everyday use. To my mind, one of the great drawbacks of *obedience* work is that it is so often divorced from reality. There is really no need for a dog to keep as close to your knee as is expected in classes or Trials, but if you want to compete at these affairs you must train for them.

4

I will give directions for training the dog for the class work, but it is wise to use two different terms for the two different types of work, because otherwise the dog will become bewildered.

If you only want the dog to be within control while you are taking an ordinary walk, you can say "Back." That means that he is not to dash forward or to leave you, but he need not be walking "at attention." For the class work you must give the order "Heel."

Your aim is to have the dog alert and gay, not dragging along with a miserable expression. Take the lead in your right hand. You must hold it loosely if you are competing, but in training you will have to hold it fairly tightly to begin with and say sharply, "Heel." Walk along quickly and at intervals bend down (the dog is at your left side) and pat his shoulder. When you turn to the left, do so quickly and you will find that the dog will turn quickly, too, because he will want to get out of your way. But when you turn to your right the dog will be very likely to slow up. The conventional aid to a quick turn is a jerk on the collar, but it doesn't do much good unless you hurt the dog. Instead of doing this, as you turn, draw him closely to your knee and give him a tasty bit of meat or something which he really likes. This not only keeps him gay and bright but it makes for smartness.

In the competitions the judge will call "Halt," and as you stop, the dog must sit beside you. Now you will see the advantage of having taught your puppy to sit when young. You need only say "Sit" when you stop and he will know what to do. In the actual competition you are not allowed to say "Sit," but by that time the dog will have learned that when you stop he must sit. Of course, you will have stopped giving him a tidbit for sitting long ago. By now he will sit when told, without any reward.

The secret of a smart worker lies in never boring a dog or working it for too long. Teaching a dog to walk smartly at "heel" is one of the most difficult of exercises, the only other more difficult one being the "retrieve." You must try to make the lesson a pleasure, not a penance, but if you are careful to do plenty of bending, so as to encourage the dog to keep close to your knee, and also encourage him to a sharp and quick right turn with a tidbit, it will not be too arduous. The "about turn" should also be rewarded, because the dog has to come round extremely quickly in order to keep pace with the handler. You *must* make these lessons very short, for the dog becomes bored very quickly, and if you get a dog "stale" once, he is apt to remember and to be on the defensive at the next lesson. About three turns each way and three about turns are ample, and then you should reward him with a good romp and *no* more orders for the rest of the walk. You can force a dog into learning an exercise, but he will always look dejected over it.

If you succeed in teaching your dog to walk smartly and cheerfully at "heel," you have done something of which you can be proud.

When you are competing in an *obedience* class you are expected to have the lead quite loose, and the only command you may give is the word "Heel," and that when you start off.

Exactly the same rules and procedure apply to "heel off the lead." I advise you when you are teaching this latter exercise to be certain that your dog does it perfectly *on* the lead before you start to take him loose. If he does it badly without the lead, put him back on the lead.

This is a purely exhibition exercise, and when you are going for an ordinary walk and you want your dog under extra control, I think it is quite unnecessary. If you use the word "Back," which he must learn to interpret as meaning that he is to keep close to you, it should be sufficient. Remember that because the word "Back" means to you to be behind, it does not necessarily convey that meaning to the dog. It is tone and association of ideas which convey meaning to an animal, and you must try to convey a sense of what you mean by your tone, as well as by your words. "Back" should be used much less peremptorily than "Heel," which is to express alertness and a lot of "theatre." Choice of words is purely arbitrary. You could say "monkey" just as effectually, so long as the dog associates the word with what is desired of him.

You must always stick to the same word, and you should

6

avoid using a word which sounds like another command. For instance, "Stand" and "Stop" both begin with "st" and may sound alike to a dog. A dog lacks the pictorial sense of words which we possess, so he depends entirely upon the sound. If you say "Halt," he will not confuse the words.

So avoid making the mistake of attributing human ideas to the dog, and when you are training him and things do not go well, try to find out some natural cause. There are only three emotions which we share with the animals—the sex impulse, the maternal impulse, and the desire for food and drink.

As with human beings, the reproductive instinct is the strongest of all emotions, followed by the maternal impulse. In both human beings and animals they are such primitive and deeply imbedded instincts that to magnify them into something wonderful and sublime is simply lush sentiment.

Forget all you have ever read about gratitude, self-sacrifice and so on, and use every endeavor to take as simple a view as you can of the dog mentality.

A dog does possess the wish to please someone of whom it is fond, but possibly because the vibrations which pass from a satisfied trainer to an obedient dog are pleasant, and when the trainer is angry the vibrations are discordant. Vibrations, I think, play a very great part in animal life, both between themselves and to a lesser degree between them and us. It seems possible that animals communicate with each other on wave lengths. You see two dogs look at each other before deciding to rush off in pursuit of another dog, and it is certain that some form of thought transference takes place. This is why it is very important to concentrate upon what you wish a dog to do. If your dog is just about to attack another dog, say "No" sharply, but throw all your will-power consciously around the dog to prevent him from disobeying you. It does make a great deal of difference in being master of the dog. Primitive peoples have this power far more highly developed than we have, and I knew an Indian who could will his dog to go right or left or straight on, as he wished, without speaking to the dog. It is possible that it was a trick, but I think it was genuine.

7

This, however, is a diversion from the purely mechanical means of training a dog, and, in any case, only a few people will agree with what I have said.

Remaining "Put"

After having perfected the dog in walking at heel both on and off the lead, it is as well to take a fairly easy exercise as the next on the list, for the dog is under a certain amount of mental strain when being trained. Indeed, in tracking it has been proved that the temperature rises one or two degrees according to the severity of the test.

As the dog knows how to "sit," you may as well continue the exercise and teach it to remain sitting for an indefinite period. If you are competing in a competition the dog must remain sitting, for if it lies down it loses marks, or else gets an 0 if it lies down at once.

From the practical point of view it does not matter if the dog lies or sits, provided it remains where it has been put, and, personally, I think that all training should be purely practical.

You have taught the dog to "sit," and now you must accustom it to the fact that you are going to move away and that it must remain there. It is really nothing but a matter of patience and repetition. You repeat the command "Sit," as you move away a foot or two, and every time the dog gets up you must go back and make him return to his original position. Be sure to make him sit in exactly the same place as before. You may have to work by inches, but if you can manage to move a yard away without the dog getting up, you have advanced a step. Continue to command "Sit" and be sure to return to the dog before you praise and pat him. Eventually he must remain sitting while you return from where you have been sent by the judge, until you have taken your place beside him and the order has been given to relax.

When the dog has remained sitting, make a great fuss over him and let him see that you are pleased, but repeat the exercise at once. There is not the same fear of the dog becoming bored and stale as there is in the "heel," because temperamentally it is so different. It is an exercise which you

8

can repeat at intervals while the dog is out walking with you, so long as he is romping about and enjoying himself between times. On no account strike the dog if it should get up or move towards you. If you do, you will find that the dog will end by running away from you, and nothing looks worse than to see a dog cringing away from its handler.

While there are a few occasions in the everyday education of a dog when it is necessary to administer punishment, there is no excuse during training for doing so.

Eventually the dog should remain sitting, however far away you may go, or however long you are away. The best place in which to teach the dog is a wood, because you can go a short distance and hide behind a tree trunk, and then if the dog gets up you can utter a stentorian "Sit." Until the dog is good at the exercise never move away behind him; always leave him looking towards where you have gone. The reason for this is that the very act of twisting his head to look for you will suggest to him that he should get up. It is not a difficult exercise and it only needs patience.

I think that in practice it does not matter at all whether the dog is standing, sitting, or lying, so long as it remains where you put it. This is a very useful and practical exercise, for it is not always desirable that your dog should be visible. Apart from these more serious considerations, it is useful in everyday life to be able to leave the dog while you go into a shop or into the house of an acquaintance. You may be going out to luncheon and the dog would enjoy a walk, but you do not want to take it into a strange house. If it is accustomed to waiting for you, there will be no difficulty.

Some of the competition exercises are almost useless; some I consider pure "theatre" and others are practical.

Whether you are teaching your dog to "stay put" from the Trial point of view, or because you want it to be useful to you, the method of teaching is the same. It is patience, and again patience. But if you are teaching it from a practical viewpoint the essential principle is that it does not move, but it is of no importance whether it is sitting, lying, or standing. Therefore, if you return and find that the dog is in the same place, you can praise it and make a fuss over it. If, however,

9

you expect it to remain at the "sit," you will have to correct it should it be lying down, which will probably be the case.

Personally, I think that insistence on the sitting attitude is pure waste of time and annoying to the dog, dissipating its brain power in a triviality. There is, I am bound to admit, another school of thought, which believes that the more you ask of a dog, the more you develop its capabilities, but when you consider the vast amount there is to teach a dog before it is even reasonably useful, it appears senseless to insist upon unnecessary "trimmings."

Outdoor Show with View of the Tent in which the Dogs are Benched.

Westminster Kennel Club Show, Madison Square Garden, Feb. 14-15, 1949
where twelve judging rings were in operation at the same time.

The Exhibition of Dogs

NOBODY should exhibit a dog in the shows unless he can win without gloating and can lose without rancor. The showing of dogs is first of all a sport, and it is to be approached in a sportsmanlike spirit. It is not always so approached. That there are so many wretched losers and so many supercilious winners among the exhibitors in dog shows is the reason for this warning.

The confidence that one's dog is of exhibition excellence is all that prompts one to enter him in the show, but, if he fails in comparison with his competitors, nobody is harmed. It is no personal disgrace to have a dog beaten. It may be due to the dog's fundamental faults, to its condition, or to inexpert handling. One way to avoid such hazards is to turn the dog over to a good professional handler. Such a man with a flourishing established business will not accept an inferior dog, one that is not worth exhibiting. He will put the dog in the best possible condition before he goes into the ring with him, and he knows all the tricks of getting out of a dog all he has to give. Good handlers come high, however. Fees for taking a dog into the ring will range from ten to twenty-five dollars, plus any cash prizes the dog may win and plus a bonus for wins made in the group.

11

Handlers do not win all the prizes, despite the gossip that they do, but good handlers choose only good dogs and they usually finish at or near the top of their classes. It is a mistake to assume that this is due to any favoritism or any connivance with the judges; they have simply chosen the best dog, conditioned them well, and so maneuvered them in the ring to bring out their best points.

The services of a professional handler are not essential, however. Many an amateur shows his dogs as well, but the exhibitor without previous experience is ordinarily at something of a disadvantage. If the dog is good enough, he may be expected to win.

The premium list of the show, setting forth the prizes to be offered, giving the names of the judges, containing the entry form, and describing the conditions under which the show is to be held, are usually mailed out to prospective exhibitors about a month before the show is scheduled to be held. Any show superintendent is glad to add names of interested persons to the mailing list.

Entries for the show close at a stated date, usually about two weeks before the show opens and no entry may be accepted under the rules after the advertised date of closing. It behooves the exhibitor to make his entries promptly. The exhibtor is responsible for all errors he may make on the entry form of his dog; such errors can not be rectified and may result in the disqualification of the exhibit. It therefore is wise for the owner to double check all data submitted with an entry. The cost of making an entry, which is stated in the premium list, is usually from three to five dollars. An unregistered dog may be shown at three shows, after which he must be registered or a statement must be made to the American Kennel Club that he is ineligible for registry and why, with a request for permission to continue to exhibit the dog. Such permission is seldom denied. The listing fee for an unregistered dog is twenty-five cents, which must be added to the entry fee for the show.

The classes opened at most shows and usually divided by sex are as follows: Puppy Class (often Junior Puppy for dogs 6 to 9 months old, and Senior Puppy for dogs 9 to 12 months); Novice Class, for dogs that have never won first in any except the Puppy Class; Bred-by-Exhibitor Class, for dogs of which the breeder and owner are the same person or persons; the American-bred Class, for dogs whose parents were mated in America; and the Open Class, which is open to all comers. The respective first prize winners of these various classes compete in what is known as the Winners Class for points toward championship. No entry can be made in the Winners Class, which is open without additional charge to the winners of the earlier classes, all of which are obligated to compete.

A dog eligible to more than one class can be entered in each of them, but it is usually wiser to enter him in only one. A puppy should, unless unusually precocious and mature, be placed in the Puppy Class, and it is unfair to so young a dog to expect him to defeat older dogs, although an exceptional puppy may receive an award in the Winners Class. The exhibitor who is satisfied merely that his dog may win the class in which he is entered is advised to place him in the lowest class to which he is eligible, but the exhibitor with confidence in his dog and shooting for high honors should enter the dog in the Open Class, where the competition is usually the toughest. The winner of the Open Class usually (but by no mean always) is also the top of the Winners Class.

The winner of the Winners Class for dogs competes with the Winners Bitch for Best of Winners, which in turn competes for Best of Breed or Best of Variety with any Champions of Record which may be entered for Specials Only. The Best of Breed or Best of Variety is eligible to compete in the respective Variety Group to which his breed belongs in the closing hours of the show; and if, perchance, he should win his Variety Group, he is obligated to compete for Best Dog in Show. This is a major honor which few inexperienced exhibitors attain and to which they seldom aspire.

Duly entered, the dog should be brought into the best possible condition for his exhibition in the show and taught to move and to pose at his best. He should be equipped with a neat, strong collar without ornaments or spikes, a leather

13

lead, sturdy enough to hold him but no wider than needful, and a bench chain of nickel with solid links with which to fasten him to his bench. Food such as the dog is used to, a bottle of the water he is accustomed to drink, and all grooming equipment should be assembled in a bag the night before departure for the show. The exhibitor's pass, on which the dog is assigned a stall number, is sent by mail by the Show Superintendent and should not be left behind, since it is difficult to have it duplicated and it enables the dog's caretaker to leave and return to the show at will.

The time of the opening of the show is stated in the premium list, and it is wise to have one's dog at the show promptly. Late arrivals are subject to disqualification if they are protested.

Examination by the veterinarian at the entrance of the show is a mere formality, and healthy dogs are quickly passed along. Once admitted to the show, it is wise to find one's bench, the number of which is on the exhibitor's ticket, to affix one's dog to the bench, and not to remove him from it until the announced exercising hour or until he is to be taken into the ring to be judged. A familiar blanket or cushion for the bench makes a dog feel at home there. It is contrary to the rules to remove dogs from their benches and to keep them in crates during show hours, and these rules are strictly enforced.

Some exhibitors choose to sit by their dog's bench, but if he is securely chained he is likely to be safe in his owner's absence. Dogs have been stolen from their benches and others allegedly poisoned in the shows, but such incidents are rare indeed. The greater danger is that the dog may grow nervous and insecure, and it is best that the owner return now and again to the bench to reassure his dog of his security.

The advertised program of the show permits exhibitors to know the approximate hour of the judging of their respective breeds. Although that time may be somewhat delayed, it may be depended upon that judging will not begin before the stated hour. The dog should have been groomed and made ready for his appearance in the show ring. When his class is called the dog should be taken unhurriedly to the entrance of the ring, where the handler will receive an arm band with the dog's number.

When the class is assembled and the judge asks that the dogs be paraded before him, the handler should fall into the counter-clockwise line and walk his dog until the signal is given to stop. In moving in a circle, the dog should be kept on the inside, so that the judge may have the opportunity to see him. He has no interest in seeing the handler. In stopping the line, there is no advantage to be gained in maneuvering one's dog to the premier position, since the judge will change the positions of the dogs as he sees fit.

Keep the dog alert and facing toward the judge at all times. When summoned to the center of the ring for examination, go briskly but not brashly. It is unwise to enter into conversation with the judge, except briefly to reply to any questions he may ask. Do not call his attention to any excellences the dog may possess or excuse any shortcomings; the judge is presumed to evaluate the exhibit's merits as he sees them.

If asked to move the dog, it is meant that the animal shall be led away from the judge and again toward the judge directly. A slow but brisk trot is the gait the judge wishes to see, unless he declares otherwise. He may ask that the movement be repeated, with which request the handler should respond with alacrity. It is best not to choke a dog in moving him, but rather to move him on a loose lead. The judge will assign or signal a dog to his position, which should be assumed without quibble.

Dog show judges are supreme in their rings and it is useless to argue with them, but they are reasonable and wish to make their awards correctly. Accept with a show of graciousness whatever award is given to one's dog, and retire from the ring without argument or contention. However unreasonable it may be, an award in a dog show, once it is made, is final and not to be changed. It is useless to ask a busy judge why one's dog has failed to win. If in doubt of the justice of the placement he has received, it is better to wait and try some subsequent show.

15

In going from the ring, it is best to inquire of the ring steward whether the dog's further presence will be required. If it is not, the dog may be returned to his bench for the remainder of the show.

It is as important that one accept a win gracefully and without undue emotion as that one may lose without rancor or other unpleasantness. There is nothing personal in a dog show award, and the winner has only done to you what you were trying to do to him. The reputation of being a bad loser is something that nobody wants and which too many acquire. This does not mean that one shall surrender one's right to one's opinion about one's dog or one's loyalty to him. It only means that one excites criticism in getting mad about the awards.

In any event, under the rules the dog is required, winner or loser, to remain on his bench until the close of the show.

Judging for Best in Show at Madison Square Garden.

16

CH. DACHSCROFT'S PLAYBOY
Sire: Ch. Moto's Pride of White Gables   Dam: Little Gates Honeybun
Breeder-Owner: Dachscroft Kennels, Mrs. David B. Doggett,
Lake Geneva, Wisconsin

CH. WHITE GABLES NUTMEG
Sire: Ch. Bucknam's Merrymaker
Owner: Mrs. Walter D. Monroe, Little Gate Kennels, Lake Forest, Illinois

CH. WHITE GABLES BASIL

Sire: Ch. Cavalier v. Marienlust   Dam: Ch. White Gables Mehitabel
White Gables Kennels, Mariam Van Court, Los Angeles, California

LITTLE GATE'S HONEYBUN

Sire: Falk v. Plater Schulhaus   Dam: White Gables Red Riding Hood
Owner: Dachscroft Kennels, Mrs. David B. Doggett, Lake Geneva, Wis.

CH. CORNHILL GOLDIE
Daughter of Ch. Eric v. Stahlhaus
White Gables Kennels, Mariam Van Court, Los Angeles, California

CH. CAVALIER v. MARIENLUST
Sire: Ch. Leutnant v. Marienlust   Dam: Moya v. Marienlust
White Gables Kennels, Mariam Van Court, Los Angeles, California

SPARLING'S DON AGAIN using typewriter
Son of Ch. Sparling's Adonis
Sparling-Louhelen Kennels in background

Josef and Maria Mehrer's Kennels
The home of Marienlust Dachshunds, West Hempstead, Long Island, N. Y.

General Care and Feeding
Constitutional Vigor

IN acquiring a dog, it is quite as essential that he shall be of sound constitution as that he shall be of the correct type of his own particular breed. This means that he must be viable. The animal that is thoroughly typical of any breed is likely to be vigorous, with a will and a body to surmount diseases and ill treatment, but the converse of this statement is not always true. A dog may have constitutional vigor and livability without breed type. We want both.

Half of the care and effort of rearing a dog is saved by choosing at the outset a puppy of sound constitution, one with a will and an ability to survive and flourish in spite of such adversity and neglect as he may encounter in life. This does not mean that the reader has any intention of obtaining a healthy dog and ill treating it, trusting its good constitution to bring it through whatever crises may beset it. It only means that he will save himself from work, and expense, and disappointment if only he will exercise care in the first place to obtain a healthy dog, one bred from sound and vigorous parents and one which has received adequate care and good food up until the present time.

How can we be sure? The answer is that absolute assurance is impossible, but that we can be careful not to load ourselves up with a dog that threatens to die on us at the smallest occasion of disaster, one with a bad digestive apparatus, or one of frail and sickly appearance.

Our first warning is not to economize too much in buying a dog. Never accept a cull of the litter at any price. The difference in first cost between a fragile, ill nourished, weedy and unhealthy puppy and a sound, vigorous one, with adequate substance and the will to survive may be ten dollars or it may be fifty dollars; but whatever it may be, it is worth it. A dog is an investment and it is not the cost but the upkeep that makes the difference. We may save fifty dollars on the first price of a dog, only to lay out twice or five times that sum for veterinary fees over and above what it would cost to rear a dog of sound fundamental constitution and structure. Money aside, the extra effort and anxiety in the care of a frail "bad-doer" is to be given consideration. If the dog dies—and an unhealthy dog is a nuisance even if we manage to keep him alive—all is lost, the original investment, however small it may have been, and all the money and work we have devoted to the hope of keeping him alive.

The vital, desirable dog, the one that is easy to rear and worth the care bestowed upon him, is active, inquisitive, and happy. He is sleek, his eyes free from pus or tears, his coat shining and alive, his flesh adequate and firm. He is not necessarily fat, but a small amount of surplus flesh, especially in puppyhood, is not undesirable. He is free from richitic knobs on his joints or from crooked bones resultant from rickets. His teeth are firm and white and even. His breath is sweet to the smell. Above all, he is playful and responsive. Puppies, like babies, are much given to sleep, but when they are awake the sturdy ones do not mope lethargically around.

An adult dog that is too thin may often be fattened; if he is too fat he may be reduced. But it is essential that he shall be sound and healthy with a good normal appetite and that he be active and full of the joy of being alive. He must have had the benefit of a good heredity and a good start in life.

Before we undertake to discuss the care of the dog, let us make sure that the dog we are to care for is worth the trouble involved. A dog without a fundamental inheritance of good vitality, or one that has been neglected throughout his growing period is seldom worth his feed. We must face these facts at the very beginning.

If the dog to be cared for has been already acquired, there is nothing to do but to make the best of whatever weaknesses or frailties he may possess; but, when it is decided to replace him with another, let us make sure that he has constitutional vigor. Spencer, in his "Essay on Education" began with the statement: "The first essential is to be a good animal." That assertion is equally applicable in the acquirement of a dog. To heed it will save the dog keeper from a world of grief.

The Feeding and Nutrition of the Adult Dog

The dog is a carnivore. This is a truism that can not be repeated too often. Dog keepers know it but are prone to disregard it, but they do so at their peril and the peril of their dogs. Dogs are carnivores—eaters of meat.

Despite all the old-wives' tales to the contrary, meat does not cause a dog to be vicious, it does not give him worms nor cause him to have fits. It is his food. This is by no means all that it is needed to know about food for the dog, but it is the essential knowledge. Give a dog enough sound meat and he will not be ill fed. The dog is a carnivore.

The dog is believed to have been the first of the animals that was brought under domestication. In his feral state he was almost exclusively an eater of meat. In his long association with man, however, his metabolism has adjusted itself somewhat to the consumption of human diet until he now can eat, even if he can not flourish upon, whatever his master chooses to share with him, be it caviar or corn pone. It is not to be denied that a mature dog can survive without ill effects upon an exclusive diet of rice for a considerable period, but it is not to be recommended that he should be forced to do so.

Even if we had no empirical evidence that dogs thrive best

upon foods of animal origin, and we possess conclusive proof of that fact, the anatomy and physiology of the dog would convince us of it. An observation of the structure of the dog's alimentary canal super-imposed upon many trial and error methods of feeding leads us to the conclusion that a diet preponderating of meat is the best food we can give a dog.

To begin with, the dental formation of the dog is typical of the carnivores. His teeth are designed for tearing rather than for mastication. He bolts his food and swallows it with a minimum of chewing. It is harmless that he should do this. No digestion takes place in the dog's mouth.

The capacity of the dog's stomach is great in comparison with the size of his body and with the capacity of his intestines. In fact, the capacity of the dog's intestines is only about three fifths that of his stomach, whereas the capacity of the intestines of the pig (an omnivore) is about two and a half times that of its stomach, and that of the horse (an herbivore) is eleven times that of its stomach.

The stomach of the dog at its lower end includes the pyloric sphincter, a powerful muscle which does not permit the passage from the stomach of partly digested food until gastric digestion is completed, and for this reason digestion in the dog's stomach requires a considerable time. The composition of the gastric juice in the dog is similar to that in mankind except for its higher content of hydrochloric acid and of pepsin.

The amounts of carbohydrates and of fats digested in the stomach are minimal. The chief function of the dog's stomach is the digestion of proteins. In the dog as in the other carnivores, carbohydrates and fats are digested for the most part in the small intestine, and absorption of food materials is largely from the small intestine. The enzymes necessary for the completion of the digestion of proteins which have not been fully digested in the stomach and for the digestion of sugars, starches, and fats are present in the pancreatic and intestinal juices. The capacity of the small intestine in the dog is not great and for that reason digestion that takes place there must be rapid.

The so-called large intestine (although in the dog it is

really not "large" at all) is short and of small capacity in comparison with that of animals adapted by nature to subsist wholly or largely upon plant foods. In the dog, the large gut is designed to serve chiefly for storage of a limited and compact bulk of waste materials, which are later to be discharged as feces. Some absorption of water occurs there, but there is little if any absorption there of the products of digestion. In comparison with the sizes, the length of the colon and rectum of the dog is less than half that of the pig, and only a little more than a quarter that of the horse.

It will be readily seen that the short digestive tract of the dog is best adapted to a concentrated diet, which can be quickly digested and which leaves a small residue. Foods of animal origin, flesh, fish, milk and eggs, are therefore suited to the digestive physiology of the dog because of the ease and completeness with which they are digested as compared with plant foods, which contain considerable amounts of indigestible structural material. The dog is best fed with a concentrated diet with a minimum of roughage.

This means meat. Flesh, milk and eggs are, in effect, vegetation partly predigested. The steer or horse eats grain and herbage, from which its long digestive tract enables it to extract the food value and eliminate the indigestible material. The carnivore eats the flesh of the herbivore, thus obtaining his grain and grass in a concentrated form suitable for digestion in his short alimentary tract. Thus it is seen that meat is the ideal as a chief ingredient of the dog's ration.

Like all other animals, the dog's diet must be made up of proteins, carbohydrates, fats, minerals, vitamins and water. None of these substances may be excluded and the dog survive. If he fails to obtain any of them from one source, it must come from another. It may be argued that before minerals were artificially supplied in the dog's diet and before we were aware of the existence of the various vitamins, we had dogs and they (some of them) appeared to thrive. However, they obtained such substances in their foods, although we were not aware of giving them to them. It is very likely that few dogs obtained much more than their very minimum of requirements of the minerals and vitamins. It is known

21

that rickets were more prevalent before we learned to supply our dogs with ample calcium, and black tongue, now almost unknown, was a common canine disease before we supplied in the dog's diet that fraction of the vitamin B complex known as nicotinic acid. There is no way for us to know how large a portion of our dogs died for want of some particular food element before we learned to supply all the necessary ones. The dogs that survived received somewhere in their diet some, though not necessarily the optimum amounts, of all of these compounds.

It is worth our while to discuss them individually.

Protein

The various proteins are the nitroginous part of the food. They are composed of the amino acids, singly or in combination. There are at least twenty-two of these amino acids known to the nutritional scientists, ten of which are regarded as dietary essentials, the others of which, if not supplied in the diet, can be compounded in the body, which requires an adequate supply of all twenty-two. When any one of the essential ten amino acids is withdrawn from the diet of any animal, growth ceases or is greatly retarded. Thus, a high protein content in any food is not an assurance of its food value if taken alone; it may be lacking in one or more of the essential ten amino acids. When the absent essential amino acids are added to it in sufficient quantities or included separately in the diet, the protein may be complete and fully assimilated.

Proteins, as such, are ingested and in the digestive tract are broken down into the separate amino acids of which they are composed. These amino acids have been likened to building stones, since they are taken up by the blood stream and conveyed to the various parts of the animal as they may be required, where they are deposited and re-united with other complimentary amino acids again to form bone and muscles in the resumed form of protein.

To correct amino acid deficiences in the diet, it is not necessary to add the required units in pure form. The same object may be accomplished more efficiently by employing proteins

22

which contain the required amino acids. It has long been known that mixtures of protein foodstuffs were desirable. Foods containing incomplete proteins should be mixed with others which, although they too may be imcomplete in themselves, will supply the mixture with adequate amounts of the essential amino acids.

Considerations of space forbid the discussion here of the details of proteins and their feeding values, but the foregoing information will serve as a warning that the protein part of a dog's diet must be complete in that it must contain all of the essential amino acids.

Foods of animal origin—meat, fish, eggs and milk—supply proteins of high nutritive value, both from the standpoint of digestibility and amino acid content. Gelatin is an exception to that statement, since gelatin is very incomplete. It does not follow that it must never be included in the diet, for it may be supplemented and completed by the addition of other food of animal origin and may be assimilated along with its compliment.

Even foods of animal origin vary among themselves in their protein content and amino acid balance. The protein of muscle meat does not rank quite as high as that of eggs or milk. The glandular tissues—such as liver, kidneys, sweetbreads or pancreas—contain proteins of exceptionally high nutritive value, and these organs should be added to the dog's diet whenever it is possible to do so. Milk contains two-thirds of an ounce (dry weight) of particularly high class protein to every pint, in addition to its minerals, vitamins, carbohydrates and fats. (The only dietary necessity absent from milk is iron.) Animal proteins have a high content of dietary-essential amino acids, which makes them very effective in supplementing many proteins of vegetable origin. The whites of eggs, while somewhat inferior to the yolks, contain excellent proteins. The lysine of milk can be destroyed by excessive heat and the growth promoting value of its protein so destroyed. Evaporated tinned milk has not been subjected to enough heat to injure its proteins.

Thus we can readily see why meat with its concentrated, balanced, and easily assimilated proteins should form the

23

major part of dry weight of a dog's ration. The proteins in meat, and the other animal products, are not only excellent in themselves but they render available and assimilable less complete proteins from other sources.

It has never been determined how much protein the dog requires in his diet. It may be assumed to vary as to the size, age and breed of the dog under consideration; as to the individual dog, some assimilating protein better, or utilizing more of it than others; as to the activity or inactivity of the subject; and as to the amino acid content of the protein employed. When wheat protein gliadin is fed as the sole protein three times as much of it is required as of the milk protein, lactalbumin. It has been estimated that approximately twenty to twenty-five percent of animal protein (dry weight) in a dog's diet is adequate for maintenance in good health, although no final conclusion has been reached and probably never can be.

Our purpose, however, is not to feed the dog the minimum ration with which he can survive or even the minimum ration with which he can flourish. It is rather to give him the maximum food in quantity and balance which he can digest and enjoy without developing a paunch. Who wants to live on a minimum diet necessary for adequate sustenance? We all enjoy a full belly of good food, and so do our dogs.

Roy G. Daggs found from experimentation that milk production in the dog was influenced by the different kinds of proteins fed to it. He has pointed out that relatively high protein diets stimulate lactation and that, in the bitch, animal proteins are better suited to the synthesis of milk than plant proteins. He concluded that liver was a better source of protein for lactation than eggs or round steak.

That the dog has an instinctive preference for a diet of meat may be seen by introducing three weeks old puppies to finely ground beef and by noticing the pleasurable enthusiasm with which they relish it. They will desert their mother's breast and attack the meat with the greatest avidity. This preference for meat, later in life, may sometimes be destroyed by feeding a dog a wholly vegetable diet for a considerable period; but when meat is again added to the

24

diet a dog soon learns to eat it and his preference for it is readily reestablished.

The Carbohydrates

The carbohydrates include all the starches, the sugars and the cellulose and hemicellulose, which last two, known as fiber, are the chief constituents of wood, of the stalks and leaves of plants, and of the coverings of seeds. There remains considerable controversy about how much carbohydrates are required or desirable in canine nutrition. It has been shown experimentally that the dog is able to digest large quantities of cornstarch, either raw or cooked. Rice fed to mature dogs in amounts sufficient to satisfy total energy requirements has been found to be 95 percent digested. We know that the various commercial biscuits and meals which are marketed as food for dogs are moderately well tolerated, especially if they are supplemented by the addition of fresh meat. There seems to be no reason why they should not be included in moderate amounts in the dog's ration.

Carbohydrates are a cheap source of energy for the dog, both in their initial cost and in the work required of the organism for their metabolism. Since there exists ample evidence that the dog has no difficulty in digesting and utilizing considerable amounts of starches and sugars for the production of energy, there is no reason why they should be excluded from his diet. Some carbohydrate is necessary for the metabolism of fats. The only danger from the employment of carbohydrates is that, being cheap, they may be employed to the exclusion of proteins and other essential elements of the dog's diet. It should be noted that meat and milk contain a measure of carbohydrates as well as of proteins.

The use of foodstuffs containing any large proportion of cellulose for the dog is not recommended.

Thoroughly cooked rice or oatmeal in moderate quantities may well be used to supplement and cheapen a meat diet for a dog without harm to him, as may crushed dog biscuit or shredded wheat waste or the waste from the manufacture of other breakfast foods. They are not required but may be used without harm. Even thoroughly cooked and mashed potatoes, especially if they contain plenty of milk, butter and gravy are good dog food (along with plenty of meat), despite that many old fashioned cranks persist in considering them harmful.

Sugar and candy, of which dogs are inordinately fond, used also to be verboten. They are an excellent source of energy—and harmless. They should be fed in only moderate quantities and only after a meal, since they tend to take the edge off the appetite. Give a dog sugar before a meal and he may refuse the meal itself. However, a finical eater may be persuaded to take his meal by mixing Karo corn syrup with his other viands, and it is harmless in reasonable quantities. Many old fashioned dog men may consider this statement as heresy, but it is none the less true.

Sugars and starches, the carbohydrates, may harmlessly be added to the meat in a dog's ration in moderate quantities for the sake of variety and to reduce the cost. Meat remains, however, the essential main element of an optimum ration.

Fats

In the dog as in man, body fat is found in largest amounts under the skin, between the muscles and around the internal organs. The fat so stored serves as a reserve source of heat and energy when the caloric value of the food is insufficient or for temporary periods when no food is eaten. The accumulation of a certain amount of fat around vital organs provides considerable protection against cold and injury.

Before fats can be carried to the body cells by means of the circulating blood it is necessary for them to be digested in the intestines with the aid of enzymes. Fats require a longer time for digestion than carbohydrates or proteins. For this reason, they are of special importance in delaying the sensations of hunger. This property of fats is frequently referred to as "staying power."

It is easily possible for some dogs to accumulate too much fat, making them unattractive, ungainly and vaguely uncomfortable. This should be avoided by withholding an excess of fats and carbohydrates from the diets of such dogs

26

whenever obesity threatens them. There is greater danger, however, that dogs may through inadequacy of their diets be permitted to become too thin.

Carbohydrates can in part be transformed to fats within the animal body. The ratio between fats and carbohydrates can therefore be varied within wide limits in the dog's ration so long as the requirements for proteins, vitamins and minerals is adequately met. Some dogs have been known to tolerate as much as forty percent of fat in their diets over prolonged periods, but so much is not to be recommended as a general practice. Perhaps, fifteen to twenty percent of fat is adequate without being too much.

Many dog keepers hold to an utterly mistaken concept that fat in a dog's diet is harmful. The dogs of such persons must obtain some fats from sources unknown to their owners, from milk or meat or elsewhere, but probably not enough for their optimum of well being.

Fat is a heat producing food, and the amount given a dog should be stepped up in the colder parts of the year and reduced in the summer months. In a ration low in fat it is particularly important that a good source of the fat-soluble vitamins be included or that such vitamins be artificially supplied. Weight for weight, fat has more than twice the full value of the other organic food groups—carbohydrates and proteins. The use of fat tends to decrease the amount of food required to supply caloric needs. The fats offer a means of increasing or decreasing the total sum of energy in the diet with the least change in the volume of food intake. To thin down an over-fat dog, the amount of fats in his diet should be reduced; to fatten a dog the amounts of fat in the diet should be increased.

It is far less important that the dog receive more than a minimum amount of fats, however, than that his ration contain an adequate amount and quality balance of proteins. Lean meat in adequate quantities will provide him with such proteins, and fats may be added to it in the form of fat meat, butter, margarine, cotton seed oil or lard. Small quantities of dog biscuits, cooked rice, or other cereals in the diet will supply the needed carbohydrates. However, cellulose or

other roughage is not required in the diet of the carnivore. It serves only to engorge the dog's colon, which is not capacious, and to increase the volume of feces, which is superogatory. The dog's digestive tract is different from that of man; and, while he can eat and digest in part a man's diet, he is better off for a diet suited to his own particular structure.

Minerals

At least eleven minerals are present in the normal dog, and there are probably others occurring in quantities so minute that they have not as yet been discovered. The eleven are as follows: Calcium (lime), Sodium chloride (table salt), copper, iron, magnesium, manganese, phosphorus, zinc, potassium and iodine.

Of many of these only a trace in the daily ration is required and that trace is adequately found in meat or in almost any other normal diet. There are a few that we should be at pains to add to the diet. The others we shall ignore.

Sodium chloride (salt) is present in sufficient quantities in most meats, although, more to improve the flavor of the food than to contribute to the animal's nutrition, a small amount of salt can be added to the ration. The exact amount makes no material difference, since the unutilized portions are eliminated, largely in the urine.

If the brand of salt used is iodized, it will meet the iodine requirements, which are very small. Iodine deficiency in dogs is rare, but food crops and meats grown in certain areas contain little or no iodine, and it is well to be on the safe side by using iodized salt.

Sufficient iron is usually found in meat and milk, but if the dog appears anemic or listless the trace of iron needed can be supplied with one of the iron salts—ferric sulphate, or oxide, or ferrous gluconate. Iron is utilized in the bone marrow in the synthesis of hemoglobin in the blood corpuscles. It is used over and over; when a corpuscle is worn out and is to be replaced it surrenders its iron before its elimination.

When more iron is ingested than can be utilized, it is stored in the liver, after which further surplus is excreted. The liver of the new born puppy contains enough iron to supply

28

several times the amount stated and an excess dosage is unlikely, it is only fair to warn the reader that it is at least theoretically possible.

Vitamin E is the so-called fertility vitamin. Whether it is required for dogs has not as yet been determined. Rats fed upon a ration from which Vitamin E was wholly excluded became permanently sterile; but the finding is not believed to pertain to all animals. Some dog keepers, however, declare that the feeding of wheat germ oil, the most abundant source of Vitamin E, has prevented early abortions of their bitches, has resulted in larger and more vigorous litters of puppies, has increased the fertility of stud dogs, has improved the coats of their dogs and furthered the betterment of their general health. Whether Vitamin E or some other factor or factors in the wheat germ oil is responsible for these alleged benefits is impossible to say.

Vitamin E is so widely found in small quantities in well nigh all foods that the hazard of its omission from any normal diet is small.

Numerous other vitamins have been discovered and isolated in recent years, and there are suspected to be still others as yet unknown. The ones here discussed are the only ones that warrant the use of care to include them in the dog's daily ration. It is well to reiterate that vitamins are not medicine, but are food, a required part of the diet. Any person interested in the complete nutrition of his dog will not neglect them.

The best and easiest way to administer vitamins to dogs is in pills or tablets in which all of the essential vitamins are included. These may be purchased at any drug store. The formula of any such preparation must be scrutinized to make sure that it contains enough of each vitamin for the purpose intended, since there is as wide a variation in the contents as in the cost of the various brands.

The tablets are tasteless or sugar coated, and may be most easily fed to the dog if they are buried in a small piece of raw meat.

It should go without saying that a dog should have access to clean, fresh, pure drinking water at all times, of which he should be permitted to drink as much or as little as he chooses. The demands of his system for drinking water will depend in part upon the moisture content of his food. Fed upon dry dog biscuits, he will probably drink considerable water to moisten it; with a diet which contains much milk or soup, he will need little additional water. That he chooses to drink water immediately after a meal is harmless. The only times his water should be limited (but not entirely withheld from him) is after violent exercise or excitement, at which times his thirst should be satisfied only gradually.

The quantities of food required daily by dogs are influenced and determined by a number of factors: the age, size, individuality and physical condition of the animal; the kind, quality, character and proportions of the various feeds in the ration; the climate, environment and methods of management; and the type and amount of work done, or the degree of exercise. Of these considerations, the age and size of the dog and the kind and amount of work are particularly important in determining food requirements. During early puppyhood a dog may require two or three (or even more) times as much food per pound of body weight as the same dog will require at maturity. A violently active dog may require almost twice as much food as a sedentary one.

Any statement we should make here about the food requirements of a dog as to weight or volume would be subject to modification. Dogs vary in their metabolism. One dog might stay fat and sleek on a given amount of a given ration, whereas his litter brother in an adjoining kennel might require twice or only half as much of the same ration to maintain him in the same state of flesh. Some dogs are gluttons and will immediately clean up all the food given to them and crave and beg for more; others have scanty appetites which have to be pampered and the dogs encouraged to eat at all. Sometimes they must be hand fed, bite by bite, and coaxed to eat. Occasionally one will be found that requires to have his meat literally stuffed down his throat like a Strasbourg goose. Dogs that refuse to eat are a trial.

The only sound determiners of how much to feed a dog are his appetite and his condition. As a general rule, a dog should have as much food for maintenance as he will readily clean up in five or ten minutes, unless he tends to lay on unwanted fat, in which case his intake of food should be reduced, especially its content of fats and carbohydrates. A thin dog should have his ration increased and be urged to eat it. The fats in his ration should be increased, and he may be fattened with a dessert of candy, sugar or sweet cake following his main meal. These should never be used before a meal, lest they impair the appetite, and they should not be given to a fat dog at all. Rightly employed, they are useful and harmless, contrary to the prevalent belief.

Growing puppies require frequent meals, as will be discussed later. Pregnant and lactating bitches and frequently used stud dogs should have at least two meals, and better three, each day. For the mere maintenance of healthy adult dogs, one large meal a day appears to suffice as well as more smaller ones. Many tender hearted dog keepers choose to divide the ration into two parts and to feed their dogs twice each day. There can be no objection offered to such a program except that it involves additional work for the keeper. Whether one meal or two, they should be given at regular hours, to which dogs soon adjust and expect their dinner at a given time.

It is better to determine upon an adequate ration, with plently of meat in it, and feed it day after day, than to vary the diet in the assumption that a dog tires of eating the same thing. There is no evidence that he does, and it is a burden upon his carniverous digestion to be making constant adjustments and readjustments to a new diet. It is well, however, that the ration chosen contains a complete balance of all the necessary food elements. The dog must be fed, not half fed either as to quality or quantity.

Most canned dog foods are inadequate. Manufactured to meet a price competition, most of them are of a cereal mush (largely water) with an inadequate amount of meat included in it. Vast numbers of dogs eat such pap, and some appear to thrive on it. It is not, however, to be recommended, at least as an exclusive diet.

There are a few brands of canned foods made of tankage

and slaughter-house waste. These appear to be relished by dogs and to nourish them. They are at least made from meat, however unappetizing its form. Except for a prejudice against the use of such substances and the odor of the food which transmits itself to the dog that eats it, there can be no objection to the feeding of such canned foods—especially if it is found to agree with the dog.

Full credence to the claims of biscuit manufacturers that their products are complete dog foods should be withheld. The best of the biscuits can be combined with meat as the carbohydrates, but they are hardly to be trusted as the sole foodstuff. Many of them contain some dried meat, which is worth taking into account in fortifying them with additional meat. There is reason to believe that the potency of the vitamins they are presumed to contain has been impaired by exposure to heat and air.

Without wholly condemning the prepared foods—the lazy man's dog foods—caution must be used to make sure that the brand used contains all the food elements needed and in adequate proportions. A dog previously well nourished requires a considerable time to exhibit the ill effects of improper feeding; and the restoration of his well being when he is changed from an incomplete diet to a complete one is equally slow.

If fish is fed, it should be boned—thoroughly. The same is true of fowl and rabbit meats. Small bones may be caught in the dog's throat or may puncture the stomach or intestines. Large, raw shank bones of beef may be given to the dog with impunity, but they should be renewed at frequent intervals before they spoil. A dog obtains much amusement from gnawing a raw bone and some nutrition. Harm does not accrue from his swallowing of bone fragments, which are dissolved by the hydrochloric acid in his stomach. Eaten in excessive amounts, bones may cause constipation which should be rectified, if it occurs, with a dose of Milk of Magnesia.

Meat for dogs may be fed raw, or may be roasted, broiled or boiled. It is not advisable to feed fried foods to dogs. All soups, gravies and juices from cooked meat must be conserved and included in the food, since they contain some of the minerals and vitamins extracted from the meat.

A well-known German physician selected a medium sized, strong, healthy bitch, and after she had been mated, he fed her on chopped horse meat from which the salts were to a large extent extracted by boiling for two hours in distilled water. In addition to this she was given each day a certain quantity of fried fat. As drink she had only distilled water. She gave birth to six healthy puppies, one of which was killed immediately, and its bones found to be strong and well built and free from abnormalities. The other puppies did not thrive, but remained weak, and could scarcely walk at the end of a month, when four died from excessive feebleness; and the sixth was killed two weeks later. The mother in the meantime had become very lean but was tolerably lively and had a fair appetite. She was killed one hundred and twenty-six days after the beginning of the experiment, and it was then found that the bones of her spine and pelvis were softened,—a condition known to physicians as osteomalacia.

The results of this experiment are highly interesting and instructive, showing clearly as they do that the nursing mother sends out to her young, in her milk, a part of her store of lime, which is absolutely essential to their welfare. They show also that if proper food is denied her, when in whelp and when nursing, not only her puppies but she as well must suffer greatly in consequence. And in the light of these facts is uncovered one of the most potential causes of rickets so common among large breeds.

It may therefore be accepted that bitches in pup must have goodly quantities of meat; moreover that while cooking may be the rule if the broth is utilized, it is a wise plan to give this food occasionally in raw state.

In advising this the writer is fully aware of the fact that he is running counter to a strong prejudice that exists among no small number of breeders, who maintain that the raw meat will cause a loss of the puppies. Such theory, however, is opposed; furthermore, experience is, that to withhold raw meat entirely must greatly intensify the danger of a loss of the offspring through the puppy-eating habit.

There is little choice among the varieties of meat, except that pork is seldom relished by dogs, usually contains too much fat, and should be cooked to improve its digestibility when it is used at all. Beef, mutton, lamb, goat and horse flesh are equally valuable. The choice should be made upon the basis of their comparative cost and their availability in the particular community. A dog suddenly changed from another diet to horse flesh may develop a harmless and temporary diarrhea, which can be ignored.

Horse flesh is likely to be deficient in fats, which may be added in the form of suet, lard, margarine, cotton seed oil or peanut oil.

The particular cuts of whatever meat is used is of little consequence. Lungs contain little of nutritional value. Liver and kidney are especially valuable and when it is possible they should be included as part of the meat used. As the only meat in the ration, liver and kidney tend to loosen the bowels. It is better to include them as a part of each day's ration, than to permit them to serve as the sole meat content one or two days a week.

It makes no difference whether meat is ground or is fed to the dog in large or medium sized pieces. He is able to digest pieces of meat as large as he can swallow. The advantage of grinding meat is that it can be better mixed with whatever else it is wished to include in the ration, the dog being unable to pick out the meat and reject the rest. There is little harm in his doing so, except for the waste, since it is the meat upon which we must depend for the most part for his nutrition.

Fresh ground meat can be kept four or five days under ordinary refrigeration without spoiling. It may be kept indefinitely if solidly frozen in deep freeze. Frozen ground horse meat for dogs is available in many markets, is low in price, and is entirely satisfactory for the purpose intended.

A suggested ration is made as follows: Two-thirds to three quarters by weight of ground meat including ten to twenty percent of fat and a portion of liver or kidney, with the remainder thoroughly cooked rice or oatmeal, or shredded wheat, or dog biscuit, or wheat germ, with a sprinkling of calcium phosphate diabasic. The vitamins may be given separately.

No vegetables are needed. Their only purpose in the ration is to supply minerals and vitamins, the latter of which are impaired by heat. Vegetables are an added burden upon the dog's digestion which is not designed for their accommodation.

If it is desired to offer the dog a second meal, it may be of shredded wheat or other breakfast cereal with plenty of milk, with or without one or more soft boiled eggs. Evaporated canned milk or powdered milk is just as good food for the dog as fresh milk. Cottage cheese is excellent for this second meal.

These are not the only possible rations for the dog, but they will prove adequate. Leavings from the owner's table can be added to either ration, but can hardly be depended upon for the entire nourishment of the dog.

The dog's food should be at approximately body heat, tepid but never hot.

Little consideration is here given to the costs of the various foods. Economies in rations and feeding practices are admittedly desirable, but not if they are made at the expense of the dog's health, efficiency and well being. Where many dogs are fed economies can be made by buying food in large quantities, and by obtaining stale bread, cracked eggs, good meat scraps, broken cereals and similar products that can not be marketed for human use but are sound, wholesome, and entirely satisfactory for dogs.

Some Brief Precepts About Feeding

Many dogs are overfed. Others do not receive adequate rations. Both extremes should be avoided, but particularly overfeeding of grown dogs. Coupled with lack of exercise, overfeeding usually produces excessive body weight and laziness, and it may result in illness and sterility. Prolonged undernourishment causes loss of weight, listlessness, dull coats, sickness and death.

An adequate ration will keep most mature dogs at a uniform body weight and in a thrifty, moderately lean condition. Observation of condition is the best guide in determining the correct amount of food. The appetite of the dog can not be accepted as a final determiner of how much he should eat. Some dogs are difficult to induce to eat enough, and many others will overeat if given the opportunity.

The axiom, "One man's meat is another man's poison," is applicable to dogs also. Foods that are not tolerated by the dog or those that cause digestive and other disturbances should be discontinued. The use of moldy, spoiled or rotten food is never good practice. Food should be protected from fouling by rats or mice, especially because rats are vectors of leptospirosis. The excessive use of food of low energy content and low biological values will often result in poor condition and may cause loss of weight and paunchiness.

All feeding and drinking utensils must be kept scrupulously clean. They should be washed after each using.

It is usually desirable to reduce the food allotment somewhat during hot weather. Dogs should be fed at regular intervals, and the best results may be expected when regular feeding is accompanied by regular, but not exhausting, exercise.

Most dogs do not thrive on a ration containing large amounts of sloppy foods, and excessive bulk is to be avoided especially for hardworking dogs, puppies, and pregnant or lactating bitches. If the ration is known to be adequate and the dog is losing weight or is not in good condition, the presence of intestinal parasites is to be suspected. However, dogs sometimes go "off feed" for a day or two. This is cause for no immediate anxiety, but if it lasts more than two or three days, a veterinarian should be consulted.

Although the dog may show no immediate or outward signs of the effects of improper feeding or malnutrition, this does not prove that no harm is done. A dog's deterioration may be so gradual as to escape the observation of the inexperienced keeper, and its improvement as the result of good food may be equally slow. A good, lively coat, bright, clear eyes, a good disposition, and an abundance of pep are reliable indications that the ration is adequate. The ultimate purpose of feeding should be to obtain a constant state of good health, happiness, and longevity.

Food For the Stud Dog

The stud dog that is used for breeding only at infrequent intervals requires only the food needed for his maintenance in good health, as is set forth above. He should be well fed with ample meat in his diet, moderately exercised to keep his flesh firm and hard, and not permitted to become either too thin or too fat.

More care is required for the adequate nutrition of the dog offered at public stud and frequently employed for breeding. A vigorous stud dog may very handily serve two bitches a week over a long period without a serious tax upon his health and strength if he is fully nourished and adequately but not excessively exercised. Such a dog should have at least two meals a day, and they should consist of even more meat, milk (canned is as good as fresh), eggs, cottage cheese, and other foods of animal origin than is used in most maintenance rations. Liver and some fat should be included, and the vitamins especially are not to be forgotten. In volume this will be only a little more than the maintenance, the difference being in its richness and concentration. Caution should be exercised never to permit a stud dog to become too fat, and it is better that he shall not be permitted to grow thin.

An interval of an hour or two should intervene between a dog's meal and his employment for breeding. He may be fed, but only lightly, immediately after he is bred.

The immediate reason why a stud dog should be adequately fed and exercised is the maintenance of his strength and virility. The secondary reason is that a popular stud dog is on exhibition at all times, between the shows as well as at the shows. Clients with bitches to be bred appear without notice to examine a dog at public stud, and the dog should be presented to them in the best possible condition; clean, hard, in exactly the most becoming state of flesh, and with a gleaming, lively coat. These all depend largely upon the highly nutritious diet the dog receives.

43

Food For the Brood Bitch

Often a well fed bitch comes through the ordeal of rearing a large litter of puppies without any impairment of her vitality and flesh. In such case she may be returned to a good maintenance ration until she is ready to be bred again. About the time she weans her puppies her coat will be dead and ready to drop out, but if she is healthy and well fed a new and vigorous coat will grow in, and she will be no worse off for her maternal ordeal. Some bitches, either from a deficient nutrition or a constitutional disposition to contribute too much of her own strength and substance to the nutrition of her puppies, are thin and exhausted at the time of weaning them. Such a bitch needs the continuance of at least two good and especially nutritious meals a day for a month or more until her flesh and strength are restored before she is returned to her routine maintenance ration, upon which she may be kept until time comes to breed her again.

At breeding time a bitch's flesh should be hard, and she should be on the lean side rather than too fat. She should be freed from any intestinal parasites she may harbor, and should be kept in clean quarters where she will not be reinfested with them. No change in her regular maintenance diet need be made until about the fourth or fifth week of her pregnancy. The growth of the fetus is small up until the middle of the pregnancy, after which it becomes rapid.

The bitch usually begins to "show in whelp" about six weeks after breeding, and her food consumption should be gradually stepped up. If she has been having only one meal a day, she should be given two; if she has had two, both should be larger. From henceforth until her puppies are weaned she must eat not merely for two, as is said of the pregnant woman, but for four or five, possibly for ten or twelve. She is not to be encouraged to grow positively fat; but, just as she was slightly on the lean side at the time of breeding, now she is to be brought slightly to the fat side and maintained in that condition, if possible, until she voluntarily weans her puppies. Especial emphasis should be laid upon her ration's content of meat, including liver, milk, calcium phosphate and Vitamins A and D, both of which are found in cod-liver oil.

44

She may refuse the last meal offered her before she whelps, which need cause no anxiety. After she has finished the delivery of her puppies, and even between the puppies' arrivals, she may be grateful for some warm (not hot) sustenance. If she likes sweets, a few pieces of candy or lumps of sugar will be readily eaten and provide the bitch with immediate strength and energy.

Some breeders destroy all but a limited number of puppies in a litter in the belief that a bitch will be unable adequately to nourish all the puppies she has whelped. In some extreme cases it may be necessary to do this or to obtain a foster mother or wet nurse to share the burden of rearing the puppies. However, the healthy bitch with normal metabolism can usually generate enough milk to feed adequately all the puppies she has produced, provided she is well enough fed and provided the puppies are fed additionally as soon as they are able to eat.

After whelping until the puppies are weaned, throughout the lactating period, the bitch should have all the nourishing food she can be induced to eat—up to four or five meals a day. These should consist largely of meat and liver, some fat, a small amount of cereals, milk, eggs, cottage cheese, calcium phosphate and vitamins, with especial reference to Vitamins A and D. At that time it is hardly possible to feed a bitch too much or to keep her too fat. The growth of the puppies is much more rapid after they are born than their growth in the dam's uterus, and the large amount of food to maintain that rapid growth must pass through the bitch and be transformed to milk, while at the same time she must maintain her own body.

If she is given enough good food, a bitch may be bred without harm to her well nigh every time she comes in heat. The long waits between litters that some breeders adhere to are largely to permit their bitches to resume their normal strength and vigor after rearing of puppies. The habit was established before we knew so much as we now know about foods and nutrition, and has been needlessly retained. Three months between weaning and breeding again is ample time for the restoration of her bodily vigor to any healthy bitch

45

of normal metabolism if she is given ample rations of the right kind.

The Feeding of Puppies

If the number of puppies in a litter is small, if the mother is vigorous, healthy and a good milker, the youngsters up until their weaning time may require no additional food over and above the milk they suck from their dam's breasts. If the puppies are numerous or if the dam's milk is deficient in quality or quantity, it is wise to begin feeding the puppies artificially as soon as they are able and willing to accept food. This is earlier than used to be realized.

It is for the sake of the puppies' vigor rather than for the sake of their ultimate size that their growth is to be promoted as rapidly as possible. Vigorous and healthy puppies attain early maturity if they are given the right amounts of the right quality of food. The ultimate size of the dog at maturity is laid down in his germplasm, and he can be stunted or dwarfed, if at all, only at the expense of his type. If one tries to prevent the full growth of a dog, by withholding from him the food he needs, one will wind up with a richitic, cow-hocked dog, one with a delicate digestive apparatus, a sterile one, or all of these shortcomings combined, even if not a dead dog.

Growth may be slowed with improper food, sometimes without serious harm to the dog; but the dog will ultimately attain the size laid down in his germplasm—either that or ruined in his structure or his constitution. He is in all ways better off if he is forced along with the best food and encouraged to attain his full adult size at an early age. Dogs of the smaller breeds usually reach their full maturity by several months earlier than those of the larger breeds. A well grown dog reaches his sexual maturity and can be safely used for limited breeding at from eight months to one year of age.

As soon as teeth can be felt with the finger in a puppy's mouth, which is usually at about seventeen or eighteen days of age, it is safe to begin to feed him. His first food (except for his mother's milk) should be of scraped raw beef at body temperature. The first day he may have two teaspoonsful, several hours apart. He will not require to be taught to eat this meat; he will seize upon it avidly and lick his chops for more. The second day he may have three or four even larger helpings, as much as a dessert-spoonful at a time. Thereafter, the amount and frequency of this feeding may be rapidly increased. By the twenty-fifth day the meat need not be scraped, but only finely ground. This process of the early feeding of raw meat to puppies not only gives them a good start in life, but it also relieves their mother of a part of her burden of providing milk for them.

At about the fourth week, some cereal (thoroughly cooked oatmeal, shredded wheat or dried bread) may be either moistened and mixed with the meat or be served to the puppies with milk, fresh or canned. It may be necessary to immerse their noses into such a mixture to teach them to eat it. Calcium phosphate and a small amount of cod-liver oil should be added to such a mixture, both of which substances the puppies should have every day until their maturity. At the fourth week, while they are still at the dam's breast, they may be fed three or four times a day upon this extra ration, or something similar, such as cottage cheese or soft boiled egg. By the sixth week their dam will be trying to wean them, and they may have four or five meals daily. One of these may be finely broken dog biscuit thoroughly soaked in milk. One or two of the meals should consist largely or entirely of meat with liver, raw or cooked.

The old advice about feeding puppies "little and often" should be altered to "much and often." Each puppy at each meal should have all the food he will readily clean up. Food should not be left in front of the puppies. They should be fed and after ten to fifteen minutes the receptacle should be taken away. Young puppies should be rolypoly fat, and kept so up to at least five or six months of age. Thereafter they should be slightly on the fat side, but not pudgy, until maturity.

The varied diet of six weeks puppies may be continued, but at eight or nine weeks the number of meals may be reduced to four, and at three months to three large rations per

47

day. After six months the meals may be safely reduced again to two a day, but they must be generous meals with meat, liver, milk, cod-liver oil and calcium phosphate. At full maturity, one meal a day suffices, or two may be continued.

The secret of turning good puppies into fine, vigorous dogs is to keep 'em growing through the entire period of their maturation. The most important item in the rearing of puppies is adequate and frequent meals of highly nourishing foods. Growth requires two or three times as much food as maintenance. Time between meals should be allowed for digestion, but puppies should never be permitted to become really hungry. Water in a shallow dish should be available to puppies at all times after they are big enough to walk.

The feeding of puppies may appear complicated in the reading about it. It is in fact very easy. It requires only common sense and the will to stick with it. Outworn practices and old wives' tales should be disregarded, and the newer findings in the science of feeding and nutrition should be taken advantage of. Beware of extremes of economy, for it is costly in the end. Puppies worth the rearing merit the cost of rearing them well.

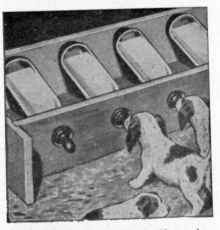

A homemade nursing rack simplifies orphan
puppy feeding.

MELINDA v. MARIENLUST
Dam of Int. Ch. Favorite v. Marienlust
Breeder-Owner: Josef and Maria Mehrer, West Hempstead, L. I., N. Y.

CH. REBECCA OF GERA
Sire: Ch. White Gables Basil   Dam: Rivenrock Doric
Owners: Mr. and Mrs. Ray E. Shultis, Van Nuys, California

CH. ANNETTE OF GERA

Sire: Admiral v. Marienlust   Dam: Aria of Gera

Owners: Mr. and Mrs. Ray E. Shultis, Van Nuys, California

OCTAVIA OF GERA

Sire: Ch. Badger Hill Nobby   Dam: Aria of Gera

Owners: Mr. and Mrs. Ray E. Shultis, Van Nuys, California

CH. HERSHEY OF HEYING-TECKEL
Sire: Ch. Leutnant v. Marienlust   Dam: Herzy v. Marienlust
Owner: Heying-Teckel Kennels, Mr. and Mrs. Fred Heying, Pacoima, Calif.

CH. CEDRIC OF HEYING-TECKEL
Sire: Ch. Favorite v. Marienlust   Dam: Cobina v. Marienlust
Owner: Heying-Teckel Kennels, Mr. and Mrs. Fred Heying, Pacoima, Calif.

CH. CINDERELLA v. MARIENLUST
Sire: Ch. Leutnant v. Marienlust   Dam: Veni v. Marienlust
Owner: Mrs. Walter D. Monroe, Little Gate Kennels, Lake Forest, Illinois

CH. CHADWICK OF CRESPI STREET
Sire: Ch. Eric Again v.d. Daniels   Dam: Ch. Queen of My Heart
Owner: Donia Bussey Cline, Crespi Street Kennels, Los Angeles, Calif.

The Breeding of Dogs

ERE, if anywhere in the entire process of the care and management of dogs, the exercise of good judgment is involved. Upon the choice of two dogs, male and female, to be mated together depends the success or failure of the future of one's dogs. If the two parties to be mated are ill chosen, either individually or as pertains to their fitness as mates one to the other, all the painstaking care to feed and rear the resultant puppies correctly is wasted. Mating together of two dogs is the drafting of the blueprints and the writing of the specifications of what the puppies are to be like. The plans, it is true, require to be executed; the puppies, when they arrive, must be adequately fed and cared for in order to develop them into the kinds of dogs they are in their germ plasm designed to become. However, if the plans as determined in the mating are defective, just so will the puppies that result from them be defective, in spite of all the good raising one can give them.

The element of luck in the breeding of dogs can not be discounted, for it exists. The mating which on paper appears to be the best possible may result in puppies that are not worth the water to drown them. Even less frequently, a good puppy may result from a chance mating together of two ill chosen parents. These results are fortuitous and unusual. However, the best dogs as a lot come from parents carefully chosen as to their individual excellences and as to their suitability as mates for each other. It is as unwise as it is unnecessary to trust to luck in the breeding of dogs. Careful planning pays off in the long run, and few truly excellent dogs are produced without it.

There is insufficient space at our disposal in this book to discuss in detail the science of genetics and the application of that science to the breeding of dogs. Whole books have been written about the subject. One of the best, clearest, and easiest for the layman to understand of these books is *The Art of Breeding Better Dogs,* by Kyle Onstott, which may be obtained from Denlinger, the publisher of this book. In it and in other books upon the subject of genetics will be found more data about the practical application of science to the breeding of live stock than can be included here.

Any superficial discussion of the Mendelian laws and neo-Mendelism and of the manner in which the hereditary characteristics of an organism are transmitted to the new generation by means of the genes and chromosomes of the cells uniting to form the new zygote are likely to be misinterpreted and misleading to the reader. Such scanty consideration is more likely to confuse than to help. This does not mean that science in the mating of dogs can profitably be ignored, for it should be studied and advantage taken of it, but it is one of those subjects of which "a little knowledge is a dangerous thing."

Some breeders without any knowledge of genetics have been successful, without knowing exactly why they succeeded. Some of them have adhered to beliefs in old wives' tales and to traditional concepts that science has long since exploded and abandoned. Such as have succeeded have done so in spite of their lack of knowledge and not because of it. There is reason to believe that ignorance of the laws of inheritance has caused many failures and that the few uninformed but lucky persons who have succeeded would have produced even better dogs if they had had more knowledge of what they were about. In these days in which so many

50

dogs of great excellence are being bred and in which the friendly competition among the owners is so intense, the breeder who disregards the available knowledge of the breeders' art is sadly handicapped in his effort to produce winning dogs.

The most that can be done here is to offer some advice soundly based upon the genetic laws. Every feature a dog may or can possess is determined by the genes carried in the two reproductive cells, one from each parent, from the union of which he was developed. There are thousands of pairs of these determiners in the life plan of every puppy, and often a complex of many genes is required to produce a single recognizable attribute of the dog.

These genes function in pairs, one member of each pair being contributed by the father and the other member of the pair coming from the mother. The parents obtained these genes they hand on from their parents, and it is merely fortuitous which half of any pair of genes present in a dog's or a bitch's germ plasm he may hand on to any one of his progeny. Of any pair of its own genes, a dog or a bitch may contribute one member to one puppy and the other member to another puppy in the same litter or in different litters. The unknown number of pairs of genes is so great that there is an infinite number of combinations of them, which accounts for the differences we find between two full brothers or two full sisters. In fact, it depends upon the genes he receives whether a dog be a male or a female.

This is not hearsay or mere belief; it is a definitely established scientific fact, however briefly and vaguely it must here be stated. We hence learn that the male dog contributes one and the bitch the other of every pair of genes that unite to determine what the puppy will be like and what he will grow into. Thus, the parents make exactly equal contributions to the germ plasm or zygote from which every puppy is developed. It was long believed that the male dog was so much more important than the bitch in any mating that the excellence or shortcomings of the bitch might be disregarded. This theory was subsequently reversed and breeders considered the bitch to be more important than the

51

dog. We now know that their contribution in every mating and in every individual puppy is exactly equal, and neither is to be considered more than the other.

It may also be deduced from our fully confirmed premise that the breeder of dogs is not blending the bloods of the two parents. He is rather constructing a mosaic of the paired genes. These genes are discrete entities, which may be separated and recombined in subsequent generations. Blood has nothing at all to do with the mating except to carry nutrition to the growing fetus.

If only the breeders could bring themselves to discard the age-old concept of the blending of bloods and to substitute for it is the correct concept of the matching of genes, the advancement of the art of breeding dogs would be astounding. The breeders are shuffling cards of which some are red and some are black; they are not blending colored liquids. In subsequent generations it will be possible to unscramble the eggs of which our omelette is composed.

There are two kinds of genes—the recessive genes and the dominant. And there are three kinds of pairs of genes: a recessive from the sire plus a recessive from the dam; a dominant from the sire plus a dominant from the dam; and a dominant from one parent plus a recessive from the other. It is the last combination that is the source of our trouble in breeding. When both members of a pair of genes are recessive, the result is a recessive attribute in the animal that carries them; when both members of the pair are dominant, the result is a pure dominant attribute; but when one member of the pair is recessive and the other member dominant, the result will be a wholly or only partially dominant attribute, which will breed true only half of the time. This explains why a dog or a bitch may fail to produce progeny that looks at all like itself.

If all the pairs of a dog's genes were purely dominant, we could expect him to produce puppies that resembled himself in all particulars, no matter what kind of mate he was bred to. Or if all his genes were recessive and he were mated to a bitch with all recessive genes, the puppies might be expected to look quite like the parents. However, a dog with mixed pairs of genes bred to a bitch with mixed pairs of genes may produce anything at all, puppies that bear no resemblance to either parent.

It is the breeder's purpose to choose for his breeding animals dogs with recessive or purely dominant gene pairs, whichever tends to produce the desired characteristics, and to avoid animals with mixed gene pairs. To make such choice of animals with matched pairs of genes for every possible attribute is perhaps impossible, but as time goes on, expert breeders are purifying their strains and matching up more and more of their dogs' genes. An absolutely pure bred dog is one with every one of his many thousand of gene pairs correctly matched, although we use the words *pure bred* to describe one with genes matched for the more telling attributes.

Long before the Mendelian laws were discovered, some dogs were known to be "prepotent" to produce certain characters, that is the characters would show up in their puppies irrespective of what their mates might be like. We now know that their prepotency was due to the union of two dominant genes for the particular character in the dog's own germ plasm. For instance, some dogs, themselves with dark eyes, might be depended upon never to produce a puppy with light eyes, no matter how light eyed the mate to which he was bred. This was true despite the fact that the dog's litter brother which had equally dark eyes, when bred to a light eyed bitch might produce a large percentage of puppies with light eyes.

We were long in learning the mechanism through which the Mendelian laws of inheritance functioned; now we know that the attributes of a plant or an animal are all determined by its genes. It is a fascinating subject and is one of which the practical breeder should possess more than the superficial knowledge it is possible to set down here.

All we can do here is to outline some of the practical breeding procedures derived from our knowledge of genetics, pending the reader's closer acquaintance with that science.

Before it is decided to breed a bitch, it is well to consider whether she is worth breeding, whether she is good enough as an individual and whether she came from a good enough family to warrant the expectations that she will produce puppies worth the expense and trouble of raising them. It is to be remembered that the bitch contributes exactly half the genes to each of her puppies; and, if she has not good genes to contribute, the time and money of breeding her and rearing her puppies will be wasted.

It is conceded that a bad or mediocre bitch when bred to an excellent dog will probably produce puppies better than herself; but while one is "grading up" from mediocre stock, other breeders are also grading upward from better stock and they will keep just so far ahead of one's efforts that one can never catch up with them. A merely pretty good bitch is no good at all for breeding. This is said with no intention to discourage the breeding of better dogs, but to save the prospective breeder from heartaches and disappointments. It is better to dispose of a mediocre bitch or to relegate her to the position of a family pet than to breed from her. It is difficult enough, with all the care and judgment one is able to muster, to obtain superlative puppies even from a fine bitch, without cluttering the earth with inferior puppies from just any old bitch.

If one will go into the market and buy the best possible bitch from the best possible family one's purse can afford and breed her sensibly to the best and most suitable stud dog one can find, success is reasonably sure. Even if for economy's sake, the bitch is but a promising puppy backed up by the best possible pedigree, it will require only a few months until she is old enough to be bred. From such a bitch, one may expect first rate puppies at the first try, whereas in starting with an inferior bitch one is merely lucky if he obtains a semblance of the kind of dog he is trying to produce in two or three generations.

Assuming it is decided that the bitch is adequate to serve as a brood bitch, it becomes necessary to choose for her a mate in collaboration with which she may realize the ultimate of her possibilities. It is never wise to utilize for stud the family pet or the neighbor's pet just because he happens to be registered in the stud book or because his service costs nothing. Any dog short of the best and most suitable (wherever he may be and whoever may own him) is an extravagance. If the bitch is worth breeding at all, she is worth shipping clear across the continent, if need be, to obtain for her a mate to enable her to realize her possibilities. Stud fees may range from ten to one hundred dollars or even more. The average value of each puppy, if well reared, should at the time of weaning approximate the legitimate stud fee of its sire. It is therefore profitable with a good bitch to lay out as much as may be required to obtain the services of the best and most suitable stud dog—always assuming that he is worth the price asked. However, it is never wise to choose an inferior or unsuitable dog just because he is well ballyhooed and commands an exorbitant stud fee.

Many dogs of only indifferent excellence are forced to the top in the show ring and then boomed and advertised out of all proportion to their merits either as show dogs or as stud dogs. The amateur breeder is well warned to watch out for such dogs and to pass them by as mates for his bitches. The fact that a dog has the word *champion* before his name may mean something or very little. Some dogs achieve considerable acclaim in the dog shows without justification and especially without the ability to transmit his breed type to his progeny. It is unwise to seek to evaluate the merits of a stud dog merely upon the basis of his awards won in the dog shows. There is no denying that a great dog is likely to be a champion of record; but that a dog is a champion, while it may mean that he is a good specimen of his breed, does not mean that he is either himself a great dog or able to transmit to his progeny whatever excellence he may possess.

There are three considerations by which to evaluate the merits of a stud dog—his outstanding excellence as an individual, his pedigree and the family from which he derived, and the excellence or inferiority of the progeny he is known to have produced.

As an individual a good stud dog may be expected to be bold and aggressive (not vicious) and structurally typical of his breed, but without any freakish exaggerations of type.

He must be sound, a free and true mover, possess fineness and quality, be a gentleman of his own breed. Accidentally acquired scars or injuries such as broken legs should not be held against him, because he can transmit only his genes to his puppies and no such accidents impair his genes.

A dog's pedigree may mean much or little. One of two litter brothers, with pedigrees exactly alike, may prove to be a superlative show and stud dog, and the other worth exactly nothing for either purpose. The pedigree especially is not to be judged on its length, since three generations is at most all that is required, although further extension of the pedigree may prove interesting to a curious owner. No matter how well bred his pedigree may show a dog to be, if he is not a good dog the ink required to write the pedigree was wasted. Most pedigrees of only three generations can be extended to six or twelve if anybody has the curiosity or the fortitude to trace them further in the stud book.

The chief value of a pedigree is to enable us to know from which of a dog's parents, grand parents, or great grand parents, he derived his merits, and from which his faults. In choosing a mate for him (or for her, as the case may be) one seeks to reinforce the one and to avoid the other. Let us assume that one of the grandmothers was upright in shoulder, whereas the shoulder should be well laid back; we can avoid as a mate for such a dog one with any tendency to straight shoulders or one from straight shouldered ancestry. The same principle would apply to an uneven mouth, a light eye, a soft back, splayed feet, cow hocks, or to any other inherited fault. Suppose, on the other hand, that the dog himself, the parents, and all the grandparents are particularly nice in regard to their fronts; in a mate for such a dog, one desires as good a front as is obtainable, but if she, or some of her ancestors are not too good in respect to their fronts, one may take a chance anyway and trust to the good fronted dog with his good fronted ancestry to correct the fault. That then is the purpose of the pedigree as a guide to breeding; more will be said about the pedigree later in this chapter.

A stud dog can best be judged, however, by the excellence of the progeny he is known to have produced, if it is possible to obtain all the data to enable the breeder to evaluate that record. A complete comparative evaluation is perhaps impossible to make, but one close enough to justify conclusions is available. Not only the number but the quality of the bitches to which the dog has been bred must enter into the consideration. A young dog may not have had the opportunity to prove his prowess in the stud. He may have been bred to few bitches and those few of indifferent merits, or his get may not be old enough as yet to hit the shows and establish a record for themselves or for their sire. Allowance may be made for such a dog.

On the other hand, a dog may have proved himself to be phenomenal in the show ring, or may have been made to seem phenomenal by means of the owner's ballyhoo and exploitation. Half of the top bitches in the entire country may have been bred to him upon the strength of his winning record. Merely from the laws of probability such a dog, if he is not too bad, will produce some creditable progeny. Some bitches are so excellent and well bred that they would produce good puppies if they were mated to a billy goat. It is necessary to take into consideration the opportunities a dog has had in relation to the fine progeny he has produced. A dog must be given a chance to prove himself.

That, however, is the chief criterion by which a good stud dog may be recognized. A dog which can sire two or three excellent puppies in every litter from a reasonably good bitch may be considered as an acceptable stud. If he has in his lifetime sired one or two champions each year, and especially if one or two of the lot are superlative champions, top members of their breed, he is a great stud dog. Ordinarily and without other considerations, such a dog is to be preferred to one of his unproved sons, even though the son be as good or better an individual. In this way one employs genes one knows to produce what one wants. The son may be only hybrid dominant for his excellent qualities.

In the choice of a stud dog no attention whatever need be paid to claims that he sires numerically big litters. The number of puppies in the litter, provided there are any puppies at all, depends entirely upon the bitch. At one service, a dog deposits enough spermatozoa to produce a million puppies, if there were so many ova to be fertilized. In any event, the major purpose should be to obtain good puppies, not large numbers of them.

There are three methods of breeding employed by experienced breeders—out-crossing, in-breeding, and line-breeding. By out-crossing is meant the breeding together of mates of which no blood relationship can be traced. It is much favored by novice breeders, who feel that the breeding together of kinsmen is likely to result in imbecility, constitutional weakness, or some other kind of degeneration. In-breeding is the mating together of closely related animals—father to daughter, mother to son, brother to sister, half-brother to half-sister. Some of the best animals ever produced have been bred from some such incestuous mating, and the danger from such practices, if they are carried out by persons who know what they are about, is minimal. Line-breeding is the mating together of animals related one to another, but less closely—such as first cousins, grandsire to granddaughter, grandam to grandson, uncle to niece, or aunt to nephew. More really fine dogs are produced from such a scheme of breeding than from both the other two schemes combined, and it is to be recommended that the inexperienced breeder adhere to it, unless he has an adequate and definite reason for using one of the other schemes or unless he has the advice of an expert and successful breeder.

Absolute out-crossing is usually impossible to do, since all the good dogs in any breed are more or less related—descended from some common ancestor in the fifth or sixth or seventh generation of their pedigrees. In any event, it is seldom to be recommended, since the results from it in the first generation of progeny are usually not satisfactory. It may be undertaken by some far-sighted and experienced breeder for the purpose of bringing into his strain some particular merit lacking in it and present in the strain of the unrelated dog. While dogs so bred may obtain an added vigor from what is known in genetics as *heterosis,* they are likely to manifest a coarseness and a lack of uniformity in the litter which is not to be found in more closely bred puppies. Good breeders never out-cross if it is possible to obtain the virtues they want by sticking to their own strain; and when they do out-cross, it is for the purpose of utilizing the out-crossed product for further breeding. It is not an end in itself.

In-breeding (or incest breeding, as it is sometimes called) involves no such hazards as are and in the past have been attributed to it. It produces some very excellent dogs when correctly employed, some very bad ones even when correctly employed, and all bad ones when carelessly used. All the standard breeds of dogs were established as uniform breeds through intense in-breeding and culling over many generations. In-breeding brings into manifestation undesirable recessive genes, the bearers of which can be discarded and the strain can thus be purged of its bad recessives.

Dogs of great soundness and excellence, from excellent parents and grandparents, all of them much alike, may be safely mated together, no matter how closely they may be related, with reasonable hope that most of the progeny will be sound and typical with a close resemblance to all the members of their ancestry. However, two such superlative and well bred dogs are seldom to be found. It is the way to make progress rapidly and to establish a strain of dogs much alike and which breeds true. The amateur with the boldness and courage to try such a mating in the belief that his dogs are good enough for it is not to be discouraged; but if his judgment is not justified by the results, let him not complain that he has not been warned. Many experienced and successful breeders make few matings without more or less intensive in-breeding as a matter of course, but such men know what they are about, and they breed enough litters that if an occasional one turns out badly they charge it to profit and loss.

Line-breeding is the safest course between the Scylla of out-crossing and the Charybdis of in-breeding for the inexperienced navigator in the sea of breeding. It, too, is to be used with care, because when it succeeds it partakes much of the nature of in-breeding. At any rate, its purpose is the pairing of like genes.

Here the pedigrees come into use. We examine the pedigree of the bitch to be bred. We hope that all the dogs named in it are magnificent dogs, but we look them over and choose the best of the four grandparents. We check this grandparent's breeding and find it good, as it probably is if it is itself a dog or bitch of great excellence. We shall assume that this best dog in the bitch's pedigree is the maternal grandsire. Then our bitch may be bred back to this particular grandsire, to his full brother if he has one of equal excellence, to his best son or best grandson. In such a fashion we compound the genes of this grandsire, and hope to obtain some puppies with his excellences intensified.

The best name in the pedigree may be some other dog or bitch, in which case it is his or her germ plasm that is to be doubled to serve for the foundation of the pedigrees of the puppies of the projected litter.

In making a mating, it is never wise to employ two dogs with the same positive fault. It is wise to use two dogs with as many of the same positive virtues as it is possible to obtain. Neither should faults balance each other, as one with a front too wide, the other with a front too narrow; one with a sway back, the other roached backed. Rather, one member of the mating should be right where the other is wrong. We can not trust to obtain the intermediate, if we overcompensate the fault of one mate with a fault of the other.

Since one wishes to be the actual, and not merely the nominal, breeder of the dogs whose pedigrees bear his name in that capacity, one should plan one's matings in accord with one's ideals and concepts. One may submit the mating to an experienced breeder for his approval, if one is available who can be trusted to be objective in his judgments. It is best to beware of the breeder who maintains a stud dog and wishes to sell its services and of the breeder who permits friendships and animosities and personalities to warp his opinions. If such a valid critical mentor can be found, his advice can be of great worth to the beginning breeder. However, before revision of one's plans already made for an intended mating, one should demand from an advisor forthright reasons why one's well laid plans may be wrong. The novice breeder's plans—especially if he has taken the trouble to study the laws of inheritance and to study his breed of dogs and what he seeks to produce—may be just as well worth execution as the vague and undefined objection to them of a more experienced man.

First read and learn all there is to be known about the breed and about the theories of breeding. And then apply what one has learned in theory. Be bold. The worst one can do is to fail and try again. Do not permit the conservative adviser to deter one from some bold and courageous policy which in one's own concept promises victory.

Negotiations to Use the Stud Dog

Plans to use a stud dog should be laid far enough in advance of the bitch's coming into heat to enable one to make sure that the services of the dog will be available when they are required. Most men with a dog at public stud publish "stud cards," on which are printed the dog's pedigree and pertinent data pertaining to its record. These should be requested for all the dogs one contemplates using. Most such owners reserve the right to refuse to breed their dogs to bitches they deem unsuitable for them; they wish to safeguard their dog's reputation as a producer of superior puppies, by choosing the bitches to which he shall be bred.

Therefore, it is advisable to submit a description of the bitch, with or without a picture of her, and her pedigree to the stud dog's owner at the time the application to use him is made. A part or all of the stud fee can be paid at the time of reservation of service, as may be arranged. In any event, unless it is agreed otherwise, payment must be made before the dog is used.

Notification should be sent to the owner of the dog as soon as the bitch begins to show in heat, and she should be taken or sent by air or by railway express to the dog's owner about the time she is first recognized to be in full heat and ready to breed. The stud dog's owner should be advised by telegram or telephone just how she has been sent and just when she may be expected, and instructions should be given about how she is to be returned.

Extreme care should be used in securely crating a bitch

for shipment when she is in heat. Such bitches are prone to chew their way out of insecure boxes and escape to be bred by some vagrant mongrel. A card containing a statement of the bitch's condition should be attached to the crate as a warning to the carrier to assure her greater security.

The Pregnancy and Whelping of the Bitch

The "period of gestation" of the bitch, by which is meant the duration of her pregnancy, is usually estimated at sixty-three days. Many bitches, especially young ones, have their puppies as early as sixty days after they are bred. Cases have occurred in which strong puppies were born after only fifty-seven days, and there have been cases that required as many as sixty-six days. However, if puppies do not arrive by the sixty-fourth day, it is time to consult a veterinarian.

For the first five to six weeks of her pregnancy, the bitch requires no more than normal good care and unrestricted exercise. For that period, she needs no additional quantity of food, although it must contain sufficient amounts of all the food factors, as is stated in the division of this book that pertains to food. After the fifth to sixth week, the ration must be increased and the violence of exercise restricted. Normal running and walking are likely to be better for the pregnant bitch than a sedentary existence but she should not be permitted to jump, hunt, or fight during the latter half of her gestation. Violent activity may cause her to abort her puppies.

About a week before she is due to whelp, a bed should be prepared for her and she be persuaded to use it for sleeping. This bed may be a box of generous size, big enough to accommodate her with room for activity. It should be high enough to permit her to stand upright, and is better for having a hinged cover. An opening in one side will afford her ingress and egress. This box should be placed in a secluded location, away from any possible molestation by other dogs, animals, or children. The bitch must be made confident of her security in her box.

A few hours, or perhaps a day or two, before her whelping, the bitch will probably begin arranging the bedding of the

62

box to suit herself, tearing blankets or cushions and nosing the parts into the corners. Before the whelping actually starts, however, it is best to substitute burlap sacking, securely tacked to the floor of the box. This is to provide traction for the puppies to reach the dam's breast.

The whelping may take place at night without any assistance from the owner. The box may be opened in the morning to reveal the happy bitch nursing a litter of complacent puppies. But she may need some assistance in her parturition; and, if it is recognized to be in process, it is best to give it to her.

As the puppies arrive, one by one, the enveloping membranes should be removed as quickly as possible, lest the puppies suffocate. Having removed the membrane, the umbilical cord should be severed with clean scissors some three or four inches from the puppy's belly. (The part of the cord attached to the belly will dry up and drop off in a few days.) There is no need for any medicament or dressing of the cord after it is cut.

The bitch should be permitted to eat the afterbirth if she so desires, and she normally does. If she has no assistance, she will probably remove the membrane and sever the cord with her teeth. The only dangers are that she may delay too long or may bite the cord too short. Some bitches, few of them, eat their new born puppies (especially bitches not adequately fed during pregnancy). This unlikelihood should be guarded against.

It is wise to remove all the puppies except one as they arrive, placing them in a box or basket lined and covered by a woolen cloth, somewhere aside or away from the whelping bed, until all have come and the bitch's activity has ceased. The purpose of this is to prevent her from walking or lying on the whelps, and the removal is to keep her from being disturbed by the puppies' whining. A single puppy should be left with the bitch to ease her anxiety.

It is best that the "midwife" be somebody with whom the bitch is on intimate terms and in whom she has confidence. Some bitches exhibit a jealous fear while they are whelping, and even viciousness. Such animals are few, and most appear grateful for gentle assistance through their ordeal.

The puppies usually arrive at intervals of one half hour to an hour until all are delivered. If the interval is greater than three hours, it is wise to call a veterinarian, whose service is seldom needed. An experienced veterinarian can usually be depended upon to withdraw an abnormally presented puppy with obstetrical forceps, although it is possible, but unlikely, that he will recommend a caesarian section. This surgery in the dog is not very grave, but it should be performed by an expert veterinarian. If one should be indicated, it is unnecessary to describe the process here, or the subsequent management of the patient, since the veterinarian will provide all the needed instructions.

Some bitches, at or immediately after their whelping period, go into a convulsive paralysis, which is called *eclampsia*. This is unlikely if the bitch throughout her pregnancy has had an adequate measure of calcium in her rations. The remedy for eclampsia, if one should be required, is the intermuscular injection of calcium gluconate, which any veterinarian is prepared to administer. The need for it should not be permitted to occur. If a veterinarian is not available, immediate action is required as eclampsia will cause death within an hour.

First, immerse the bitch in ice cold water, covering the entire body up to her neck. It is not required to hold her in the water for long. The idea is to shock the nervous system. Next, she must be put completely to sleep with an injection of nembutal, one c.c. to each five pounds of body weight or if the owner does not have the sterile solution of nembutal on hand, give any of the barbital compounds by mouth, two grains for each five pounds of body weight.

When the bitch comes out of her sleep, the puppies can be put back to nurse for a few minutes but care must be exercised and she must never be left with her litter for long periods as a reoccurrence of eclampsia will follow.

Assuming that the whelping has been normal and without untoward incident, all of the puppies are returned to the bitch, and put, one by one, to the breast, which strong puppies will accept with alacrity. The less handling of

CH. MOTO'S PRIDE OF WHITE GABLES
Son of Int. Ch. Cid, Jr., of Lakelands
Owner: Mrs. Walter D. Monroe, Little Gate Kennels, Lake Forest, Illinois

CH. MERRYMAN OF LITTLE GATE
Son of Ch. Bucknam's Merrymaker
Owner: Mrs. Walter D. Monroe, Little Gate Kennels, Lake Forest, Illinois

CH. LIMELIGHT BRESLAUERLICHT, A-378985
Wirehaired chocolate, 8½ pounds, out of Ch. Christel v. d. Bunzlauer
Heide-Limelight by Cito v. Blucherbruch
Owner: Lyman R. Fisher, M.D., Ithaca, N. Y.

CH. ROTCOD v. TENROC, A-876651
Owner: Dr. L. A. Cornet   Breeder: A. Bywaters

CH. de SANGPUR WEE ALLENE
Long-haired Miniature Dachshund
Sire: Tinyteckel Black Silk   Dam: Shantee Linda de Sangpur
Breeder and owner: Mrs. William Burr Hill, Hicksville, L. I., N. Y.

CH. ALICIA OF EDLIDGE
Sire: Ch. Sunset of Hohenburg   Dam: Gold Seal of Edlidge
Breeder and Owner: Mrs. Edward A. Anthony, Whitman, Mass.

AUDRAN'S MERRY-MIX-UP OF JO-NOR
Sire: Ch. Bucknam's Merrymaker
Dam: Ch. Brumbaugh's Teckelheim Tanya
Owner: Kathleen A. Beaty, Audran's Kennels, La Mesa, Calif.

CH. MAX ROSSMAN v. NOTFORT
Sire: Ch. White Gables Basil   Dam: Ramsay's Tanya
Owner: Jack and Luci Ward Nateford, North Hollywood, Calif.

puppies for the first four or five days of their lives, the better. However, the litter should be looked over carefully for possible defectives and discards, which should be destroyed as soon as possible. There is no virtue in rearing hare-lipped, crippled, or mismarked puppies. Drowning is as good a method of disposing of the unwanted young as any other.

It is usually unwise to destroy sound, healthy puppies just to reduce the number in the litter, since it is impossible to sort young puppies for excellence and one may be destroying the best member of the litter, a future champion. Unless a litter is extraordinarily numerous, the dam, if well fed, can probably suckle them all. If it is found that her milk is insufficient, the litter may be divided, and the surplus placed on a foster mother if it is possible to obtain one. The foster mother need not be of the same breed as the puppies, a mongrel being as good as any. She should be approximately the same size as the actual mother of the puppies, clean, healthy, and her other puppies should be of as nearly the same age as the ones she is to take over as possible. She should be removed from her own puppies (which may well be destroyed) and her breasts be permitted to fill with milk until she is somewhat uncomfortable, at which time her foster puppies can be put to her breasts and will usually be accepted without difficulty. Unless the services of the foster mother are really required, it is better not to use her.

The whelping bitch may be grateful for a warm meal even between the arrivals of her puppies. As soon as her chore is over, she should be offered food in her box. This should be of cereal and milk or of meat and broth, something sloppy. She will probably not leave her puppies to eat and her meals must be brought to her.

It is wise to give her a mild laxative for her bowels, also milk of magnesia. She will be reluctant to get out of her box even to relieve herself for about two days, but she should be urged, even forced, to do so regularly. A sensible bitch will soon settle down to care for her brood and will seldom give further trouble. She should be fed often and well, all that she can be induced to eat during her entire lactation.

Acid Milk

Occasionally a bitch is found that produces early milk (colostrum) so acid that it disagrees with, sometimes, kills, her puppies. The symptoms of the puppies are whining, disquiet, frequently refusal to nurse, frailty, and death. It is true that all milk is slightly acid, and it should be, turning blue litmus paper immersed in it a very light pink. However, milk harmfully on the acid side will readily turn litmus paper a vivid red. It seems that only the first two or three days milk is so affected.

This is not likely to occur with a bitch that throughout her pregnancy has received an adequate supply of calcium phosphate regularly in her daily ration. That is the best way to deal with the situation—to see to the bitch's correct nutrition in advance of her whelping.

If it is found too late that her milk is too acid, the puppies must be taken from her breasts and either given to a foster mother or artificially fed from bottle or by medicine dropper. Artificial feeding of very young puppies seldom is successful. Sometimes the dam's milk can be rectified by giving her large doses of bicarbonate of soda (baking soda), but the puppies should not be restored to her breasts until her milk ceases to turn litmus paper red.

The owner has only himself to blame for the bitch's too acid milk, since adequate calcium in advance would have neutralized the acid.

Rearing the Puppies

Puppies are born blind and open their eyes at approximately the ninth day thereafter. If they were whelped earlier than the full sixty-three days after the breeding from which they resulted, the difference should be added to the nine days of anticipated blindness. The early eye color of young puppies is no criterion of the color to which the eyes are likely to change, and the breeder's anxiety about his puppies' having light eyes is premature.

There is little to do about normal puppies except to let them alone and permit them to grow. The most important thing about their management is their nutrition, which is discussed in another chapter. The first two or three weeks, they will thrive and grow rapidly on their mother's milk, after which they should have additional food as described. The principal thing is to keep them well fed and to encourage them to grow rapidly. Puppies sleep much of the time, as do other babies, and they should not be frequently awakened to be played with. They grow more and more playful and sportive as they mature.

After the second week their nails begin to grow long and sharp. The mother will be grateful if the puppies' nails are blunted with scissors from time to time that in their pawing of the breast they do not lacerate it. Sharp nails tend to prompt the mother to wean the whelps early, and she should be encouraged to keep them with her as long as she will tolerate them. Even the small amount of milk they can drain from her after the weaning process is begun is the best food they can obtain. It supplements and makes digestible the remainder of their ration.

Many bitches, after their puppies are about four weeks of age, eat and regurgitate food, which is eaten by the puppies. This food is warmed and partly digested in the bitch's stomach. This practice, while it may appear disgusting to the novice keeper of dogs, is perfectly normal and should not be discouraged. However, it renders it all the more necessary that the food of the bitch be sound, clean and nutritious.

It is all but impossible to rear a litter of puppies without their becoming infested with round worms. Of course, the bitch should be wormed, if she harbors such parasites, before she is bred, and her teats should be thoroughly washed and disinfected just before she whelps to free them from the eggs of round worms. Every precaution must be taken to reduce the infestation of the puppies to a minimum; but, in spite of all it is possible to do, puppies will have round worms. These pests hamper growth, reduce the puppies' normal resistance to disease, and may kill them outright unless the worms are eliminated. The worming of puppies is discussed in the chapter entitled "Intestinal Parasites and Their Control."

67

The Dog's Teeth

The dog, like the human being, has two successive sets of teeth, the so-called milk teeth or baby teeth, which are shed and replaced later by the permanent teeth. The temporary teeth, which begin to emerge at two and a half to three weeks of the puppy's age, offer no difficulty. The full set of milk teeth (consisting usually of six incisors and two canines in each jaw, with four molars in the upper jaw and six molars in the lower jaw) is completed usually just before weaning time. Except for some obvious malformation, the milk teeth may be ignored and forgotten about.

At about the fourth month the baby teeth are shed and gradually replaced by the permanent teeth. This shedding and replacement process may consume some three or four months. This is about the most critical period of the dog's life—his adolescence. Some constitutionally vigorous dogs go through their teething easily, with no seeming awareness that the change is taking place. Others, less vigorous, may suffer from soreness of the gums, go off in flesh, and require to be pampered. Puppies at these ages should be particularly protected from exposure to infectious diseases and should be fed on nutritious foods, especially meat and milk.

The permanent teeth normally consist of 42—six incisors and two canines (fangs) in each jaw, with twelve molars in the upper jaw and fourteen in the lower jaw. Occasionally the front molars fail to emerge; this deficiency is considered by most judges to be only a minor fault, if the absence is noticed at all.

Dentition is a heritable factor in the dog, and some dog's have soft, brittle and defective permanent teeth, no matter how excellent the diet and the care given them. The teeth of those dogs which are predisposed to have excellent sound ones, however, can be ruined by an inferior diet prior to and during the period of their eruption. At this time, for the teeth to develop properly, a dog must have an adequate supply of calcium, phosphate and vitamin D, besides all the protein he can consume.

Often the permanent teeth emerge before the shedding of the milk teeth, in which case the dog may have parts of both sets at the same time. The milk teeth will eventually drop out, but as long as they remain they may deflect or displace the permanent analogues in the process of their growth. The incisors are the teeth in which a malformation may result from the late dropping of the baby teeth. When it is realized just how important a correct "bite" may be deemed in the show ring, the hazards of permitting the baby teeth to deflect the permanent set will be understood.

The baby teeth in such a case must be dislodged and removed. The roots of the baby teeth are reabsorbed in the gums, and the teeth can usually be extracted by firm pressure of thumb and finger, although it may be necessary to employ forceps or to take the puppy to the veterinarian.

The permanent teeth of the puppy are usually somewhat overshot, by which is meant that the upper incisors protrude over and do not play upon the lower incisors. Maturity may be trusted to remedy this apparent defect unless it is too pronounced.

An undershot mouth in a puppy, on the other hand, tends to grow worse as the dog matures. Whether or not it has been caused by the displacement of the permanent teeth by the persistence of the milk teeth, it can sometimes be remedied (or at least bettered) by frequent hard pressure of the thumb on the lower jaw, forcing the lower teeth backward to meet the upper ones. Braces on dog teeth have seldom proved efficacious, but pressure and massage are worth trying on the bad mouth of an otherwise excellent puppy.

High and persistent fevers, especially from the fourth to the ninth month, sometimes result in those discolored, pitted and defective teeth, commonly called "distemper teeth." They often result from maladies other than distemper. There is little that can be done for them. They are unpleasant to see and are subjected to penalty in the show ring, but are serviceable to the dog. Distemper teeth are not in themselves heritable, but the predisposition for their development appears to be. At least the offspring from distemper toothed ancestors seem to be especially prone to fevers at the teething age which impairs their dentition.

Older dogs, especially those fed largely upon carbohydrates, tend to accumulate more or less tartar upon their teeth. The tartar generally starts at the gum line on the molars and extends gradually to the cusp. It usually causes no unpleasantness to the dog or injury to his health, but fastidious owners will not tolerate it. The remedy is scaling, which may be done at home, but is best accomplished by the veterinary dentist.

The cleanliness of a dog's mouth may be brought about and the formation of tartar discouraged by the scouring of the teeth with a moist cloth dipped in a mixture of equal parts of table salt and baking soda. The dentine of the dog's tooth is not covered with enamel, and the dog is little given to caries.

A hard biscuit is often recommended as a means of cleansing the teeth, but it is a sales argument of the biscuit makers, and the biscuit fails to scour the tartar from the teeth. In fact, the increase of carbohydrate in the diet may further the growth of tartar instead of removing it. A large raw bone for the dog to gnaw on may tend to erode the tartar, and is at least useful in the cutting of the second teeth.

A dog's age after his maturity can not be estimated with any degree of certainty from the examination of his teeth. The incisors of some dogs may be worn down almost to the gums by three years of age, whereas others may retain a full set of unworn ivory teeth until an advanced age. This seems not to depend upon the dog's nutrition after his teeth are fully formed. The age of a puppy may be guessed approximately from the stage of the eruption of his teeth, but the teeth of some dogs emerge earlier than others and there is no assurance in such an estimate.

Care of the Nails

The nails of the dog should be kept shortened and blunted right down to the quick—never into the quick. If this is not done, the toes may spread and the foot may splay into a veritable pancake. Some dogs have naturally flat feet, which they have inherited. No pretense is made that the shortening of the nails of such a foot will obviate the fault entirely and make the foot beautiful or serviceable. It

70

will only improve the appearance and make the best of an obvious fault. Short nails do, however, emphasize the excellence of a good foot.

Some dogs keep their nails short by digging and friction. Their nails require little attention, but it is a rare dog the foot of which can not be bettered by the artificial shortening of its nails.

Nail clippers are available, made especially for the purpose. After using them, the sides of the nail should be filed away as much as is possible without touching the quick. Carefully done, it causes the dog no discomfort; but, once the quick of a dog's nail has been injured, he may forever afterward resent and fight having his feet treated or even having them examined.

The obvious horn of the nail can be removed, after which the quick will recede to permit the removal of more horn the following week. This process may be kept up until the nail is short and blunt as it can be made, after which nails will need attention only at six weeks or two months intervals.

Some persons clip the nails right back to the toes in one fell swoop, disregarding injury to the quick and pain of the dog. The nails bleed and the dog limps for a day or two, but infection seldom develops. Such a procedure should not be undertaken without a general anesthetic. If an anesthetic is used, this forthright method does not prejudice the dog against having his feet handled.

The nails of some dogs grow more rapdily than those of others and require more frequent attention. As a rule, the dogs with the best feet develop large, slow growing, naturally blunt nails, which need only a minimum of trimming. Thin, flat, splayed feet can be much improved by eliminating the horn of the nails.

The Spaying of Bitches

First, let us say, that the spaying (castration) of bitches is not recommended. However, it is frequently done.

Before having such an operation performed, the owner must realize that the spayed bitch can never be bred and is disqualified for exhibition. The pedigree had as well be burned, for it is useless. The only purpose spaying serves is to prevent this bitch from coming into heat. It is best done, if ever, on a bitch before her full maturity.

The whole nature of the bitch is liable to change after her spaying. She may lose her pep, grow fat, lazy and dependent. These conditions may, however, be prevented or rectified by hypodermic injections of the female hormones from time to time, as they may be required.

The operation, in the hands of an expert veterinarian, is not difficult and seldom dangerous. It should be undertaken only with the full realization that the bitch's reproductive functions will be forever destroyed, and with a full knowledge of the effects of the operation upon her character and appearance.

The Castration of Dogs

Castrated dogs are monstrosities, even worse than spayed bitches. The horrible practice of castration is mentioned here only to declare that it should never be done, except as it may be to remove testes irreparably injured in an accident or fight or to remove a malignant growth. Emasculation alters a dog's entire internal economy, causes him to grow fat, lethargic, lazy and misshapen. It serves no possible purpose.

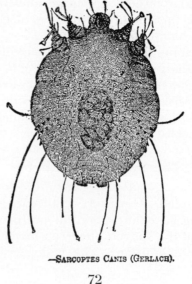

—Sarcoptes Canis (Gerlach).

72

External Vermin and Parasites

THE bugs that attach themselves to the hair and hides of dogs and feed upon or otherwise irritate their hosts are numerous. Here, only four kinds will be considered, the most frequently found and the hardest to get rid of—fleas, lice, ticks and flies. Since DDT has been made freely available to the public, these vermin are a lesser problem. While discussion still continues about the harmful effects of the application directly to the skin. such a process will not be recommended. That harm appears to be minimal, if it exists at all, but it is not urged upon the reader. The vermin can rather easily be removed from the bodies of the dogs themselves by other methods. The purpose of the DDT is to clean up the surroundings and to prevent reinfestations of the dog. By keeping the premises thoroughly sprayed at freqeunt intervals with the magic DDT, insects are repelled or killed before they attack the dog. The duration of the effective action of DDT varies with the thoroughness with which it is used, the temperature and the humidity. A reasonably thorough application in a spray gun of a 10% solution of DDT should control insect pests for from two to six weeks, after which it should be repeated.

Fleas

Neglected dogs are too often beset by hundred of blood-thirsty fleas, which do not always confine their attacks to the dogs but also sometimes feast upon their masters. Unchecked, they overrun kennels, homes and playgrounds. Moreover, they are the intermediate hosts for the development of the kind of tapeworm most frequently found in dogs, as will be more fully discussed under the subject of *Intestinal Parasites*. Fleas are all around bad actors and nuisances. Although it need hardly concern us in America, where the disease is not known to exist, fleas are the recognized and only vectors of bubonic plague.

There are numerous kinds and varieties of fleas, of which we shall discuss here only the three species often found on dogs. These are the human flea (*Pulex irritans*), the dog flea (*Ctenocephalides canis*), and the so-called chicken flea or sticktight flea (*Echidnophaga gallinacea*).

Of these the human flea prefers the blood of man to that of the dog, and unless humans are also bothered they are not likely to be found on the dog. They are small, nearly black animals, and occur mostly in the Mississippi Valley and in California. Their control is the same as for the dog flea.

The dog flea is much larger than his human counterpart and is dark brown in color. It seldom bites mankind. On an infested dog these dog fleas may be found buried in the coat of any part of his anatomy, but their choicest habitat is the area of the back just forward from the tail and over the loins. On a badly neglected dog, especially in summer, fleas by the hundred will be found on that part of the dog intermixed with their dung and with dried blood. They may cause the dog some discomfort or none. It must not be credited that because a dog is not kept in a constant or frequent agitation of scratching that he harbors no fleas. The coats of pet animals are soiled and roughened by the fleas and torn by the scratching that they sometimes induce. Fleas also appear to be connected in some way with summer eczema of dogs; at least the diseased condition of the skin often clears up after fleas are eliminated.

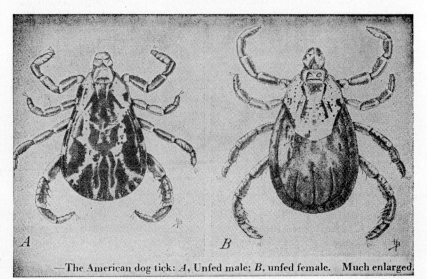

—The American dog tick: *A*, Unfed male; *B*, unfed female. Much enlarged.

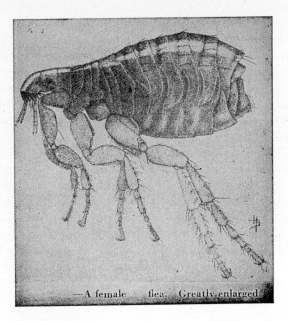

—A female flea. Greatly enlarged.

Fleas do not reproduce themselves on the dog. Rather, their breeding haunts are the debris, dust and sand of the kennel floor, and especially the accumulations of dropped hair, sand and loose soil of unclean sleeping boxes. Nooks and cracks and crannies of the kennel may harbor the eggs or maggot-like larvae of immature fleas. The adults seldom remain long away from the dog's body.

This debris and accumulation must be eliminated—incineration of it is best—after which all possible breeding areas should be thoroughly sprayed with a DDT solution. The adult dog that harbors fleas may be merely bathed, the fleas combed from him and washed down the drain or killed with kerosene, DDT, gasoline, or otherwise. A more thorough and perhaps more lasting method is, after the dog is bathed and dried, to dust and work into his coat derris powder, or by washing or soaking the dog in a solution containing one ounce of soap (or detergent) and two ounces of derris powder to the gallon of water, permitting the solution to remain in the coat without rinsing. Care should be used not to permit derris solution to get into the dog's eyes.

The treatment for young puppies (and for adult dogs) is to work into their coats fresh, finely ground pyrethrum powder, which is harmless even to the youngest puppy. Pyrethrum only suffocates the fleas, however, and causes them to drop off the dog, apparently but not actually dead. They may be caught upon a newspaper or sheet as they fall, after which they should be flushed down the drain or otherwise destroyed.

Sticktight fleas are minute, but are to found, if at all, in patches on the dog's head and especially on the ears. They remain quiescent and do not jump, as the dog fleas and human fleas do. Their tiny heads are buried in the dog's flesh. To force them loose from the area decapitates them and the head remains in the skin which is prone to fester from the irritation. They may be dislodged by placing a cotton pad or thick cloth well soaked in ether, or alcohol over the flea patch, which causes them immediately to relinquish their hold, after which they can be easily combed loose and destroyed.

76

These sticktights abound in neglected, dirty and abandoned chicken houses, which, if the dogs have access to them should be cleaned out thoroughly and sprayed with DDT.

Fleas, while a nuisance, are only a minor problem. They should be eliminated not only from the dog but from all the premises he inhabits. Dogs frequently are reinfested with fleas from other dogs with which they play or come in contact. Every dog should be occasionally inspected for the presence of fleas, and, if any are found, immediate means should be taken to rid him of them.

Lice

There are even more kinds of lice than of fleas, although as they pertain to dogs there is no reason to differentiate them. They do not infest dogs, except in the events of gross neglect or of unforeseen accident. Lice reproduce themselves on the body of the dog. To rid him of the adult lice is easy. A bath with derris will suffice like that for fleas. However, the eggs and "nits" are harder to remove.

It is insufficiently known that a rinse with vinegar, which is permitted to dry on the coat, will dissolve the outer covering of the nits and leave them ineffective. Subsequently, they may be bathed away or will disappear of themselves.

Rare as the occurrence of lice upon dogs may be, they must be promptly treated and got rid of.. To know that one's dogs are infested with lice is more embarrassing even than with fleas. Lice also serve as intermediate hosts for canine tapeworms; but, because they are less numerous than fleas, are less likely to be the source of tapeworms in the dog.

The dog's quarters are to be thoroughly sprayed with DDT after a siege of lice, just as after a siege of fleas. However, because lice breed directly upon the dog and seldom detach themselves from him the kennel premises are less liable to infestation.

Ticks

The term "wood ticks" and "dog ticks," as usually employed, refer to at least eight different species, whose appearances and habits are so similar that none but entomologists are likely to know them apart. It is useless to

77

attempt to differentiate between these various species here, except to warn the reader that the Rocky Mountain spotted fever tick (*Dermacentor andersoni*) is a vector of the human disease for which it is named, as well as of rabbit fever (tularemia), and care must be employed in removing it from dogs lest the hands be infected. Some one or more of these numerous species are to be found in well nigh every state in the Union, although there exist wide areas where wood ticks are seldom seen and are not a menace to dogs.

All the ticks must feed on blood in order to reproduce themselves. The eggs are always deposited on the ground or elsewhere after the female, engorged with blood, has dropped from the dog or other animal upon which she has fed. The eggs are laid in masses in protected places on the ground, particularly in thick clumps of grass. Each female lays only one such mass, which contains 2500 to 5000 eggs. The development of the American dog tick embraces four stages: the egg, the larva or seed tick, the nymph, and the adult. The two intermediate stages in the growth of the tick are spent on rodents, and only in the adult stage does it attach itself to the dog. Both sexes affix themselves to dogs and to other animals and feed on their blood; the males do not increase in size, although the female is tremendously enlarged as she gorges. Mating occurs while the female is feeding. After some five to thirteen days, she drops from her host, lays her eggs and dies. At no time do ticks feed on anything except the blood of animals.

The longevity and hardihood of the tick are amazing. The larvae and nymphs may live for a full year without feeding, and the adults survive for more than two years if they fail to encounter a host to which they may attach. In the Northern United States the adults are most active in the spring and summer, few being found after July; but in the warmer Southern States they may be active the year around.

Although most of the tick species require a vegetative cover and wild animal hosts to complete their development, at least one species, the brown tick (*Rhipicephalus sangui-*

.—Fully engorged female. American
dog tick. Much enlarged.

—Engorged female depositing eggs. Much enlarged.

nius), is adapted to life in the dryer environment of kennels, sheds and houses, with the dog as its only necessary host. This tick is the vector of canine piroplasmosis, although this disease is at this time almost negligible in the United States.

This brown dog tick often infests houses in large numbers, both immature and adult ticks lurking around baseboards, window casings, furniture, the folds of curtains, and elsewhere. Thus, even dogs kept in houses are sometimes infested with hundreds of larvae, nymphs, and adults of this tick. Because of its ability to live in heated buildings, the species has become established in many northern areas. Unlike the other tick species, the adult of the brown dog tick does not bite human beings. However, also unlike the other ticks, it is necessary not only to rid the dogs of this particular tick but also to eliminate the pests from their habitat, especially the dogs' beds and sleeping boxes. A spray with a 10% solution of DDT suffices for this purpose. Fumigation of premises seldom suffices, since not only are brown dog ticks very resistant to mere fumigation, but the ticks are prone to lurk around entry ways, porches and out buildings, where they can not be reached with a fumigant. The spraying with DDT may not penetrate to spots where some ticks are in hiding, and it must be repeated at intervals until all the pests are believed to be completely eradicated.

Dogs should not be permitted to run in bushy areas known to be infested with ticks, and upon their return from exercise in a place believed to harbor ticks, dogs should be carefully inspected for their presence.

If a dog's infestation is light, the ticks may be picked individuallly from his skin. If the infestation is heavy, it is easier and quicker to saturate his coat with a derris solution, such as that described for the treatment of fleas (one ounce of soap and two ounces of derris powder dissolved in one gallon of water). The derris should be of an excellent grade containing at least 3% of rotenone, the active insecticide principle. The mixture may be used and reused, since it retains its strength for about three weeks if it is kept in a dark place.

CH. RIVENROCK MANHATTAN "Hattie"
Sire: Ch. Eric Again v.d. Daniels   Dam: Rivenrock Leda
Owner: Donia Bussey Cline, Crespi Street Kennels, Los Angeles, Calif.

CH. RIVENROCK TEAK
Sire: Dreadnaught v. Dachshafen   Dam: Rivenrock Russet
Owner: Nancy Ann Bussey Oberg, Crespi Street Kennels,
Los Angeles, California

CH. FAR STAR'S SIRIUS
Sire: Ch. Leutnant v. Marienlust   Dam: Furstin v. Zauberberg
Owner: Sigmaringen Kennels, G. A. Plummer, Dallas, Texas

CH. STANDARD OF HEYING-TECKEL
Sire: Am. and Can. Ch. Favorite v. Marienlust
Dam: White Gables Brenda
Owner: C. A. Dusse, New Orleans, Louisiana

BLACK STAR OF LAMBROS

Sire: Ch. Bronze v. d. Daniels   Dam: Ch. Miss Ruby Daniels of Pal-Mar

Owner: Raymond S. Hill, Phoenix, Arizona

CRESPI CAPTAIN CARLSEN

Sire: Ch. Chadwick of Crespi Street   Dam: Ch. Rivenrock Teak

Owner: Donia Cline, Los Angeles, California

Puppies owned by Dale Daniels, Gilroy, California
Sired by Ch. Arri v.d. Daniels

DACHSCROFT'S MOONPLAY
Sire: Ch. Dachscroft's Playboy
Dam: Bucknam's Moonglow

DACHSCROFT'S TUFFET
Ten weeks old
Sire: Dachscroft's Moonplay
Dam: Little Gates Honeybun

Breeder and Owner: Dachscroft Kennels,
Mrs. David B. Doggett, Lake Geneva, Wisconsin

If possible, the dip should be permitted to dry on the dog's coat. It should not get into a dog's eyes. The dip will not only kill the ticks that are attached to the dog, but the powder drying in the hair will repel further infestation for two or three days and kill most if not all the boarders. These materials act slowly, requiring sometimes as much as twenty-four hours to complete the kill.

If the weather is cold or the use of the dip should be otherwise inconvenient, derris powder may be applied as a dust, care being taken that it penetrates the hair and reaches the skin. Breathing or swallowing derris may cause a dog to vomit, but he will not be harmed by it, although the dust as well as the liquid should be kept from his eyes.

Since the dog is the principal host on which the adult tick feeds and since each female lays several thousand eggs after feeding, treating the dog regularly will not only bring him immediate relief but will limit the reproduction of the ticks. Keeping underbrush, weeds and grass closely cut tends to remove protection favorable to the ticks. Burning vegetation accomplishes the same results.

Many of the ticks in an infested area may be killed by the thorough application of a spray made as follows: Four tablespoonfuls of nicotine sulphate (40% nicotine) in three gallons of water. More permanent results may be obtained by adding to this solution four ounces of sodium fluride, but this will cause some injury to the vegetation. Ticks often concentrate on the sides of roads and paths, and such places may be most in need of treatment.

Besides the ticks that attach themselves to all parts of 'he dog, there is another species that infests the ear specifically and that is known as the spinose ear tick. This pest penetrates deep into the convolutions of the ear and often causes irritation and pain, as evidenced by the dog's scratching its ears, shaking its head or holding it on one side.

One part derris powder (5% rotenone) mixed with ten parts of medicinal mineral oil (liquid parafine) and dropped into the ear will kill the spinose ear ticks. Only a few drops of the material is required, but it is best to massage the base of the ear to make sure that the remedy penetrates to the deepest part of the ear to reach all the ticks.

Flies

Flies can play havoc with dogs in outdoors kennels, stinging them and biting the ears until they are raw. Until recently the only protection against them was the screening of the entire kennel. The breeding places of flies, which are damp filth and stagnant garbage, are in most areas now happily abated, but the chief agent for control of the pest is DDT.

A spray of a 10% solution of DDT over all surfaces of the kennel property may be trusted to destroy all the flies that light on those surfaces for from two weeks to one month. It must, of course, be repeated from time to time when it is seen that the efficacy of the former treatment begins to diminish. It is the same as for the other insect pests, all of which may be brought under control with a single thorough spraying.

Intestinal Parasites and Their Control

The varieties of worms that may inhabit the alimentary tract of the dog are numerous. Much misapprehension exists, even among experienced dog keepers, about the harm these parasites may cause and about the methods of getting rid of them. Some dog keepers live in terror of these worms and continually treat their dogs for them whether they are known to be present or not; and others ignore the presence of worms and do nothing about them. Neither policy is justified.

Too many dog owners are so parasite conscious that they feel that their dogs should be dosed or wormed at regular intervals regardless of whether such treatment is necessary. Promiscuous dosing, without the certainty that the dog harbors worms or what kind he may have, is a practice fraught with danger for the well-being of the animal. All drugs for the expulsion or destruction of parasites are poisonous or irritant to a certain degree and should be administered only when it is known that the dog is infested by parasites and what kind. It is hardly necessary to say that when a dog is known to harbor worms he should be cleared of them, but in most instances there is no such urgency as is sometimes manifested.

Many of the symptoms associated with parasitic infections also occur in connection with other diseases, and worms are often accused of conditions they do not in fact produce. On the other hand, an adult dog may harbor some kinds of worms for many months and exhibit no recognizable symptoms of them at all. Many dogs go through their entire lives without being wormed and with no apparent harm from the neglect.

It may be assumed that puppies at weaning time are more or less infested with intestinal round worms or ascarids (*Toxocara canis*), and that such puppies need to be treated for worms. It is all but impossible to rear a litter of puppies to weaning age free from those parasites. Once the puppies are purged of them, it is amazing to see the spurt of their growth and the renewal of their thriftiness. Many neglected puppies surmount the handicap of their worms and at least some of them survive. This, however, is no reason why good puppies—puppies that are worth saving—should go unwormed and neglected.

Aside from weanling puppies, dogs should not be treated for worms without the assurance that they have them and a knowledge of the variety of parasite that is being dealt with. There can be no doubt that worms are responsible for some morbid symptoms in some adult dogs, but many of the dull coats and dull eyes and much of the unthriftiness and langor that are charged to worms are caused by other diseases or by malnutrition.

The ways to find out that a dog actually has worms are to see some of the worms themselves in the dog's droppings or to submit a sample of his feces to a veterinarian or to a biological laboratory for microscopic examination. From a report of such an examination, it is possible to know whether or not a dog is a host to intestinal parasites at all and intelligently to undertake the treatment and control of the specific kind he may harbor.

All of the vermifuges, vermicides, and anthelmentic remedies tend to expel all other worms besides the kind for which they are specifically intended, but it is better to employ the remedy particularly effective against the individual kind of parasite the dog is known to have, and to refrain from worm treatments unless or until it is known to be needed.

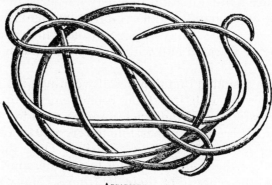

'.—ASCARIDES

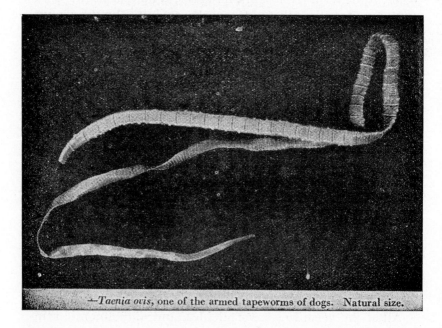

—Taenia ovis, one of the armed tapeworms of dogs. Natural size.

Intestinal Worms
Roundworms

HE ascarids, or large intestinal roundworms, are the largest of the worm parasites occurring in the digestive tract of the dog, varying in length from 1 to 8 inches, the females being larger than the males. The name "spool worms," which is something applied to them, is derived from their tendency to coil in a springlike spiral when they are expelled, either from the bowel or vomited, by their hosts. There are at least two species of them which frequently parasitize dogs, *Toxocara canis* and *Toxascaris leonina*, but they are so much alike except for some minor details in the life histories of their development that it is not practically necessary for the dog keeper to seek to distinguish between them.

It is the first named species, *Toxocara canis*, that is almost unavoidably found in young puppies and untreated young dogs, whereas *Toxascaris leonina* usually confines its infestation to older animals. Neither requires an intermediate host for its development. Numerous eggs are deposited in the intestinal tract of the host animal; these eggs are passed out by the dog in his feces and are swallowed by the same or another animal, and hatching takes place in its small

85

intestine. Their development requires from twelve to sixteen days under favorable circumstances.

It has been shown to be possible that puppies before their birth may be infested by roundworms from their mother. This accounts for the occasional finding of mature or nearly mature worms in very young puppies. It can not occur if the mother is entirely free from worms, as she should be.

These roundworms are particularly injurious to young puppies. The commonest symptoms of roundworm infection are general unthriftiness, digestive disturbances, and bloat after feeding. The hair grows dead and lusterless, and the breath may have a peculiar sweetish odor. Large numbers of roundworms may obstruct the intestine, and may have been known to penetrate the intestinal wall. In heavy infestations the worms may wander into the bile ducts, stomach, and even into the lungs and upper respiratory passages where they may cause pneumonia, especially in very young animals.

They are sometimes (but not always) the cause of "running fits" in older puppies and mature dogs, but they are less likely to cause serious harm to grown dogs than to puppies.

The control of intestinal roundworms depends primarily upon prompt disposal of feces, keeping the animals in clean quarters and on clean ground, and using only clean utensils for feed and water. Dampness of the ground favors the survival of worm eggs and larvae. There is no known chemical treatment feasible for the destruction of eggs in contaminated soil, but prolonged exposure to sunlight and drying has proved effective.

Numerous remedies have been in successful use for roundworms, including turpentine, which has a recognized deleterious effect upon the kidneys; santonin, an old standby; freshly powdered betel nut and its derivative, arecoline, both of which tend to purge and sicken the patient; oil of chenopodium, made from American wormseed; carbon tetrachloride, widely used as a cleaning agent; tetrachlorethylene, closely related chemically to the former, but less toxic; and numerous other medicaments. While all of them are effective as vermifuges or vermicides, if rightly employed, to each of them some valid objection can be interposed.

The best and most harmless remedy for roundworms so far discovered appears to be normal butyl chloride. The effective dosage for roundworms of normal butyl chloride is as follows:

Amount of the Drug	*Weight of Dog*
0.5 cc. (8 drops)	less than 3 pounds
1.0 cc. (15 drops)	3 to 5 pounds
2.0 cc. (½ fluid dram)	5 to 10 pounds
3.0 cc. (¾ fluid dram)	10 to 20 pounds
4.0 cc. (1 fluid dram)	20 to 40 pounds
5.0 cc. (1¼ fluid drams)_____	more than 40 pounds

This remedy is best administered in the early morning after a night spent without food or water. A purgative dose of castor oil one hour after the normal butyl chloride will hasten the action of the drug and should cleanse the intestine of roundworms. If it is doubted that the entire infestation has been dispelled, it is well to wait a week or ten days until the dog has recovered from the effects of his purge and to repeat the dose. No further treatment need be given.

The formulas of many proprietary vermifuges for dogs have been changed to include normal butyl chloride, and most such vermifuges are trustworthy if used according to directions printed on the package. These proprietary preparations are more expensive and no better than normal butyl chloride. In the directions printed on the package, the need to administer the remedy on an empty intestinal tract and to follow it with a purge are omitted. The remedy will be found more effective if these additional precautions are taken.

Hookworms

Hookworms are the most destructive of all the parasites of dogs. There are three species of them—*Ancylostoma caninum, A. braziliense,* and *Uncinaria stenocephalia*—all to be found in dogs in some parts of the United States. The first named is the most widespread; the second found only in the warmer parts of the South and Southwest; the last named, in the North and in Canada. All are similar one to another and to the hookworm that infests mankind (*Ancylostoma uncinariasis.* For purposes of their eradication, no distinction need be made between them.

It is possible to keep dogs for many years in a dry and well drained area without an infestation with hookworm, which are contracted only on infested soils. However, unthrifty dogs shipped from infested areas are suspect until it is proved that hookworm is not the cause of their unthriftiness.

Hookworm males seldom are longer than half an inch, the females somewhat larger. The head end is curved upward, and is equipped with cutting implements, which may be called teeth, by which they attach themselves to the lining of the dog's intestine and suck his blood.

The females produce numerous eggs which pass out in the dog's feces. In two weeks or a little more these eggs hatch, the worms pass through various larval stages, and reach their infective stage. Infection of the dog may take place through his swallowing the organism, or by its penetration of his skin through some lesion. In the latter case the worms enter the circulation, reach the lungs, are coughed up, swallowed, and reach the intestine where their final development occurs. Eggs appear in the dog's feces from three to six weeks after infestation.

Puppies are sometimes born with hookworms already well developed in their intestines, the infection taking place before their birth. Eggs of the hookworm are sometimes found in the feces of puppies only thirteen days old. Assumption is not to be made that all puppies are born with hookworms or even that they are likely to become infested, but in hookworm areas the possibility of either justifies precautions that neither shall happen.

Hookworm infestation in puppies and young dogs brings about a condition often called kennel anemia. There may be digestive disturbances and blood streaked diarrhea. In severe cases the feces may be almost pure blood. Infected puppies fail to grow, often lose weight, and the eyes are sunken and dull. The loss of blood results in an anemia with pale mucus membranes of the mouth and eyes. This anemia is caused by the consumption of the dog's blood by the worms and the bleeding that follows the bites. The worms are not believed to secrete a poison or to cause damage to the dog except loss of blood.

There is an admitted risk in worming young puppies before weaning time, but it is a risk that must be run if the puppies are known to harbor hookworms. The worms, if permitted to persist, will ruin the puppies and likely kill them. No such immediacy is needful for the treatment of older puppies and adult dogs, although hookworm infestation will grow steadily worse until it is curbed. It should not be delayed and neglected in the belief or hope that the dog can cure himself.

As in the treatment for roundworms, normal butyl chloride appears to be the best and most nearly harmless remedy so far discovered for hookworm. The dosage is the same as for roundworms. It should be given on an empty stomach, but for hookworm need not be followed by a purge.

Brine made by stirring common salt (sodium chloride) into boiling water, a pound and a half of salt to the gallon of water, will destroy hookworm infestation in the soil. A gallon of brine should be sufficient to treat eight square feet of soil surface. One treatment of the soil is sufficient unless it is reinfested.

Tapeworms

The numerous species of tapeworm which infect the dog may, for practical purposes, be divided into two general groups, the armed forms and the unarmed forms. Species of both groups resemble each other in their possession of a head and neck and a chain of segments. They are, however, different in their life histories and in the best manner to deal with them. This is unfortunately not well understood, since to most persons a tapeworm is a tapeworm.

The armed varieties are again divided into the single pored forms of the genera *Taenia, Multiceps,* and *Echinococcus,* and the doubled pored tapeworm, of which the most widespread and prevalent among dogs in the United States is the so-called dog tapeworm, *Dipylidium caninum.* This

89

is the variety with segments shaped like cucumber-seeds. The adult rarely exceeds a foot in length, and the head is armed with four or five tiny hooks. This is the only tapeworm of which it is necessary to take particular cognizance for the person with well cared for and protected dogs.

The dog tapeworm requires but a single intermediate host for its development, which in most cases is the dog flea or the biting louse. Thus, by keeping dogs free from fleas and lice the major danger of tapeworm infestation is obviated.

The egg of the tapeworm is expelled by the dog in his feces and is swallowed by the flea or louse. The louse or flea is in turn swallowed by the same or another dog and the tapeworm develops in its intestine. This life cycle of the tapeworm is interesting as a matter of natural history, but for the practical purpose of keeping the dog free of tapeworms that is all we need to know about it.

The egg of the tapeworm cannot be found by a microscopic examination of the feces. It is secreted in the segment which breaks off and passes with the stool.

It is well to be suspicious of a finicky eater—a dog that refuses all but the choicest meat and shows very little appetite.

The injury produced by this armed tapeworm to the dog that harbors it is not well understood. Frequently it produces no symptoms at all, and it is likely that it is not the actual cause of many of the symptoms attributed to it. At least, it is known that a dog may have one or many of these worms over a long period of time and apparently be no worse for their presence. Nervous symptoms or skin eruptions, or both, are often charged to the presence of tapeworm, which may or may not be the cause of the morbid condition.

Tapeworm-infected dogs sometimes involuntarily pass segments of worms and so soil floors, rugs, furniture or bedding. The passage by dogs of a segment or a chain of segments via the anus is a frequent cause of the dog's itching, which he seeks to allay by sitting and dragging himself on the floor by his haunches. The segments or chains are sometimes mistakenly called pinworms, but pinworms are a kind of round worm to which dogs are not subject.

It is believed by many experienced persons that tapeworm in the dog may result in loss of weight, unthriftiness, staring coat, skin lesions, and other ills. On the other hand, dogs have harbored tapeworm for years on end without recognized ill effects. Despite that they may do him no harm, few dog owners care to tolerate tapeworm in their dogs. These worms, it has been definitely established, are not transmissible from dog to dog or to man. Without the flea or the louse, it is impossible for the adult dog tapeworm to reproduce itself, and by keeping dogs free from fleas and lice it is possible to keep them also free from dog tapeworm.

The various unarmed species of tapeworm find their intermediate hosts in the flesh and other parts of various animals, fish, crustacians and crayfish. Dogs not permitted to eat raw the officially uninspected meats never have these worms, and it is needless here to discuss them at length. Hares and rabbits are the intermediate hosts of some of these worms and dogs should not be encouraged to feed upon those animals.

Little is known of the effects upon dogs of infestations of the unarmed tapeworms, but they are believed to be similar to the effects (if any) of the armed species.

The prevention of tapeworm infection may be epitomized by saying: Do not permit dogs to swallow fleas or lice nor to feed upon uninspected raw meats. It is difficult to protect dogs permitted to run at large from such contacts, but it is to be presumed that persons interested enough in caring for dogs to read this book will keep their dogs at home and protect them.

The several species of tapeworm occurring in dogs are not all removable by the same treatment. The most effective treatment for the removal of the armed species, which is the one most frequently found in the dogs, is arecoline hydrobromide. This drug is a drastic purgative and acts from fifteen to forty-five minutes after its administration. The treatment should be given in the morning after the dog has fasted overnight, and food should be withheld for some three hours after dosing.

Arecoline is not so effective against the double-pored tapeworm as against the other armed species, and it may be necessary to repeat the dose after a few days waiting, since some of the tapeworm heads may not be removed by the first treatment and regeneration of the tapeworm may occur in a few weeks. The estimatedly correct dosage is not stated here, since the drug is so toxic that the dosage should be estimated for the individual dog by a competent veterinarian, and it is better that he should be permitted to administer the remedy and control the treatment. While the control of roundworms and hookworms with normal butyl chloride may be well undertaken at home, for the control of tapeworm professional aid is indicated.

For the unarmed species of tapeworm, the same statement holds true. For them, the remedy is oleoresin of male fern, which is also a toxic agent and not safely employed by the amateur. It should be given after a fast of eighteen hours and should be followed by a non-oily purgative. While either of these remedies is comparatively safe to employ at home, the dosage should be prescribed by the veterinary who takes into consideration the size, weight, age, and condition of the patient.

Whipworms

The dog whipworm (*Trichuris vulpis*) is so called from its fancied resemblance to a tiny whip, the front part being slender and hairlike and the hinder part relatively thick. It rarely exceeds three inches in its total length. Whipworms in dogs exist more or less generally throughout the world, but few dogs in the United States are known to harbor them. They are for the most part confined to the cecum, from which they are hard to dislodge, but sometimes spill over into the colon, whence they are easy to dislodge.

The complete life history of the whipworm is not well established, but it is known that no intermediate host is required for its development. The eggs appear to develop in much the same way as the eggs of the large roundworm, but slower, requiring from two weeks to several months for the organisms to reach maturity.

It has not as yet been definitely established that whipworms are the true causes of all the ills of which they are accused. In many instances they appear to cause little damage, even in heavy infestations. A great variety of symptoms of an indefinite sort have been ascribed to whipworms, including digestive disturbances, diarrhea, loss of weight, nervousness, convulsions, and general unthriftiness, but it remains to be proved that whipworms were responsible.

The incidence of whipworm infestation is comparatively rare. Many old-established kennels have never been known to have them at all.

To be effective in its removal of whipworms, a drug must enter the cecum and come into direct contact with them; but the entry of the drug into this organ is somewhat fortuitous, and to increase the chances of its happening, large doses of a drug essentially harmless to the dog must be used. Normal butyl chloride meets this requirement, but it must be given in doses about four times as large as is indicated for roundworms. Even then, complete clearance of whipworms from the cecum can not be expected; the best to be hoped is that their numbers will be reduced and the morbid symptoms for which the treatment is given will subside.

Before treatment the dog should be fasted for some eighteen hours, although he may be fed in two hours after being treated. It is wise to follow the normal butyl chloride in one hour with a purgative dose of castor oil. This treatment, since it is not expected to be wholly effective, may be repeated at monthly intervals until it is believed that the dog is free from whipworms.

The only known means of the complete clearance of whipworms from the dog is the surgical removal of the cecum, which of course should be undertaken only by a veterinary surgeon and only after it is found to be imperative. The marked improvement in the health of some dogs after such operations tends to support the belief that whipworms, at least in some cases, may be definitely harmful to the dog.

Hydrogen peroxide, 1.5 percent solution, as an enema has been found useful in the removal of all species of worm parasites from the intestinal tract of dogs—roundworms, tapeworms, hookworms, and whipworms. The dosage is approximately an ounce and a half for dogs of two pounds, to twenty-four ounces for dogs of sixty pounds. This treatment demands that the dog shall be induced to vomit; to facilitate the reaction a few ounces of the solution are administered by stomach tube just before the enema is given. Caution is recommended in the use of this treatment in dogs suffering from diseases of the heart or other vital organs.

Heart Worms

Heart worms (*Dirofilaria immitis*) in dogs are rare. They occur largely in the South and Southeast, but their incidence appears to be increasing and cases have been reported along the Atlantic Seaboard as far north as New York. The various species of mosquitoes are known to be its vectors, although the flea is also accused of spreading it.

The symptoms of heart worm are somewhat vague, and include coughing, shortness of breath and collapse. In advanced cases, dropsy may develop. Nervous symptoms, fixity of vision, fear of light, and convulsions may develop. However, all such symptoms may occur from other causes and it must not be assumed that because a dog manifests some of these conditions that he has heart worms. In fact, the only way to be sure is a microscopic examination of the blood and the presence or absence of the larvae. Even in some cases where larvae have been found in the blood, post mortem examinations have failed to reveal heart worms in the heart.

Both the diagnosis and treatment of heart worm are functions of the veterinarian. They are beyond the province of the amateur. The drug used in the treatment of heart worm is a derivative from antimony known as fuadin, and many dogs are peculiarly susceptible to antimony poisoning. If proper treatment is used by a trained veterinarian, a large preponderance of cases of heart worm make a complete recovery; but even the most expert of veterinarians may be expected to fail in the successful treatment of a percentage of heart worm infections. The death of some of its victims is to be anticipated.

Less Frequently Found Worms

Besides the intestinal worms that have been enumerated, there exist in some dogs numerous other varieties and species of worms which are of so infrequent occurrence that they require no discussion in a book for the general dog keeper. These include, esophageal worms, lungworms, kidney worms, and eye worms. They are in the United States, indeed, so rare as to be neglible.

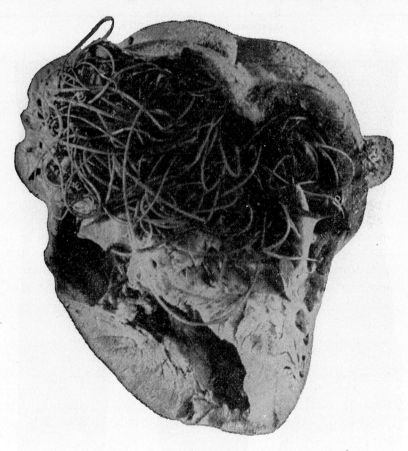

—Heart of a dog, showing heavy heart worm infection.

95

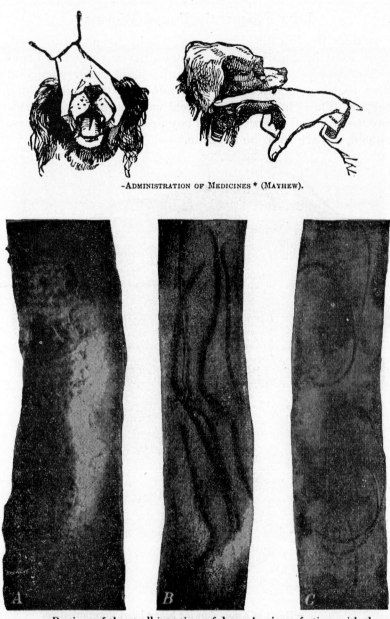

−ADMINISTRATION OF MEDICINES * (MAYHEW).

.—Portions of the small intestines of dogs, showing infections with three of the common roundworms: *A*, The common hookworm, *Ancylostoma caninum; B* and *C*, the large roundworms, *Toxascaris leonina* and *Toxocara canis.*

Litter of Puppies sired by Dolf v. d. Daniels ex Nita v. d. Daniels
Breeder: Jean Fletcher, New Westminster, British Columbia, Can.

Litter of Puppies—McIntyre's Fiagal, Ferus, and Fiona
Sire: MacGonigal of Arden   Dam: Bucknam's Winnie Winkle
Owners: Mr. and Mrs. H. G. McIntyre, Vancouver, Can.

AM. and CAN. CH. HARBORVALE ALADIN
Sire: Am. and Can. Ch. Aristo v. Marienlust
Dam: Sunset v. Marienlust
Owner: Raymond S. Hill, Phoenix, Arizona

Skin Troubles

HERE is a disposition on the part of the amateur dog keeper to consider any lesion of the dog's skin to be mange. Mange is an unusual condition in clean, well fed, and well cared for dogs. Eczema is much more frequent and is more difficult to control than sarcoptic mange, which with care is easy to cure.

Mange or Scabies

There are at least two kinds of mange that affect dogs— sarcoptic mange and demodectic or red mange, the latter rare indeed and difficult to cure.

Sarcoptic mange is caused by a tiny spider-like mite (*Sarcoptes scabiei canis*) which is similar to the mite that causes human scabies or "itch." Indeed, the mange is almost identical with scabies and is transmissible from dog to man. The mite is approximately one 1/100th of an inch in length and just visible to acute human sight without magnification.

Only the female mites are the cause of the skin irritation. They burrow into the upper layers of the skin, where each lays twenty to forty eggs, which in three to seven days hatch into larvae. These larvae in turn develop into nymphs which later grow into adults. The entire life cycle requires

97

from fourteen to twenty-one days for completion. The larvae, nymphs and males do not burrow into the skin, but live under crusts and scabs on the surface.

The disease may make its first appearance on any part of the dog's body, although it is usually first seen on the head and muzzle, around the eyes, or at the base of the ears. Sometimes it is first noticed in the armpits, the inner parts of the thighs, the lower abdomen or on the front of the chest. If not promptly treated it may cover the whole body and an extremely bad infestation may cause the death of the dog after a few months.

Red points which soon develop into small blisters are the first signs of the disease. These are most easily seen on the unpigmented parts of the skin, such as the abdomen. As the female mites burrow into the skin, there is an exudation of serum which dries and scabs. The affected parts soon are covered with bran-like scales followed with grayish crusts. The itching is intense, especially in hot weather or after exercise. The rubbing and scratching favor secondary bacterial infections and the formation of sores. The hair may grow matted and fall out, leaving bare spots. The exuded serum decomposes and gives rise to a peculiar mousy odor which increases as the disease develops and which is especially characteristic.

Sarcoptic mange is easy to confuse with demodectic (red) mange, ringworm, or with simple eczema. If there is any doubt about the diagnosis, a microscopic examination of the scrapings of the lesions will reveal the true facts.

It is easy to control sarcoptic mange if it is recognized in its earlier stages and treatment is begun immediately. Neglected, it may be very difficult to eradicate. If it is considered how rapidly the causative mites reproduce themselves, the necessity for early treatment becomes apparent. That treatment consists not only of medication of the infected dog but also of sterilization of his bedding, all tools and implements used on him, and the whole premises upon which he has been confined. Sarcoptic mange is easily and quickly transmissible from dog to dog, from area to area on the same dog, and even from dog to human.

In some manner which is not entirely understood, an inadequate or unbalanced diet appears to predispose a dog to sarcoptic mange, and few dogs adequately fed and cared for ever contract it. Once a dog has contracted mange, however, improvement in the amount or quality of his food seems not to hasten his recovery.

There are various medications recommended for sarcoptic mange, sulphur ointment being the old standby. However, it is messy, difficult to use, and not always effective.

A bath made by dissolving four ounces of derris powder (containing at least 5% rotenone) and one ounce of soap in one gallon of water has proved effective, especially if large areas of the surface of the dog's skin are involved. All crusts and scabs should be removed before its application. The solution must be well scrubbed into the skin with a moderately stiff brush and the whole animal thoroughly soaked. Only the surplus liquid must be taken off with a towel and the remainder permitted to dry on the dog. This bath should be repeated at intervals of five days until all signs of mange have disappeared. Three such baths will usually suffice.

The advantage of such all over treatment is that it protects uninfected areas from infection. It is also a precautionary measure to bathe in this solution uninfected dogs which have been in contact with the infected one.

Isolated mange spots may be treated with oil of lavender. Roll a woolen cloth into a swab with which the oil of lavender can be applied and rubbed in thoroughly for about five minutes. This destroys all mites with which the oil of lavender comes into contact.

Another method of spot treatment is with a solution made with one pint grain alcohol, one ounce white carbolic acid, and 3 ounces balsam of Peru True. Mix the ingredients in a bottle with a wide mouth and use the cork as an applicator. This solution not only destroys the mange mite but it instantly quiets all itching and so seals the surface as to prevent secondary invasions. It is slightly gummy, but dries in a few minutes after its application, and it may discolor the coat temporarily.

Even after a cure is believed to be accomplished, vigilance

must be maintained to prevent fresh infestations and immediately to treat new spots as soon as they appear.

Demodectic or Red Mange

Demodectic mange, caused by the wormlike mite *Demodex canis,* which lives in the hair follicles and the sebaceous glands of the skin, is difficult to cure. It is a baffling malady of which the prognosis is not favorable. The life cycle of the causative organism is not well understood, the time required from the egg to maturity being so far unknown. The female lays eggs which hatch into young of similar appearance to the adult, except that they are smaller and have but three pairs of legs instead of four.

One peculiar feature about demodectic mange is that some dogs appear to be genetically predisposed to it and the others do not contract it whatever their contact with infected animals may be. Young animals seem to be especially prone to it, particularly ones with short hair. The first evidence of its presence is the falling out of the hair on certain areas of the dog. The spots may be somewhat reddened, and they commonly occur near the eyes, on the hocks, elbows, or toes, although they may be on any part of the dog's body. No itching occurs at the malady's inception, and it never grows so intense as in sarcoptic mange.

In the course of time, the hairless areas enlarge, and the skin attains a copper hue; in severe cases it may appear blue or leadish gray. During this period the mites multiply and small pustules develop. Secondary invasions may occur to complicate the situation. Poisons are formed by the bacteria in the pustules, and the absorption of toxic materials deranges the body functions and eventually affects the whole general health of the dog, leading to emaciation, weakness, and the development of an acrid, unpleasant odor.

This disease is slow and subtle in its development, runs a casual course, and frequently extends over a period of two or even three years. Unless it is treated, it usually terminates in death, although spontaneous recovery occasionally occurs, especially if the dog has been kept on a nourishing diet. As in other skin diseases, correct nutrition plays a major part in recovery from demodectic mange, as it plays an even larger part in its prevention.

It is possible to confuse demodectic mange with sarcoptic mange, fungus infection, acne, or eczema. A definite diagnosis is possible only from microscopic examination of skin scrapings and of material from the pustules. The possibility of demodectic mange, particularly in its earlier stages, is not negated by the failure to find the mites under the microscope, and several examinations may be necessary to arrive at a definite diagnosis.

The prognosis is not entirely favorable. It may appear that the mange is cured and a new and healthy coat may be re-established only to have the disease manifest itself in a new area, and the whole process of treatment must be undertaken afresh. It appears that nourishing food with adequate vitamins and minerals, laxatives, and warm, comfortable quarters facilitates recovery, but many dogs fail to recuperate whatever the treatment.

Persistent use of the derris wash recommended for sarcoptic mange, applied every second day for two weeks and once a week thereafter for four weeks has been known to effect a cure. Perseverance is necessary, and even then failure is possible. One recommended remedy is a one percent solution of rotonone in alcohol or oil. The rotonone is to be dissolved in a small amount of acetone to which the alcohol or oil is added. This is applied daily to the affected parts, in connection with the derris bath already described. Good results have also been claimed to result from X-radiation.

Ear Mites or Ear Mange

The mites responsible for ear mange (*Ododectes cynotis*) are considerably larger than the ones which cause sarcoptic mange. They inhabit the external auditory canal and are visible to the unaided eye as minute, slowly moving, white objects. Their life history is not known, but is probably similar to that of the mite that causes sarcoptic mange.

These mites do not burrow into the skin, but are found deep in the ear canal, near the eardrum. Considerable irritation results from their presence, and the normal secretions of the ear are interfered with. The ear canal is filled with inflammatory products, modified ear wax, and mites, causing the dog to scratch and rub its ears and to shake its head. While ear mange is not caused by incomplete washing or inefficient drying of the ears, it is encouraged by such negligence.

The ear mange infestation is purely local and is no cause for anxiety. An ointment of one part of derris powder (5% rotonone) in ten parts of olive oil has been found effective in this condition. Usually two treatments, a week apart, are required, but treatments should continue until a cure is effected.

Eczema

Eczema is the most common skin disease (if it may be called a disease) with which dogs are afflicted. It is frequently mistaken for ringworm and mange, with which it has no kinship whatever. Eczema is not of parasitic origin, is not contagious or infectious, and can not be conveyed from dog to dog or from dog to human. This does not mean that the malady is easy to control or that it may be neglected.

Eczema is characterized by erythema, the development of papules, vesicles, and pustules, a serous discharge, formation of crusts, intense itching, appearance of scurf, loss of hair, and a marked tendency to become chronic. The most common site for the development of eczema is the region around the base of the tail and spreading along the back line to the shoulders and neck. No part of the body, however, is exempt from its beginning lesions. The skin around the scrotum or the vulva is often affected. A moist form of eczema with a brownish discharge often attacks the ear canal and the skin between the toes.

Eczema occurs in two forms; one is an acute moist condition referred to as weeping eczema, the other and most common is a dry condition that tends to be chronic. In the moist, acute form the development of the disease is rapid. Its principal characteristics are an intense reddening of the skin, persistent itching, the formation of vesicles, an exudate of serum, loss of hair, and a glistening, moist appearance of the skin. The chronic type usually begins with a simple dermatitis which slowly develops and grows more intense. It is characterized by inflammation and eruptions of the skin, intense itching, loss of hair, and the formation of scurf, crusts, and scabs.

The disease is nost prevalent during the summers, especially in hot, humid weather. In some dogs it has a tendency to clear up spontaneously during the winter months, only to reappear again in the following spring and summer. On account of its seasonal occurrence, this form is often referred to as summer eczema or periodic eczema. It may be surmised, however, that the heat and humidity of summer does not so much produce eczema as they tend to aggravate its cause and bring about the major manifestations of its lesions. The predisposing cause may remain through the winter months in which the skin may appear more nearly normal.

There is no cure for eczema except to find and remove the cause of it. That cause may be obscure and difficult to discover. The cause removed, the malady tends to disappear of its own accord.

The cause to be searched for is usually to be found in the dog's diet. It may be the absence from the diet of some essential element, some particular protein or amino acid, one of the vitamins, or one or more of the minerals. When the missing essential substance is added to the ration, the eczema will disappear. Or, on the other hand, the eczema may be caused by the presence in the diet of a factor that the system of the individual dog can not tolerate with impunity. This superfluous, and to the individual dog poisonous, factor is usually some particular carbohydrate or an excess of the various carbohydrates in the diet. When the causative carbohydrate is removed from the ration or the excess of the various carbohydrates is reduced, the eczema begins spontaneously to heal without further treatment.

It must be taken into consideration that all eczemas have not the same cause. What is one dog's food may be another dog's poison. Dogs possess food idiosyncracies, just as persons do. A food that may produce eczema in one dog may be a wholesome part of another dog's ration. Each case of canine eczema must be considered as individual, and a separate and distinct cause of the malady must be sought in each dog.

Many fat, obese, and overfed dogs, especially old animals, are eczemous. Their skins usually clear up well when they are reduced to a normal state of flesh and kept so.

Eczema may result from the irritations brought about by infestations of fleas, lice, or ticks, or from filthy or unsanitary quarters. These conditions do not primarily produce eczema, but they conduce to its manifestation. Too frequent bathing with harsh or medicated soaps sometimes bring about a dermatitis that may become chronic and called eczema, or the skin of some dogs may be sensitive to medication, such as phenol dips used to destroy fleas or lice.

Another possible cause of eczema is infestation with intestinal parasites. It is wise to have the feces of an eczemous dog examined for their presence, and to worm him if any are found.

There can no longer be any doubt that some dogs have an hereditary predisposition to eczema and require especial care to thwart its manifestations. This predisposition appears to exist in certain strains in all the breeds. The dog with general constitutional vigor is usually exempt from that predisposition, but may develop eczema from some other aggravated cause.

Eczema may be caused by some unsuspected plant or other factor in the dog's environment, usually a protein substance. For instance, one otherwise healthy dog developed skin irritation when permitted to exercise in a field of alfalfa, although his kennel mates exhibited no such allergy. Trial and error checks should be made until the cause of the eczema is found and removed.

Little other treatment is usually indicated. Mild lotions, ointments, and dusting powders may be used externally to allay itching and heal lesions, but they can not be depended upon as curative agents. Mild antiseptics hinder the secondary invasions of disease-causing organisms, although these secondary invasions may be discouraged with ordinary cleanliness and sanitation.

In cases of eczema where diet is suspected of being the cause (as it well may be), the ration may be reduced entirely to raw meat, milk, or cottage cheese, with vitamins and minerals. After a week on such an exclusive diet, if the lesions have begun to heal, the customary ingredients may be added one by one to the ration until eczema begins to reappear. It is often possible in such a manner to isolate the cause. Once found, the element should be permanently excluded from the ration of the particular dog it affects. It does not follow, however, that the causative factor for eczema in one dog will produce the malady in other dogs.

General measures for the control of eczema include reducing the carbohydrate content of the rations, decrease of the food intake of overfed dogs, less frequent bathing with irritating soaps, regular brushings and combings to keep the hair and skin clean, keeping the affected dogs in cool, dry, well ventilated quarters free from flies and other insect pests, regular exercise in the cool part of the day, regular evacuation of the bowels and bladder, and keeping the animal free from internal parasites. Regular mild purges with milk of magnesia, if the bowels are costive, often reduce skin irritation, or small daily doses between meals of bicarbonate of soda (Arm and Hammer baking soda) allay acidity which sometimes reflects itself in eczema lesions.

Touching the lesions with the alcohol and balsam of Peru mixture, for which the formula is given in the discussion of sarcoptic mange in this book, is useful in eczema to allay itching and to close open lesions. It is not recommended as a cure, however.

Ringworm

Ringworm is a communicable disease of the skin of dogs, readily transmissible to man and to other dogs and animals. The disease is caused by specific fungi, which are somewhat similar to ordinary molds. The lesions caused by ringworm usually first appear on the face, head or legs of the dog, but they may occur on any part of the surface of his body.

The disease in dogs is characterized by small, circular areas of dirty gray or brownish-yellow crusts or scabs partially devoid of hair, the size of a dime. As the disease progresses, the lesions increase both in size and in number and merge to form larger patches covered with crusts containing broken off hairs. A raw, bleeding surface may appear when crusts are broken or removed by scratching or rubbing to relieve itching. In some cases, however, little or no itching is manifested. Microscopic examination and culture tests are necessary for accurate diagnosis.

If treatment of affected dogs is started early, when only a few lesions are present, the progress of the disease can be immediately arrested. Treatment consists of clipping the hair from around the infected spots, removing the scabs and painting the spots with tincture of iodine, five percent salicylic acid solution, or other fungicide two or three times weekly until recovery takes place. In applying these remedies it is well to cover the periphery of the circular lesion as well as its center, since the spots tend to expand outward from their centers. Scabs, hair and debris removed from the dog during his treatments should be burned to destroy the causative organisms and to prevent reinfection. Precautions in the handling of animals affected with ringworm should be observed, since the disease is transmissible to man and other animals. Isolation of affected dogs is not necessary if the treatment is thorough.

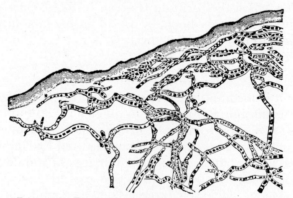

.--Tricophyton Tonsurans, the Vegetable Parasite causing Ringworm, Magnified 400 Diameters (after Payne).

Internal Canine Diseases and Their Management

THE word *management* is employed in this title heading rather than *treatment*, since the treatment of disease in the dog is the function of the veterinarian, and the best counsel it is possible to give the solicitous owner of a sick dog is to submit the case to the best veterinarian available and to follow his instructions implicitly. In general, it may be said, the earlier in any disease the veterinarian is consulted, the more rapid is the sick animal's recovery and the lower the outlay of money for the services of the veterinarian and for the medicine he prescribes.

Herein are presented some hints for the prevention of the various canine maladies and for their recognition when they occur. With dogs of great constitutional vigor, fed as well as they should be, and kept in a normal environment, the incidence of disease may well be rare, if at all. In kennel husbandry, disease is a minor problem, and, if preventive methods are employed, it is one that need not be anticipated.

Distemper

Distemper, the traditional bug-bear of keeping dogs, the veritable scourge of dog-kind, has at long last been well conquered. Compared with twenty years ago when "over distemper" was one of the best recommendations for the purchase of a dog, the incidence of distemper in well bred and adequately cared for dogs is minimal. Time was when the exhibition of a puppy in a dog show was to invite distemper, and it was hazardous to take a young dog upon the streets lest he contract the dreaded malady.

The difference between then and now is that we now have available preventive sera, vaccines, and viruses, which may be employed to forestall distemper before it ever appears. There are valid differences of opinion about which of these measures is best to use and at what ages of the dog they are variously indicated. About the choice of preventive measures and the technique of administering them, the reader is advised to consult his veterinarian and to accept his advice. There can be no doubt, however, that any person with a valued or loved young dog should take immediate steps to have him immunized.

Up until a dog is about four months old, injection of distemper serum at two weeks intervals is indicated. This may be continued indefinitely if the dog should not be in perfect health or should be having trouble with his teething. After four months of age for a dog in the bloom of health, either of two other protective methods against distemper should be undertaken. One is the injection of distemper vaccine, which must be renewed every six months. The other is inoculation with the virus of distemper after the dog has been fortified with serum or vaccine, or both.

The last named method induces a very mild case of distemper, which may be communicated to other dogs that are not immune to the disease. However, it establishes a permanent immunity of the inoculated dog to recurrence of distemper, and, having been done successfully, the dog is safe from distemper for the remainder of his life.

This inoculation with virus should not be undertaken after a dog has been exposed to distemper or while he is in bad health from any cause. Occasionaly, but rarely indeed, a sever case of distemper results from the virus inoculation, and this has sometimes resulted in the dog's death. This is seldom to be feared if the dog's health and condition is good, and if he is properly fortified beforehand with serum or vaccine. It may be assumed that a dog that develops a severe distemper from his inoculation is highly susceptible to the disease and would later contract it in its most virulent form. The experienced veterinarian is the best person to decide upon the dog's fitness to receive the virus inoculation and to administer it.

Distemper is essentially a disease of young dogs, although no dog is immune to it until he has either had it or until he has had his inoculation with virus. Once having the disease confers immunity against further attack from it. Some dogs are reputed to have had distemper twice or three times, but it is believed that diagnosis has been faulty after the initial distemper.

Canine distemper is an acute, highly contagious, febrile disease caused by a filterable virus. It is characterized by a catarrhal inflammation of all the mucous membranes of the body, frequently accompanied by nervous symptoms and pustular eruptions of the skin. Its human counterpart is influenza, which, though not identical with distemper, is very similar to it in many respects. Distemper is so serious and complicated a disease as to require expert attention; when a dog is suspected of having it, a veterinarian should be consulted immediately. It is the purpose of this discussion of the malady rather to describe it that its recognition may be possible than to suggest medication for it or means of treating it.

Distemper is known in all countries and all parts of the United States in all seasons of the year, but it is most prevalent during the winter months and in the cold, damp weather of early spring and late autumn. No breed of dogs is immune. Puppies of low constitutional vigor, pampered, overfed, unexercised dogs, and those kept in overheated, unventilated quarters contract the infection more readily and suffer more from it than hardy animals, properly fed and living in a more natural environment. Devitalizing influences which decrease the resistance of the dog, such as rickets, parasitic infestations, unsanitary quarters, and especially an insufficient or unbalanced diet, are factors predisposing to distemper.

While puppies as young as ten days or two weeks have been known to have true cases of distemper, and very old dogs in rare instances, the usual subjects of distemper are between two months (after weaning) and full maturity at about eighteen months. The teething period of four to six months is highly critical. It is believed that some degree of temporary protection from distemper is passed on to a nursing litter through the milk of the mother.

As was first demonstrated by Carré in 1905 and finally established by Laidlaw and Duncan in their work for the Field Distemper Fund in 1926 to 1928, the primary causative agent of distemper is a filterable virus. The clinical course of the disease may be divided into two parts, produced respectively by the primary Carré filterable virus and by a secondary invasion of bacterial organisms which produce serious complicating conditions usually associated with the disease. This is also true of human influenza. It is seldom true that uncomplicated Carré distemper would cause more than a fever with malaise and indisposition if the secondary bacterial invasion could be avoided. The primary disease but prepares the ground for the secondary invasion which produces the havoc and all too often kills the patient.

Although it is often impossible to ascertain the source of infection in outbreaks of distemper, it is known that the infection may spread from affected to susceptible dogs by either direct or indirect contact. The disease, while highly infectious throughout its course, is especially easy to communicate in its earliest stages, even before clinical symptoms are manifested. The virus is readily destroyed by heat and by most of the common disinfectants in a few hours, but it resists drying and low temperatures for several days, and has been known to survive freezing for months.

The period of incubation (the time between exposure to infection and the development of the first symptoms) is variable. It has been reported to be as short as three days and as long as two weeks. The usual period is approximately one week. The usual course of the disease is about four weeks, but seriously complicated cases may prolong themselves to twelve weeks.

The early symptoms of distemper, as a rule, are so mild and subtle as to escape the notice of any but the most acute observer. These first symptoms may be a rise in temperature, a watery discharge from the eyes and nose, an impaired appetite, a throat-clearing cough, and a general sluggishness. In about a week's time the symptoms become well marked, with a discharge of mucus or pus from the eyes and nose, and complications of a more or less serious nature, such as broncho-pneumonia, hemorrhagic inflammation of the gastro-intestinal tract, and disturbances of the brain and spinal cord, which may cause convulsions. In the early stages of distemper the body temperature may suddenly rise from the normal 101°F. to 103°. Shivering, dryness of the nostrils, a slight dry cough, increased thirst, a drowsiness of expression, reluctance to eat, and a desire to sleep may follow. Later diarrhea (frequently streaked with blood or wholly of blood), pneumonia, convulsions, paralysis, or chorea (a persistent twitching condition) may develop. An inflammation of the membranes of the eye may ensue; this may impair or destroy the sight through ulceration or opacity of the cornea. Extreme weakness and great loss of body weight occur in advanced stages.

All, any, or none of these symptoms may be noticeable. It is believed that many dogs experience distemper in so mild a form as to escape the owner's observation. Because of its protean and obscure nature and its strong similarity to other catarrhal affections, the diagnosis of distemper, especially in its early stages, is difficult. In young dogs that are known to have been exposed to the disease, a rise of body temperature, together with shivering, sneezing, loss of appetite, eye and nasal discharge, sluggishness, and diarrhea, (all or any of these symptoms) are indicative of trouble.

There is little specific that can be done for a dog with primary distemper. The treatment is largely concerned with alleviating the symptoms. No drug or combination of drugs is known at this time that has any specific action on the disease. Distemper runs a definite course, no matter what is done to try to cure it. None of the nostrums advanced as so-called quick cures have any value.

111

Homologous anti-distemper serum, administered sub-cutaneously or intravenously by the veterinarian, is of value in lessening the severity of the attack. The veterinarian may see fit to treat the secondary pneumonia with penicillin or one of the sulpha drugs, or to allay the secondary intestinal infection with medication. It is best to permit him to manage the case in his own way. The dog is more prone to respond to care in his own home and with his own people, if suitable quarters and adequate nursing are available to him. Otherwise, he is best off in a veterinary hospital.

The dog affected with distemper should be provided with clean, dry, warm but not hot, well ventilated quarters. It should be given moderate quantities of nourishing, easily digested food—milk, soft boiled eggs, cottage cheese, and scraped lean beef. The sick dog should not be disturbed by children or other dogs. Discharges from eyes and nose should be wiped away. The eyes may be bathed with boric acid solution, and irritation of the nose allayed with greasy substances such as petrolatum. The dog should not be permitted to get wet or chilled; and he should have such medication as the veterinarian prescribes and no other.

When signs of improvement are apparent, the dog must not be given an undue amount of food at one meal, although he may be fed at frequent intervals. The convalescing dog should be permitted to exercise only very moderately until complete recovery is assured.

In the control of distemper, affected animals should be promptly isolated from susceptible dogs. After the disease has run its course, whether it end in recovery or death, the premises where the patient has been kept during its illness should be thoroughly cleaned and disinfected, as should all combs, brushes, or other utensils used on the dog, before other susceptible dogs are brought in.

After an apparent recovery has been made in the patient, the germs are present for about four weeks and can be transmitted to susceptible dogs.

Chorea or St. Vitus Dance

A frequent sequela of distemper in chorea, which is characterized by a more or less pronounced and frequent twitch-

AM. AND CAN. CH. SHIP'S MASCOT MISS PEACHES
Sire: Seigfried v. Marienlust   Dam: Fredacea of Romanald
Owner: Mr. and Mrs. A. C. Spraggins, Rock Manor Kennels,
Walnut Creek, California

CH. JEFFREY OF HEYING-TECKEL
Sire: Ch. Favorite v. Marienlust   Dam: Jubilee of Heying-Teckel
Owner: Heying-Teckel Kennels, Mr. and Mrs. Fred Heying, Pacoima, Calif.

CH. BLACKIE DOCKIE, SON OF CH. GUNTHER v. MARIENLUST AND
SUSIE v. MAGDEBURG
Bred and owned by Mrs. Katrina Walter

Wheaton Walter holding Ferdinand v. Magdeburg, and Katrina Walter,
publisher of The Kennel Crier, with Susie v. Magdeburg, mother of Ch.
Blackie Dockie, in their home, Babylon, New York.

CH. CALIDOX LUIGI
Sire: **Int. Ch.** Favorite v. Marienlust   Dam: Dinah of Heying-Teckel
Owner: Raymond S. Hill, Phoenix, Arizona

Litter of six weeks old puppies
Sire: **Ch. Cavalier** v. Marienlust   Dam: Little Lady **v. Cavalier**
Owner: Mildred L. Hill, Phoenix, Arizona

INT. CH. MIRA—ERLENMARK OF SETON
Sire: Ch. Michael von Wälder   Dam: Mona Lisa von Wälder
Best, all coats, Scottish Dachshund Club's Ch. Show, 1946
Owner: John Pollard, Southport, Lancs., England

AM. AND CAN. CH. ARISTO v. MARIENLUST
Sire: Bruce v. Marienlust   Dam: Freda O'Red Bairn
Owner: Mrs. Lancaster Andrews, West Hempstead, Long Island, N. Y.

ing of a muscle or muscles. There is no known remedy for the condition. It does not impair the usefulness of a good dog for breeding, and having a litter of puppies often betters or cures chorea in the bitch. Chorea is considered a form of unsoundness and is penalized in the show ring. The condition generally becomes worse.

Running Fits or Fright Disease

Running fits, variously known as fright disease, barking fits, and canine hysteria, is a nervous affection of dogs, occurring in dogs of all breeds, all ages, both sexes, and at all times of the year. More or less prevalent throughout the United States, it seems more common in the Southern States than elsewhere. Whether it should be denominated a disease is still open to doubt.

The condition, whatever it may be, is characterized by periodic attacks of running and barking or howling, with manifestations of excitement and terror, and evidences of acute pain. Between attacks, the dog appears normal, though it sometimes is dull and listless. Usually the first symptoms are restlessness, a staring expression, and fright. Then the affected animal suddenly starts to run as if pursued, with excited barking interspersed with howling. The attacks last from a few minutes to half an hour, may occur at intervals of days, weeks, or months over a period of years.

In mild attacks, after a short period of terrified running and barking, the dog will hide in a dark place, from which it will later emerge seemingly normal. Severe attacks may include spasms, the champing of the jaws, a flow of saliva with or without involuntary passage of feces or urine. Sometimes the dog will remain timid or in a state of fear, will snap at and fail to recognize the owner or keeper.

A baffling characteristic of running fits is that other dogs in the menage are likely to be also affected, and through sympathy or immitation evince a like state at the same time. This is true despite the unlikelihood of similar causes producing a similar condition at the identical minute.

The fits or convulsions of puppies heavily infested with intestinal parasites or cutting their permanent teeth are

113

not to be confused with running fits. The symptoms of running fits are sometimes by the uniformed believed to be those of rabies, although the two conditions are not in fact alike.

In cases of prolonged attacks, the brain becomes affected, the fits come oftener and for longer duration and eventually the dog will be unable to lift his head, in which case it is best to put him to sleep as recovery is an impossibility. In the case of a very valuable dog where an early attempt at a cure is made, recovery is sometimes effected by keeping the subject under the influence of a narcotic for several days, only allowing him to come out long enough to eat small portions of easily digested food, but as a rule, a dog so affected will never regain its normal mentality.

The basic cause of running fits is still unknown and much disputed. The preponderance of evidence is that they are caused by fault or faults in the diet. It has been observed that a long continued diet composed largely of meal, cereals, breadstuffs, or dog biscuit may produce a condition identical with or similar to running fits, particularly in dogs kept in close confinement. Dogs that have liberty to run and whose ration includes ample meat are seldom affected. It has also been suggested that running fits are caused by an insufficiently of vitamins A and B_1 in the diet. They have also been charged to an hereditary predisposition, which seems an unlikely theory, since the trouble can be controlled and cured.

During the immediate attack, the victim should be placed in a dark room and kept free from annoyance and molestation. Following recovery, he should be kept quiet to avoid recurrence of the symptoms. Nerve sedatives may be given, as may seem advisable.

Reduction of the carbohydrates in the diet, the substitution of sound meats, and the addition of a plentiful amount of vitamin A and B_1 appear the best methods of preventing occurrence or recurrence of the trouble.

As prolonged fits are liable to affect the brain, time does not permit the administration of Vitamin B by mouth. It is recommended that injections of Vitamin B be given each day by a veterinarian.

Eclampsia or Whelping Tetany

Convulsions of bitches before, during or shortly after their whelping are called eclampsia. It seldom occurs to a bitch receiving a sufficient amount of calcium and vitamin D in her diet during her pregnancy. The symptoms vary in their severity from nervousness and mild convulsions to severe attacks which may terminate in coma and death. The demands of the nursing litter for calcium frequently depletes the supply in the bitch's system.

Eclampsia can be controlled by the hyperdermic administration of calcium gluconate. Its recurrence is prevented by the addition to the bitch's ration of readily utilized calcium and vitamin D.

Rickets, or Rachitis

The failure of the bones of puppies to calcify normally is termed rickets, or more technically rachitis. The condition is due to the neglect of the diet of the puppies after they are weaned or the diet of their dam during her pregnancy and lactation. Perhaps more otherwise excellent puppies are killed or ruined by rickets than by any other disease. It is essentially a disease of puppies, but the malformation of the skeleton produced by rickets persists through the life of the dog.

The symptoms of rickets include lethargy, arched neck, crouched stance, knobby and deformed joints, bowed legs, and flabby muscles. The changes characteristic of defective calcification in the puppy are most marked in the growth of the long bones of the leg, and at the cartilaginous junction of the ribs. In the more advanced stages of rickets the entire bone becomes soft and easily deformed or broken. The development of the teeth is also retarded.

Rickets results from a deficiency in the diet of calcium, phosphorous, or vitamin D. It may be prevented by the inclusion of sufficient amounts of those substances in the puppy's diet. It may also be cured, if not too far advanced, by the same means, although distortions in the skeleton that have already occured are seldom rectified. It is very important that the puppy's ration include ample amounts of

115

these substances. The requirements of vitamin D to be artificially supplied are greater for puppies raised indoors and with limited exposure to sunlight or to sunlight filtered through window glass.

(It is possible to give a dog too much vitamin D, but very unlikely without deliberate intent.)

Adult dogs that have had rickets in puppyhood and whose recovery is complete may be bred from without fear of their transmission to their puppies of the malformations of their skeletons produced by the disease. The same imbalance or absence from their diet that produced rickets in the parent may produce it in the progeny; but the disease in such case is reproduced and not inherited.

The requirements of adult dogs for calcium, phosphorus and vitamin D are much less than for puppies and young dogs, but a condition called osteomalacia, or late rickets, is sometimes seen in grown dogs as the result of the same kind of nutritional deficiency that causes rickets in puppies. In such cases a softening of the bones leads to lameness and deformity. The remedy is the same as in the rickets of puppyhood, namely the addition of calcium, phosphorus, and vitamin D to the diet. It is especially essential that bitches during pregnancy and lactation have included in their diets ample amounts of these elements, both for their own nutrition and for the adequate skeletal formations of their fetuses and the development of their puppies.

Blacktongue

Blacktongue (the canine analogue of pellagra in the human) is no longer to be feared in dogs fed upon an adequate diet. For many years, it was a recognized scourge among dogs, and its cause and treatment were unknown. It is now known to be caused solely by the insufficiency in the ration of vitamin B complex and specifically by an insufficiency of nicotinic acid. (Nicotinic acid is vitamin B_2, formerly known as vitamin G.)

Blacktongue may require a considerable time for its full development. It usually begins with a degree of lethargy, a lack of appetite for the kind of food the dog has been re-

116

ceiving, constipation, often with spells of vomiting, and particularly with a foul odor from the mouth. As the disease develops, the mucous membranes of the mouth, gums, and tongue grow red and become inflamed, with purple splotches of greater or lesser extent, especially upon the front part of the tongue, and with ulcers and pustules on the lips and the lining of the cheeks. Constipation may give way to diarrhea as the disease develops. Blacktongue is an insidious malady, since its development is so gradual.

This disease is unlikely to occur except among dogs whose owners are so unenlightened, careless or stingy as to feed their dogs exclusively on a diet of cornmeal mush, salt pork, cowpeas, sweet potatoes, or other foodstuffs that are known to be responsible for the development of pellagra in mankind. Blacktongue is not infectious or contagious, although the same deficiency in the diet of dogs may produce the malady in all the inmates throughout a kennel.

Correct treatment involves no medication as such, but consists wholly in the alteration of the diet to include foods which are good sources of the vitamin B complex, including nicotinic acid; such food as the muscles of beef, mutton, or horse, dried yeast, wheat germ, milk, eggs, and especially fresh liver. As an emergency treatment, the hypodermic injection of nicotinic acid may be indicated. Local treatments of the mouth, its cleansing and disinfection, are usually included, although they will avail nothing without the alteration in the diet.

Leptospirosis or Canine Typhus

Leptospirosis, often referred to as canine typhus, is believed to be identical with Weil's disease (infectious juandice) in the human species. It is not to be confused with non-infectious jaundice in the dog, which is a mere obstruction in the bile duct which occurs in some liver and gastric disorders. Leptospirosis is a comparatively rare disease as yet, but its incidence is growing and it is becoming more widespread. It rarely is found in dogs under eight months of age, but it spreads rapidly and is often fatal.

117

It is caused by either of two spirocheates, *Leptospira canicola* or *Leptospira icterohenorrhagiae*. These causative organisms are found in the feces or urine of infected rats; and the disease is transmitted to dogs by their ingestion of food fouled by those rodents. It is therefore wise in rat in-fested houses to keep all dog food in covered metal containers to which it is impossible for rats to gain access. It is also pos-sible for an ill dog to transmit the infection to a well one, and, it is believed, to man. Such cases, however, are rare.

Symptoms of leptospirosis include high fevers, vomiting, bleeding of the gums, loss of appetite, gastroenteritis, bloody diarrhea, jaundice, and excessive depression. The disease is one for immediate reference to the veterinarian whenever it is suspected.

Prognosis is not entirely favorable, especially if the dis-case is neglected in its earlier stages. Taken in its incipience. treatment with penicillin has produced excellent results, as has antileptospiral serum and vaccine.

Control measures include the extermination of rats in areas where the disease is known to exist, and the cleaning and disinfection of premises where infected dogs have been kept.

Metritis

Metritis is the acute or chronic inflamation of the uterus of the bitch, caused by retention of the fetal membranes, infection introduced at time of whelping, or wounds and in-juries to the mucous membranes of the vagina and uterus. Cold damp quarters also are conducive to metritis.

In acute metritis the symptoms include a swelling and congestion of the vulva and vagina with a brownish or blood-stained, fetid discharge from the vagina, fever, loss of ap-petite, vomiting, and tenderness in the region of the uterus.

Treatment in mild cases consists of irrigation of the uterus with mild antiseptics, such as douching with a salt solution, one tablespoonful of salt to one quart of warm water. Severe acute cases and chronic cases require surgery, for which recourse should be had to the veterinarian.

Conjunctivitis or Inflammation of the Eye

Certain irritants, injuries or infections, and many febrile diseases, such as distemper, produce an inflammation of the membranes lining the lids of the dog's eyes, known as conjunctivitis. It manifests itself first as a congestion of the membranes and a watering of the eyes, followed by a discharge of mucus and later of pus.

The remedies to be used are freshly prepared argyrol (10 percent solution), sulfate of zinc (1 percent solution), opthalmic yellow oxide of mercury (2 percent), and opthalmic sulphathiazol (5 percent). These remedies should be dropped or pressed directly into the eye in small quantities two, three, or four times each day. Any one of them will usually suffice in mild cases, although in aggravated cases two or more of these remedies may be alternated in use. The application of borated petrolatum jelly to the edges of the eyelids will prevent their being stuck together by the accumulated discharge.

The remedies are the same, whether the cause be mere irritation or some systemic disease. In the latter case the conjunctivitis may be expected to continue until the disease is cured. The purulent conjunctivitis of distemper and some other diseases may result in suppurative keratitis (ulceration of the cornea) which in turn may bring about partial or total blindness. Successful treatment of severe cases requires professional veterinary care.

Turned-In and Turned-Out Eyelids

The inversion, or turning-in of the eyelids against the cornea, is technically called entropion. The turning-out of the eyelids is called ectropion. Both are to be found in certain strains and are heritable. Surgery is never satisfactory to completely remedy these conditions, although the remedies recommended for conjunctivitis tend to allay temporarily the inflammation of the lids which results from these conditions. Neither before nor after their surgical rectification should dogs with such defective eyelids be employed for breeding. This condition is encountered mostly in small eyed breeds such as terriers.

119

Rabies or Hydrophobia

There is no disposition here to disparage whatever anxiety
the reader may have about rabies, otherwise known as hydrophobia or mad dog. It is a disease which, after its development and manifestations, is invariably fatal, and nothing can be done to remedy or cure it. However, it may be
said, rabies is rare, so rare that among well protected dogs
confined to their owner's premises the incidence of the disease is well nigh negligible.

Several generally credited misapprehensions about rabies
need to be corrected, to the end of allaying the needless
fears of the disease. First, all warm-blooded animals are
subjects for rabies when infected, and the disease is not
confined merely to dogs and men. It is believed that many
of the rabies "scares" or epidemics are begun by some infected wild animal, wolf, fox, or coyote, biting a domestic
dog, which in turn bites other dogs and other animals.

The virus of rabies is transmitted only by the saliva of the
infected animal injected into the blood stream of the uninfected. This may occur from an infected dog's licking a small
abrasion; but there is no danger of infection from mere contact with an infected animal's outer surfaces.

The old concept of the mad dog galloping down the street,
snapping to right and left at all and sundry, is false. The
rabid dog usually seeks refuge in a dark, quiet place and
remains there. The disease takes at least two forms, the so
called "furious" rabies, and the "dumb" rabies. In the
furious form, the dog is somewhat aggressive and will snap
at and bite various objects placed before it, especially objects in motion. In this form, too, the dog's tendency is to
roam restlessly. When confined in a cage, it may attack
the bars with such vigor as to break its teeth. Many dogs
affected with rabies exhibit none of these symptoms. The
manifestation of the disease may be more or less masked,
and may be only an eventual paralysis and death.

Many dogs suffering only from thirst or from convulsions
caused by intestinal worms have been shot in the erroneous
belief that they were "mad".

The dumb form of rabies is of much higher incidence than

120

the furious form. In it the paralytic symptoms are the outstanding feature. The dog is not vicious, has no tendency to bite or to roam, and is not excitable; in fact, it may be the opposite. The most noteworthy symptom of dumb rabies is the paralysis of the lower jaw—the so called "dropped jaw." The dog's mouth can be closed with the hands, but he has lost the power to close his own mouth. Many times this has been mistaken for a bone lodged in the throat, and persons have exposed themselves to rabies infection in their effort to extract the bone. A dog with a dropped jaw should be viewed with suspicion and no examination of the throat should be made. Such an animal should be taken immediately to the veterinarian for examination. In addition to the dropped jaw, in the dumb form of rabies, the animal shows evidence of paralysis of the hindquarters, of the forequarters, or of both within a few days. It eventually becomes completely paralyzed and dies.

The course of the disease in both its forms is usually short, and the animal dies after three to seven days. No treatment is recognized to be of any value after the symptoms are manifested.

Persons bitten by dogs believed to be infected with rabies should present themselves to their physicians and should submit to the so called Pasteur treatment immediately. That treatment, if taken before the onset of the disease, eliminates the probability of its development.

The word *hydrophobia* implies the fear of water. It is a mistaken application to the rabid dog, who may have difficulty in drinking, although it may make an effort to lap water. The convulsions produced by that unsuccessful effort to drink lead some observers to believe it is "fear".

It is mistakenly believed that the incidence of rabies increases in the summer months—during the "dog days". In no time of the year is the disease more prevalent than at any other time. Dog days are a mere myth.

The prophylactic vaccination of dogs against rabies infection has been proved to produce an immunity to the disease for a limited time in at least a percentage of the dogs so vaccinated. The disease is so rare that it is difficult to obtain sufficient animals for experimentation. Nobody as yet can be sure of the percentage of vaccinated dogs that develop immunity nor how long the immunity lasts.

What is said here about rabies is intended only to allay anxieties. Rabies is no problem for the person who does not permit his dogs to run at large. Many experienced dog keepers, who have owned and cared for literally thousands of dogs, have never so much as seen a case of rabies.

Statistics prove that rabies in dogs is more prevalent on Army posts where inoculations are required, than in civilian life.

Clogged Anal Glands

On either side of the anus of the dog is situated an anal gland, which secretes a lubricant that better enables the dog to expel the contents of the rectum. These glands are subject to being clogged, and in them accumulates a fetid mass. This accumulation is not, strictly speaking, a disease —unless it becomes infected and purulent. Almost all dogs have it, and most of them are neglected without serious consequences. However, they are better if they are relieved. Their spirits improve, their eyes brighten, and even their coats gradually grow more lively if the putrid mass is occasionally squeezed out of the anus.

This is accomplished by seizing the tail with the left hand, encircling its base with the thumb and forefinger of the right hand, and pressing the anus firmly between thumb and finger. The process results in momentary pain to the dog and often causes him to flinch, which may be disregarded. A semi-liquid of vile odor is extruded from the anus. The operation should be repeated at intervals of from one week to one month, depending on the rapidity of glandular accumulation. No harm results from the frequency of such relief, although there may be no apparent results if the anal glands are kept free of their accumulations.

If this process of squeezing out of the glands is neglected, the glands sometimes become infected and surgery becomes necessary. This is seldom the case; but, if needful at all, it must be entrusted to a skillful veterinary surgeon.

Housing For Dogs

VERY owner will have, and will have to solve, his own problems about providing his dog or dogs with quarters best suited to the dog's convenience. The special circumstances of each particular owner will determine what kind of home he will provide for his dogs. Here it is impossible to provide more than a few generalities upon the subject.

Little more need be said than that fit quarters for dogs must be secure, clean, dry, and warm. Consideration must be given to convenience in the care of kennel inmates by owners of a large number of dogs, but by the time one's activities enlarge to such proportions one will have formulated one's own concept of how best to house one's dogs. Here, advice will be predicated upon the maintenance of not more than three or four adult dogs with accommodations for an occasional litter of puppies.

First, let it be noted that dogs are not sensitive to aesthetic considerations in the place they are kept; they have no appreciation of the beauty of their surroundings. They do like soft beds of sufficient thickness to protect them from the coldness of the floors. These beds should be secluded and covered to conserve body heat. A box or crate of adequate

123

size to permit the dog to lie full length in it will suffice. The cushion may be a burlap bag, lightly stuffed with long straw, which should be occasionally renewed. Long wheat straw or rice straw loose in such a box will serve as well but it is liable to scatter and require frequent sweeping up. Wood shavings, excelsior, and sawdust are not recommended for the purpose, because they are likely to be swallowed and wood is not digestible.

The kennel should be light, except for a retiring place; and, if sunshine is available at least part of the day, so much the better. Boxes in a shed or garage with secure wire runs to which the dogs have ready access suffice very well, are very inexpensive, and are easy to plan and to arrange. The runs should be made of wire fencing strong enough that the dogs are unable to tear it with their teeth and high enough that the dogs are unable to jump or climb over it. In-turning flanges of wire netting at the tops of the fences tend to obviate jumping. Boards, rocks, or cement buried around the fences forestall burrowing to freedom.

These pens need not be large, if the dogs are given frequent respites from their captivity and an opportunity to obtain needed exercise. However, they should be large enough to relieve them of the aspect of cages. Concrete floors for such pens are admittedly easy to keep clean and sanitary. However, they have no resilience, and the feet of dogs confined for long periods on concrete floors are prone to spread and their shoulders to loosen. A further objection to concrete is that it grows hot in the summer sunshine and is very cold in winter. If it is used for flooring at all, a low platform of wood, large enough to enable the dogs to sprawl out on it full length, should be provided in each pen.

A well drained soil is to be preferred to concrete, if it is available; but it must be dug out to the depth of three inches and renewed occasionally, if it is used. Otherwise, the accumulation of urine will make it sour and offensive. A floor of cork tile is excellent, but expensive.

Gates, hinges, latches and other hardware must be trustworthy. The purpose of such quarters is to confine the dogs and to keep them from running at large; and unless it serve

124

such a purpose it is useless. One wants to know when one puts a dog in his kennel, the dog will be there when one returns. An improvised kennel of old chicken wire will not suffice for one never knows whether it will hold one's dogs or not.

Frequently two friendly bitches may be housed together, or a dog housed with a bitch. Unless one is sure of male friendships, it is seldom safe to house two adult male dogs together. It is better, if possible, to provide a separate kennel for each mature dog; but, if the dogs can be housed side by side with only a wire fence between them, they can have companionship without rancor. Night barking can be controlled by confining the dogs indoors or by shutting them up in their boxes.

Adult dogs require artificial heat in only the coldest of climates, if they are provided with tight boxes of long straw, placed under shelter. Puppies need heat in cold weather up until weaning time, and even thereafter if they are not permitted to sleep together. Snuggled together in a tight box with long straw, they can withstand much cold without discomfort. All dogs in winter without artificial heat should have an increase of their rations—especially as pertains to fat content.

Whatever artificial heat is provided for dogs should be safe, fool-proof, and dog-proof. Caution should be exercised that electric wiring is not exposed, that stoves can not be tipped over, and that it is impossible for sparks from them to ignite the premises. Many fires in kennels, the results of defective heating apparatus or careless handling of it, have brought about the deaths of the inmates. It is because of them that this seemingly unnecessary warning is given.

No better place for a dog to live can be found than the home of its owner, sharing even his bed if permitted. So is the dog happiest. There is a limit, however, to the number of dogs that can be tolerated in the house. The keeper of a small kennel can be expected to alternate his favorite dogs in his own house, thus giving them a respite to confinement in a kennel. Provision must be made for a place of

125

exercise and relief at frequent intervals for dogs kept in the house. An enclosed dooryard will serve such a purpose, or the dog may be exercised on a lead with as much benefit to the owner as to the dog.

That the quarters of the dog shall be dry is even more important than that they shall be warm. A damp, drafty kennel is the cause of much kennel disease and indisposition. It is harmless to permit a dog to go out into inclement weather of his own choice, if he is provided with a sheltered bed to which he may retire to dry himself.

By cleanness, sanitation is meant—freedom from vermin and bacteria. A little coat of dust or a degree of disorder does not discommode the dog or impair his welfare, but the best dog keepers are orderly persons. They at least do not permit broken straw and old bones to accumulate in a dog's bed, and they take the trouble to spray with antiseptic or wash with soap and water their dog's house at frequent intervals. The feces in the kennel runs should be picked up and destroyed at least once, and better twice, daily. Persistent filth in kennels can be counted on as a source of illness sooner or later. This warning appears superfluous, but it isn't; the number of ailing dogs kept in dirty, unsanitary kennels is amazing. It is one of the axioms of keeping dogs that their quarters must be sanitary or disease is sure to ensue.

Readers who desire a more thorough discussion of kennel buildings and their construction than can be given here are referred to the volume entitled *Complete Kennel Construction* by Milo G. Denlinger, published by Denlinger's, Silver Spring, Maryland.

That Doggy Odor

Many persons are disgusted to the point of a refusal to keep a dog by what they fancy is a "doggy odor". The fact is that the mild emanations from a clean and well fed dog are, like that of a clean child, rather pleasant. The unpleasant smell associated with the dog is not in fact the odor of the dog, but rather the stench of his external dirt and the exudations of unsound rations with which he is fed.

Putrifying accumulations in the dog's intestines, the ex-

126

pulsions of his flatulence, the odor of his putrid breath, whether from mucous coated teeth or from a stomach over-loaded with decomposing carbohydrates, can be very un-pleasant to human olfactories, and the accumulation of dirt and detritus on the skin or in the hair, especially when damp, can cause one to hold one's nose. It is no worse, however, than the smell of the unwashed human with digestive dis-orders.

The remedy with the dog is to give him a bath, to clean him out internally, and to see to it that he has only good, sound, digestible and clean smelling food. It is not to be denied that dogs carry an odor, but it is not strong or unpleasant unless it is aggravated with dirt. Claims are made for cer-tain breeds that they "do not smell", but they all have odors, little different one from another. Kept clean, internally and externally, the odor of none of them is offensive. An ill-smelling dog in good health is the mark of careless dog keeping and is inexcusable. Unclean anal glands also cause an odor. Certain diseases, such as distemper and mange, have characteristic odors, but it is not the smells of sick dogs to which objection is made.

Bathing the Dog

There is little to say about giving a bath to a dog, except that he shall be placed in a tub of warm (not hot) water and thoroughly scrubbed. He may, like a spoiled child, object to the ordeal, but if handled gently and firmly he will submit to what he knows to be inevitable.

The water must be only tepid, so as not to shock or chill him, and such a bland and unmedicated soap as Ivory or Palmolive is best. Such soaps do not irritate the skin or dry out the hair. Even better than soap is one of the pow-dered detergents marketed under such trade names as "Vel" and "Tide". They rinse away better and more easily than soap, and, in any event, do not leave the coat gummy or sticky.

The best beginning is with the face which should be thor-oughly and briskly washed with a cloth. Care should be taken not to get the soap or cleaning solvent into the dog's eyes, not because they are likely to cause permanent harm, but because an eye full of soap is unpleasant to the dog and prone to prejudice him against future baths. The interior of the ear canals should be thoroughly cleansed until they not only look clean but also until no unpleasant odor comes from them. The head may then be rinsed thoroughly and dried, before proceeding to the body. Especial attention should be given to the drying of the ears, inside and outside. Many ear infections arise from failure to dry the canals completely.

With the head bath finished and the surplus water removed from that part, the body must be soaked thoroughly with water. This is best done either with a hose or by dipping the water from the bath with a small pan and pouring it over the dog's back until he is totally wetted. Thereafter, apply the soap or detergent and rub the dog until he lathers freely. A stiff brush is useful in penetrating the coat and getting the soap right down to the skin. It is not sufficient to wash only the back and sides, but the belly, neck, legs, feet and tail must all be scrubbed thoroughly down to the skin.

If the dog is very dirty, it may be well to rinse him lightly and repeat the soaping process and scrub again. Thereafter, the dog must be rinsed with warm (tepid) water until all soap and soil come away. This is more easily done if detergent is used instead of soap. If a bath spray is available, the rinsing is an easy matter. If the dog must be rinsed in standing water, it will be needful to renew it two or three times to get all of the soap from the coat.

When he is thoroughly rinsed, it is well to remove such surplus water as may be squeezed with the hand, after which he in enveloped with a turkish towel, lifted from the tub, and rubbed until he is dry. This will probably require two or three dry towels. In the process of drying the dog, it is well to return again and again to the interior of the ears.

HOME OBEDIENCE TRAINING
By Fred Spooner
$3.00

In writing this book, Fred Spooner has directed his efforts primarily to the one-dog owner who is not particularly interested in obedience trials but wishes to educate his dog for good behavior in the home; to teach him to sit and stay on command; to lead, on and off leash.

There are chapters on running away, jumping on people, car sickness and hurdling and guard work.

While this book is written primarily for the home dog, there are chapters on obedience trials as Mr. Spooner feels that once an owner has experienced the thrill of having an obedient dog, he will want to go further and take up the trials at the various dog shows.

Mr. Spooner has been engaged in the training of dogs all his life and during the recent war was a member of the K-9 Corps. He now maintains a training kennel at Madison, New York, and under the auspices of the University of Kansas, is touring the Middle West, lecturing on dog training at the schools and colleges.

If the reader is interested in training, he will do well to obtain a copy of this book, Home Obedience Training, which is the most recent publication on this subject and contains the latest A. K. C. rules and methods which have been adopted universally for training dogs. Mr. Spooner's style of writing is very pleasing and his method of explanation is clear and understandable to the amateur.

COMPLETE KENNEL CONSTRUCTION
By Milo G. Denlinger
$3.75

The purpose of this book is to furnish a practical guide and reference for those who would undertake their own building improvements, but who are handicapped more or less by a limited knowledge of building construction. Its topics are prepared especially for the kennel operator and deal with every phase of the erection and remodeling of buildings to be used as kennels with the utmost economy and efficiency.

There are chapters on preparing plans and specifications, figuring the materials required, staking out the structure and building the foundation, concrete construction, framing the building, enclosing walls, shape, framework and coving the roof, erecting the trim, fencing, making repairs and tables of weights and measures.

There are 150 drawings illustrating the various stages of construction, together with complete diagrams of modern kennels, 308 pages, cloth bound, gold stamped.

GROOMING AND SHOWING INSTRUCTIONS
By Milo Denlinger
$2.00

Are you ashamed of your dog's appearance? Are you one of those persons who would like to keep your dog looking his best —like him to be a credit to his breed and to you? Would you keep him fit, if only you knew how? Maybe you'd like to exhibit him in the next dog show. Do you know how to go about it?

WELL, HERE'S HOW!

This is a practical book—a "how to" book, with detailed instructions that you can follow. Whether the breed is a wire-haired terrier, a poodle, a collie, a dachshund, or a cocker, this book tells you how to trim and condition him, either for the show or to make him presentable before your friends.

These instructions are fresh, up-to-date, clear, and understandable. They are something to work from. It was written for the amateur, but many a professional can obtain valuable ideas from its contents.

The owner who is proud of a good dog can't afford to miss this book.

THE ART OF BREEDING BETTER DOGS
By Kyle Onstott
$4.50

Read this book and escape from the old fashioned ideas of the mixing of bloods, and substitute for them the union of the genes. The book opens up a concept of the reproductive process wholly new to most dog breeders, and it is all founded on scientific truths. It is a serious book, written for serious people who take seriously the art of breeding dogs. It is for those persons who are no longer satisfied with mediocre puppies.

This book considers the breeding of dogs as a creative art. It makes clear the meaning of Mendelism, and it shows how the fundamental laws of the science of genetics can be applied to the practical breeding of fine dogs. It clears the atmosphere of all the superstition, and pseudo-science, and old wives' tales that have cluttered up breeding practices time-out-of-mind.

This is no mere "how to" book. It goes behind the "how to" and explains the "why". It enables you to plan your matings in the light of biology.

Don't expect a lot of empirical drivel about how to take care of puppies. And this is not a picture book. It is about BREEDING, and ONLY ABOUT BREEDING. It dispels a lot of misapprehensions and replaces them with scientific facts.

Some of the subjects discussed are: Dog Breeding as a Creative Art; the Mechanics of Reproduction; the Pre-Natal Life of the Dog; Mendelism and What It Is; the Chromosomes and their Genes; Neo-Mendelism; the Implications of Mendelism; the Determination of Sex; Sterility, Impotence, and Cryptorchidism; In-Breeding, Line-Breeding, and Out-Breeding; the Pedigree; Knowing What You Want; Heredity and Environment; Superstitions and Things That Are Not True; the Choice of a Brood Bitch; the Choice of a Stud Dog.

Don't fool along with out-worn methods. Get your copy right away of THE ART OF BREEDING BETTER DOGS, by Kyle Onstott. It will open your eyes.

OTHER BOOKS PUBLISHED BY DENLINGER'S

Airedale for Work and Show, by A. F. Hochwalt_____

Art of Breeding Better Dogs, by Kyle Onstott_____

Complete Beagle, Wm. Denlinger_____

Complete Boxer, by Milo G. Denlinger_____

Complete Bull Dog (Englisn), Wm. Denlinger_____

Complete Care of Your Dog, by Milo Denlinger_____

Care and Breeding Manual, by Milo Denlinger_____

Complete Book of the Cat, by Milo Denlinger_____

Complete Book of Siamese Cat, by Milo Denlinger_____

Complete Chihuahua, by Milo Denlinger_____

Your Cocker Puppy, Care and Training, by Milo Denlinger_____

Complete Cocker Spaniel, by Milo Denlinger_____

Complete Collie, by Milo Denlinger_____

Complete Dachshund, by Milo Denlinger_____

Complete Dalmatian, by Milo Denlinger_____

Complete Doberman, by Milo Denlinger_____

Englishe Dogges, Reprint of 1576_____
    First Book Ever Written on Dogs

Complete English Setter, by Davis H. Tuck_____

Complete German Shepherd, by Milo Denlinger_____

German Shorthaired Pointer, Trans. from the German_____

Complete German Shorthaired Pointer, by Seiger and von Dewitz__

Complete Great Dane, by Milo Denlinger_____

Grooming and Showing Instructions, by Milo Denlinger_____

Irish Setter in Word and Picture, Wm. C. Thompson_____

Irish Setter Champion List, Wm. C. Thompson_____

Irish Setter, by Lt. Col. Corn. Schilbred_____

Complete Irish Setter, by Milo Denlinger_____

Complete Kennel Construction, by Milo Denlinger_____

Complete Kerry Blue Terrier, by Dr. E. S. Montgomery_____

Complete Pomeranian, by Milo Denlinger_____

Complete Pitbull or Staffordshire Terrier, by Milo Denlinger_____

Complete Pekingese, by Milo Denlinger_____

A Living in Dogs, by Milo Denlinger_____

Complete Poodle, by Lydia Hopkins_____

Complete Pug, by Milo Denlinger_____

Complete Saint Bernard, by Milo Denlinger_____

Home Obedience Training, by Fred Spooner_____

Training the Dog for Guard Work, Arundel_____

Spaniel Training for Sport and Field, by Carlton_____

Complete Toy Manchester Terrier, by Dixie Dempsey_____

Complete Weimaraner, Wm. Denlinger_____

Our Puppy's Baby Book, arranged along the lines of a real baby book
    32 pp. illustrated with drawings, handsomely bound in Blue for
    Boy Dogs, Pink for Girl Dogs_____

Complete Book of Tropical Fish_____

Complete Book of Tropical Fish, edited by Milo Denlinger_____

Parakeets, Their Breeding, Training and Manage-
    ment, edited by Milo Denlinger_____